Teaching and learning
in the primary school

Edited by Andrew Pollard and Jill Bourne
at The Open University

London and New York
in association with
The Open University

First published 1994
by Routledge
11 New Fetter Lane, London EC4P 4EE

Simultaneously published in the USA and Canada
by Routledge
29 West 35th Street, New York, NY 10001

Selection and editorial matter: © 1994 The Open University

Typeset in Garamond by Florencetype Ltd, Kewstoke, Avon
Printed and bound in Great Britain by
Biddles Ltd, Guildford and King's Lynn

British Library Cataloguing in Publication Data
A catalogue record for this book is available from the British Library.

Library of Congress Cataloging in Publication Data
Teaching and learning in the primary school/edited by Andrew Pollard
and Jill Bourne.
    p.   cm.
'Open University Postgraduate Certificate of Education' – Galley.
Includes bibliographical references and index.
1. Education, Elementary – Great Britain.   2. Elementary school
teaching – Great Britain.   3. Learning.   I. Pollard, Andrew.
II. Bourne, Jill. 1947–.
LA633.T43   1994
372.941 – dc20   93–5056
                                                         CIP

ISBN 0–415–10258–8

Teaching and learning
in the primary school

The Open University Postgraduate Certificate of Education

The readers in the PGCE series are:

Thinking Through Primary Practice
Teaching and Learning in the Primary School
Teaching and Learning in the Secondary School
Teaching English
Teaching Mathematics
Teaching Science
Teaching Technology
Teaching Modern Languages
Teaching History

All of these readers are part of an integrated teaching system; the selection is therefore related to other material available to students and is designed to evoke critical understanding. Opinions expressed are not necessarily those of the course team or of the University.

If you would like to study this course and receive a PGCE prospectus and other information about programmes of professional development in education, please write to the Central Enquiry Service, PO Box 200, The Open University, Walton Hall, Milton Keynes, MK7 6YZ. A copy of *Studying with the Open University* is available from the same address.

Contents

Foreword   ix

Introduction: teaching and learning in the 1990s   1
Andrew Pollard

Part I Learners

1 How children learn . . . and fail   7
John Holt

2 Towards a sociology of learning in primary schools   12
Andrew Pollard

3 Wally's story   28
Vivian Gussin Paley

4 Bilingual by rights   32
Helen Savva

5 Sex roles in the formative years   42
Sara Delamont

6 Learner needs or learner rights?   53
Caroline Roaf and Hazel Bines

Part II Teachers

7 The teacher as a person   67
Michael Fullan and Andy Hargreaves

8 Teacher expertise   73
David Berliner

9 Teaching as a professional activity   80
James Calderhead

10 Those who understand: knowledge growth in teaching   84
Lee Shulman

11 A first try: starting the day   89
Carol Cummings

12 Akemi   95
Vivian Gussin Paley

13 Teacher expectations   99
*Peter Mortimore, Pamela Sammons, Louise Stoll,
David Lewis, and Russell Ecob*

Part III Classrooms

14 Life in classrooms   113
Philip Jackson

15 Characteristics of good practice   119
Her Majesty's Inspectors of Schools

16 The rise and fall of primary education   123
Ellen Yeo

17 The 'three wise men' and after   132
David Hutchinson

18 Teaching strategies   142
Robin Alexander

19 An approach to personal and social education in the
primary school: or how one city schoolteacher tried to
make sense of her job   157
Jane Needham

Part IV Curriculum

20 The core curriculum: an international perspective   167
Martin Skilbeck

21 The national curriculum: origins, context, and implementation   172
Bob Moon

22 Coherence and manageability: reflections on the national
curriculum and cross-curricular provision   184
David Hargreaves

23 The evolution of the topic   188
Trevor Kerry and Jim Eggleston

24 Preserving integration within the national curriculum in
primary schools: approaching a school development plan 194
Anna Ryan

25 Successful topic work 206
OFSTED

26 The classteacher and the curriculum 207
Robin Alexander

27 Teachers' subject knowledge 213
Ted Wragg

28 Assessment and the improvement of education 219
*Wynne Harlen, Caroline Gipps, Patricia Broadfoot,
and Desmond Nuttall*

29 Target setting with young children 228
Yolande Muschamp

Part V Schools

30 The organisation of the primary school 239
Charles Handy and Robert Aitken

31 Key factors for effective junior schooling 250
*Peter Mortimore, Pamela Sammons, Louise Stoll,
David Lewis, and Russell Ecob*

32 The culture of collaboration 258
Jennifer Nias, Geoff Southworth, and Robin Yeomans

33 St Andrew's Church of England Primary School 273
Miriam Wilcock

34 Involving the whole staff in developing a maths curriculum 283
Richard McTaggart

35 Primary–secondary transfer after the national curriculum 293
Brian·Gorwood

36 Parents' choice of school
Martin Hughes, Felicity Wikeley, and Tricia Nash 298

37 Involving parents 302
Alastair Macbeth

Acknowledgements 314

Notes on sources 317

Index 319

Foreword

The form of teacher education is one of the most debated educational issues of the day. How is the curriculum of teacher education, particularly initial, pre-service education to be defined? What is the appropriate balance between practical school experience and the academic study to support such practice? What skills and competence can be expected of a newly qualified teacher? How are these skills formulated and assessed and in what ways are they integrated into an ongoing programme of professional development?

These issues have been at the heart of the development and planning of the Open University's programme of initial teacher training and education – the Postgraduate Certificate of Education (PGCE). Each course within the programme uses a combination of technologies, some of which are well tried and tested, while others, on information technology for example, may represent new and innovatory approaches to teaching. All, however, contribute in an integrated way towards fulfilling the aims and purposes of the course and programme.

All of the PGCE courses have readers which bring together a range of articles, extracts from books, and reports that discuss key ideas and issues, including some specially commissioned chapters. The readers also provide a resource that can be used to support a range of teaching and learning in other types and structures of course.

This series from Routledge, in supporting the Open University PGCE programme, provides a contemporary view of developments in primary and secondary education and across a range of specialist subject areas. Its primary aim is to provide insights and analysis for those participating in initial education and training. Much of its content, however, will also be relevant to ongoing programmes of personal and institutional professional development. Each book is designed to provide an integral part of that basis of knowledge that we would expect of both new and experienced teachers.

Bob Moon
Professor of Education, The Open University

Introduction
Teaching and learning in the 1990s

Andrew Pollard

This collection reflects the major influences and challenges which face teachers in primary schools in the 1990s, but it also identifies the very important continuities in their professional work with young children.

One influence comes from the development over the past decades of an appreciative understanding of the skills, judgement, and knowledge which are involved in high quality teaching. This has been complemented by the development of increasingly sophisticated views of children's learning. Such approaches recognise the significance of the social context in which learning takes place, the importance of clearly stated curricular aims, the vital role of teachers, with appropriate subject expertise, in assisting the development of understanding, and the constructive role of both pupil and teacher assessment. These arguments have been most explicitly set out in research findings and in the work of educationalists and, appropriately, we draw on such work in the collection.

However, a second and perhaps even more significant source of influence has come from the teaching profession itself. Moving beyond simplistic ideas of 'progressive' or 'traditional' teaching, primary schoolteachers have developed repertoires of teaching approaches, skills at diagnostic and formative assessment, and subject expertise. Above all, teachers have increasingly embraced processes of self-evaluation and critical reflection on their own classroom and school practice. Thus, professional development now often involves the collection and sharing of evidence with colleagues and the discussion of future developments in terms of whole-school goals.

Such influences on professional work have developed gradually since at least the mid-1970s. However, recent years have also been characterised by successive challenges to teacher autonomy by national government. The impact of such challenges has been different in each country within the United Kingdom but the central thrust of the changes, initiated by the Education Reform Act of 1988, has been to produce national structures for curriculum and assessment and to render schools and teachers more accountable to parents through exposing them to market forces.

The implementation of such educational reforms has been highly complex. In some respects, teachers have endorsed them and seen them as complementing other constructive professional influences on the development of quality provision. In other respects, successive waves of legislated change have been seen as damaging to quality, to teacher commitment and to professionalism.

In the midst of this ebb and flow of change and debate there are many continuities in the practical classroom work of primary schoolteachers. Though the importance of subject expertise and the need for new forms of organisation to share this across schools is increasingly recognised, responsibility for a class of children has remained at the core of the primary teacher's role. Key factors are still the size of classes and the specific learning needs of the children – factors which almost inevitably pose severe dilemmas for teachers as they try to decide on priorities. Teachers also continue to assert the vital importance of maintaining good relationships with their pupils in underpinning classroom order, in sustaining a positive atmosphere for learning, and in providing mutual fulfilment.

Another continuity concerns the basic reality of classroom decision making, for, whatever the research analysis, professional advice, or government requirements, complex decisions have to be made with extraordinary rapidity in primary school classrooms. This expertise is learned through extensive practice and experience, though there is an important role for discussion, reading, and analysis in developing an understanding of the issues and in achieving levels of effective competence.

This collection contains articles which provide both analysis of issues and examples of teachers at work. This mix, in each section, is important – for no analysis can, by its very nature, express the full, holistic complexity of the issues which teachers face in practice. Conversely, when managing such complexity, teachers can find it hard to think rigorously about some of the specific issues which are raised. The papers are thus intended to complement and enrich each other. In particular, we have included some papers where teacher intuition, judgement, and sensitivity are apparent. *Study* of teaching, in itself, can seem to emphasise the technical skills and competencies which are necessarily involved, but these are not sufficient, particularly for work with young children.

The section on *learners* starts with some classic material from John Holt which conveys both the risks and the potential achievements of learning in school. Other papers address the influence of social context on teaching-learning processes, demonstrate the facilitative skill of a teacher at work, and consider equal opportunities issues involved in bilingualism, gender, and special educational needs.

We begin the section on *teachers* with four papers which set out various facets of teachers' role and expertise. Once again, these are illustrated in action through articles by teachers and the section concludes with a consideration of issues raised by work on the expectations which teachers may have of children of particular social groups.

Classrooms is a section in which we begin to enter into some recent debates about classroom pedagogy. Following Jackson's paper on the complexity of classroom life, we have an account of 'good practice' by Her Majesty's Inspectors of Schools. This is followed by a critique of 'progressivism' and a counterblast from an educationalist concerned at political intervention in education. We then visit some influential research evidence by Robin Alexander and then consider a teacher's reflections on the realities of her classroom work. The latter provides some interesting contrasts with some of the arguments presented in earlier papers.

The section on *curriculum* offers papers which review the major issues which are involved in the introduction of national curricula. The international trend towards this is noted and various features of national curriculum planning and implementation in the United Kingdom are discussed, including the problems of achieving coherence and manageability. Beyond the specification of a syllabus, the importance of teachers' subject expertise in supporting learning is emphasised by Wragg, though, as a headteacher reports, even this cannot overcome some of the severe problems of whole-school planning where the curriculum is overcrowded. The section concludes with two papers on assessment. The first explores some of the most important issues and controversies which have emerged in the introduction of national systems, while the second, with a much more practical orientation, reports on constructive ways of involving pupils in self-assessment.

In the section on *schools* we have provided two articles which focus on the issue of effectiveness in school management and practice, followed by a report of findings on the 'culture of collaboration' which can sometimes be found among primary school staffs. The section continues with articles by a headteacher and a curriculum co-ordinator on how they actually carry out their school development responsibilities and a discussion on issues of transfer between primary and secondary schools.

The book concludes with two chapters on parents and the school – the first looking at parents' choice of school, the second outlining parents' legal responsibilities and rights.

Part I

Learners

Chapter 1

How children learn . . . and fail

John Holt

This chapter contains extracts from two classic books on learning. John Holt looks at learning in the classroom context from the perspective of the learner and draws attention to the ways in which the school can be a 'place where children learn to be stupid'. He argues that school routines can create contexts in which children can feel so afraid to make mistakes that they learn to make themselves dependent on the teacher. They begin to lack confidence to trust their own perceptions, to correct their own mistakes. In this fear of 'failing', they do not see school as a place where they can put their own knowledge and curiosity to work, but become 'frozen' in what Holt calls a 'school stupidity'. Holt calls for schools to try to make themselves places where children are encouraged to be independent, to say 'I see it, I get it, I can do it!'

What we must remember about the ability of children to become aware of mistakes, to find and correct them, is that it takes time to work, and that under pressure and anxiety it does not work at all. But at school we almost never give it the time. When a child at school makes a mistake, say, in reading aloud in a reading group, he gets an instant signal from the environment. Perhaps some of the other children in the group, or class, will giggle, or cover their mouths with their hands, or make a face, or wave their hands in the air – anything to show the teacher that they know more than the unfortunate reader. Perhaps the teacher herself will correct the mistake, or will say, 'Are you sure?' or will ask another student, 'What do you think?' Perhaps, if the teacher is sympathetic and kindly, as many are, she will only smile a sweet, sad smile – which from the point of view of the child is one of the severest punishments the school has to offer, since it shows him that he has hurt and disappointed the person on whose support and approval he has been trained to depend. At any rate, something will happen to tell the child, not only that he goofed, but that everyone around him knows he goofed. Like almost anyone in this situation, he will feel great shame and embarrassment, enough to paralyse his thinking. Even if he is confident enough to keep some presence of mind in the face of this public failure, he will not be given time to seek out, find, and correct his mistake. For teachers not only like right answers, they like them right away. If a child can't correct his mistake immediately, someone else will correct it for him.

The result of this is a great loss. The more a child uses his sense of consistency, of things fitting together and making sense, to find and correct his own mistakes, the more he will feel that his way of using his mind works, and the better he will get at it. He will feel more and more that he *can* figure out for himself, at least much of the time, which answers make sense and which do not. But if, as usually happens, we point out all his mistakes as soon as he makes them, and, even worse, correct them for him, his self-checking and self-correcting skill will not develop, but will die out. He will cease to feel that he has it, or ever had it, or ever could have it. He will become like the fifth-graders I knew – many of them 'successful' students – who used to bring me papers and say, 'Is it right?' and when I said, 'What do you think?' look at me as if I were crazy. What did *they* think? What did what *they* thought have to do with what was right? Right was what the teacher said was right, whatever that was. More recently I have heard much older students, also able and successful, say very much the same thing. *They* could not make any judgements about their own work; it was up to the teachers to decide.

One of the most important things teachers can do for any learner is to make the learner less and less dependent on them. We need to give students ways to find out for themselves whether what they have done is correct and makes sense.

The other day I decided to talk about what happens when you don't understand what is going on. We had been chatting about something or other, and everyone seemed in a relaxed frame of mind, so I said, 'You know, there's something I'm curious about and I wonder if you'd tell me.' They said, 'What?' I said, 'What do you think, what goes through your mind, when the teacher asks you a question and you don't know the answer?'

It was a bombshell. Instantly a paralysed silence fell on the room. Everyone stared at me with what I have learned to recognise as a tense expression. For a long time there wasn't a sound. Finally Ben, who is bolder than most, broke the tension, and also answered my question, by saying in a loud voice, 'Gulp!'

He spoke for everyone. They all began to clamour, and all said the same thing, that when the teacher asked them a question and they didn't know the answer they were scared half to death. I was flabbergasted – to find this in a school which people think of as progressive; which does its best not to put pressure on little children; which does not give marks in the lower grades; which tries to keep children from feeling that they're in some kind of race.

I asked them why they felt gulpish. They said they were afraid of failing, afraid of being kept back, afraid of being called stupid, afraid of feeling themselves stupid. Stupid. Why is it such a deadly insult to these children, almost the worst thing they can think of to call each other? Where do they learn this?

Even in the kindest and gentlest of schools, children are afraid, many of them a great deal of the time; some of them almost all the time. This is a hard fact of life to deal with. What can we do about it?

This makes me think about written work. Some say that children get security from large amounts of written work. Maybe. But suppose every teacher in the school were told that he had to do ten pages of addition problems, within a given time limit and with no mistakes, or lose his job. Even if the time given was ample for doing all problems carefully with time over for checking, the chances are that no teacher would get a perfect paper. Their anxiety would build up, as it does in me when I play the flute, until it impaired or wholly broke down their co-ordination and confidence. Have you ever found yourself, while doing a simple arithmetic problem, checking the answer over and over, as if you could not believe that you had done it right? I have. If we were under the gun as much as the kids in our classes are, we would do this more often.

Perhaps children need a lot of written work, particularly in maths; but they should not get too much of it at one time. Ask children to spend a whole period on one paper and anxiety or boredom is sure to drive them into foolish errors. It used to puzzle me that the students who made the most mistakes and got the worst marks were so often the first ones to hand in their papers. I used to say, 'If you finish early, take time to check your work, do some problems again.' Typical teacher's advice; I might as well have told them to flap their arms and fly. When the paper was in, the tension was ended. Their fate was in the lap of the gods. They might still worry about flunking the paper, but it was a fatalistic kind of worry, it didn't contain the agonising element of choice, there was nothing more they could do about it. Worrying about whether you did the right thing, while painful enough, is less painful than worrying about the right thing to do.

To a very great degree, school is a place where children learn to be stupid. A dismal thought, but hard to escape. Infants are not stupid. Children of one, two, or even three throw the whole of themselves into everything they do. They embrace life, and devour it, it is why they learn so fast and are such good company. Listlessness, boredom, apathy – these all come later. Children come to school *curious*; within a few years most of that curiosity is dead, or at least silent. Open a first or third grade to questions, and you will be deluged; fifth-graders say nothing. They either have no questions or will not ask them. They think, 'What's this leading up to? What's the catch? Last year, thinking that self-consciousness and embarrassment might be silencing the children, I put a question box in the classroom, and said that I would answer any questions they put into it. In four months I got one question – 'How long does a bear live?' While I was talking about the life-span of bears and other creatures, one child said impatiently, 'Come on, get to the point.' The expressions on the children's faces seemed to say, 'You've got us here in school; now make us do whatever it is that you want us to do.' Curiosity, questions, speculation – these are for outside school, not inside.

Boredom and resistance may cause as much stupidity in school as fear. Give a child the kind of task he gets in school and, whether he is afraid of it, or resists it, or is willing to do it but bored by it, he will do the task with only a small part of his attention, energy, and intelligence. In a word, he will do it stupidly – even if correctly. This soon becomes a habit. He gets used to working at low power; he develops strategies to enable him to get by this way. In time he even starts to think of himself as being stupid, which is what most fifth-graders think of themselves, and to think that his low-power way of coping with school is the only possible way.

It does no good to tell such students to pay attention and think about what they are doing. I can see myself now, in one of my ninth-grade algebra classes in Colorado, looking at one of my flunking students, a boy who had become frozen in his school stupidity, and saying to him in a loud voice, 'Think! Think! Think!' Wasted breath; he had forgotten how. The stupid way – timid, unimaginative, defensive, evasive – in which he met and dealt with the problems of algebra were, by that time, the only way he knew of dealing with them. His strategies and expectations were fixed; he couldn't even imagine any others. He really was doing his dreadful best.

We ask children to do for most of a day what few adults are able to do even for an hour. How many of us, attending, say, a lecture that doesn't interest us, can keep our minds from wandering? Hardly any. Not I, certainly. Yet children have far less awareness of and control of their attention than we do. No use to shout at them to pay attention. If we want to get tough enough about it, as many schools do, we can terrorise a class of children into sitting still with their hands folded and their eyes glued on us, or somebody; but their minds will be far away. The attention of children must be lured, caught, and held, like a shy wild animal that must be coaxed with bait to come close. If the situations, the materials, the problems before a child do not interest him, his attention will slip off to what does interest him, and no amount of exhortation or threats will bring it back.

A child is most intelligent when the reality before him arouses in him a high degree of attention, interest, concentration, involvement – in short, when he cares most about what he is doing. This is why we should make schoolrooms and schoolwork as interesting and exciting as possible, not just so that school will be a pleasant place, but so that children in school will act intelligently and get into *the habit* of acting intelligently. The case against boredom in school is the same as the case against fear: it makes children behave stupidly, some on purpose, most because they cannot help it. If this goes on long enough, as it does in school, they forget what it is like to grasp at something, as they once grasped at everything, with all their minds and senses; they forget how to deal positively and aggressively with life and experience, to think and say, 'I see it! I get it! I can do it!'

Chapter 2

Towards a sociology of learning in primary schools

Andrew Pollard

This chapter considers children as learners within a social context. Beginning by drawing contrasts between psychological and sociological approaches to learning, it goes on to argue that many recent policies focus too much on curriculum and teaching and pay insufficient attention to social factors in learning. This is illustrated with reference to a longitudinal study of pupil learning in an infant school.

The chapter strongly implies that primary schoolteachers should try to understand and work with each child as a whole person, being aware of the cultural influences which are reflected through family and peers. No primary schoolteacher deals simply with some asocial category of 'pupils': each child has particular circumstances in their lives and such experiences will affect the approach which is adopted to school learning.

LEARNING IN PRIMARY SCHOOLS

A review of the sociology of primary schooling and of the psychology of young children's learning over the past twenty years or so reveals a curious picture. On the one hand, sociologists have continued, in one way or another, to focus their attention on issues of social differentiation. Certainly the emphasis has developed from that of social class to include increasing attention to issues of race and gender, and theoretical refinements have accumulated too. However, the overriding impression left by work such as Hartley (1985), Pollard (1985), Sharp and Green (1975), Lubeck (1985), King (1978), and King (1989), is that learning processes are, at best, tangential to issues such as typification, group formation, and the consequences of differentiation. Returning over a decade earlier, and to a different theoretical perspective, reveals a similar story – as is illustrated by the way in which Dreeben's *On What is Learned in School* (1968) concerns itself with socialisation of children into norms but makes no attempt to consider the sociological factors which influence the learning of knowledge, concepts, and skills.

Sociologists' focus on differentiation in the past has, until recently, been matched by the naive individualism of much child psychology which derived from the work of Piaget. Piaget's work was directed, in an overarching sense, towards the study of 'genetic epistemology', but the route towards this analysis was through many detailed studies of children's thinking and behaviour. Careful development and use of the clinical method over many years enabled Piaget to generate a model of learning processes based on the interaction between individuals and their environment and involving development through successive stages of equilibration, each of which was taken to be associated with particular capacities and ways of thinking. This model was powerfully adopted by primary schoolteachers in the UK in the years following the Plowden Report (CACE 1967) and was used as a professional legitimation for 'progressive' classroom practices which, ostensibly, gave children a large degree of control over their learning.

However, while it is impossible to overestimate Piaget's influence within developmental psychology over the past decades, it is also true to say that Piaget's ideas have increasingly been modified by the gradual emergence of a new paradigm – 'social constructivism'.

Thus, the previously dominant model, which implicitly conceptualised children as *individual* 'active scientists', has begun to be superseded by an image of children as *social* beings who construct their understandings (learn) from social interaction within specific socio-cultural settings. They are thus seen as intelligent social actors who, although their knowledge base may be limited in absolute terms, are capable in many ways. For instance, processes of 'intellectual search' have been identified in young children (Tizard and Hughes 1987), as have children's capacities to develop sophisticated forms of representation for meaning and understanding. Such findings are being arrived at with younger and younger children as research goes on.

The theoretical basis of such psychological research is strongly influenced by Vygotsky (1962, 1978). Of particular importance is his comparative work on the interrelations of thought, language, and culture and, at another level, on the role of adults in scaffolding children's understanding across the 'zone of proximal development' – the extension of understanding which can be attained with appropriate support from others. According to Bruner and Haste (1987), this social constructivist approach has brought about a 'quiet revolution' in developmental psychology in the last decade and this is certainly borne out by the impact in education of work such as that by Donaldson (1978), Hughes (1986), Bruner (1986), and Edwards and Mercer (1987).

A key thrust of such new approaches is to recognise the way in which the social context influences perspectives and behaviour. One particularly interesting way of conceptualising this has been provided by Helen Haste (1987) in her model of 'intra-individual', 'interpersonal' and 'socio-historical' factors affecting learning (Figure 2.1).

The intra-individual domain is the province of the cognitive psychologists who have accumulated so many insights into the ways in which individuals

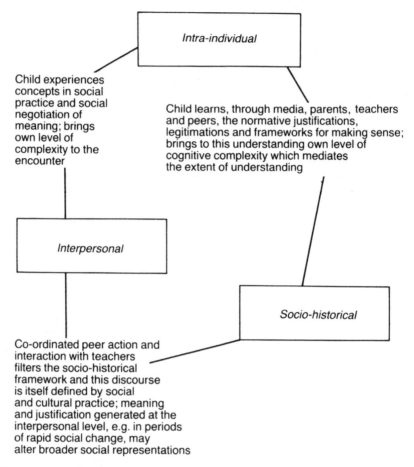

Figure 2.1 The relationship between intra-individual, interpersonal and socio-historical factors in learning

Source: Haste 1987: 175

assimilate experiences and construct understanding. The interpersonal is the domain of social interaction – the area in which meanings are negotiated and through which cultural norms and social conventions are learned. The socio-historical is the domain of culturally defined and historically accumulated justification and explanation. It is a socio-historical resource for both inter-personal interaction and intra-individual reflection.

Such conceptualisation of factors and domains affecting learning begins to make it possible to break out of the individualist assumptions which have been common in child psychology, so that wider social issues can be addressed. Sociologists could have much to offer here for, as Apple has argued:

We do not confront abstract 'learners' in schools. Instead, we see specific classed, raced and gendered subjects, people whose biographies are intimately linked to the economic, political and ideological trajectories of their families and communities, to the political economies of their neighbourhoods.

(Apple 1986: 7)

In other words, intra-individual learning cannot really be understood without reference to both interpersonal experiences and socio-historical circumstances.

I suspect that there is some way to go in the development of working relationships and analytical tools before psychologists and sociologists concerned with children's learning are able to take on the full import of Haste's framework and Apple's suggestion in detailed empirical investigations. However, a growing consensus about the interrelatedness of such factors does seem to be emerging and this is underpinned, not just by theory and empirical research, but also by the common-sense and lived experiences of millions of children, teachers, parents, and others. If we are to investigate the issue of learning in valid ways, then our first problem, as social scientists, is really to find ways of bridging the artificial disciplinary boundaries which dissipate our energies.

I want to suggest that one way of developing such collaborative work could be through the linking of social constructivist psychology and symbolic interactionist sociology.

These approaches share a basic assumption that people are active and make decisions on the basis of meanings. However, while social constructivist work has begun to identify the processes by which people 'make sense' in social situations, and thus come to 'know', symbolic interactionist studies promise to provide more detailed and incisive accounts of the dynamics and constraints of the contexts in which learning takes place. The two approaches are, arguably, complementary.

Some years ago I began to toy with this potential sociological contribution through the publication of a collection of papers which highlighted the influence of social contexts in schools on children's thinking and learning (Pollard 1987). This collection of case studies includes material from 3–12-year-olds and provides a degree of 'thick description' which invites further theorisation regarding the nature of such complementarity – a task which I have begun through the work on an ethnography and which is reflected in this paper.

However, before addressing the study and the theoretical issue directly, it is appropriate to place the topic of 'learning in primary schools' in the context of recent policies in England and Wales and in relation to other approaches to classroom teaching/learning processes. In particular, I will have regard below to the work of Neville Bennett because of the sustained quality and impact of his research into classroom teaching and learning over many years.

POLICY AND SUBSTANTIVE CONTEXTS

In recent years, major thrusts of government policy in England and Wales have been directed towards the streamlining of the management of schools, increasing the effectiveness and accountability of teachers, and restructuring the curriculum (e.g. Education Act 1986; Education Reform Act 1988). We do not yet know whether such initiatives will achieve their aims in terms of the delivery of the curriculum. However, irrespective of this, it can be argued that far too little attention has been paid to the actual reception of the curriculum by learners. Indeed, by focusing on the issue of learning, one could claim to be anticipating a policy debate of the future – a claim based on the proposition that when the dust of reforms of teacher and curriculum management has settled and we are still chasing that ever-receding Holy Grail of 'educational standards', more detailed attention to learning and the learners in schools will be perceived as necessary.

The issue also has implications for teachers in primary schools in a more general way concerning the theoretical underpinning of practice. Over the past decade or so, there has been a gradual erosion of the primacy of the Plowden Report's (CACE 1967) philosophy of 'child centredness', which underpinned much primary school practice. As Piaget's work has been questioned and research evidence has accumulated about actual classroom behaviour, so primary school practice has begun to be seen to lack a 'theoretical base' (Sylva 1987). I would suggest that a fusion of social constructivism and symbolic interactionism, suitably applied, has the potential to offer a new legitimation – indeed, I think there are many forms of innovative curriculum practice which, perhaps unwittingly, appear to be based on such precepts.

In the past twenty years a considerable amount of research has been conducted with the aim of identifying factors which enable teachers to be 'effective'. However, as Bennett (1987) has argued, while the initial work, emphasising teaching styles, identified some interesting patterns and descriptions, it lacked explanatory power and made few connections with actual practice. It was superseded in the mid-1970s by an 'opportunities to learn' model in which the teacher was seen as the manager of the attention and time of the pupils. A key indicator became the amount of time which the pupil was 'on task'. More recently, the focus has also turned to the analysis of what is termed 'quality' of classroom tasks – defined in terms of the degree of appropriate match with children's capacities (e.g. Bennett et al. 1984).

Neville Bennett's work represents a sustained and consistent attempt to develop and test a model of teaching and learning. His successive studies have focused on different parts of an emerging model and his work continues through his present Leverhulme Project on the quality of teachers' subject knowledge and ability to diagnose learning difficulties.

Bennett and his co-author, Joy Kell, express the model particularly clearly below:

> Teaching is, we argue, a purposeful activity: teachers provide tasks and activities for their children for good reasons. These reasons or, as we call them in the model, teacher intentions, will inform the teacher's selection of tasks/activities. Once chosen these are presented to children in some way, e.g. to individuals, groups or the whole class, together with the necessary materials. The children then get on with their work, demonstrating, through their performances, their understanding (or misconceptions) of it. When they have completed their activity it might be expected that the teacher will assess it in some way in order to judge children's developing competencies, and it might also be expected that the information gained from those assessments will inform the teacher's next intentions.
>
> (Bennett and Kell 1989)

The very important point which Bennett has empirically documented is that breakdowns can and do occur regularly between each stage in the 'task process cycle' and it is unfortunate that this can sometimes come across as an unappreciative critique of teachers. Rather, I would suggest that it should be seen, more constructively, as providing a detailed testimony of just how difficult the job is.

Having said that though, I would also argue that such work seriously underplays the importance of the socio-cultural situation in which teaching and learning take place and fails to trace the full impact of the subjectivity of the participants. There is no specific emphasis on learners with reference to their responses to the social influences and teaching/learning situations which they experience. The model thus appears as a technical model of teaching – one which is dominated by the teacher, with pupils 'performing' to externally determined tasks.

In terms of the issues raised by Helen Haste, Bennett's analysis is very partial. It is worthwhile and necessary, but it is not sufficient and should be complemented by other work – work which is more informed by sociological perspectives.

Among other related issues which have emerged regularly in recent research and in HMI surveys has been that of the routine nature of many of the activity structures and classroom tasks in which children engage – particularly in the 'basic' curriculum areas (Alexander 1984). In an attempt to address this issue and to be appreciative of the concerns of teachers, Woods (1990) has drawn on coping strategies theory (e.g. Pollard 1982) to identify problems of the limited 'opportunities to teach' in classrooms.

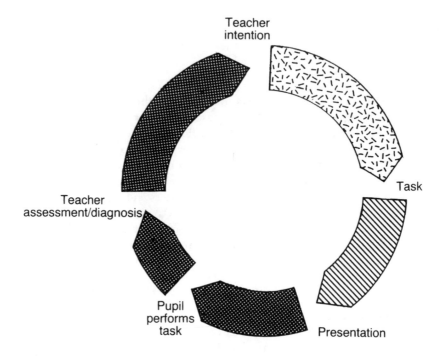

Figure 2.2 A model of classroom task processes

Source: Bennett and Kell 1989: 7

These are constrained by the inadequate resourcing of schools and by the enormous current expectations of teachers.

However, it is also clear that the routinisation of tasks and activity structures is not simply the result of a transmission process for which teachers are solely responsible. Indeed, Doyle (1979) has suggested that many pupils seek tasks which are 'low risk' and 'low ambiguity' and both the ORACLE researchers' identification of 'intermittent working' and 'easy riding' (Galton *et al.* 1980) and my own identification of pupil 'drifting' (Pollard and Tann 1987) suggest that pupils' learning stances and strategies could be of considerable significance. Arguably, this is particularly import-ant in the context of the national concern for improvement in the level of learning achievements, given the psychological evidence on the contribution of risk-taking to learning (Claxton 1984) and Dweck's socio-cognitive re-search on motivation (1986). As Galton's review of the field in the last twenty years concludes:

> if advances [in our understanding] are to be made, there will [need to] be
> greater concentration on the social factors affecting pupil learning and

[on] the ways in which teachers can create classroom climates which allow situations of 'high risk' and 'high ambiguity' to be coped with successfully.

(Galton 1989: 44)

This statement underlines a key point in social constructivist models of learning about control of the learning process. Since understanding can only be constructed in the mind of the learner, it is essential that learners exercise a significant degree of control of the process – a point to which I will return below.

I turn now, though, to introduce the empirical study around which my thinking on this topic has developed.

A LONGITUDINAL ETHNOGRAPHY

In 1987 I began a research programme, a longitudinal ethnography, which was designed to explore the potential for linking social interactionism and social constructivism.

I aimed to monitor the primary school careers of a small cohort of ten children at one primary school by using a variety of qualitative methods and I started from the children's entry to the school at the age of four. I particularly focused on the social factors which were likely to influence the children's stance, perspectives, and strategies regarding learning. Data were thus collected from parents about family life, sibling relationships, and the children's emergent identities; from peers and playground contexts concerning peer-group relations; and from teachers with regard to classroom behaviour and academic achievements.

At the heart of the study was regular classroom observation so that the progression of organisation, activity structures, and routine tasks in each class which the children passed through could be documented – together with the responses of the children to such provision. The main sources of data were: field-notes from participant observation, interviews, teacher records, parent diaries, school documents, photographs, video recordings, sociometry, and examples of children's work.

Before I focus directly on the emerging analysis, an indication of the data is provided below by a brief illustrative account of the educational experiences, over their first two school years, of just two of the children whom I studied.

This is highly condensed 'account', in almost narrative form, and was written initially for an audience of governors and parents (Pollard 1990). The judgements expressed in it rest on a detailed analysis of data, but the main point which I wish to make requires a holistic understanding, for which narrative documentary is a proven vehicle. I thus hope that the account below serves its purpose in highlighting the importance of contextual factors in learning and in providing a bridge to the theoretical analysis in the final section of this paper.

LEARNING AND DEVELOPING AN IDENTITY

The two children on whom this illustration is based began their school careers together, with twenty-four others, in the same 'reception' class.

The first child, a girl called Sally, was the youngest of the two children of the school caretaker. Her mother also worked in the school as a School Meals Services Assistant and as a cleaner. Her parents had always taken enormous pleasure and pride in Sally's achievements. They celebrated each step as it came but did not seem overtly to press her. Life, for them, seemed very much in perspective. Sally was physically agile and had a good deal of self-confidence. She had known the school and the teaching staff for most of her life. She felt at home. She was very sensitive to 'school rules' and adult concerns and she engaged in each new challenge with zest. Over the years, with her parents' encouragement, she had developed a considerable talent for dancing and had won several competitions. In school she had also taken a leading role in several class assemblies and had made good progress with her reading and other work. The teachers felt she was a delightful and rewarding child to teach – convivial and able, but compliant too. Her friends were mainly girls though she mixed easily. She was at the centre of a group which was particularly popular in the class and which, over the years since play-group, had developed strong internal links and friendships through shared interests, for instance, in 'My Little Pony', playing at 'mummies and daddies', and reciprocal home visits.

The second child, Daniel, was the fifth and youngest in his family. His father was an extremely busy business executive and his mother had devoted the previous sixteen years to caring for their children, which she saw as a worthwhile but all-absorbing commitment. She was concerned for Daniel who had had some difficulties in establishing his identity in the bustle of the family with four older children. She also felt that he had 'always tended to worry about things' and was not very confident in himself. For many years he had tended to play on being the youngest, the baby of the family, a role which seemed naturally available. At playgroup he was particularly friendly with a girl, Harriet, who was later to be in his class at school. However, over their first year at school, distinct friendships of boys and girls began to form. It became 'sissy' to play with girls. Daniel, who had found the transition from the security of home hard to take and who had to begin to develop a greater self-sufficiency, thus found the ground-rules of appropriate friendships changing, as the power of child culture asserted itself. He could not play with Harriet because she was a girl, nor was he fully accepted by the dominant groups of boys.

This insecurity was increased when he moved from the structured and

'motherly' atmosphere of his reception class into the more volatile environment of his 'middle infant' class. There were now thirty-one children in his
class, most of whom were from a parallel reception class – within which a
group of boys had developed a reputation for being 'difficult'. The new
teacher thus judged that the class 'needed a firm hand to settle them down
after last year' and, as a caring but experienced infant teacher, decided to
stand no nonsense. It also so happened that this teacher was somewhat
stressed, as a lot of teachers in England and Wales have been in the late
1980s. She sometimes acted a little harshly and in other ways which were
against her own better judgement.

The environment which Daniel experienced was therefore one which was
sometimes a little unpredictable. While he was never one of the ones who
'got into trouble', he was very worried by the possibility that he might
'upset Miss'. Daniel would thus be very careful. He would watch and listen
to the teacher, attempting to 'be good' and do exactly what was required. He
would check with other children and, on making a first attempt at a task, try
to have his efforts approved before proceeding further. Occasionally, at
work with a group and with other children also pressing, the teacher might
wave Daniel away. He would then drift, unsure, watching to take another
opportunity to obtain the reinforcement which he felt he needed. As the
year progressed, Daniel became more unhappy and increasingly unwilling to
go to school.

Daniel's mother was torn as this situation developed – was the 'problem'
caused by Daniel's 'immaturity' or was it because he was frightened of the
teacher? She felt it was probably a bit of both but school-gate advice
suggested that discussion in school might not go easily. She delayed and the
situation worsened, with Daniel making up excuses to avoid school, insisting
on returning home for lunch, and becoming unwilling to visit the homes of
other children. Daniel's mother eventually and tentatively visited the school
where the issues were aired.

Over the following weeks the teacher worked hard to support Daniel and
to help him settle. Daniel's confidence improved a little, particularly when
he found a new friend, a boy, from whom he then became inseparable. Even
so, as his mother told me towards the end of the year, 'we are holding on and
praying for the end of term'.

These two children attended the same school and were part of the same
classes – yet as learners they had quite different characteristics. While Sally
was confident, keen to 'have a go', and would take risks, Daniel was
insecure, fearful lest he 'got things wrong' in a world in which he felt
evaluated and vulnerable. The accident of birth into a small or large family
may have been an influence too, with Sally having had the psychological
space to flourish and the day to day support of both her parents all around
her, while Daniel had to establish his place in a large family in which both
parents faced considerable pressure in their work – be it in an office or

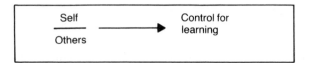

Figure 2.3 Individual, context, and learning: an analytic formula

domestically. Perhaps too, Daniel's initial solutions to his position, which had stood him in good stead in his infancy, while at home, would simply not transfer into the less bounded environment of school.

TOWARDS AN ANALYTICAL FRAMEWORK

The data which underpin an account such as that reviewed above are highly complex and, in attempting to make sense of them, one can easily lose direction or become distracted. For the purposes of this study, it was crucial to retain the focus on identity and learning while also structuring the comparison of cases across settings – with twenty-seven interrelated data sets formed by the nine children and three major settings. Building on what I take to be key interactionist and constructivist principles, I evolved a simple analytical formula which I found to be powerful and which could be applied to data and cases derived from any setting (see Figure 2.3).

The relationship between self and others expresses the key symbolic interactionist focus, with its recognition of the importance of social context in the formation of meaning and self. A sense of control in social situations is seen as a product of this. It is an indication of the success, or otherwise, of a child's coping strategies in the politico-cultural context of any particular social setting – home, classroom, playground – and thus reflects the interplay of interests, power, strategies, and negotiation. However, it is also a necessary element of the learning process as conceived by social constructivist psychologists. Only children themselves can 'make sense', understand, and learn. They may be supported and instructed by others, but, once their understanding has been scaffolded in such ways, it must stand on its own foundations – foundations which can only be secure when the child has been able to control the construction itself.

Teaching and other forms of support by adults are necessary, but they are not sufficient. Learning also requires conditions which enable each child to control the assembly and construction of their understanding.

I have elaborated a model by Rowland (1987) in order to express this point (see Figure 2.4).

It is worth dwelling a little on the importance of the role of an adult as a 'reflective agent' in this model, providing meaningful and appropriate guidance and extension to the cognitive structuring and skill development arising from the child's initial experiences. This, it is suggested, supports the child's

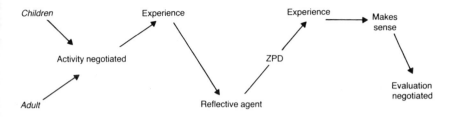

Figure 2.4 A social-constructivist model of the teaching/learning process

attempts to 'make sense' and enables them to cross the zone of proximal development (ZPD). Their thinking is thus *restructured* in the course of further experiences. Of course, the concept of 'reflective agent' is not unrelated to that of 'reflective teaching' (Pollard and Tann 1987), which is becoming a new orthodoxy in terms of course rationales for teacher education in the UK. However, as with sociology of education, present work on reflective teaching is relatively weak on the issue of learning itself. Of great interest, too, is the fact that carrying out the role of a reflective agent effectively is dependent on sensitivity *and* accurate knowledge of each child's needs. It thus places a premium on formative teacher assessment (TGAT 1988) and could be greatly facilitated in England and Wales by the requirements of new legislation – if it is appropriately implemented, a condition which, unfortunately, we cannot take for granted.

To recap – in Figure 2.4, we see the need for appropriate adult support and instruction and its relationship to children's control over their learning. The two are not contradictory. Indeed, I would argue that both are necessary but neither is sufficient for high quality learning. In the cases of Sally and Daniel, Sally was able to negotiate, control, and cope with the variety of domestic, classroom, and playground settings which she encountered with relative ease. She was confident in tackling new learning situations and achieved a great deal. Daniel found things much more difficult in each setting, but particularly in the classroom. He developed two key strategies regarding this learning. First, to watch, check, and recheck to make sure that he 'was doing it right' so that he could avoid 'trouble with Miss'. Second, to stay away from school. His learning achievements over the two years were relatively modest.

Of course, the simple formula (Figure 2.3) and the social constructivist model of interaction in learning (Figure 2.4) express only a small part of the story, and I have developed them further to begin to reflect on the outcomes and consequences of the learning process (see Figure 2.5).

This model expresses the recursive nature of experience. Self-confidence, together with other attributes and other contextual factors (e.g. Bennett's work on the quality of tasks set), produces particular learning outcomes – successful or otherwise – and with them associated perspectives. These, it is

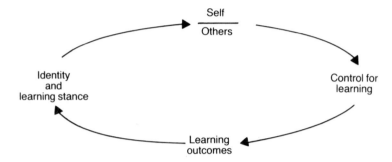

Figure 2.5 A model of learning and identity

suggested, contribute cumulatively to each child's sense of identity and to their learning stance, and it is with these which, for better or worse, they enter the next setting. Over time, as this cycle moves forward, it tends to develop in patterned ways into what can be identified more clearly as 'pupil career'.

Thus in the case of Sally and Daniel, we might speculate that Sally's pupil career will go from strength to strength, founded on the confidence of her learning stance, while Daniel's progress may be more halting. In fact, of course, such speculation is premature. Time will bring new social contexts and experiences and the factor of social class may influence the children's development. This is where the longitudinal design of the study should be significant.

Whatever the empirical outcomes, the nature of the patterns in pupil learning and career is of consequence for both psychologists and sociologists. For psychologists, it highlights processes of learning in context. For sociologists, it begins to relate factors such as social class, gender, and race, through the processes of learning and identity formation, and on to long-term social differentiation, career, and life chances.

I am attempting to apply the basic formula, Figure 2.3 above, in relation to the settings of classrooms, playground, and the home, through the application of some key elements of the model of coping strategies which I developed some years ago (Pollard 1985). Four important aspects of this are:

1 An individual's structural position: their power, influence, and capacity to take active decisions.
2 An individual's interests-at-hand: the immediate concerns of a person in processes of interaction, given their goals and structural position within a particular social setting.
3 The working consensus: the social rules and understandings which tend to become established in any particular setting as a result of interaction. Such understandings often involve a negotiated 'trade-off' between the participants.

4 Strategic action: strategies used by individuals as a means of coping with different settings. These include conformity, negotiating, and rejecting and may or may not be transferred across different settings.

In the case of both the children illustrated, we see the influence of each of the three major social settings and significant others in their lives – family, peers, and teachers.

For Sally, the particular, overlapping configuration of the self/other relationship between home and school gave her self-confidence on which she was able to build in her relationships with her peers and which enabled her to exercise considerable control over her classroom learning. Other data clearly show how this control was obtained, in large part, through her social awareness and negotiating skills. She contributed directly to the working consensus in both classes. Her structural position was strong, her interests-at-hand could be accommodated within teacher goals and she acted with skill and strategic awareness to achieve expected learning outcomes and a positive identity – despite the risks associated with life in her second class.

For Daniel, the situation was more difficult. His structural position was weak both in his family and then, almost as a knock-on effect of his strategies in the home setting, among his peers. He felt insecure, in one way or another, in each of the three main settings in his life and he thus developed relatively defensive strategies in order to protect his interests. At its most obvious, this involved trying to avoid coming to school but, once there, it was manifested by extreme caution in his dealings with teachers and a reluctance to take any sort of risk or exercise control over his learning. Preferring to keep a low profile, he participated little in the establishment of classroom understandings and the working consensus. Learning outcomes were affected and, with them, Daniel's identity began to develop and to be registered with both his teachers, parents, and peers.

Of course, these patterns are related to the particular classroom settings in which Daniel worked and to the teachers concerned and, unfortunately, the teacher of Daniel's middle infant class seemed to compound some of his difficulties. It remains perfectly possible that Daniel will develop more poise and belief in himself as he gets older and he has many abilities and social advantages. The question is an empirical one about which, for the moment, we must be open-minded.

The story of these two children is not just about learning in a narrow academic sense. Additionally, it is about the ways in which Sally and Daniel began to develop their identities as people. As was suggested by Figure 2.5, identity and self-confidence in stances towards future learning develop alongside skills, knowledge, and other learning outcomes. They thus feed back, recursively, into future actions and experiences and as the biography and career of each child is gradually constructed.

This brief illustration of the cases of Sally and Daniel demonstrates the importance of the social context in which learning takes place and suggests that it will impact on children irrespective of their individual capabilities. Interestingly, it also reinforces the suggestion that there is no necessary connection between social class factors or income levels and the quality of the learning environment which parents can provide.

SUMMARY AND CONCLUSION

This analysis has significant policy implications for parents, teachers, and school governors since they bear very heavy responsibilities for children's learning and careers. This is so because children develop their perspectives, strategies, and, thus, identities in response to their need to cope with circumstances which such adults control. If adults fail to co-operate, to liaise, to negotiate, or to think their actions through, then it is the children who will suffer. Their lives are, literally, an ongoing test of the continuity and support which adults provide. Certainly such vulnerability deserves our attention and can, I would argue, best be addressed by focusing on the nature of the learning provision in different settings and by recognising the integrated nature of experience.

It is interesting that, at the present time in England and Wales, such issues are far down the educational agenda – an agenda which is dominated by curriculum, assessment, accountability, and management issues. One day, when policies are sought with a more secure foundation on learning processes, it is to be hoped that sociologists will be able to contribute to the available understanding about this extremely important issue.

REFERENCES

Alexander, R. (1984) *Primary Teaching* (London, Cassell).
Apple, M. (1986) *Teachers and Texts* (London, Routledge).
Bennett, N. (1987) 'The search for the effective primary school teacher', in: S. Delamont (Ed.) *The Primary School Teacher* (Lewes, Falmer Press).
Bennett, N. *et al.* (1984) *The Quality of Pupil Learning Experiences* (London, Lawrence Erlbaum).
Bennett, N. and Kell, J. (1989) *A Good Start? Four Year Olds in Infant Schools* (Oxford, Basil Blackwell).
Bruner, J. (1986) *Actual Minds, Possible Worlds* (London, Harvard University Press).
Bruner, J. and Haste, H. (1987) *Making Sense* (London, Methuen).
CACE (1967) *Children and their Primary Schools* (the Plowden Report) (London, HMSO).
Claxton, G. (1984) *Live and Learn* (London, Harper & Row).
Donaldson, M. (1978) *Children's Minds* (London, Fontana).
Doyle, W. (1979) 'Classroom tasks and student abilities', in: P. Peterson and H. Walberg (Eds) *Research on Teaching: concepts, findings and implications* (Berkeley, CA, McCutchan).
Dreeben, R. (1968) *On What is Learned in School* (London, Harvard).
Dweck, C. (1986) 'Motivational processes affecting learning', *American Psychologist*, October, pp. 1040–1048.

Edwards, D. and Mercer, N. (1987) *Common Knowledge* (London, Methuen).

Galton, M. (1989) *Teaching in the Primary School* (London, David Fulton).

Galton, M., Simon, B. and Croll, P. (1980) *Inside Primary Schools* (London, Routledge).

Hartley, D. (1985) *Understanding Primary Schools* (London, Croom Helm).

Haste, H. (1987) 'Growing into rules', in: J. Bruner and H. Haste (Eds) *Making Sense* (London, Methuen).

Hughes, M. (1986) *Children and Number* (Oxford, Basil Blackwell).

King, R. A. (1978) *All Things Bright and Beautiful* (London, Wiley).

King, R. A. (1989) *The Best of Primary Education* (Lewes, Falmer Press).

Lubeck, S. (1985) *Sandbox Society* (Lewes, Falmer Press).

Pollard, A. (1982) 'A model of coping strategies', *British Journal of Sociology of Education*, Vol. 3, No. 1, pp. 19–37.

Pollard, A. (1985) *The Social World of the Primary School* (London, Cassell).

Pollard, A. (1987) *Children and their Primary Schools, A New Perspective* (Lewes, Falmer Press).

Pollard, A. (1990) *Learning in Primary Schools* (London, Cassell).

Pollard, A. and Tann, S. (1987) *Reflective Teaching in the Primary School* (London, Cassell).

Rowland, S. (1987) 'Child in control', in: A. Pollard (Ed.) *Children and their Primary Schools* (Lewes, Falmer Press).

Sharp, R. and Green, A. (1975) *Education and Social Control* (London, Routledge).

Sylva, K. (1987) 'Plowden: history and prospect – research', *Oxford Review of Education*, Vol. 13, No. 1, pp. 3–11.

Task Group on Assessment and Testing (1988) *National Curriculum Report* (London, Department of Education and Science).

Tizard B. and Hughes, M. (1987) 'The intellectual search of young children', in: A. Pollard (Ed.) *Children and Their Primary Schools: a new perspective* (Lewes, Falmer Press).

Vygotsky, L. S. (1962) *Thought and Language* (New York, Wiley).

Vygotsky, L. S. (1978) *Mind in Society* (London, Harvard).

Woods, P. (1990) *Teacher Skills and Strategies* (Lewes, Falmer Press).

Chapter 3

Wally's story

Vivian Gussin Paley

This short vignette of a somewhat disruptive 5-year-old boy in class graphically illustrates the challenge of teaching young children. Wally has a vivid and fast-moving imagination which many other children seem to understand but which his teacher can only observe. His energy, motivation, and interest are tied to this imaginative world rather than to a teacher-specified curriculum and set of classroom procedures. He is thus difficult to manage in school.

In trying to support Wally's learning, what should the teacher's strategy be? Should she discipline him, work through the flow of his imagination, or develop some combination of the two? What skills would be needed?

Most young children have a strong imagination and school life often constrains it. How, though, can it be harnessed for development and learning?

'He did that on purpose! You knocked my tower down on purpose!' Fred grabs Wally's leg and begins to cry.

Wally pushes Fred away. 'I'm a dinosaur. I'm smashing the city.'

'You didn't ask me. You have to ask.' The tears have stopped.

'Dinosaurs don't ask.'

I swoop down, dinosaurlike, and order Wally to the time-out chair. This will give me a ten-minute respite from his fantasies. His quick smile that is a silent laugh and his laugh that is a lion's roar are gone. He stares past me at the window, hunched over on the chair. Wally has come to our school after two and a half years in a day-care centre. Nothing in the school report suggests the scope of his imagination. It is a customary 'bad boy' report: restless, hyperactive, noisy, uncooperative. Tonight the children will give their mothers a similar description: there's a boy Wally who growls like a lion; the teacher yells at him but not at me.

'Are you being bad, Wally?' asks Rose. Rose is from the same day-care centre as Wally, and she once told me that he got spanked there every day.

'Were you bad, Wally?' she asks again.

'I was a dinosaur.'

'Oh.'

Wally cannot understand why I don't admire him when he is a dinosaur. Before he goes home he'll ask me if he was good. He has to tell his mother, and he is never sure. The time-out chair is not connected to his perception of events.

'Was I good today?' he asks. I am tying his shoes at the top of the outside steps.

'You were OK except for the playground.'

'What did I do?'

'You knocked down that first-grade boy.'

'The black boy? Jason? We were superheroes.'

'You were too rough.'

'He's still my friend.'

Fred is still his friend, too. As Wally changes from dinosaur to superhero to lion, Fred keeps an eye on him. He examines Wally's behaviour and then watches my reaction. Wally, however, never watches me. He seldom takes his cues from adults, bringing forth his own script for being a 5-year-old. He is never bored, except when he's on the time-out chair, and even then his head dances with images and stories.

'Whoever sits in the time-out chair will die for six years until the magic spell is broken,' he says one day after a session on the chair.

'They turn into a chair,' Eddie decides, 'and then God breaks the spell.'

'Not God,' corrects Wally. 'God is for harder things.'

'Fairies could do it,' says Lisa. 'Not the tooth kind.'

'It *is* a fairy,' Wally agrees. 'The one for magic spells.'

The children like Wally's explanations for events better than mine, so I give fewer and fewer interpretations each day and instead listen to Wally's. The familiar chord he strikes stimulates others to speak with candour, and I am the beneficiary. However, Wally does not always teach me what I want to learn. He is a lightning rod, attracting the teacher's negative sparks, keeping them from landing on others. It is a role that receives little credit.

'You're riding too fast, Wally,' I caution.

'OK.'

'Don't crash into the wall.'

'OK.'

'Do *not* slam into things, Wally!'

'I didn't see it.'

When I begin to play the piano, he leaps over Lisa and Rose to get to the piano first, but before the song is finished he is on the outer edge of the rug, growling.

'Don't make that noise, Wally,' I say.

'It's a warning growl.'

'Not at piano time.'

'I'm guarding the lions,' he whispers. 'The growl means I hear a suspicious noise.' The children stop squirming and watch Wally as he crouches in concentration. Several boys copy his pose and give low growls.

One day at lunch Wally says, 'I'm going to be a mother lion when I grow up.'

'A mother lion?' I ask. 'Can you become a mother lion?'

'Sure. The library has everything. Even magic. When I'm eight I can learn magic. That's how.'

'Why a mother lion?'

'Because I would have babies and do the mommy work. They stay home and take care of babies. Daddy lions go to work and have to walk fast.'

Deana has been listening. 'People can't turn into animals.'

'That's true,' Wally says.

'You changed your mind, Wally?' I ask.

'It *is* true, what she said. But I'm going to use magic.'

'Oh, I didn't hear him say that.' Deana leans forward. 'If he uses magic he might. Maybe. It's very hard to do.'

Fred joins in. 'I might become a daddy crocodile. Every time a person tries to kill them they can swat at their guns.'

'Fred,' I ask, 'do you believe Wally can become a mother lion?'

'No. Only if he practises very hard.'

Eddie and Lisa are in the doll corner when I bring up the subject. 'Wally has decided to become a lion when he grows up.' They look up and laugh hesitantly. 'He intends to learn magic,' I add.

'Oh, that way,' says Eddie. 'It depends how hard he studies. That's the hardest thing to do.'

'It's impossible,' Lisa argues. 'You can't turn into a lion. That's too big. Maybe a mouse or a cat.' She pauses. 'But he can dress up to look like a lion.'

I turn to Earl. 'Do you suppose a boy could become a mother?'

'He can put on a dress and a wig,' Earl answers.

'And a mask,' says Lisa.

'How about a lion? Can Wally become a lion?'

'No,' answers Earl. 'He has to be a huge man with sideburns.'

'What if he uses magic?'

'Oh, I thought you meant ordinary. He could do it with magic,' says Earl.

'But it *would* be very hard,' says Lisa.

The next day I ask Andy, 'Do you think it's interesting to be a father?'

'Sure. If a robber comes, the father punches him in the nose.'

'Wally wants to become a lion, Andy. What do you think?'

Andy is quiet for a moment. 'He can't. Unless he becomes an actress. Or he can wish for it, and if God wants you to become that then you can do it. Wait. I'm not too sure about lions. I know he could become a smaller thing. But he could dress up like a lion.'

'Would he *be* a lion if he dressed up like a lion?'

'I mean just until he learns to do that trick.'

Wally frowns and squirms beside me on the playground bench. A hot flush gives his brown skin a reddish tone. His black curly hair is coated with sand, sweat, and dirt.

'You get into fights out here every day,' I say. 'You keep making me punish you.'

'I don't care,' he shrugs.

'I know you care. You'd rather be running around.'

'I don't care.'

Later he dictates a story.

Once upon a time there was a little lion and he lived alone because his mother and father was dead and one day he went hunting and he saw two lions and they were his mother and father so he took his blanket to their den because it was bigger.

'But weren't the mother and father dead?' I ask. He has a quick answer. 'They came alive again because he only thought they were dead. They really went out shopping and he didn't recognise them because they were wearing different clothes.'

'Can I be the father in your story?' Fred asks. We usually acted out stories as soon as they were written and books as soon as they were read.

'Okay,' says Wally. 'Fred will be the father, Rose is the mother, I'm the little brother, and Eddie is the magician.'

'There's no magician in your story,' I remind Wally, who doesn't read yet.

'Yes, there is. I just didn't tell you about him.'

A few days later a first-grade teacher complains about Wally.

'This is embarrassing,' I tell Wally and the whole class. 'I don't know what else to do about you, Wally.'

'Just keep reminding him,' says Lisa.

'But I continually warn him,' I tell her.

'Remind him nicely.'

'Lisa, he made you cry today.'

'Keep telling Wally not to be rough,' she says.

Eddie agrees. 'Say to him, "Be good, Wally, will you?" '

I turn to Wally. 'Your classmates don't want you to be punished.'

He smiles shyly. 'That's because we're friends.'

Chapter 4

Bilingual by rights

Helen Savva

Helen Savva draws attention to the challenges which bilingual children face in primary schools. She argues that school practices can be harmed by lack of awareness and by teacher indifference but that much more positive and appreciative teaching is possible. Of particular concern is the way in which the national curriculum structures the teaching of English and Savva suggests that there can be no genuine equality of opportunity for bilingual pupils in schools unless the whole of their language competence is recognised and supported.

Operating in more than one language is normal. It is not in itself a problem and it certainly does not constitute a learning difficulty. Yet those of us who live in England live in a country in which monolingualism is still regarded as the norm. This is both a cause and an effect of official attitudes towards bilingualism and bilingual children. Most recently, we have had national curriculum provisions placed before us which, whatever their good qualities in other respects, are still inadequate regarding the education of bilingual children in England.

Bilingualism is a sensitive issue. It arouses strong emotions in teachers. They can feel defensive, threatened, guilty; they can feel that they are doing their best in difficult circumstances and with very little guidance or support. Quite often when I talk to teachers about bilingualism, some say (and they say it as though they have really caught me out): 'But my parents only want their children to learn English at school', and/or: 'But the bilingual children in my class won't admit that they can speak another language.' And I always want to ask: 'Well, why do you think that might be? Just ask your-self why.'

POSITIVE PRACTICE AND NEGATIVE ATTITUDES

Satvinder, who is 9 years old, wrote the story of Jethro Banks in Punjabi. She wrote it at the invitation of a bilingual advisory teacher who had been working in her classroom. This was the very first occasion on which

Satvinder had been encouraged to use her knowledge of her home language at school.

Activities which led up to Satvinder's piece of writing included listening to the story of Jethro Banks being told in English and Punjabi, followed by the class collaborating in groups to re-work the story and present it in dramatic form. In undertaking this work, the children were invited to draw upon their whole linguistic repertoire (language/s, accents, dialects). Having written her story in Punjabi, Satvinder produced another version in English. Satvinder explained to her teacher that it would be impossible to write a literal translation since differences in language structures would render the second version nonsensical. She was able to discuss the differences in language structures between Punjabi and English and thus explore her knowledge of two language systems explicitly.

In the transcript which follows, Satvinder and a group of friends in her class discuss their experience of being bilingual with the advisory teacher.

TEACHER: Do you speak Punjabi more at home or do you speak it more at school?

JASWANT: I speak it more at home like we come from an Indian family and so we speak it mostly at home 'cos like they're Indian and they speak Indian so I speak Indian.

TEACHER: And what about the children in your class, do you speak Punjabi to them?

JASWANT: No.

TEACHER: Why is that?

JASWANT: 'Cos most of them are English and my Indian friends and I don't speak Indian with them like I sort of get shy speaking to them.

SHARAN: Yeah. Sometimes like we are talking in the playground and someone English comes along then like we kind of stop and start talking English 'cos I think I'm going to get the mick taken out of me and things like that.

TEACHER: Do you get a lot of that?

ALL: Yeah! Yeah! They start saying 'bard, bard' and stuff like that.

TEACHER: What do they start saying?

SHARAN: 'Bard, bard', 'ding, ding' and all that and putting on, making fun.

SHEREKHA: That's what J – does, she goes: 'ardi, ardi, ardi'.

SHARAN: They make up stupid words and that, and they swear and that.

TEACHER: Do they?

ALL: Yeah.

SATVINDER.: 'Cos they reckon that what you are saying is something about them.

SHARAN: They think that if you're talking in Indian and we look at them they start saying horrible things. Some of them don't even know what we're talking about then they go and tell the teacher and some of the teachers will say don't talk in your own language because other people can't understand it.

JASWANT AND
SHEREKHA: Yeah, they say it's an English school.

SHARAN: Yeah, and the children say to you there is no place for Indians in this school and country and things. They say go back to your own country so that people can understand you.

It may be that teachers at the school would be both surprised and alarmed to learn about the overt racism which is the shared experience of the children who contributed to this discussion.

I would want to say to people who insist that bilingual children won't admit that they speak another language that we have to provide an environment in which children feel they can. In order to use their whole linguistic repertoire in schools, children have to be secure in the knowledge that their languages have a legitimate role to play in their learning. If they come to understand that languages other than English can only ever be peripheral or suspect, that racism will be countenanced or ignored, they will remain silent. On the other hand, if we open up our classrooms linguistically and culturally, we will be surprised just how forthcoming bilingual children and their parents can be.

MULTILINGUAL DIVERSITY

Tacko was a small boy of 4 when I knew him. He attended nursery school in Deptford. Tacko and his parents were Kurdish refugees. His mother took him to school every morning. Steve Cummings, his teacher, was genuinely interested in the linguistic and cultural experiences of all the children. Tacko was therefore prepared to share some of his experiences with Steve.

Steve made a recording of Tacko who wanted to sing a song; this turned out to be a Kurdish resistance song which Tacko sang with genuine feeling. A conversation followed during which Tacko revealed a surprisingly sophisticated grasp of the situation in Kurdistan, for one so young.

STEVE: What do the people of Kurdistan want to happen? Do they want the war to finish?

TACKO: They want to don't fight. Know what? We say: 'We shall fight!

We shall win! Viva, viva, Kurdistan!' You know why we said
that? Because the soldiers got our house at Kurdistan.

STEVE: Does your family want to go back? If they could live in
Kurdistan without fighting?

TACKO: No.

STEVE: Aren't they going to go back to Kurdistan?

TACKO: No, they won't because the soldiers will kill us. They won't let
us into our house, they've got our house as their house.

STEVE: What if the soldiers go away and never come back? Would your
parents go back to Kurdistan?

TACKO: Yes . . . yes, if there was no fighting . . . all the soldiers killed
and in hospital . . . they would go back to Kurdistan, if there
was no fighting and get our house back.

Tacko took the tape home. Two days later, Tacko's mother brought Steve a
videotape which had been smuggled out of Kurdistan because she wanted
him to understand more about the situation there and how it affected her
family.

That kind of trust doesn't just happen. We have to earn it. With luck,
Tacko will hold on to his very strong sense of personal identity and his
commitment to his home language and culture. Meanwhile, his knowledge
of the English language and of the interplay of cultures revealed through
English will develop and become increasingly sophisticated. Tacko has the
right to choose how the languages and cultures which are part of his life
should exist and operate in relation to each other. And it is different for each
child.

One of the key lessons to be learnt about bilingual children is that they are
not a homogeneous group. There is a tendency to discuss them and their
needs as though they were identical. Linguistically, socially, culturally,
politically, the lives of bilingual children are complex and their experiences
diverse. They operate along a continuum of language competencies in
English and a home language or languages, ranging from virtual beginners to
full competence. Some are literate in languages other than English; others
only speak those languages. Some are members of established and organised
communities. Others belong to groups in a state of flux, unsettled and on the
move. Some bilingual children attend multilingual schools; others attend
predominantly mono-ethnic schools where English is the only language
recognised; others attend schools where they constitute a linguistic majority.

An example will help to illustrate this diversity. It is from a multilingual
school in the East End of London where I worked as co-ordinator of the
national writing project in the ILEA. It was a school that did more than
value linguistic and cultural diversity; it placed it at the centre of children's
learning. It was there in the range of languages spoken, on the notices and
displays around the school, in the activities of the parents and other adults in

the school, in the resources in the classrooms and in the library, and in the children's work.

Here I met Runa and Jharna, two young girls who were constant companions in and out of the classroom. At the age of 7 they were fluently bilingual, speaking both English and Sylheti at school. At home they spoke Sylheti with their families. (Sylhet is a region in north-eastern Bangladesh whose language is sufficiently different from standard Bengali to be considered a distinct language rather than a dialect of Bengali.) Runa and Jharna attended community school every afternoon and there they learnt standard Bengali and, for religious purposes, Arabic. They were linguistically competent and sophisticated at the age of 7. They had that confidence in part because they attended a mainstream school where they were taught by adults who genuinely valued their bilingualism and in part because they attended a local community school.

Those of us who work in mainstream schools need closer contact with community schools and a clearer understanding of the work they do. Community languages should be taught in mainstream schools and should be made available to all children; but this will never replace the work of community schools. Bilingual children are greatly helped by access to both. Community schools enable children not only to learn the home language, but to learn through the home language about the culture and history of the country of origin. These schools provide intensive cultural experience and a special degree of parental involvement and commitment.

Tacko, Runa, and Jharna are examples of the most positive thing that the Cox Report has to say about bilingual children. It appears in Chapter 6: 'Many pupils are bilingual and sometimes biliterate and quite often literally know more about language than their teachers, at least in some respects.'

If we truly value children's linguistic competencies we will take the trouble to find out what they do know about language. If we don't value their linguistic competencies, neither they nor their parents are likely to tell us what they know.

BILINGUALISM AND THE NATIONAL CURRICULUM

Chapter 10 of the Cox Report, entitled 'Bilingual Children', is not about how best to serve the interests of bilingual children as a whole; it is simply about teaching English as a second language. The report at least gives its support to the now familiar idea that developing bilinguals learn best in the mainstream classroom. But in paragraph 10.10 we discover the sole purpose of this enlightened position:

> The implications are therefore that, where bilingual pupils need extra help, this should be given in the classroom as part of normal lessons and there may be a need for bilingual teaching support and for books and

other written materials to be available in the pupils' mother tongues until such time as they are competent in English.

It would appear that resources which reflect linguistic diversity should be made available only to bilingual children and then only to those bilingual children who are in need of extra help. In addition, these resources should be withdrawn when bilingual children become competent in English. This is transitional, not full bilingualism. It is not the development and mutual enrichment of two or more languages and cultures but the idea that development must involve the eventual supremacy of one language and the neglect of others.

In Wales, there is official recognition that bilingual education extends cultural and social choice (not so in England). We know how hard-won that right was. Research quoted in Chapter 13 of the Cox Report about the growth of language competencies among bilingual Welsh- and English-speaking children tells us that full, balanced bilingualism does benefit children's intellectual development, at least in Wales. The Cox Report maintains, however, that the positions in England and Wales are not comparable: 'In Wales, Welsh is an official language and a core subject of the National Curriculum.'

ASSESSMENT

We now understand that children who are learning English as an additional language should be actively encouraged to use their proficiency in one language in order to learn the new language and simultaneously learn about other things. Jim Cummins (1984) and others have stressed the creative interplay between languages and have pointed out that, although surface features between, say, Gujerati and English are clearly separate, there is an underlying proficiency which is common across languages. This common proficiency makes it possible to transfer linguistic and other knowledge.

This influential idea has had a positive impact on classroom practice. It has certainly helped to quash the foolish notion that bilingual children go about their business in the world in a state of perpetual linguistic confusion. But the interactive development of competence in more than one language takes time – too much time, apparently, for national curriculum testing procedures.

Currently, teachers have the 'choice' – not really a choice at all – of disapplying bilingual children from the national curriculum and its testing procedures if they have only the beginnings of English, or accepting, if children are at a transitional stage of learning English, that their test results (their levels) are going to be, certainly in English, lower than those of their monolingual peers, even though they are engaged in essential cognitive activity of a high order.

Statutory orders on assessment arrangements at key stage 1 allow children to be assessed in home languages in mathematics and science, where circumstances allow. The orders prohibit this in English. We can understand the argument which says: 'English is English. English can't be a language other than English.' The problem lies in the decision not to recognise that, for bilingual children, the development of competence in English is complementary to the development of competence in a home language or languages. For this and other reasons (like the inappropriateness of the idea of subject English to most primary school curricula and developments in the secondary school subject which now include within English the study of media and communications, for example), it would be much better to rename 'English'. 'Language and Communications' would be an improved alternative.

The government currently proposes that when bilingual children gain lower levels than they would gain if operating in their strongest language, that is simply an indication that they need more support. According to the Cox Report, to record a low level of achievement would not reflect a child's general ability, but indicate that he or she needed 'special help in English language skills' to 'overcome their problems with the English language'. We are presented here with a deficit view of bilingual children and an inadequate model of their language learning and development. No mention is made of the crude, invidious comparisons likely to be made within and between schools as a result.

There is no way round this problem at present. The position of those bilingual children for whom English is still the weaker language, in the face of levels, is unjust and unacceptable. We must make sure, at least, that the systems we develop for teacher assessment during a key stage are of the sort which build up an authentic picture of a child's achievements and needs over time, including references to cognitive breakthroughs which a teacher can see developing bilingual children making.

THE MULTILINGUAL CLASSROOM

Much of what I have written, especially about the national curriculum, has been critical. I have highlighted commonly held misconceptions which can undervalue and obstruct bilingual children's achievements. It is equally important, however, to acknowledge the excellent work carried out in many LEAs, schools, and classrooms by teachers who succeed in valuing and extending children's multilingualism. In the hands of informed and imaginative teachers (whether bilingual or monolingual), the multilingual classroom can provide the most challenging and intellectually stimulating environment for all children.

In conclusion, I offer three principles which we should adopt in order to construct such an environment, and provide examples in support of them.

1. Create the conditions which enable children to gain access to the whole curriculum by encouraging them to use, as appropriate, their strongest or preferred language.

Ozlem is a bilingual child who is a virtual beginner in English. She attends junior school, where she is the only Turkish speaker in her class. However, Ozlem has access to the curriculum and can operate at an appropriate cognitive level because her teacher encourages her to learn through her strongest and preferred language. As well as speaking Turkish, she reads and writes it fluently.

Ozlem takes an active part as her class carries out science experiments which test different fabrics. Although she does not understand English yet, she can observe the experiments as they are carried out. The synthesising and internalising of ideas is done in Turkish; so is the recording of data and information.

Ozlem is making connections between and across languages. This ability to reflect on the structure of language has to be advantageous to the learner. Children who are learning English as a second language can enter school at any point in their educational career. The fact that they may not as yet speak, read, or write English fluently does not mean that their intellectual development should come to an abrupt end. They may, for example, have a great deal of knowledge about mathematics, science, or literature. When working in a comprehensive school in the East End of London, I was told a story about a fourth-year pupil who had arrived recently from Bangladesh. Withdrawn from his mainstream mathematics lesson, he was taken to work with a small group on 'extra maths'. After completing a series of elementary calculations which the teacher provided, he pushed himself angrily from the table, chalked a complex algebraic equation on the blackboard and said: 'In Bangladesh, me!'

2. Take every opportunity to promote children's understanding of cultural diversity by presenting a world view through the curriculum and through the materials selected to resource it.

A class of year 6 children was embarking on a term's topic on 'Communication'. Since mathematics is a universal form of communication and since it owes its development to many cultures, the teacher, Bet Lowe, decided to make it a significant part of the topic. In particular, Bet wanted children to examine some of the contributions made to maths by many cultures. In considering the names of numbers and the way names used could reflect the base used (5 and 10 generally), and why this was so, the children examined the number systems of the Egyptians, Babylonians, Abyssinians, and Mayans. Bet Lowe writes:

> The Mayan system interested us most – it is a base 360 system, based on a year. It facilitated calculations of the seasons. This made us aware of how

closely number systems are bound to culture. We looked at numbers in many languages to see what patterns could be found. From this, children were asked to develop their own counting system, having first decided which base they would use, and to develop names and symbols for their numerals. This was followed by groups of children setting problems for other groups to solve.

The children were thoroughly fascinated by the realisation that there are more numbers and number systems than the ones commonly known and learnt about. In fact, there is a wealth of knowledge that we don't acknowledge; there are whole areas of number development that we have forgotten about.

3. Take every opportunity to ensure that the curriculum both reflects and makes authentic use of the linguistic diversity in our schools and the rest of society.

In her infant classroom, Avril Bristow produced dual-text story books with her pupils, their parents, and other adults. The children worked on the original text and on the illustrations. The adults participating in the project produced a second version of the text in a variety of home languages.

The next sequence of activities was part of a term's work on the theme of texts, designed by Lorraine Dawes and Derek Hoddy for two year 4 classes. They outline here their reasons for planning a cross-curricular theme on this subject:

> We wanted a theme that would develop the children's awareness of the multiracial and multilingual society they live in, and develop their ability to think critically. Redbridge Junior School in the London Borough of Redbridge is mixed: approximately a third of the children are Jewish, and another third are of Asian origin. Such diversity is only a resource when it is actively utilised; children (or adults) do not spontaneously volunteer information about their cultural, linguistic or religious background unless encouraged to do so, in the confidence that such information will be positively received. How often can ethnic minority pupils think to themselves as they are learning: 'That's my history, that's my language, that's my culture'? The curriculum has to create the climate for discussion that invites all children to share their experience. We wanted to make the most of every opportunity.
>
> Another concern was that children tend to accept everything they read at face value, while subconsciously absorbing the hidden messages. We wanted to give them the habit of thinking critically about their reading, by developing the language they need to manipulate such ideas.

The activities, spanning several weeks, included a study of how a book is made (incorporating the idea that books are published in many languages).

The classes discussed the kinds of stereotyping sometimes found in books and the ways in which our perceptions of people can be influenced by such stereotypes. They read fairy tales and considered how alternative readings could be achieved by challenging the writers' intentions. They examined newspapers published in languages other than English, both abroad and locally, and discussed the needs of people in Britain for newspapers in their community languages.

A SUCCESSFUL BALANCE

There is a sense of community in the successful multilingual classroom. Linguistic and cultural similarities and differences between children are central to the learning that goes on there. It would be simplistic and naive to suggest that tensions do not exist in such classrooms, or that children do not experience conflict and contradiction, or that racism is not a factor. However, I do believe that children are empowered if that which is shared and common, as well as that which is personal and individual, has status in the classroom.

Meanwhile, we have the national curriculum. On the whole, it fails to provide the positive framework for the successful multilingual classroom that we might have hoped for. However, we must do our best to interpret the statutory requirements in ways which increase bilingual children's sense of achievement and affirmation and increase all children's knowledge of the linguistic diversity which is a permanent feature of our society.

REFERENCE

Cummins, J. (1984) 'Bilingualism and Special Education: Issues in Assessment and Pedagogy', *Multilingual Matters*, 6.

Chapter 5

Sex roles in the formative years

Sara Delamont

In this chapter, Sara Delamont reminds us that children are never seen and treated simply as 'children' in school, but as gendered. Her review of research shows that teachers seem to have different expectations of girls and boys, and that girls and boys systematically receive different forms of interactions from the adults around them. The reinforcement of gender differences can be seen in classroom management techniques and the teaching children receive. Not surprisingly, as the children grow, they assimilate these gender stereotypes themselves. In trying to ensure equal opportunities in the classroom, and in the light of the evidence presented in this chapter, what should the teacher's strategy be?

From their earliest hours, boys and girls are brought up in different ways, to reinforce different behaviours and punish or prevent 'wrong' activities. There is no real evidence on how far parents, teachers, and others are conscious or unconscious of dividing and segregating the young in this way. There is important evidence about teachers' expectations for boys and girls, and their performance on tests and in ordinary schoolwork, which needs summarising here. At the infant and primary stages girls are more successful than boys in every subject except mathematics (Douglas 1964; Davie *et al.* 1972; Mortimore *et al.* 1988) and are rated more highly for good behaviour and personality by teachers. Ingelby and Cooper (1974) collected teacher ratings on 180 West Indian, Asian, Anglo-Saxon, Cypriot, and other white London primary children. Girls received more favourable ratings than boys on all the scales except sociability. Girls were seen as superior in character, brightness, schoolwork, home background, and language skills. During the school year the gap between boys and girls narrowed on all the scales except schoolwork. Ethnic minority children had worse ratings than Anglo-Saxons throughout, but the gender gap was equally pronounced within each group. That is, West Indian girls were rated better than West Indian boys, Cypriot girls better than Cypriot boys, and so on. Hartley (1978) collected data on 393 infant school pupils. The teacher rated the working-class pupils as untidier, noisier, and less able to concentrate than middle-class pupils, and, within each class, boys were rated rougher, noisier, untidier, and less able to concentrate than girls. Thus girls from non-manual homes were most favourably perceived by teachers, and manual working-class boys were rated worst. Hartley also got the pupils to rate each other, and their ratings showed clear sex differences in the same direction as the teachers'. Hartley also found that the sex differences were greater in the middle class than the working class. He concludes that 'the pre-school sex-roles of children within the same social class background do not equally prepare them for the pupil role' (p. 81).

Teacher ratings of children are important if they relate to teacher behaviour or are communicated to the children. There is considerable evidence that teachers' expectations for children do influence their interactions with them. Brophy and Good (1974) showed that pupils believed to be clever were given longer to answer teacher questions, and more prompts and hints to help their thinking, than pupils who were believed to be stupid. The subsequent research is summarised in Mortimore *et al.* (1988: 163–75), Good (1987), and Brophy (1985).

CLASSROOM MANAGEMENT

Teachers in many nursery, infant, and junior schools regularly use sex and gender as an organising principle and a management strategy within their classrooms. King (1978: 52) offers some fine examples, such as the teacher saying, 'Boys close eyes. Girls creep out, quietly get your coats. Don't let the boys hear you!' This shows a teacher using sex segregation to motivate and to control children, a combination which is extremely common. Later King quotes a mistress ridiculing a child with the comment 'Oh, Philip is a little girl. He's in the wrong queue' (p. 68) as a disciplinary strategy. This is a common teacher usage.

Exactly similar patterns were found in Gryll Grange and Guy Mannering among 9-year-olds. For example, at Gryll Grange the pupils had to complete a worksheet which asked them to measure features of the room such as the length of the window sills, the height of the doors, and so on. Throughout one morning the teacher encouraged the class to hurry and complete this work, and her incentive was a race between boys and girls:

> Miss Tweed announces, 'I'm still waiting for most of the boys to do that measuring . . .'. (Later) Yvette has finished measuring her worksheet. Miss Tweed says, 'Another girl finished'. . . . (Later when Tammy and Stephanie are up) Miss Tweed says, 'Only seven girls to go'. Someone asks how many boys and the answer is lots. . . . Later when Kenneth is up for marking Miss Tweed says, 'Only five girls to go now'. 'How many boys?' 'Nearly all of them.'

This was Gryll Grange, a 'progressive' school, but Guy Mannering was equally characterised by gender-typing. For example, in a cookery lesson the home economics teacher said:

> *Boys* – is it boys who are making so much noise or is it a group of girls? . . . Be careful boys that you get your tables all nice and straight.

Incidentally, cookery may nowadays be done by both boys and girls, but as King (1978: 43) also shows, they are clearly distinguished in the school kitchen. He quotes:

> TEACHER: What must you do before any cooking?
> CHILDREN: Roll up your sleeves and wash your hands.
> TEACHER: Right, girls go first.

The boys put on green-striped aprons and girls flowery ones. A number of further incidents will show how typical sex separation is in discipline, motivation, and control.

> Communal singing in the Hall. Two teachers and all six first year classes (180 pupils). Towards the end of the lesson they sing *There's a Hole in My Bucket* with the sexes divided. Boys are told to 'pretend to be a bit gormless. I know you're not'. (*Guy Mannering*)

> (In Maths) There is a wasp in the room. Mrs Forrest asks a boy to get rid of it. He kills it. (*Guy Mannering*)

> Music with Mr Vaughan. Has pupils clapping rhythms – has two girls doing it alone, then two boys. After playing part of *Peter and the Wolf* has scale singing – competing boys versus girls. (*Gryll Grange*)

> Miss Tweed's class are going to have their school photographs taken. The girls are sent first. (The photographer is in the foyer with a blue backcloth hung up). . . . Kenneth has made 82 + 47 equal over 300. Held up for public ridicule, told he should be the Chancellor of the Exchequer and that 'Scotsmen don't usually make mistakes over money'. Girls are told 'You've done enough fussing. I know you're all filmstars' and asked about the photographer, 'Did he faint with delight at such loveliness?' (*Gryll Grange*)

This last extract shows the use of gender labelling in discipline, where boys are shamed by reference to adult males in responsible positions, while girls are exhorted to be beautiful. These kinds of controlling strategies shade into teaching, where gender roles are again clearly separated, as the next section will show.

TEACHING

Teachers in nursery, infant, and primary schools value instruction both in basic skills and in social and emotional development (Ashton *et al.* 1975; Ashton 1981). In both kinds of instruction they are, on the evidence available, polarising and differentiating boys and girls and reinforcing quite different behaviour patterns. Lisa Serbin (1978) spent five years observing fifteen pre-school classrooms in New York working in four schools. She offers the following account of the build-up to Easter in 1971 as a typical example of teacher instruction in social behaviour. The teacher played *Here Comes Peter Cottontail* while the boys hopped all over the room. Then the girls had a turn as rabbits. Next the teacher played *In Your Easter Bonnet* while the girls paraded. The teacher said, solemnly:

> Ladies, that isn't the way we have a parade. When we have a parade, we all walk very nicely, and we pick up our feet so we don't make lots of noise on the floor, and we all walk like little ladies. Now let's do it again.

She played again and the girls tiptoed. A boy asked for a second turn for boys. So the teacher played *Here Comes Peter Cottontail* again. No one said the boys should be quiet.

Serbin's observations show a typical incident with young schoolchildren, where the teaching is about social behaviour as much as any intellectual content, and the social behaviour is highly stereotyped. Other observations Serbin made were that boys got a great deal more teacher attention than girls whether they were physically close to the teacher or not, while girls got attention only when they were physically close to the teacher. The staff told Serbin that little girls were boring, and clung too closely to them, while boys were more independent. These teachers did not realise that their own interaction patterns were reinforcing the very behaviour they disliked. Little *girls* had to stay close behind the teacher to get any attention, while boys did not. The kind of teacher–pupil interaction was also different for boys and girls. Boys got more teacher interaction, more ticking off, more praise, and a different type of instruction. Boys got 'more detailed step-by-step instruction in how to solve a problem or how to do something for themselves'. Serbin found that boys got eight times as much instruction as girls, and, when teachers were faced with this, they said that girls picked up things by themselves, while boys needed teaching.

Serbin also looked at what children chose to play with, and found that those pre-school children who played with bricks, trucks, and climbing apparatus were better at all the problem-solving tasks involving visual spatial reasoning. In contrast, children who played with dolls and housekeeping materials were better at fine motor tasks. Among these children the two sets of abilities were not totally sex specific, although it was predominantly boys who played with the bricks, trucks, and climbing apparatus, and primarily girls who played at housekeeping tasks. Serbin found that teachers were reinforcing the incipient sex segregation. When there were three new toys in the classes, a fishing game, a sewing game, and a counting puzzle, the staff told the classes that they could go fishing like Daddy and sewing like Mommy. Then they got boys to demonstrate the fishing game and girls to demonstrate the sewing game. Serbin was also aware that the staff had a biased pattern of object usage. They spent their time among the 'teaching tasks' and did not go over to the bricks and trucks. This meant that girls, who stayed close to the teachers, never went near the bricks or cars. The researchers then asked the teachers to go to the area where the bricks were, and, when they did, the girls went with them and began playing with bricks and cars. Similarly, teachers spent little time with dolls, but if a teacher did go and work with them, boys would follow her there. Serbin says, 'In about ten minutes the whole block corner was occupied by boys and girls, half the children had never been in that area before'. In other words if the teacher encouraged girls to play with 'male' toys by going to work with them herself, girls would play with them, and girls who did improved their spatial reasoning. Yet before the researchers showed the teachers how they were failing to get all children involved in all kinds of tasks, teachers were unaware of it. If Serbin's observations are true in Britain (and the work of Adelman (1979) suggests they might be) then some action research to encourage each gender to develop all its skills by trying all toys and games seems a priority.

King's work on infant schools shows how instruction in social skills and academic matters are closely tied together. For example:

(A boy has found a snail in the wet sand box)
When a girl went to touch it, the teacher said, 'Ug, don't touch it, it's all slimy. One of the boys, pick it up and put it outside'.

(King 1978: 43)

Just the thing to encourage scientific curiosity.

A similar pattern was common in the lessons for 9-year-olds at Gryll Grange, as the following extracts show:

In Mrs Hind's class, pupils are writing their own sentences, each one including three words from the board. The word trios are:
boy football window
gorilla cage keeper
monkeys coconuts hunters
soldier army tank
Several ask her about the words so she reads through them.
Says of 'soldier army tank'
'That's one for the boys really I suppose.'

Here we see an entirely gratuitous comment by a teacher implying only boys are interested in warfare. It adds nothing to the lesson, and indeed detracts from it. (It might be good to offer pupils less stereotyped sets of words such as 'girl football window', 'WRAC army tank', just to see what pupils did.)

> French with Miss Tweed. Miss Tweed can get lots of pupil involvement in French by saying 'C'est une fille' and pointing to a boy, and vice versa. . . . When we get on to individual children answering one girl says she doesn't know whether Ralph is a girl or a boy. Miss Tweed makes a great joke about it, 'been here a week and a half and you don't know if "it" is a boy or a girl'.
>
> Sammy can reduce the whole class to laughter by pointing to Kenneth and saying Voilà Maman. Nanette can do the same thing, and the joke does not pall. . . . Duncan calls Malcolm a girl which is very funny to the class.
>
> Go back to tape. Miss Tweed divides them into boys and girls, the boys are to copy the man on the tape, the girls are to copy the woman.
>
> 11.24 P.E. as Mr Valentine appears to take the boys to football, Miss Tweed says C'est Maman and gets laughter.

French, a language with gender-differentiated words, is a new idea to the pupils. Teaching the crucial difference between une fille and un fils using the pupils' sense of humour may be good instructional technique. However, it reinforces the idea that males and females are completely different, and any confusion is a source of hilarity. Sometimes there is not even an instructional strategy. Mr LeGard at Guy Mannering managed to put sex stereotyping into a library lesson on 'The Book':

> He tells them on the title page there will be the author's name, and that tells you something about the book. You may recognize the author and therefore know he is a good one. 'If you get a chemistry book by a senior master at a big school he ought to know what he is talking about but if it is by someone who is just a housewife, well!'

Clearly the housewife must stick to her real job, and not branch out.

At Kenilworth, in a music lesson Mr Tippett was introducing the stringed instruments:

> Mr Tippett gave out a large number of broken and derelict violins. He said they were not all complete but they would do for drawing. . . . He began by saying that violins were like young ladies: they are fairly big at the top, they are small-waisted, and they have got . . . err 'Big bums' says a child.
>
> 'Yes, that is right, large bottoms' says Mr Tippett.
>
> Then he asked what the family the violin belonged to was called. Luella said 'The strings'.

In Mrs Hind's class. Boy is up at her desk. She reads aloud from book 'Mary says she likes looking after people who are ill. What would she like to be when she grows up?' The answer is, of course, 'a nurse'. Doctor is not mentioned as a possible answer. . . . Mrs Hind tells Kenton to show his book to Janice to help her draw an aeroplane. (*Gryll Grange*)

Here we see a highly stereotyped piece of teaching material, an English comprehension book. Women are nurses, not doctors. It is also noticeable that the teacher does not add the idea of a woman being a doctor to counteract the sexism of the book, which she could easily do. We also see an example of one pupil being asked to teach another, which is a feature of a 'progressive' school. However, the particular example shows an assumed male superiority in the sphere of machinery/transport. The girl is not told to find out about aeroplanes, but to ask a male.

In Miss Tweed's class for a Maths test. There are mixed questions, straight calculations and problems such as 'If you were sent by your mother to buy half a dozen eggs, how many would you bring her?'

This is again an example of unnecessary sex typing in academic materials. Why say it is 'mother' who sends for food and is responsible for providing meals? It could just as easily be 'Dad' sending for the eggs, but it is not. Teaching materials are full of such implicit sexism, which is never counterbalanced by maths problems about Dad going shopping or Mum digging a trench.

PUPILS' VIEWS

Of course it would be ridiculous to suggest that teachers are enforcing sex differentiation upon pupils to whom it is unknown. Pupils come to school with clearly stereotyped ideas about boys and girls. Guttentag and Bray (1976: 284) found that among 10-year-olds each sex stereotyped the other. Boys thought girls were neat, sensitive, gentle, cautious, good looking, obedient, quiet, apt to cry a lot, and weak! The children actually operated a triple standard. Both sexes were committed to the idea that they could try anything as individuals, that their same-sex peers could break the rules of masculinity and femininity to some extent, but that children of the opposite sex must be rigidly conventional. So it was, in David's eyes, fine for him to be a ballet dancer, but not really suitable for his mates, and unthinkable for Karen to be an airline pilot.

Best (1983) and Clarricoates (1987) have many examples of children's stereotypes impinging on their peers. Clarricoates was told about Michael:

When Miss Mackeson asked him what he wanted to be when he grew up he said he wanted to be a butterfly. He's just a great big sissy.

(Clarricoates 1987: 191)

Minns (1985) transcribed a taped discussion of pupils' responses to *Charlotte's Web*, during which children 'explained' why girls cried:

CLAYTON: Only the boys didn't cry 'cos they were brill. . . . We don't cry like girls. They're babies.

KAREN: Miss, I think why the boys didn't cry is because the girls are more sensitive than boys at stories like that.

TRACY: I think I know why girls sometimes cry, 'cos they take things more serious than boys do.

CLAYTON: . . . Men don't cry when spiders die. Women do, they're so stupid.

Best's (1983) book is called *We've All Got Scars*, because the 8-year-old boys at Pine Hill told her scars marked a proper male. Jonathan told Best that to be in a high status boys' clique scars were a prerequisite, because they showed the boy had fought and climbed and fallen.

Children not only hold stereotyped views about the opposite sex, they also segregate themselves. Joffe (1971) saw three girls who had climbed on top of a large structure in the playground. A (male) comes over and C screams, 'Girls only!' to which A screams back, 'No, boys only!'. Similar incidents are reported in Sussman (1977), Clarricoates (1987), and Paley (1984). Karkau (1976) found that boys and girls of 9 rarely mixed: forming separate groups, playing different games, and rarely talking to each other. His pupils even had a taboo on touching or approaching a person of the opposite sex. Girls told him that if they went near boys 'People will think you're "in love" ', and boys said 'If you touch a girl you get "cooties" or "girl-touch" ' which Karkau describes as 'a mysterious quality which can only be removed by saying "no gives" '. When Karkau asked his class about segregation in the playground the boys said that girls *could* play soccer with them, but the girls pointed out that the boys never asked, only boys were captains of teams, the boys did not pass the ball to girls, and, if a girl scored, the boys did not cheer. The boys agreed that all these criticisms were true. Similar observations are recorded in Best (1983) and Clarricoates (1987).

Rivalry between boys and girls is revealed in the following incidents:

This morning there was obvious sex rivalry in racing to get changed after swimming – as pupils were waiting in the foyer for their classmates to emerge from the changing rooms so they could all come back to school there were occasional whispers from the girls: 'Three boys and four girls, we're winning. Oh now we're not' as more boys emerge from their changing room. (*Gryll Grange*)

They do competitive counting. All stand up and say numbers in French in turn. If wrong they sit down. Davina is the last one on her feet. When Maurice was the only boy left there were mutters from other boys that he should win for the boys. (*Gryll Grange*)

English with Mr Evans. Pupils can have one book between two. Dominico and another boy are given the books to distribute. Told to give one between two and then give out spares, Dominico and the other boy give out one between two, and Mr Evans says that they must not give all the spare copies to the boys, but must be 'democratic' – he finds a girl for the last spare copy. (*Guy Mannering*)

One consequence of the pupils' views and behaviour is that when mixed groups were formed, the task did not get done, as in the following extract from notes on a PE lesson at Guy Mannering:

Pupils are told to get into threes. Girls organise themselves but boys don't. Teacher puts Terence with Coral and Lauretta to the giggles of other boys. The threes are told to get a bench and place it in a specific locality (to do exercises on).

Terence, Coral, and Lauretta did not co-operate well; no PE was done by that trio. There is evidence that the more 'progressive' the class, the more polarisation there is. Sussman (1977) studied 'progressive' elementary schools in the USA to investigate the hypothesis that where there is 'partial withdrawal of the teacher's authority' (p. xiii) the vacuum is filled by peer group authority. After observation in a variety of schools she found that:

(In a black ghetto school first grade class)
The children's groupings in the room seemed during observation to be quite fluid. . . . The only line of segregation was between the sexes. Ironically, when children are left to group themselves, there is more sex segregation than in teacher-made groups. (p. 138)

(In the second grade class of the same school)
In this classroom, there was a fairly clear-cut division of peer groups, not only by sex, but by ethnicity and ability as well. (p. 148)

Sussman studied an upper-class school where the 'underground' life pre-occupied the pupils and

There was an intensive struggle for control of a 'fort' which the boys had built on the playground. They would not let 'outsiders' in. Outsiders included all girls. . . . Girls who tried to gain entry on one day were physically attacked by the boys, knocked to the ground, and had their coats torn off. (p. 178)

(In the fifth and sixth grade)
We remarked that it was interesting, for instance, that when she gave her pupils a chance to change their seats at tables all the shifts were in the directions of segregating girls and boys more completely. (p. 193)

Sussman found this sex polarisation disturbing, and makes it one major indictment of 'progressive' classrooms. Readers may argue that if pupils separate themselves in this way, it is because such divergence is 'natural' and schools should accept it. All kinds of things may be done 'naturally' by the pupils which schools will not tolerate for a moment, and such segregation should be one of them. After all no school would allow pupils to build a fort for 'black children only', 'council house children only', 'Catholics only', or 'Band A children only'. Any school which heard those cries would attempt to democratise the fort. Yet children are allowed to be sexist even in 'progressive' schools. Clarricoates (1987) has shown in her comparative study of four infant schools with intakes from different social classes that gender divisions are manifested in contrasting ways.

Data from the ORACLE project (Tann 1981) give an academic reason for worrying about pupils' own hostilities. Systematic observation shows that when mixed groups of pupils are required to co-operate upon tasks in the classroom they do not. Teachers who want boys and girls to co-operate on tasks must, therefore, struggle to overcome pupils' sex segregation and hostility.

REFERENCES

Adelman, C. (1979) Unpublished material on nursery education.

Ashton, P. (1981) 'Primary teachers' aims 1969–1977', in B. Simon and J. Willcocks (eds) *Research and Practice in the Primary Classroom*, London: Routledge & Kegan Paul.

Ashton, P. *et al.* (1975) *The Aims of Primary Education*, London: Macmillan.

Best, R. (1983) *We've All Got Scars*, Bloomington, IN: Indiana University Press.

Brophy, J. (1985) 'Interactions of male and female students with male and female teachers', in L.C. Wilkinson and C.B. Marrett (eds) *Gender Influences in Classroom Interaction*, Orlando, FL: Academic Press.

Brophy, J.E. and Good, T.L. (1974) *Teacher–Student Relationships*, New York: Holt Rinehart & Winston.

Clarricoates, K. (1987) 'Child culture at school: a clash between gendered worlds?', in A. Pollard (ed.) *Children and their Primary Schools*, London: Falmer.

Davie, R. *et al.* (1972) *From Birth to Seven*, London: Longman.

Douglas, J. W. B. (1964) *The Home and the School*, London: MacGibbon & Kee.

Good, T. L. (1987) 'Teacher expectations', in D. Berliner and B. Rosenshine (eds) *Talks to Teachers*, New York: Teachers College Press.

Guttentag, M. and Bray, H. (eds) (1976) *Undoing Sex Stereotypes. Research and Resources for Educators*, New York: McGraw-Hill.

Hartley, D. (1978) 'Sex and social class: A case study of an infant school', *British Educational Research Journal* 4 (2): 75–82.

Ingelby, J. D. and Cooper, E. (1974) 'How teachers perceive first-year schoolchildren', *Sociology* 8 (3): 463–73.

Joffe, C. (1971) 'Sex role socialization and the nursery school', *Journal of Marriage and the Family* 33 (3).

Karkau, K. (1976) 'A student teacher in 4th grade', in M. Guttentag and H. Bray (1976) (eds) *Undoing Sex Stereotypes. Research and Resources for Educators*, New York: McGraw-Hill.

King, R. (1978) *All Things Bright and Beautiful*, Chichester: Wiley.

Minns, H. (1985) 'Boys don't cry', *Times Educational Supplement* 5 April: 18.

Mortimore, P., Sammons, P., Stoll, L., Lewis, D. and Ecob, R. (1988) *School Matters*, Wells, Somerset: Open Books.

Paley, V. G. (1984) *Boys and Girls: Superheroes in the Doll Corner*, Chicago: The University Press.

Serbin, L. A. (1978). 'Teacher, peers, and play preferences', in B. Sprung (ed.) *Perspectives in Non-Sexist Early Childhood Education*, New York, Teachers College Press, and in S. Delamont (ed.) (1984) *Readings on Interaction in Classroom*, London: Methuen.

Sussman, L. (1977) *Tales out of School*, Philadelphia: Temple University Press.

Tann, S. (1981) 'Grouping and group work', in B. Simon and J. Willcocks (eds) *Research and Practice in the Primary Classroom*, London: Routledge & Kegan Paul.

Chapter 6

Learner needs or learner rights?

Caroline Roaf and Hazel Bines

While the last chapter began to explore the way in which gender is constructed and maintained in the classroom, this chapter considers the idea of 'special needs'. In the past, children identified as having 'special educational needs' were seen as requiring special and separate provision, not compatible with what was defined as 'normal' education. More recently, a new discourse of 'equal opportunities' has focused not on the individual, but on the environment, attempting to make the 'mainstream' classroom more accessible for children with a wider range of needs. However, Caroline Roaf and Hazel Bines warn that an exclusive focus on the environment can lead to a 'difference blindness', resulting in some pupils not receiving the extra resources that they need within this 'mainstream context' to realise their potential. They therefore propose that a discourse of 'rights' and 'entitlement' should be integrated with an equal opportunities approach.

The central contention of this chapter is that the concept of 'need' is inadequate on its own as a means of achieving the goals of education for those identified as having special needs. Instead, we argue that the addition of the discourse of equal opportunities and rights, with its emphasis on entitlement, would provide a more effective basis for policy and practice. In explaining these ideas, this chapter begins by reviewing past and present trends in special education, with reference to needs, equality and rights, and opportunities before going on to look at these concepts in more detail. Finally, we suggest that the way forward lies through an approach in which all three concepts can be interrelated.

PAST AND PRESENT TRENDS IN SPECIAL EDUCATION

Needs

The development of special education during the last hundred years has traditionally focused on handicap and needs. It has involved efforts to expand provision for children and young people whose impairments or difficulties are not adequately catered for in ordinary schools or who may need additional help to cope with the demands of mainstream curricula and schooling. Such growth has been seen as the best means of focusing and securing special resources and expertise. Progress has also largely been measured in terms of expansion of the range, as well as the amount, of special provision available for children and young people in order to cater for an increase in number and a wider range of handicaps and difficulties or needs.

Nevertheless, during the last decade there have been a number of changes in the ways in which this development of special needs provision and curricula has been viewed and secured. In particular, the language and categories of handicap have been replaced by the more generic and flexible concept of special educational need. This new concept, as developed by the Warnock Report (DES 1978) and incorporated into the 1981 Education Act, represented an attempt to remove formal distinctions between handicapped and non-handicapped students and to replace categories through an expanded and more flexible definition of special need. This could potentially incorporate one-fifth of the whole school population, including children and young people in both ordinary and special schools. It also reflected a shift in emphasis from medical or psychological criteria of assessment and placement towards an educational, interactive, and relative approach which would take into account all the factors which have a bearing on educational progress (DES 1978: para 3.6).

This change has been accompanied by a range of new approaches to curricula and provision. For example, there is now an increasing emphasis on the development and modification of mainstream curricula to make them more appropriate for, and accessible to, children and young people with special needs. Similarly, special needs provision is no longer defined primarily in terms of special, usually segregated, provision, but rather in terms of a continuum which includes both specialised and mainstream settings, with an increasing emphasis on the latter.

These developments have had a number of implications for policy and practice in both special and mainstream education. Integration as a policy principle and the development of the 'whole school approach' have emphasised the role and contribution of mainstream schools in relation to special needs provision (Dessent 1987). It is also now considered that special needs should be viewed not just in individual or deficit terms, but in relation to the requirements of curriculum and schooling. Thus, inappropriate teaching materials and techniques may be seen as having generated or at least exacerbated the range of learning difficulties experienced by students.

The work of special needs teachers has consequently been redefined. In order to ensure that special needs are properly catered for in mainstream settings, special needs teachers have been asked to take on the role of a 'change agent', concerned with developing the mainstream curriculum through working with colleagues and providing advice and support (Bines 1986; Dessent 1987; NARE 1985). This means, as Clough and Thompson (1987) have noted, that curriculum is beginning to replace psychological theory and practice as the theoretical basis of special education with a consequent change in concepts of what should comprise 'special expertise'. Although such expertise is still often traditionally seen in terms of knowledge of assessment and *special* teaching materials and techniques, it now also includes the capacity to understand learning and learning difficulties in the light of mainstream education.

These substantial changes in special education have provided a liberating and enabling framework for a much greater emphasis on the interactive nature of learning difficulties and on the reform of mainstream provision and curricula (Hegarty 1987). However, although now widely accepted as the current basis of provision and practice, 'special educational needs' remains a problematic term, with a number of meanings and implications. As will shortly be discussed, the language and concept of special educational needs have not overcome all the difficulties of terminology in special education, nor has the apparent potential for change in provision and curricula been realised. This may in part be due to the difficulties of implementing change in special education (Bines 1986; Jeffs 1988) and to constraints on resources. However, it could be argued that, despite its interactive implications, the new concept of special educational need still reflects an individualistic approach to difficulties and handicaps which also clouds issues of values, power, and function (Tomlinson 1982). Moreover, despite intentions to limit stigma and labelling, it has become a new euphemism for failure.

We do, therefore, have to question the value of the concept of special educational need, and at two levels of analysis. Firstly, there is the issue of whether current usage and practice can be improved to overcome some of the problems outlined above. Secondly, there is the question of whether the 'concept of need' is an appropriate or sufficient basis for developing special education or whether we should be thinking of additional or alternative approaches.

Equality and rights

The current emphasis on needs may have obscured other aspects in the development of special education, such as the degree to which equality of opportunity has been a significant dimension of debate and policy. There has, for example, been considerable concern about the issue of equal access to education, notably in regard to children with severe and multiple difficulties, who were finally brought into the education system in 1970. Similarly, debate over segregation and placement in special schooling has been related to lack of equal educational opportunity. The increasing focus on integration as the model of good practice thus represents not just a new approach to fulfilling needs but also an intention to secure equal access to a common schooling for all children. Current approaches to curriculum can also be linked to equal opportunities, particularly the concern to ensure that mainstream teaching is accessible to all and to improve educational outcomes as well as access. Indeed, it could now be argued that egalitarianism in special education has been strengthened by the convergence which has taken place between two avenues of thought, one arising from the history and development of special education to the period of the Warnock Report and the 1981 Act, the other arising from the period of the Sex Discrimination Act (1975) and the Race Relations Act (1976) and the development of the concept of equal opportunities in education from the mid-1970s onwards (ILEA 1985; Potts 1986).

The issue of equal outcomes has been most clearly evidenced in demands for additional resources and specialised teaching for special educational needs and in the conception of special education as compensatory in nature, concerned with overcoming and improving educational, social, and other disadvantages. Other aspects of egalitarianism have also informed the debate about special education, in particular, the stress laid on valuing all students equally and considering integration as the extension and fulfilment of comprehensive principles (Booth 1983).

All these developments suggest changes in the ways needs, rights, and opportunities may be viewed and brought together. For example, the curricular approach suggests that needs should be seen in relation to mainstream curricula and schooling, while sociological perspectives stress that needs have both social and educational dimensions, reflecting not just inappropriate teaching or curricula, but also vested social interest. Needs are thus linked to structural disadvantage and inequality. In relation to equal opportunity, the curricular approach suggests that opportunity cannot be created just by extending the range of special provision, but also requires change in curriculum, pedagogy, and organisation. Sociological perspectives would also argue that we need to alter relationships and beliefs in society as a whole in order to secure opportunity and that the establishment of rights may involve tackling professional vested interests as well as social inequality. These new perspectives therefore posit a change in the interrelationship between the issues of needs, rights, and opportunity, so that increasingly need is seen in relation to equality and rights. Certainly, despite many current problems of terminology, policy, and practice, there is a range of ideas and perspectives to be examined. The three themes of needs, opportunity, and rights will thus now be considered in more detail.

THE CONCEPT OF NEEDS

Despite the changes in definition of special educational need, it remains a very difficult and complex concept in practice. It has the appearance of simplicity and familiarity, yet its use in so many contexts, the fact that it appears to have both normative and non-normative meaning and that it is essentially concerned with values and priorities, should alert us to its complexity. Thus, the greatest care is required in evaluating needs, in prioritising them and in being clear in whose interest they are being stated. This is especially true at the present time when we are already a long way from the days when it was only handicapped children who were perceived as having needs.

Firstly, the term *needs* is often used in relation to the development and learning of all children. Given their individuality and idiosyncrasy, defining what constitutes a *special* educational need in any particular case can be difficult. However, if special education is to be used as a basis for special resource allocation, the difference between special and other educational needs would seem to have to be acknowledged. Although the 1981 Act emphasises the relationship between learning difficulty and special educational need, learning difficulty in the past has largely been used in relation to remedial provision. Since this has been somewhat separate from other special education, its more general use for all forms of special needs is ambiguous. In addition, although 'special educational needs' is now the generic term, the number of specific descriptive categories has not been reduced. Indeed the Warnock Report and 1981 Act, while attempting to remove differences between handicapped and non-handicapped students, did not take special education out of the realm of handicap. Instead, more students have been brought within its brief under the much broader and ill-defined category of learning difficulty, and further divisions have emerged, particularly between students who are subjects of Statements and those who are not.

Secondly, the relativism of needs as currently understood can lead to haphazard and unequal provision. 'Special educational need' is a legal and administrative term as well as an educational and descriptive one, thus taking on different meanings according to the context in which it is used. Such relativism is also a feature of the legislative definitions within the 1981 Education Act, where need is defined in terms of the level of difficulty experienced by other children and the kind of educational provision available. Being considered to have a special educational need may, therefore, largely depend on which school is attended and in which locality, leading to considerable variations in assessment, placement, and subsequent educational treatment. Because needs in themselves do not necessarily indicate or define teaching approaches, or the extent of special provision, current conceptions of needs have been developed as enabling rather than prescriptive and very much depend on current conceptions of good practice. Although there may at present be an emphasis on necessary change in the curricula and schools, the concept of needs in itself gives no protection or assurance that such a definition of good practice will be sustained. Since special needs are seen to be relative to those of other children and are also relative to current knowledge and conceptions of good practice, there is always the danger that different definitions may prevail. Unless we are very particular about what constitutes need, and associated provision, we may thus deny both general equal educational opportunity and equal special educational opportunity (Brennan 1981).

Thirdly, as indicated by this relativism, needs are a matter of professional and value judgement. The moral and political bases of such judgements are usually neglected because we still focus on the *receiver* – the individual or group with needs. Yet hidden within these conceptions of needs are social interests, for example, to make the disabled productive or control troublesome children, together with a range of assumptions about what is *normal* (Tomlinson 1982). When we focus on needs and particularly when we take our assumptions about the nature of those needs for granted, we do not ask who has the power to define the needs of others. We do not enquire why it is professionals who mostly define needs, as opposed to parents or the students themselves. Nor do we fully explore the normative nature of our assumptions, for example, that they are grounded in conceptions of 'normal' cognitive development or behaviour whether such assumptions are informally operated, by teachers in the classroom, or more formally operated, by normative testing. We focus on what seem to be the genuine needs of the individual who lacks something and who has a need. However, we do not consider how needs may be generated by valuing certain aspects of development and attainment more than others. For example, if we did not value certain cognitive skills, would there be the needs currently identified as 'special' in schools (Hargreaves 1983).

Finally, the term 'needs' has now become a euphemism for labelling individuals as 'special'. This is due partly to its hidden implications and partly to limited change in traditional approaches and practice. The idea of having a difficulty suggests something can be done about it (or even that the cause may be the difficulty of the learning on offer). Similarly, handicap, particularly if we apply the distinction between impairment, disability, and handicap (the last being societal in character) suggests some social context. Needs, however, tends to refocus on individuals as a bottomless pit of problems to be overcome or filled up. The concept of needs remains deficit-based, despite attempts to relate it to context, with an inbuilt tendency to slippage back towards individuals and their problems. It is not always easy, for example, to make the distinction between those who have learning difficulties of one kind or another, and may require special provision, and those who need special provision but do not have learning difficulties. The classic example is of those for whom English is not the first language, but there are others. Needs are largely now special and seen as such, despite the potential radicalism of the approach with which they are currently associated, and are often little more than a new label for old practices and problems.

OPPORTUNITY AND EQUALITY

Given that 'needs' is a problematic concept, 'opportunity' would seem to offer a better approach to special education. Firstly, there is a much more explicit focus on context: 'opportunity' raises questions of system rather than individual failure. When linked with equality, to make 'equality of opportunity', it also raises issues of discrimination and disadvantage. Equality of opportunity is also a widely known and understood rationale, given the importance of egalitarianism in educational policies until recently. Even in the current political climate, egalitarianism remains in our educational thinking. Therefore, it may be easier for the majority of teachers and policy makers to relate to opportunity rather than needs or at least to see the educational, social and political implications of requiring that equal opportunity be extended to those with impairments and difficulties. Notions of opportunity and equality are also relevant to mainstream settings in that they are comprehensive, in rhetoric if not reality, and thus we should be able to argue for improved and integrated special education using the comprehensive principle (Booth 1983).

However, there are problems with opportunity, particularly when put forward as *equal opportunity*. Firstly, there has been much confusion generally between liberal (access) and radical (outcomes) versions of the equality debate (Evetts 1973). It can also be difficult to achieve equality of opportunity without encountering contradictions such as the difficulty of balancing normalisation with the need for positive discrimination and provision. Such difficulties may be even more pertinent to debates about special educational needs because physical and other impairments may mean not just overcoming structural disadvantage and discrimination but also providing compensatory measures. By contrast, the equality debate in relation to class, gender, and race supposes all groups to have the same basic qualities. When different resources, teaching, and provision are required, this raises a central area of confusion for teachers for whom a 'difference blind' or 'normalisation' approach is more familiar than a 'social justice' perspective to equality concerned with realisation of potential.

It is important to be very clear as to what form of equality of opportunity is being argued. Basic issues of access and integration have still not been solved and many educational opportunities continue to be denied just through a lack of resources, such as access for the physically disabled. Achieving such access would in itself be a major gain in some instances. It would also seem to be beneficial to operate the more radical notion of opportunity, arguing for positive discrimination in terms of staffing or resources in order to ensure that children and young people experiencing impairment or other difficulties do get full benefit from ordinary education. It would also seem worthwhile to make the connections between disadvantage arising out of class, race, or gender and disadvantage arising out of special needs as traditionally perceived. Nevertheless, equality of opportunity still seems to imply being dependent on the gift of others and on making the best of yourself, which not all young people can do.

Finally, using the equality of opportunity approach to developing special education rests on certain political and moral assumptions and beliefs which are not accepted by all. Thus, even though egalitarianism is embedded in educational thinking, élitism is just as powerful an ideology, and increasingly so. Equality of opportunity may not, therefore, be the most effective rationale for developing provision or curriculum.

RIGHTS

'Rights' as a basis for developing special education policy and practice would seem to have a number of advantages. As Kirp (1983) has suggested, comparing British and American special education policies and legislation, thinking about special education in terms of political and legal rights makes one reappraise resource allocation, relationships among the affected parties, the level and amount of dispute, and the very conception of handicap. In respect to resource allocation, for example, the American structure of rights does not formally treat resource limits as constraining what can be provided. Whereas the British approach weighs the interests of special and ordinary children, the American orientation on rights places the burden of adjustment on the ordinary school. The greater disputes engendered by a rights approach, including increased litigation, may make for a more dynamic policy and lead school authorities to offer more than would otherwise have been provided. In respect to the disabled themselves, rights should encourage a stronger definition and assertion of self and interests, reducing professional power and paternalism.

THE VALUE OF AN INTEGRATED APPROACH

Taken separately, therefore, there are advantages but also limitations to needs, rights, and opportunity. In searching for the best way forward we suggest the following starting points.

We have to look at the current context and recognise that, despite the inadequacies of the concept of needs, any shift in emphasis towards equality of opportunity and rights has not in fact found teachers abandoning needs as a basis for policy and practice. There are several reasons for this, including the existence of an established range of resources with which to meet identified and agreed needs and the long tradition of focusing on needs as the rationale for expanding provision. There is also the weight and influence of the Warnock Report and 1981 Act, which, by introducing and broadening special educational needs, overcame certain previous contradictions and problems and brought in a more appropriate practice. We should recognise, however, that where the desire to meet needs has developed and expanded into debates about opportunity, it has tended to be weak unless buttressed by the language of rights and social justice.

A shift from needs as an approach to developing special education is, therefore, unlikely to occur or to be totally effective. Nor will opportunity or rights be sufficient in themselves. We require an integrated approach where all three themes stand in a proper relationship with each other to achieve educational outcomes which are just and fair.

CONCLUSION

The picture which is emerging, then, is essentially one of progressively developing ideas about community and the extent to which it is possible to bring about a state of affairs in which people value each other with something approaching equality of esteem and concern. This raises a number of questions. How, for example, is a balance to be achieved between rights and responsibilities? On what basis is the distinction to be made between needs which can be met and those which cannot? In the past attempts to resolve these problems stemmed from philanthropy and empathy for others but were characterised by the spasmodic and indiscriminate attention typically bestowed upon minority, disadvantaged, and powerless groups by powerful groups. This approach also allowed too readily for damage limitation, with those in power not needing to be more generous, observant, or humane than was convenient to them. These new perspectives advocated here would seem to provide a more secure framework in which to define needs and assert rights.

However, although we have stressed the problems and limitations associated with a philanthropic approach, certain aspects of it should not be abandoned entirely. Caring for anyone is important, as are notions of duty and responsibility, neither of them far from the language of rights. Egalitarian and equal opportunity approaches have widened this but can be effective only when coupled with a strong emphasis on rights and anti-discrimination and a developing understanding of the effect of interpersonal, institutional, and structural prejudice and discrimination (Lynch 1986).

It is significant that the debates and dilemmas which we have been discussing in relation to young people who, in the pre-Warnock days were regarded as handicapped, have also been seen in relation to race and gender. In connection with ethnic minorities, a needs-based perspective emphasising assimilation and integration characterised the 1950s and 1960s within which the needs of the immigrant communities were those defined by the host community. In turn this was succeeded by a perspective emphasising diversity. This was an improvement, conferring a greater sense of community and equality of opportunity but in a notably 'weak' form. It has had to be strengthened by policies emphasising the active reduction of prejudice and unfair discrimination, through the courts, both national and European if necessary. The gender debate has been characterised by a broadly similar succession of perspectives.

These developments in relation to special education could do much to move provision and curriculum from traditional, deficit-based, and paternalistic approaches towards approaches which would embrace and protect the interests of all minority groups. We need to be aware, however, that the language used in the discourse and debate to promote a sense of community, in which social justice prevails, is open to a range of interpretations and can be all too readily moulded to the political climate of the time. Needs, rights, and opportunity are powerful words with different meanings for different interest groups. They will have to be further clarified before they can be used to best effect and the implications and processes of change be well monitored and evaluated to ensure desired outcomes are being achieved. The issues are difficult and may not all be resolved but, without the discussion of the strengths and limitations of current and potential approaches which this chapter hopes to generate, gains which have been made in special education will remain precarious and vulnerable.

REFERENCES

Bines, H. (1986) *Redefining Remedial Education*, London, Croom Helm.

Booth, T. (1983) 'Integrating special education', in Booth, T. and Potts, P. (Eds) *Integrating Special Education*, Oxford, Blackwell.

Brennan, W. K. (1981) *Changing Special Education*, Milton Keynes, Open University Press.

Clough, P. and Thompson, D. (1987) 'Curricular approaches to learning difficulties: problems for the paradigm', in Franklin, B. (Ed.) *Learning Disability: Dissenting Essays*, Lewes, Falmer Press.

Department of Education and Science (1978) *Special Educational Needs (Warnock Report)*, London, HMSO.

Dessent T. (1987) *Making Ordinary Schools Special*, Lewes, Falmer Press.

Evetts, J. (1973) *The Sociology of Educational Ideas*, London, Methuen.

Hargreaves, D. (1983) *The Challenge for the Comprehensive School*, London, Routledge & Kegan Paul.

Hegarty, S. (1987) *Meeting Special Needs in Ordinary Schools*, London, Cassell.

Inner London Education Authority (ILEA) (1985) *Educational Opportunities for All? (Fish Report)*, London, ILEA.

Jeffs, A. (1988) 'The appearance and reality of change within special educational needs', in Barton, L. (Ed.) *The Politics of Special Educational Needs*, Lewes, Falmer Press.

Kirp, D. (1983) 'Professionalization as policy choice: British special education in comparative perspective', in Chambers, R. G. and Hartman, W. T. (Eds) *Special Education Policies*, Philadelphia, Temple University Press.

Lynch, M. (1986) *Multicultural Education: Principles and Practice*, London, Routledge & Kegan Paul.

National Association for Remedial Education (NARE) (1985) *Teaching Roles for Special Needs Guidelines, No. 6*, Stafford, NARE.

Potts, P. (1986) 'Equal opportunities: the fourth dimension', *Forum for the Discussion of New Trends in Education*, 29, 1, pp. 13–15.

Tomlinson, S. (1982) *The Sociology of Special Education*, London, Routledge & Kegan Paul.

Part II

Teachers

Chapter 7

The teacher as a person

Michael Fullan and Andy Hargreaves

This edited extract takes externally imposed staff development activities as a starting point for its major argument that teachers must be appreciated and understood in terms of their purposes, as people, and in terms of their work context – as 'total teachers'. Teachers, in other words, should not be seen as mere technicians, 'delivering' a national curriculum or anything else. Teaching involves skill, values, and expertise. It draws on the whole person of teachers who must be valued as people if they are to give of their best. Teaching takes place in contexts which are challenging and diverse and which call for expertise and judgement in resolving the dilemmas which are posed.

Many staff development initiatives take the form of something that is done *to* teachers rather than *with* them, still less by them. Such top-down approaches to staff development embody a passive view of the teacher, who is empty, deficient, lacking in skills, needing to be filled up and fixed up with new techniques and strategies.

Approaches of this kind seriously underestimate what teachers already think, know, and can do. They underestimate the active way that teachers relate to their work. They ignore the way that teachers' approaches to their work are deeply grounded in the accumulated learning of experience, in the meaning that their work and the way they approach it has for them as people. They do not recognise the important moral and social purposes they want to fulfil through their teaching.

Teachers are more than mere bundles of knowledge, skill, and technique. There is more to developing as a teacher than learning new skills and behaviours. As teachers sometimes say to their students, they are not wheeled out of a cupboard at 8.30 am in the morning and wheeled back in at 4.00 pm. Teachers are people too. You cannot understand the teacher or teaching without understanding the person the teacher is (Goodson 1992). And you cannot change the teacher in fundamental ways, without changing the person the teacher is, either. This means that meaningful or lasting change will almost inevitably be slow. Human growth is not like rhubarb. It can be nurtured and encouraged but it cannot be forced. Teachers become the teachers they are not just out of habit. Teaching is bound up with their lives, their biographies, with the kinds of people they have become.

Many factors are important in the making of a teacher. Among them are the times in which teachers grew up and entered the profession, and the value systems and dominant educational beliefs that went with those times (compare the 1960s with the 1980s here, for instance). Also important is the stage in life and career that teachers are at, and the effect this has on their confidence in their own teaching, their sense of realism, and their attitudes to change. The teacher's sex is another factor, in particular the way that teaching and work in general for men and women are often bound up with very different sorts of lives and interests.

This view of the teacher as a person has crucial implications for our understandings of change, professional development, and working relationships between teachers and their colleagues. We want to focus on two of these implications: the ways we often misjudge the competence, commitment, and capacity of our colleagues; and the excessive and unrealistic expectations we sometimes have of our colleagues concerning their involvement in schools and their commitment to change.

First, in teaching, as in life, we are quickest to judge those who fail rather than those who succeed. When teachers are new to the job, incompetence can be excused or at least tolerated. They are, after all, only learning. Experienced teachers, who should have matured with their years in the classroom, get away less lightly. Where incompetence is persistent rather than temporary, it is rarely excusable. Almost every reader of this book will have known at least one teacher in mid- to late-career whose competence and commitment have been in doubt among their colleagues. We have a glossary of graphic labels for such teachers – 'dead wood', 'burned out', 'time-servers', and 'past-it'! Such labels do not really explain these teachers' difficulties, though. They explain them *away*. They are not labels that invite action, that suggest solutions. They are labels that legitimise inaction, that signal abandonment of hope. The fault is presumed to be in the teacher, deeply ingrained in their personality. Little point, therefore, in trying to change them. Not much you can do about bad teachers, especially bad *old* teachers, except wait for them to leave, retire, or die! 'If only I could get some new teachers . . .' or 'wait until my new teachers arrive . . .' – these are heads' stock responses to this apparently irremediable problem.

Yet have you ever wondered what these 55-year-old 'time servers' were like when they were 35, or 25? Were they just ticking over then too? Were they that cynical? Is it possible that they were once as bright-eyed and idealistic as many of their younger colleagues are now? And if they were, what happened to them in the meantime? Why did they change? Have you ever wondered what it might be like to be one of these people, ever wondered about the man or the woman behind the mask?

Some of the reasons for the transformation, of course, have to do with ageing. Sikes' (1985) analysis of the ageing process within the 'life-cycle of the teacher' is instructive. One of the age-phases she describes is between 40 and 50 or 55:

> It is during this phase that it becomes apparent whether or not the work of establishing occupational career, family and identity begun in the twenties and thirties has been successful; and it tends to involve self re-appraisal, questioning what one has made of one's life.
>
> (Sikes 1985: 52)

This is when disappointment can set in. It is also a time, particularly towards the later years, of sheer decline in physical powers which puts morale and enthusiasm very much to the test. As one of Sikes' teachers expressed it: 'The kids are always the same age and you gradually get older and older . . . And unfortunately too, their capacity for life, their energy remains the same as yours diminishes.'

Disillusion and disappointment tend to go with the ageing process in the teacher's unfolding career. But there is nothing natural or inevitable about this. Much depends on the particular experiences these teachers have had, on how their schools have treated them. To some extent, ageing is a cultural process of learning, of interpreting the ways that other people repeatedly treat you. The disillusioned are partly products of their own mortality, but they are also products of their schools' management – responsible as such management is for the quality of experiences and treatment these teachers receive over the years. Trees do not kill themselves. 'Dead wood', rather, is usually the product of an infertile, undernourished environment. In this sense, schools often end up with the staffs they deserve.

Age, stage of career, life experiences, and gender factors make up the total person. They affect people's interest in and reaction to innovation and their motivation to seek improvement. When we introduce new teaching methods, we often ignore these differences and treat teachers as if they were a homogeneous lot. In the process, we often devalue large segments of the teaching population. This problem is especially important at a time when many new teachers are entering the profession, new teachers on whom many an eager head is staking his or her hopes for future improvement. Heads have been waiting a long time for infusion of new blood into the system. It is clear that a serious and unexpected danger looms ahead also – the danger of ostracising and alienating existing staffs of more mature teachers who may not embrace with as much eagerness and energy as their junior colleagues the new methods and approaches favoured by their heads. These teachers deserve both our understanding and respect in a system which should be cautious about granting inflated importance to very particular approaches to teaching, like 'active' learning, at the expense of all others which have preceded them. Without such understanding it is likely that many teachers will disengage from their work, will ignore or resist change, and will help create divided schools of 'old' and 'new' teachers, polarised into opposing factions.

At the other end of the spectrum, the failure to recognise the special needs and contributions of beginning teachers can also have a disastrous, lasting impact on their motivation and confidence to become good teachers and good colleagues. Mentors are not just there to support their protégés but also to learn from them. Teaching is inherently difficult. Even the most experienced need help. From their recent training, their university subject knowledge and their willingness to try things out under the right conditions, new teachers will have much to give to experienced teachers. We must also be careful not to take advantage of new teachers and their seemingly endless energy by loading them with extracurricular responsibilities and giving them the worst classes. This is a sure path to early burn-out.

A second sense in which reform often glosses over the personal lives, interests, and backgrounds of teachers concerns the expectations we have for change and commitment. Teaching is very important. However, there is more to life than school. Life interests and responsibilities beyond teaching must also be recognised. In our enthusiasm to involve staff more and more in the life of the school, and to commit them to change within it, we should not forget the other legitimate calls on their time and commitments, which in the long run may well make them better people and teachers for it.

There are important gender implications here. In dealing with gender irregularities in teaching, much of the policy emphasis has been on encouraging more women to apply for promotion. But the focus is very much on making the characteristically male educational career more available to women. What analysis of the experience of women teachers also suggests is that individual development of all teachers, men and women, may also be well served by questioning and revising our norms in schools and educational systems of what constitutes proper commitment for a teacher, of how much involvement in the wider affairs of the school life is reasonable and desirable, given various personal circumstances. Commitment to continuous improvement is important. Becoming a professionally omnivorous workaholic is not!

So we should fight for a broadening of expectation, for an acknowledgement that there are several versions of excellence and more than one route to achieving them. We should also temper some of our expectations in the pursuit of excellence, not as an act of defeatism, but as an exercise in realism where we abandon the pursuit of swift, drastic change for change which is more modest in its scope, yet more widespread and enduring in its impact. Put another way, sweeping blanket reforms, running to tight timelines, that are insensitive to the wider aspects of the teacher's life and career and that do not address the teacher as a person, are unlikely to be successful.

What, in summary form, have we learned from this discussion of the teacher as a person?

1 That teaching behaviours are not just technical skills to be mastered, but behaviours that are grounded in the kinds of people teachers are.
2 That among the many factors which shape what kind of people and teachers, teachers become, one of the most important is how their schools and their heads treat them.
3 That schools often get the teachers they deserve. Teachers who are devalued, discarded, and disregarded become bad teachers. Ironically, such an approach also permits the seriously incompetent to be ignored.
4 That we need to value and involve our teachers more. There is something to value in almost every teacher. We should identify it, recognise it, and reward it.
5 That valuing our colleagues involves more than being more caring and sympathetic. It also involves extending what we value. Faddish innovations, narrow views of excellence, rolling bandwagons of active learning or performance-based assessment, which presume only one good way to teach, divide insiders from outsiders and create alienation and incompetence among those who are excluded.
6 That, while not any route to excellence will do, many routes are possible. Salvation has more than one road. This applies to teaching methods and to professional development alike.
7 That extensive involvement in school decision making does not constitute the highest level of professional development for all teachers. Maintaining a balance between work and life, concentrating on expanding one's own classroom repertoire rather than getting consumed by school-wide innovation, is just as worthy a form of professional development for many teachers.
8 That massive commitment to whole-school change is an unrealistic goal for many teachers – for many of those in later career, for instance. Modest but persistent attempts to expand teaching repertoires and to improve practice in association with colleagues may be a more realistic objective.
9 That meaningful and lasting change is slow. Changing people is not achieved overnight. It requires patience and humility on the part of administrators.

Acknowledging the teacher's purpose and understanding and valuing the teacher as a person, we want to suggest, should therefore be vital elements underpinning any strategy of staff development and school improvement. It is one of the keys to unlocking motivation and to helping teachers confront what it means to be a teacher.

REFERENCES

Goodson, I. (1992) 'Sponsoring the teacher's voice: teachers' lives and teacher development', in Hargreaves, A. and Fullan, M. (eds) *Understanding Teacher Development*, London, Cassell.

Sikes, P. (1985) 'The lifestyle of the teacher', in Ball, S. and Goodson, I. (eds) *Teachers' Lives and Careers*, Philadelphia, Falmer Press.

Chapter 8

Teacher expertise

David Berliner

David Berliner offers a rather different perspective on what makes a teacher from that provided by Fullan and Hargreaves in the last chapter. He focuses on the 'expertise' which a teacher develops over a professional career. The chapter suggests that teaching for the 'novice' is very different from teaching for the 'expert'. In what ways would this analysis suggest that beginning teachers and their mentors might have difficulties in reaching understandings about what is happening in classrooms? How might this analysis help a beginning teacher to understand the mentor's perspective, and to develop her or his own?

Experts in areas as divergent as chess, bridge, radiology, nursing, air-traffic control, physics, racehorse handicapping, and pedagogy show certain kinds of similarities. Despite their apparent diversity, experts in these fields seem to possess similar sets of skills and attitudes and to use common modes of perceiving and processing information (Chi, Glaser, and Farr 1986; Berliner 1986). These abilities are not found among novices. Experience allows experts to apply their extensive knowledge to the solution of problems in the domain in which they work. To the novice, the expert appears to have uncanny abilities to notice things, an 'instinct' for making the right moves, an ineffable ability to get things done and to perform in an almost effortless manner.

Although we have gained some insight into the differences between experts and novices in various fields, we have only the scantiest knowledge about the ways that one progresses from novice to expert within a field. In part, this is because scientific knowledge about expertise is relatively new. But such research also requires longitudinal studies, and these studies are among the most difficult for which to get support.

Despite the shortage of scientific research in this area, some thoughtful speculation about the ways in which one becomes expert in a particular field is needed, because the planning of instruction for novices and the evaluation of others in a field are inherently related to theories of the development of expertise within the field. If we focus on the field of teaching, then answers to questions about what to teach novices, when to teach it, and how to teach it depend in part on implicit theories about the role of experience in the ability to learn the pedagogical skills, attitudes, and ways of thinking that teacher educators believe to be desirable. The evaluation of teachers also depends on such implicit theories of development. What one chooses to observe or test for, when one expects to see it, how it should be measured, and the criteria by which successful performance is judged all depend on some notions, perhaps fragmentary, about the development of ability in pedagogy. To make these often implicit and incomplete theories more explicit and complete, I report here on a general theory about the development of expertise.

A THEORY OF SKILL LEARNING

There are five stages to consider in the journey one takes from novice to expert teacher. We begin with the greenhorn, the raw recruit, the *novice*. Student teachers and many first-year teachers may be considered novices. As experience is gained, the novice becomes an *advanced beginner*. Many second- and third-year teachers are likely to be in this developmental stage. With further experience and some motivation to succeed, the advanced beginner becomes a *competent* performer. It is likely that many third- and fourth-year teachers, as well as some more experienced teachers, are at this level. At about the fifth year, a modest number of teachers may move into the *proficient* stage. Finally, a small number of these will move on to the last stage of development – that of *expert* teacher. Each of these stages of development is characterised by some distinctive features.

Stage I: Novice This is the stage at which the commonplace must be discerned, the elements of the tasks to be performed must be labelled and learned, and a set of context-free rules must be acquired. In learning to teach, the novice is taught the meaning of terms such as higher-order questions', 'reinforcement', and 'learning disabled'. Novices are taught context-free rules such as 'Give praise for right answers', 'Wait at least three seconds after asking a higher-order question', 'Never criticize a student', and that old standby, 'Never smile until Christmas'. The novice must be able to identify the context-free elements and rules in order to begin to teach. The behaviour of the novice, whether that person is an automobile driver, chess player, or teacher, is very rational, relatively inflexible, and tends to conform to whatever rules and procedures the person was told to follow. Only minimal skill should really be expected. This is a stage for learning the objective facts and features of situations and for gaining experience. And it is the stage at which real-world experience appears to be far more important than verbal information, as generations of drivers, chess players, and student teachers have demonstrated.

Stage 2: Advanced beginner This is when experience can meld with verbal knowledge. Similarities across contexts are recognised and episodic knowledge is built up. Strategic knowledge – when to ignore or break rules and when to follow them – is developed. Context begins to guide behaviour. For example, advanced beginners may learn that praise doesn't always have the desired effect, such as when a low-ability child interprets it as communicating low expectations. The teacher may also learn that criticism after a bad performance can be quite motivating to a usually good student. Experience is affecting behaviour, but the advanced beginner may still have no sense of what is important. Benner (1984: 23–4) makes this point in describing the difference between novice and advanced beginner nurses on the one hand and competent nurses on the other:

> I give instructions to the new graduate, very detailed and explicit instructions: When you come in and first see the baby, you take the baby's vital signs and make the physical examination, and you check the I. V. sites and the ventilator and make sure that it works, and you check the monitors and alarms. When I would say this to them, they would do exactly what I told them to do, no matter what else was going on. . . . They couldn't choose one to leave out. They couldn't choose which was the most important. . . . They couldn't do for one baby the things that were most important and then go on to the other baby and do the things that were most important, and leave the things that weren't as important until later on. . . . If I said, you have to do these eight things . . . they did those things, and they didn't care if their other kid was screaming its head off. When they did realize, they would be like a mule between two piles of hay.

The novice and the advanced beginner, though intensely involved in the learning process, may also lack a certain responsibility for their actions. This occurs because they are labelling and describing events, following rules, and recognising and classifying contexts, but not actively determining through personal action what is happening. The acceptance of personal responsibility for classroom instruction occurs when personal decision making, wilfully choosing what to do, takes place. This occurs in the next stage of development.

Stage 3: Competent There are two distinguishing characteristics of competent performers. First, they make conscious choices about what they are going to do. They set priorities and decide on plans. They have rational goals and choose sensible means for reaching the ends they have in mind. In addition, they can determine what is and what is not important – from their experience they know what to attend to and what to ignore. At this stage, teachers learn not to make timing and targeting errors. They also learn to make curriculum and instruction decisions, such as when to stay with a topic and when to move on, on the basis of a particular teaching context and a particular group of students.

Because they are more personally in control of the events around them, following their own plans, and responding only to the information that they choose to, teachers at this stage tend to feel more responsibility for what happens. They are not detached. Thus they often feel emotional about success and failure in a way that is different and more intense than that of novices or advanced beginners. And they have more vivid memories of their successes and failures as well. But the competent performer is not yet very fast, fluid, or flexible in his or her behaviour. These are characteristics of the last two stages in the development of expertise.

Stage 4: Proficient This is the stage at which intuition and know-how become prominent. Nothing mysterious is meant by these terms. Consider the microadjustments made in learning to ride a bicycle – at some point, individuals no longer think about these things. They develop an 'intuitive' sense of the situation. Furthermore, out of the wealth of experience that the proficient individual has accumulated comes a holistic recognition of similarities. At this stage, a teacher may notice without conscious effort that today's mathematics lesson is bogging down for the same reason that last week's spelling lesson bombed. At some higher level of categorisation, the similarities between disparate events are understood. This holistic recognition of similarities allows the proficient individual to predict events more precisely, since he or she sees more things as alike and therefore as having been experienced before. Chess masters, bridge masters, expert air-traffic controllers, and expert radiologists rely on this ability. The proficient performer, however, while intuitive in pattern recognition and in ways of knowing, is still analytic and deliberative in deciding what to do. The proficient stage is the stage of most tournament chess and bridge players. But the grand masters are those few who move to a higher stage, to the expert level.

Stage 5: Expert If the novice, advanced beginner, and competent performer are rational and the proficient performer is intuitive, we might categorise the experts as often arational. They have both an intuitive grasp of the situation and a nonanalytic and nondeliberative sense of the appropriate response to be made. They show fluid performance, as we all do when we no longer have to choose our words when speaking or think about where to place our feet when walking. We simply talk and walk in an apparently effortless manner. The expert martial artist in combat, the expert chess master, and the expert teacher in classroom recitations all seem to know where to be or what to do at the right time. They engage in their performance in a qualitatively different way than does the novice or the competent performer, like the race-car driver who talks of becoming one with her machine or the science teacher who reports that the lesson just moved along so beautifully today that he never really had to teach. The experts are not consciously choosing what to attend to and what to do. They are acting effortlessly, fluidly, and in a sense this is arational, because it is not easily described as deductive or analytic behaviour. Though beyond the usual meaning of rational, since neither calculation nor deliberative thought is involved, the behaviour of the expert is certainly not irrational. The writings of Schon (1983) about knowledge in action characterise the behaviour of the expert practitioner.

Experts do things that usually work, and thus, when things are proceeding without a hitch, experts are not solving problems or making decisions in the usual sense of those terms. They 'go with the flow', as it is sometimes described. When anomalies occur, things do not work out as planned, or something atypical happens, they bring deliberate analytic processes to bear on the situation. But when things are going smoothly, experts rarely appear to be reflective about their performance.

FINDINGS AND IMPLICATIONS

1. There are differences in the ways that teachers at various levels of experience and expertise interpret classroom phenomena. Because of a lack of experience, those near the novice end of the developmental continuum can be expected to have trouble interpreting events. Until episodic knowledge is built up and similarities can be recognized across contexts, confusion may characterize the interpretations of classroom phenomena made by novices and advanced beginners. Experts are more likely than those with less ability to discern what is important from what is not when interpreting classroom phenomena. And we should also expect that experts will show more effortless performance and rely more on experience for interpreting information. We obtained data supportive of these ideas in some of our studies.

2. There are differences in the use of classroom routines by teachers at various levels of expertise and experience. The effortless and fluid performance that often characterises the experts' performance may be due, in part, to their use of routines. Adherence to routines by teachers and students makes classrooms appear to function smoothly. In studying elementary school mathematics lessons, Leinhardt and Greeno (1986) compared an expert's opening homework review with that of a novice. The expert teacher was found to be quite brief, taking about one-third less time than the novice did. This expert was able to pick up information about attendance, about who did or did not do the homework, and was also able to identify who was going to need help later in the lesson. She elicited correct answers most of the time throughout the activity and also managed to get all the homework corrected. Moreover, she did so at a brisk pace and never lost control of the lesson. She also had developed routines to record attendance and to handle choral responding during the homework checks and hand raising to get attention. This expert also used clear signals to start and finish the lesson segments. In contrast, when the novice was enacting an opening homework review as part of a mathematics lesson, she was not able to get a fix on who did and did not do the homework, she had problems taking attendance, and she asked ambiguous questions that led her to misunderstand the difficulty of the homework. At one time the novice lost control of the pace. She never did learn which students were going to have more difficulty later in the lesson. It is important to note that the novice showed lack of familiarity with well-practised routines. She seemed not to act in habitual ways.

3. There are differences in the emotionality displayed by teachers at various levels of expertise and experience. When the developmental stage of competence is reached, it is said to be accompanied by a qualitatively different kind of emotionality and sense of responsibility for the work of the performer. We have some evidence for that, obtained in a curious way, in the study in which experts, advanced beginners, and novices planned and then taught a lesson [in a university-based laboratory context] (Berliner 1988). The novices in that study were quite happy about their performance, although we did not rate it highly. Advanced beginners were generally affectless in describing their experience. They had a task to do and they did it. The experts, however, were quite angry about their participation in the task and disappointed about their performance.

In retrospect, and on the basis of our interviews, it appears that we had inadvertently taken away some of the experts' edge. First, we had created an artificial teaching situation. Second, according to their standards, they did not have enough time to prepare the lesson. Third, the students were not trained in the routines that make the experts' classrooms hum. One expert expressed his anger by walking out of the study. Another stopped in the middle of the lesson and had to be coaxed to continue. One started crying during the playback of her videotape. All were upset. Two weeks after the study, one expert, when asked what she remembered of her experience, said:

> I just remember it as the worst experience in my entire life, and I was depressed. . . . The things that stick out in my mind are the negative things. I remember just being frustrated the whole time I taught the lesson. . . . I don't like what happened. I've been real depressed and down [since then].

Other comments by experts were about their feelings of uncomfortableness, stress, terror, and so forth. In this situation, advanced beginners and novices were virtually untouched at any deep emotional level, but our experts were affected deeply. In addition, they felt that in some way they had let us down – their sense of responsibility played a part in their feelings. Expert teachers, apparently like other experts, show more emotionality about the successes and failures of their work.

SUMMARY

A growing body of literature is documenting the ways in which individuals at different levels of experience in classroom teaching and other fields differ in their interpretive abilities, their use of routines, and the emotional invest-ment that they make in their work. From this one can extract a general principle, namely, that very important qualitative differences exist in the thinking and the performance of novices, experts, and all those who fall between these two points on the continuum. The developmental sequence involved in the acquisition of expertise, however, is not yet as clearly described. The five-stage theory of the development of expertise presented above is intended to help us think more about that issue and is well supported by data that were collected for other purposes.

REFERENCES

Benner, P. (1984) *From Novice to Expert*, Reading, MA, Addison-Wesley.

Berliner, D. C. (1986) 'In pursuit of the expert pedagogue', *Educational Researcher*, 15, pp. 5–13.

Berliner, D. C. (1988) 'Memory for teaching as a function of expertise', paper presented at meetings of the American Educational Research Association, New Orleans, April.

Chi, M. T. H., Glaser, R., and Farr, M. (eds) (1986) *The Nature of Expertise*, Hillsdale, NJ, Erlbaum.

Leinhardt, G. and Greeno, J. (1986) 'The cognitive skill of teaching', *Journal of Educational Psychology*, 78, pp. 75–95.

Schon, D. (1983) *The Reflective Practitioner*, New York, Basic Books.

Chapter 9

Teaching as a professional activity

James Calderhead

This chapter continues the discussion of the teacher's role, exploring in what ways teaching can be said to be a 'professional' activity. It recognises the conflicting expectations which society holds of teachers and the consequent dilemmas which teachers face within the complexities of the classroom. It suggests that it is the teachers' knowledge base – content, pedagogical and curricular – which enables them to juggle and balance the range of demands made upon them during the school day. This suggests that what we observe in the 'expert' teacher's classroom (see Berliner, Chapter 8) is 'knowledge-in-action', even where the skilled teacher may find it difficult to analyse and explain to others the basis and rationales for those actions. How far do you think it may be possible for a new teacher to begin to bring theory alive by reflecting critically on reading in relation to observations of skilled teaching in action? How might this be helped by joint analysis with an experienced teacher 'mentor'?

Teaching is a complex process that can be conceptualised in many different ways, using alternative models, metaphors, and analogies. One metaphor that acknowledges the intentional, problem-solving aspects of teachers' work is that of teaching as a reflective, thinking activity. This highlights several key characteristics of teaching, which it shares with many other professions such as medicine, law, architecture, and business management. Consequently, the metaphor sometimes used is that of teaching as a professional activity.

According to this metaphor, teachers possess a body of specialised knowledge acquired through training and experience. Just as a doctor possesses formal knowledge of physiology and pathology, together with knowledge acquired from experience about patient behaviour and the various combinations of symptoms that complicate the task of diagnosis, the teacher has acquired knowledge about the curriculum, teaching methods, subject matter, and child behaviour together with a wealth of other particular information resulting from the experience of working with children in numerous contexts and with different materials. Like other professionals, teachers rely upon this specialist knowledge in their daily work.

A second feature of professional activity is its goal-orientation in relation to its clients. Doctors aim to cure their patients, lawyers to defend their clients' interests, architects to design buildings to suit their clients' specifications. In the case of teaching, who the clients are is a little more ambiguous. Although much of teachers' activity may be oriented to the education of their pupils, teachers, more so than many professionals, are also answerable to a number of others, including parents, administrators, advisers, inspectors, employers, curriculum development agencies, and politicians. These individuals and agencies are in a position to influence what teachers do by controlling the provision of materials, curriculum guidelines, and finance, and in the determination of the conditions in which teachers work. Influence might also be exerted at an ideological level through the perpetuation of beliefs and ideologies of good classroom practice. There is rarely any consensus among teachers' 'clients' on what constitutes good practice. Consequently, teachers may encounter numerous expectations that can be in conflict with each other as well as with the beliefs of the individual teacher. The fact that there are no agreed goals for education and that there are several interest groups to whom teachers may be held accountable frequently results in teachers facing impossible dilemmas. Consider, for instance, the recently popular call for the school curriculum to return to basics, coupled with the equally popular demand for schools to prepare children for a future, technological, computer-oriented society.

A third characteristic is that the problems professionals deal with are often complex and ambiguous, and professionals must use their expert knowledge to analyse and interpret them, making judgements and decisions as they formulate a course of action intended to benefit their client. A lawyer, for instance, may encounter an array of conflicting evidence. His knowledge of court practice and legal procedures, together with his previous experience and knowledge of how witnesses and juries typically respond, enables him to make judgements about the plausibility of alternative lines of argument. He can decide how best to interpret and present evidence in court, which features to emphasise, and when doubts might be implied about particular points of fact in order to advantage his client.

Teachers similarly face complex situations, and this is well described by Doyle (1986), who concisely summarises the complexity of the classroom environment in terms of six general features: *multidimensionality, simultaneity, immediacy, unpredictability, publicness*, and *history*. Classrooms are busy places. At any one time, teachers may be faced with a series of incidents to manage – keeping the class working quietly, for instance, while dealing with one particular child's difficulty and postponing or redirecting other children's requests for attention. As a result, teachers face competing demands and often teaching decisions are a compromise among multiple costs and benefits. For instance, in deciding whether to carry out a particular activity in groups or as a class, teachers may have to weigh the possible benefits of encouraging co-operative work and perhaps obtaining greater pupil satisfaction against the costs of more preparation, the risk of some pupils opting out and leaving others to do the work, and greater demands on teachers' managerial skill. The pace of teachers' activity in the classroom is necessarily rapid. There is also considerable uncertainty in the teachers' world. Unexpected events, distractions, and interruptions threaten to disturb the normal course of events. Lessons don't always go as expected, and children's behaviour is sometimes unpredictable. In addition, teachers, for much of the day, are 'on show'. How they are seen to cope with classroom situations can influence how individual children assess them and respond to them in the future. And as a result of classroom interactions, particularly those occurring early in the year when teachers and children are first assessing one another, each class develops its own norms, its own ethos, its own work routines, a history that shapes the ways in which it copes and responds to activities in the present.

Given this complexity of the teaching task, it indeed seems a remarkable achievement that teaching and learning occur in schools at all. The school and classroom environment clearly place a heavy burden upon teachers to attend to and process a large volume of information and continually to juggle conflicting and competing interests. Teachers must use their knowledge to cope with a constant barrage of complex situations.

In classroom teaching, however, there is often little opportunity to reflect upon problems and to bring one's knowledge to bear upon their analysis and interpretation. Teachers must often respond immediately and intuitively. This relates to a fourth feature of professional activity, namely that it involves skilful action that is adapted to its context. Through repeated practice and reflection on practice, the professional has developed various specialist and 'knowledgeable' skills. The lawyer, for instance, in his skills of cross-examination demonstrates a keen knowledge of human behaviour in a legal context and an awareness of alternative questioning strategies. The professionals' expert knowledge enables them to perceive significant features in their work and to respond to them. Teachers have extensive knowledge about children, curriculum materials, classroom organisation, and approaches to instruction. This knowledge helps them to establish relationships with children, manage the class, decide how best to teach a particular topic, maintain the children's interest, and instruct them. The teachers' knowledge and experience of children in a classroom context has in some cases become so closely tied to their practice that they can, for instance, notice a child's inattention to work and readily identify it as a case of difficulty in understanding, attention-seeking, lack of interest, tiredness, or the child having an 'off-day', and respond appropriately, when to an outsider the same cues may be lost in a blur of classroom noise and activity.

Schön (1983) uses the term 'knowledge-in-action' to describe the knowledge that is embedded in the skilled action of the professional. Knowledge-in-action is sometimes inaccessible directly to professionals themselves in the sense that, although they can demonstrate it in action, they are unable to disclose it verbally. Just as expert tennis players, who might return shots in rapid succession, intuitively calculated to land at particular spots on the court, often cannot describe the knowledge of ball control that lies in their skilled performance, neither can lawyers in their skills of cross-examination or teachers in their classroom interaction.

In some respects, teaching sits uneasily alongside professions such as medicine, law, or architecture. Teachers, for instance, are not self-employed, in most countries they do not have their own professional association that oversees a standard of good practice, nor generally do they have high status or high salaries. In fact, it has sometimes been suggested that teachers' claims to professionalism can be viewed as status-enhancing strategies or as a means of defending competence, autonomy, and individualism from outside interference (Hargreaves 1981; Lortie 1975). Nevertheless, in terms of the types of activities in which professionals engage, there seem to be some enlightening similarities, and the metaphor may be a valuable one in helping us to conceptualize and explore further the nature of teachers' practice. Such a metaphor illuminates crucial aspects of teaching by guiding us towards an exploration of the nature of teachers' knowledge and the influences on its formation, how it is applied to the analysis of teaching situations, and how it has come to be embedded in teachers' actions.

REFERENCES

Doyle, W. (1986) 'Classroom organization and management', in Wittrock, M.C. (ed.) *Handbook of Research on Teaching* (3rd edn), New York, Macmillan.
Hargreaves, D.H. (1981) 'The occupational culture of teachers', in Woods, P. (ed.) *Teacher Strategies*, London, Croom Helm.
Lortie, D.C. (1975) *Schoolteacher*, Chicago, University of Chicago Press.
Schön, D.A. (1983) *The Reflective Practitioner*, London, Temple Smith.

Chapter 10

Those who understand
Knowledge growth in teaching

Lee Shulman

Is a teacher's role essentially expertise in teaching itself, regardless of the content; or is it rather to be the transmitter of valued knowledge? The chapter from which this extract is taken argues that there has been an overemphasis in the preparation of new teachers on how to teach, with too little attention paid to the content to be taught. It argues for a more equal balance to be achieved between developing expertise in teaching techniques and the organisation and management of classrooms and developing expertise within the subjects to be taught. In the extract below, Lee Shulman lays out a taxonomy of the different types of knowledge required by the teacher, who must, he argues, not only know how to teach, but also what to teach and why. We shall return to the discussion of teachers' knowledge of curriculum content in Part 4 of this book on the curriculum.

How might we think about the knowledge that grows in the minds of teachers, with special emphasis on content? I suggest we distinguish among three categories of content knowledge: (a) subject matter content knowledge, (b) pedagogical content knowledge, and (c) curricular knowledge.

Content knowledge This refers to the amount and organisation of knowledge *per se* in the mind of the teacher.

In the different subject matter areas, the ways of discussing the content structure of knowledge differ. To think properly about content knowledge requires going beyond knowledge of the facts or concepts of a domain. It requires understanding the structures of the subject matter in the manner defined by such scholars as Joseph Schwab (see his collected essays, 1978).

For Schwab, the structures of a subject include both the substantive and the syntactic structures. The substantive structures are the variety of ways in which the basic concepts and principles of the discipline are organised to incorporate its facts. The syntactic structure of a discipline is the set of ways in which truth or falsehood, validity or invalidity, are established. When there exist competing claims regarding a given phenomenon, the syntax of a discipline provides the rules for determining which claim has greater warrant. A syntax is like a grammar. It is the set of rules for determining what is legitimate to say in a disciplinary domain and what 'breaks' the rules.

Teachers must not only be capable of defining for students the accepted truths in a domain. They must also be able to explain why a particular proposition is deemed warranted, why it is worth knowing, and how it relates to other propositions, both within the discipline and without, both in theory and in practice.

We expect that the subject matter content understanding of the teacher be at least equal to that of his or her lay colleague, the mere subject matter major. The teacher need not only understand *that* something is so; the teacher must further understand *why* it is so, on what grounds its warrant can be asserted, and under what circumstances our belief in its justification can be weakened and even denied. Moreover, we expect the teacher to understand why a given topic is particularly central to a discipline whereas another may be somewhat peripheral. This will be important in subsequent pedagogical judgements regarding relative curricular emphasis.

Pedagogical content knowledge A second kind of content knowledge is pedagogical knowledge, which goes beyond knowledge of subject matter per se to the dimension of subject matter knowledge *for teaching*. I still speak of content knowledge here, but of the particular form of content knowledge that embodies the aspects of content most germane to its teachability.[1]

Within the category of pedagogical content knowledge I include, for the most regularly taught topics in one's subject area, the most useful forms of representation of those ideas, the most powerful analogies, illustrations, examples, explanations, and demonstrations – in a word, the ways of representing and formulating the subject that make it comprehensible to others. Since there are no single most powerful forms of representation, the teacher must have at hand a veritable armamentarium of alternative forms of representation, some of which derive from research whereas others originate in the wisdom of practice.

Pedagogical content knowledge also includes an understanding of what makes the learning of specific topics easy or difficult: the conceptions and preconceptions that students of different ages and backgrounds bring with them to the learning of those most frequently taught topics and lessons. If those preconceptions are misconceptions, which they so often are, teachers need knowledge of the strategies most likely to be fruitful in reorganising the understanding of learners, because those learners are unlikely to appear before them as blank slates.

Curricular knowledge If we are regularly remiss in not teaching pedagogical knowledge to our students in teacher education programmes, we are even more delinquent with respect to the third category of content knowledge, *curricular knowledge*. The curriculum is represented by the full range of programmes designed for the teaching of particular subjects and topics at a given level, the variety of instructional materials available in relation to those programmes, and the set of characteristics that serve as both the indications and contraindications for the use of particular curriculum or programme materials in particular circumstances.

The curriculum and its associated materials are the *materia medica* of pedagogy, the pharmacopoeia from which the teacher draws those tools of teaching that present or exemplify particular content and remediate or evaluate the adequacy of student accomplishments. We expect the mature physician to understand the full range of treatments available to ameliorate a given disorder, as well as the range of alternatives for particular circumstances of sensitivity, cost, interaction with other interventions, convenience, safety, or comfort. Similarly, we ought to expect that the mature teacher possesses such understandings about the curricular alternatives available for instruction.

FORMS OF KNOWLEDGE

A conceptual analysis of knowledge for teachers would necessarily be based on a framework for classifying both the domains and categories of teacher knowledge, on the one hand, and the forms for representing that knowledge, on the other. I would like to suggest three forms of teacher knowledge: *propositional knowledge*, *case knowledge*, and *strategic knowledge*.

Recall that these are 'forms' in which each of the general domains or particular categories of knowledge previously discussed – content, pedagogy, and curriculum – may be organised. (There are clearly other important domains of knowledge as well, for example, of individual differences among students, of generic methods of classroom organisation and management, of the history and philosophy of education, and of school finance and administration, to name but a few. Each of these domains is subdivided into categories and will be expressible in the forms of knowledge to be discussed here.)

Much of what is taught to teachers is in the form of propositions. When we examine the research on teaching and learning and explore its implications for practice, we are typically (and properly) examining propositions. When we ask about the wisdom of practice, the accumulated lore of teaching experience, we tend to find such knowledge stored in the form of propositions as well.

The research-based principles of active teaching, reading for comprehension, and effective schools are stated as lists of propositions. The experience-based recommendations of planning five-step lesson plans, never smiling until Christmas, and organising three reading groups are posed as sets of propositions. In fact, although we often present propositions one at a time, we recognise that they are better understood if they are organised in some coherent form, lodged in a conceptual or theoretical framework that is generative or regenerative. Otherwise they become terribly difficult to recall or retrieve.

The roots of the 'case method' in the teaching of law in this country, certainly the best-known approach to employing cases as vehicles for professional education, lie in their value for teaching theory, not practice.

Case knowledge is knowledge of specific, well-documented, and richly described events. Whereas cases themselves are reports of events or sequences of events, the knowledge they represent is what makes them cases. The cases may be examples of specific instances of practice – detailed descriptions of how an instructional event occurred – complete with particulars of contexts, thoughts, and feelings. On the other hand, they may be exemplars of principles, exemplifying in their detail a more abstract proposition or theoretical claim.

I have referred to *strategic knowledge* as the third 'form' of teacher knowledge. Both propositions and cases share the burden of unilaterality, the deficiency of turning the reader or user towards a single, particular rule or practical way of seeing. Strategic knowledge comes into play as the teacher confronts particular situations or problems, whether theoretical, practical, or moral, where principles collide and no simple solution is possible.

Strategic knowledge must be generated to extend understanding beyond principle to the wisdom of practice. We generally attribute wisdom to those who can transcend the limitations of particular principles or specific experiences when confronted by situations in which each of the alternative choices appears equally 'principled'. Novice bridge players rapidly learn the principles of the game, embodied in such maxims as 'Lead fourth highest from your longest and strongest suit', and 'Never lead away from a king'. But when you must lead away from a king to lead fourth highest, then propositional knowledge alone becomes limited in value. Strategic knowledge (or judgement) is then invoked.[2]

When strategic understanding is brought to bear in the examination of rules and cases, professional judgement, the hallmark of any learned profession, is called into play. What distinguishes mere craft from profession is the indeterminacy of rules when applied to particular cases. The professional holds knowledge, not only of how – the capacity for skilled performance – but of what and why. The teacher is not only a master of procedure but also of content and rationale, and capable of explaining why something is done. The teacher is capable of reflection leading to self-knowledge, the metacognitive awareness that distinguishes draughtsman from architect, bookkeeper from auditor. A professional is capable not only of practising and understanding his or her craft, but of communicating the reasons for professional decisions and actions to others (see Shulman 1983).

NOTES

1 There is also pedagogical knowledge of teaching – as distinct from subject matter – which is also terribly important, but not the object of discussion in this paper. This is the knowledge of generic principles of classroom organisation and management and the like that has quite appropriately been the focus of study in most recent research on teaching. I have no desire to diminish its importance. I am simply attempting to place needed emphasis on the hitherto ignored facets of content knowledge.

2 It may well be that what I am calling strategic *knowledge* in this paper is not knowledge in the same sense as propositional and case knowledge. Strategic 'knowing' or judgement may simply be a process of analysis, of comparing and contrasting principles, cases, and their implications for practice. Once such strategic processing has been employed, the results are either stored in terms of a new proposition (e.g., 'Smiling before Christmas may be permissible when . . .') or a new case. These then enter the repertoire of cases and principles to be used like any others. In that sense, it is possible that strategic analysis occurs in the presence of the other forms of knowledge and is the primary means for testing, extending, and amending them.

REFERENCES

Schwab, J. J. (1978) *Science, Curriculum and Liberal Education*, Chicago, University of Chicago Press.

Shulman, L. S. (1983) 'Autonomy and obligation: the remote control of teaching', in Shulman, L. S. and Sykes, G. (eds) *Handbook of Teaching and Policy*, New York, Longman.

Chapter 11

A first try
Starting the day

Carol Cummings

An infant school teacher provides an account of her first attempt to collect and analyse 'objective' data on her own classroom practice. In fact, she taped, and then transcribed, a registration session with her class. She reflects on her self-consciousness and on the insights which she obtained from the activity, noting its value as self-evaluation. *This is an edited account which, for reasons of space, does not include the actual transcript but the process of teacher-controlled enquiry is evident.*

INTRODUCTION

Self-evaluation can be frightening. Some teachers will honestly feel that they have, through lengthy experience, 'found *the* answers'. The less confident might perceive the whole notion as a threat, and those who vary approach and method in an attempt to follow ever-changing trends might see self-evaluation as yet another 'solution'.

It obviously requires some degree of courage and an honest desire to look more closely at what happens in one's classroom, to overcome the initial trepidation. The threat is probably greatest to those who feel most confident in their teaching; honest evaluation of what has *actually* taken place may provide some surprises and disappointments – it may shake confidence. However, it cannot be denied that for any teacher it may also provide a basis for change and pointers towards greater effectiveness.

For those who might view the approach to self-evaluation being advocated as a 'latest trend' to follow, a word of warning. This type of self-evaluation may be valuable and enlightening, but following it does not bring easy solutions. It requires no initial changes of approach, but may point the way to modifications that the individual teacher hopes will remedy perceived shortcomings. It cannot be seen as a universal panacea, it leaves the evaluation and any consequent changes to the individual. Perhaps, then, such changes might better suit the individual than blanket changes in philosophy or practice evolved 'up there' and 'imposed' on the chalk-face practitioner.

It is probably true that the majority of teachers look at what they are doing, judge their effectiveness, and plan future strategies based on their evaluation of past successes and failures anyway. But they generally do this work almost subconsciously, often haphazardly and most frequently unsystematically. It was with these thoughts that I, an infant teacher, decided to tape-record the early part of a typical school day.

As any infant teacher will know, especially if, like me, they plan their work around the 'integrated day' (whatever that phrase is taken to mean!), there are likely to be only two times in the day when one finds all the children with the teacher, and when taping is likely to be comparatively uninterrupted and free from excessive background noise. That doesn't mean to say these are the only times teaching activities can be taped but they do present possibly the easiest place to start. These times are story-time and the start of the day. I chose to look at the start of the day because I felt that it was a relatively unstructured get-together and because I wanted to look, in more depth, at the way I used the time, at what I felt the children might be gaining, at how they handle and manage the occasion and at how I could make the time more effective.

Why do I, in common with most teachers of young children, reserve the first part of the day for general, usually child-initiated talk? I think that infant teachers are perhaps more aware of home/school links than teachers in other kinds of schools, particularly as many schools, in common with my own, encourage parents to bring their children into the classroom, and because the children have not yet been taught to keep home and school apart. Later in their school careers, one gets the impression that 'out-of-school' talk is discouraged in the classroom as irrelevant to the business of 'learning'. In common with most infant teachers, I base the children's learning on their own experiences, on the things they seem to find relevant, and find the early morning an appropriate time to discover those things.

RECORDING

I found the actual recording to present no real problems as I have often used a tape-recorder in the classroom to record children's conversation, and very few children noticed the recorder after the first few moments. More difficult, though, was my own slight self-consciousness. I felt, during the session, that I was, perhaps, being 'the good infant teacher' to a greater extent than usual. I was probably a little more solicitous, answered children's questions a little more thoroughly and expanded the talk more than I might on a 'bad' day, but with the same sort of zealousness as I might if there were a stranger present. This self-awareness, though, was spasmodic; at times I completely forgot about the presence of the 'black box'; at others I was acutely aware, although I had previously promised myself that a complete disaster could, and would be erased. When I listened to the tape, I found no such utter disasters, although the reader is at liberty to disagree! Nevertheless, 'disasters' could be fruitful events to have on tape. Perhaps one would learn more from them, but it would have needed more than my meagre supply of courage and confidence to display them publicly at this stage in my career as self-evaluator.

The most time-consuming part of the exercise is the transcription, and one could be tempted to pass on this onerous task to others. It would be a mistake. I feel that I gained as many useful insights into what actually happened during the slow and repetitive task of transcription as during subsequent evaluation. The first impressions were very telling and answered many of my initial questions, such as how many of the children took part in the session, which children dominated the talk, did I talk too much, and did my questions lead the children to gain new or deeper understanding, knowledge, or skills.

Having read transcripts of other people's recordings, one thing became increasingly clear as I made my own. Useful as the transcripts of others may be, using a transcript without the benefit of knowing the situation, the children and the ethos of the session does seem to have less potential for fruitful analysis. I was there, I can remember much of the background and circumstances of the session, the personalities of the children and my own reactions to them. The tape *added to* my perception, rather than *providing* a perception of an unknown situation. Nevertheless, the dangers inherent in such 'knowledge' must also be acknowledged. The fact that I was there makes the assumption of a position of 'anthropological strangeness' doubly difficult to achieve. Not only do I 'know' what 'everybody' knows about classrooms, and teachers and children, but I also have more explicit knowledge about these particular children, this particular teacher, and the circumstances within which this episode occurred. The methodology employed here presents the reader with the opportunity to draw different conclusions, to place different emphases, and to use the materials presented as they wish. For myself, it required great effort to attempt to 'see' the transcript without the 'knowledge' I had, and led me to think about the nature, validity, and reliability of that knowledge. One assumes that one 'knows' both oneself and the children. Our 'knowledge' of children is based on both hearsay and personal observation. But usually one only observes what is presented for observation (and how often do overheard playground remarks show us a different 'side' to the children we know so well!); rarely does one question, as a 'stranger', occurrences that have become commonplace and routine. Thus, although familiarity with the situation can heighten awareness and deepen perception, an attempt to divorce oneself from the situation, to assume an attitude of 'unknowingness' facilitates the discovery of some of the seen, but unnoticed, features of the interaction.

SOME EARLY OBSERVATIONS

As I transcribed the tape, my first impression was of a very disjointed session with many more interruptions than I was conscious of at the time. Perhaps these are so routine and so expected that they are dealt with, in most cases, without interrupting the 'real' work of the session. I also noticed how easily the conversation seemed to 'jump' from interaction between myself and one child or small group of children to another such individual or group, while the majority of children either listened, chattered among themselves or read a book. Perhaps when we are the only adult and, therefore, generally the focus to which the children come, we remember only those parts of a session when we are personally involved; it would be interesting to have placed another recorder closer to those children farthest away, to catch their conversation.

In a session theoretically based on the need for *children* to talk, show their 'treasures', and generally guide the conversation, I was surprised at how much I talked, although, on reading through the transcript, most of the talk *was* child-initiated.

The session seemed to be very much a question/answer one, with me feigning ignorance in order to draw out from the children the knowledge and ideas they possessed, interspersed with information giving and 'mothering' on my part. Although the child questioned generally seemed able to provide an adequate (in my opinion!) answer to my questioning, I suppose that this conversation might benefit others, although I had not really thought about why I use this approach. As with many things in the classroom, it seems to be appropriate and is based, I suppose, on some sort of belief in the child's need to display his knowledge and his desire to share his experiences with others.

Such 'discussion' interactions seem to be regularly interspersed with 'control' episodes – it is apparent, through explicit instructions and the almost inviolate 'teacher speaks, child speaks' sequencing of the conversation, that children accept the teacher's right to speak, and that their right to speak is governed by the teacher's will. Explicit control appears throughout the transcript although, as all the children were not expected to sit and listen throughout the session, it might be less in evidence than in a more formal situation where all children are expected to listen quietly. Nevertheless, some administrative jobs, such as registration, are an integral part of such a session, and for this and other times when I thought all the children could gain by listening, they were called to order. It is noticeable that the teacher feels entitled to do this and that the children unquestioningly accept that entitlement. Parents and children accept the authority of the teacher in the classroom. Those children who came with messages for other children and those parents who arrived in the classroom with their children after the start of the session felt the 'rightness' of speaking to me first.

How, one wonders, does this come about? The classroom is continually referred to as 'our' classroom, implying a sharing relationship, but the children obviously accept the inequality inherent in the situation. Although this is not something that I had previously considered in any explicit sense, I suppose within the notion of 'class control' lies a sense of differential status. In common with many recently qualified teachers, I would have named class control and organisation as my overriding concerns in my early years and, indeed, great emphasis was placed on the need for such control as a prerequisite for teaching/learning during training. Perhaps the concept of the teacher authority can be seen to be more deeply rooted than that. One remembers one's own school days with the authoritarian teacher only too well – teachers are seen to hold authority over children and even the youngest child entering school has, more than likely, been briefed to 'be good and do what teacher says'. And, although we may not like to think of ourselves as 'controllers', perhaps such degree of order as emerges from the tape would not have come about if all concerned did not accept this notion.

The device, previously unnoticed, of 'feigning ignorance' is interesting too in this context. It can be seen as a manipulative (and almost dishonest!) method of drawing information and conversation from children. I can think of a few instances when one might employ such strategies with co-equals (in an attempt to 'trip someone up', or in an interview situation), but even then the parties involved are not really interacting on a basis of equality. Here, the teacher is 'playing tricks' on the children, some of whom may be aware of the nature of such 'ignorance' in a way that produces the specialised kind of talk that occurs in classrooms. The implication that emerges is one of inequality, with the teacher controlling and manipulating the talk towards specific ends. The children do not have such power, either in this situation or over conversation generally, seem largely unaware of the device, and so are not, in this sense, practising adult conversation, but are perhaps learning a little more about the strategies adults employ.

DISCUSSION AND CONCLUSIONS

This exercise in analysing tape-recorded classroom data has proved fascinating. It has highlighted techniques which were used unconsciously and has shown their effectiveness in achieving the classroom ethos in which I like to work. There are, nevertheless, certain disquieting aspects of the session. On reflection I feel that not enough children spoke, and particularly not the more passive children, who could perhaps have been given more encouragement and opportunity. I also feel that we tended to 'flit' from one topic to another, although on analysing the progression from one to another, and the content within each topic, in some ways control and orderliness were maintained, and perhaps the depth was great enough for such young children, whose thinking and activity is demonstrably of this butterfly nature.

Indeed, at times, some of what was said may well have been unintelligible, especially to the youngest children.

I was struck by the competence of the children to communicate their ideas in an intelligible and, mostly, grammatically correct way, and by their cognisance of the rules of talk. For the most part, unless a general response was invited, they took turns, and interruptions were remarkably few. The morning routine seems to have been accomplished and interruptions dealt with, without 'wasting' too much 'teaching' time; and this time, 'children's time', although controlled by the teacher, does seem to have been largely child-initiated and centred around their interests.

I set off on this voyage of discovery with extreme trepidation. After all, one can never have such supreme confidence in one's ability and methodology that a deeper look will not be disturbing. At the outset, I worried about what might emerge from the tape which memory would otherwise have expunged, and which I might regret. However, as I began to look more closely at the transcript, feelings of personal involvement began to fade; I began to look at the tape as impersonal, and at the interaction as involving 'the teacher', often losing sight of the fact that 'the teacher' was me.

The emerging structure of the session and the competence of the children were surprises which I do not think I could have discovered without this analysis. Neither would I have perceived the strategies employed by both the children and myself to widen and deepen both interactional competence and the acquisition of knowledge.

I found the experience interesting and enlightening and well worth while. We, as teachers, *can* do our own research, and can use such research to understand and, perhaps, answer our own problems. After all, we *do* the teaching, we must be in the most favourable position to look to that teaching in an attempt to understand what we do and to improve our ways of doing it.

Chapter 12

Akemi

Vivian Gussin Paley

This account of a young Japanese girl, Akemi, and her struggle to speak confidently in English, is again drawn from Vivian Paley's account of her kindergarten class in the United States. At first sight it may not seem to be about 'teachers' and may thus seem to be misplaced in this section. However, try reading it for the almost invisible support and guidance which is offered to Akemi as she begins to flourish in engaging with English. One then sees the importance of holistic teacher skills, judgement, and sensitivity as appropriate interventions, provision, and support are offered. The teacher provides the conditions for, and harnesses, the child's imagination and the 'magic' begins to work.

Rose, Kim, and Akemi began school with language problems, different in nature but similar in consequence; they could not explain their ideas easily. Rose lacked practice in putting consecutive thoughts into completed sentences; she had not understood the exacting connections between ideas and words. Kim's vocabulary and sentence structure were well developed, but self-consciousness in public often made her withdraw and bury her thoughts. Akemi's language problems stemmed from a vastly different cause. Having mastered one language, she alone of the three knew the pleasure of easy communication and was loath to flounder and stumble in a new language.

For all three girls, the lure of becoming a character in a story proved stronger than their resistance to public speaking. This attraction seems almost magical. If the child's belief in magic is based on the assurance of being changed into something else in the future, then dramatics is the immediate representation of this idea.

Play provides a similar opportunity but lacks the powerful certainty of outcome. The printed story, whether by an adult or a child, promises dependability. The soldier will always kill the witch; the lost child will invariably find his parents; everyone will live happily ever after.

Stories have yet another magical quality: fully developed sentences borrowed from someone else. The dialogue can change a child from inarticulate embarrassment to confidence, as if by a magic wand. The only task required is to memorise the words. With enough practice, anyone can do this, because the practice is part of the reward.

'Akemi does not permit herself mistakes,' her father had said on the first day of school, 'so she won't practise English.' He watched his daughter as she sat alone, drawing with her new school crayons. 'If she learned English better she wouldn't be so disagreeable with the children. She was so angry when the nursery school children did not understand her.'

The Nakamotos had come to America from Japan the year before. They were disappointed with Akemi's adjustment to school. 'In Japan she loved school,' Mr Nakamoto continued. 'She reads and writes in Japanese like a 7-year-old.'

Mr Nakamoto was right about Akemi. She was not comfortable with the children and she was afraid to speak English. What neither of us foresaw was the speed with which she began to use English in order to act in a play.

The first character she wanted to be was the woman in *The Funny Little Woman*. This Japanese folktale concerns an old woman's attempt to retrieve a rice dumpling that rolls through a crack in the earth down to a place where 'statues of the god' live alongside monstrous creatures called 'wicked oni'. The old woman tricks the oni, steals their magic rice paddle, and returns safely to the world above.

The old woman's habit of saying 'tee-hee-hee' made Akemi laugh despite a determined effort to remain the solemn outsider. She took the role immediately and produced a barely audible 'tee-hee-hee', but it was enough to make her wish for more.

'Read me,' she would insist, following me around with the book in her hands. Each time I read the story, Akemi repeated more of the dialogue. 'My dumpling, my dumpling! Has anyone seen my dumpling?' became Akemi's leitmotif. She had accomplished her first complete English sentence, and since everyone knew the story she did not have to explain herself further.

By Monday of the second week, Akemi was ready to add to her repertoire. She walked directly to the library corner and began leafing through a pile of books. When she came to *A Blue Seed*, our only other Japanese story, she examined it carefully.

'If I be this?' she asked, pointing to the fox.

'Can I be the fox?' I repeated her question.

'If I can be fox?' she asked again.

'Yes, you can. We'll read the book at piano time.'

Akemi's choices were uncanny. The funny little woman went about laughing 'tee-hee-hee', the very thing Akemi would not allow herself to do. Next she was the fox screaming out, 'Listen everyone! This is *my* house. No one can come in without my permission. Everyone get out at once!' What an opportunity for the child who fears that this schoolroom will never feel like *her* house.

I took four Japanese stories out of the library, but Akemi, after a quick glance, passed them by. Her commitment was not to Japanese stories but to magic. She wanted characters who looked the way she wanted to look and said what she needed to say.

In *Tico and the Golden Wings*, the wishingbird said the right words for Akemi. 'I am the wishingbird. Make a wish and it will come true.' From the wishingbird she went to Kurochka, the heroine of *The Little Hen and the Giant*. On her way to kill the giant, Kurochka said to everyone who got in her way, 'If you don't stop laughing right this minute, I will gobble you up!'

'Drakestail' gave Akemi a couplet she liked even better. 'Quack, quack, quack, when shall I get my money back?' Akemi carried her memorised lines around like gifts, bestowing them on children in generous doses. 'Quack, quack, quack, when shall I get my money back?' she would say, dipping a brush into a jar of paint. Soon everyone at the painting table would be chanting along with her.

'I am the wishingbird,' she said, flying gracefully into the doll corner. 'I wish for a golden crown,' Jill responded, whereupon Akemi delicately touched her head with an invisible wand.

Adults who go about quoting poetry seldom receive encouragement, but the children rewarded Akemi by repeating her phrases and motions. She correctly interpreted this as friendship. Whenever a child copied her, Akemi would say, 'OK. You friend of me.'

Her triumph came just before Halloween. She wanted a witch story but none of the Halloween stories pleased her. She told the librarian, 'Witch story but not Halloween', and was given *Strega Nona*, an Italian folktale about a kindly old witch who owns a magic pasta pot.

Akemi memorised the magic verse at home.

Bubble bubble, pasta pot,
Boil me up some pasta, nice and hot.
I'm hungry and it's time to sup,
Boil enough pasta to fill me up.

Wally came running over, 'What's that from, Akemi?'
'Witch book not Halloween,' she replied. 'You can read.'
'I can't read yet,' said Wally. 'Mrs Paley'll read it to us.'
By the end of the day almost everyone knew the entire verse, and Akemi was ready to tell her first story. 'Now I telling story, OK?' In only six weeks, Akemi had become a story teller in English. 'Is Halloween story,' she began.

One day four colours walking. But one witch sees four colours. Witch with four hands. Witch holds four colours. 'Let go, let go!' Four colours running. Witch running. Four colours running home. Is Mother. Oh, good.

In Akemi's next story just two weeks later, she had made considerable progress.

> One day is magic cherry tree. A nice skeleton is coming. The cherry tree says, 'We are playing.' A black cloud is coming. The cherry tree says, 'We are playing also.' They are playing all day. The mother comes. 'You are coming home.'

On Rose's birthday in January, Akemi dictated a story to be acted out at Rose's party. 'Rose is the magic princess,' she told us.

> Once there is castle has everything. Even nine princesses and nine dogs. When winter comes the boy came and hurt the princess in the night except princess is magic and doesn't get hurt. And then two robbers coming take two princesses home and tied them up. The next night is good-guy prince but he is lost and the magic princess find him and marries him inside her castle because it is so beautiful. But then the bad king came and stole the magic princess but she is not afraid. The king is magic but she makes him unmagic so he can't use his magic. She makes him into a frog and makes herself into a magic shark and she ate up his castle. Then the good-guy prince comes back and she makes him magic too so he is never afraid forever.

Akemi was conquering English, and I was learning an important principle: magic can erase the experiential differences between children. It can make the difficult simple and the simple rewarding. Akemi's princess made the good-guy prince magic 'so he is never afraid forever'. When magic is accepted and encouraged, the children are not afraid to think and speak.

Chapter 13

Teacher expectations

*Peter Mortimore, Pamela Sammons, Louise Stoll,
David Lewis, and Russell Ecob*

*Teachers do not influence classroom learning only through their planned
curriculum and their teaching. It seems clear, after decades of research into
classrooms, that teacher expectations have a strong impact on pupil performance. We looked at this earlier, in Chapter 5, in relation to teachers' different
expectations of boys and girls. However, research also suggests that many
effects are very subtle indeed. The following extract is taken from a large-
scale study of junior school classrooms undertaken for the now defunct Inner
London Education Authority. In some ways, the study refutes claims made
about the impact of low teacher expectations on certain social groups.
However, a careful reading indicates the ways in which low expectations are
transmitted, even where teachers are making positive efforts not to discrimi-
nate among their pupils. In what ways might such a critical awareness of
classroom processes help teachers to act to bring about changes in their own
teaching?*

Every classroom inevitably contains pupils of differing personalities, abilities, and backgrounds. Previous research findings demonstrate that, for
some teachers at least, the expectations they have for their pupils can
influence the children's future academic performance and self-perception
(see, for example, Pilling and Kellmer Pringle 1978; Meyer 1982). Nash
(1973) suggests that the teachers' behaviour is affected by their expectations,
and 'somehow the teacher's mental attitudes to the child are . . . being
communicated' (p. 12). Thus, different pupils may be presented with quite
different psychological environments by their teachers.

Inevitably, many predictions about pupil achievement are based on past
experience and may well reflect accurate teacher expectations. Furthermore,
as Brophy and Good (1974) pointed out, not all teachers will allow their
expectations to interfere with their ability to treat pupils appropriately.
Some studies, however, have shown that certain teachers do treat children
differently according to differential beliefs about them (see Pilling and
Kellmer Pringle 1978). We have been able to consider whether teacher
behaviour, particularly in terms of individual contacts with pupils, varied

towards different groups of children. These groups are defined by age, sex, social class, ethnic background, perceived ability, and behaviour.

AGE DIFFERENCES

The attainment of younger pupils within a year group was generally poorer than that of their older peers, although there was no difference in their progress in cognitive skills. Teachers, however, were found consistently to have judged pupils born in the summer months as being of lower ability and having more behaviour difficulties. Younger pupils themselves also were found to have a less positive view of school than their older peers.

Pidgeon (1970) has suggested that teachers 'know' that older children are capable of doing more advanced work and – albeit subconsciously – expect more from them. In order to test out this theory, teachers' communications with pupils of different ages were analysed. The youngest pupils (those born in the summer term) were found to have received the least feedback on their behaviour, while the oldest received the most. This is surprising, given that the youngest pupils were rated as having the most problems and were also observed to be distracted from their work more frequently than the older ones. This finding suggests that Pidgeon's explanation may need to be adapted. It may be that teachers have expectations of pupils' behaviour in that they 'know', subconsciously, that older pupils are more mature. They may be less prepared, therefore, to accept disobedience from older children.

Teachers also listened to autumn-born pupils read more frequently than they listened to their younger peers, even though the older children scored more highly in the reading assessments and were rated as being of higher ability. No other statistically significant differences in interaction, however, between teachers and pupils of different ages were identified.

In mixed-age classes covering more than one year group, less than a third of the teachers reported that they usually gave younger and older pupils different work in language and mathematics sessions. In project work, only 9 per cent of the teachers took age into account when planning work. Given that younger children achieve less well in the cognitive assessments, it is likely that they may be even more at risk in mixed-age classes where all the pupils are given the same work. However, it is also possible that older pupils are held back because work is pitched at too low a level for them. This could also occur in single-age classes where all pupils work on the same task.

SOCIAL CLASS DIFFERENCES

The influence of pupils' background upon teacher behaviour in the class-room has concerned researchers for some time (see Pilling and Kellmer Pringle (1978) for a review). Opinion is divided. Some studies have found no social class effect (Nash 1973; Murphy 1974; Croll 1981). Others, however, indicate that social class is one of the major sources of expectations teachers hold for their pupils (Goodacre 1968; Barker Lunn 1970; Dusek and Joseph 1983) and that teachers' behaviour can vary according to a child's background. For example, Sharp and Green (1975) found that pupils whom teachers regarded as more 'successful' were given greater attention than other children. These pupils invariably came from a 'good area'. The influence of social class may not always be relevant, particularly if teachers know little about a child's home circumstances. None the less, other cues, such as speech, physical appearance, and eligibility for free school meals, may also be indicators of social class.

The fact that pupils from non-manual backgrounds had higher attainments in most of the cognitive assessments and made more progress in reading and writing has already been pointed out. They were also rated by their teachers as of higher ability, even after account had been taken of their attainment. Those from unskilled manual backgrounds and from homes where the father was absent were perceived by their teachers as having a greater incidence of behaviour problems. Thus, it appears that some teachers have different expectations of pupils from different social class backgrounds, irrespective of the children's performance on cognitive assessments.

Teachers' contacts with pupils were observed systematically at set periods throughout each observation day. In the second year, observation time over three days totalled four and a quarter hours, almost the equivalent of one whole day's teaching time. During this time the average number of individual contacts between teachers and each pupil was approximately eleven. This covered a wide range, with one child experiencing only one contact, whereas, at the other extreme, a teacher communicated with a particular pupil on sixty-three occasions. Children from one-parent families had, on average, just over fifteen contacts with the teacher, a figure which is half as much again as that for the non- or skilled manual backgrounds.

There was no significant difference between groups in the number of discussions they had with the teacher about the content of their work. The non-manual and those of skilled manual backgrounds, however, were told significantly less often how to set about and organise their work. There may have been less need for teachers to supervise these latter pupils' work, given their higher attainments in the cognitive assessments.

There was only one significant difference between the social class groups in the frequency with which they were observed reading to their teachers. Pupils whose fathers were not working read to their teachers more often than those who lived with only one parent.

Teachers spent a significantly greater proportion of their time discussing non-work (routine) matters with the pupils whose fathers were absent. This is in line with their ratings of these pupils' behaviour. Routine comments included, for example, advice on the use or location of materials, telling pupils where and with whom they should be sitting, and feedback on behaviour, whether positive, neutral, or negative. The particular emphasis on behaviour control also related to the poorer concentration observed among pupils in the father-absent group.

Thus, teacher expectations did not appear to affect their behaviour with regard to the depth of discussion on work-related issues. However, in line with their perceptions that pupils who did not come from non-manual backgrounds were less likely to be of above-average ability, teachers devoted more time to the supervision of these pupils' work.

SEX DIFFERENCES

There is already considerable evidence of differences in teacher action towards, and judgements of, girls and boys (Palardy 1969; Good and Brophy 1971; Whyte 1983). The reinforcement of sex-stereotyping in the classroom has also been referred to as part of the 'hidden curriculum' (Serbin 1983). Thus, teachers may well be completely unaware of their own behaviours that encourage and sustain stereotyping and that, subsequently, may have an effect upon the academic progress and behavioural development of girls and boys.

It will also be seen that girls had higher attainments in reading and writing throughout their junior schooling and slightly higher attainment in mathematics by the third year. There were few other sex differences in pupil performance or progress. Although it did not reach statistical significance, teachers tended to rate boys' ability slightly higher than that of girls, when account was taken of their attainments in cognitive areas. This was surprising, because boys were consistently assessed as having more behaviour difficulties, and were also found to be less positive in their attitude to school. They were also observed to be less involved with their work by the field officers.

The ILEA's primary record summary, completed by teachers at the end of infant school, and at the end of the first and second junior years, was examined for all children individually. Significantly more girls than boys were rated as demonstrating marked ability in the four areas of written language: personal statements; factual statements; imaginative writing; and using information from various sources of reference. Conversely, more boys were rated as showing serious and persistent difficulties in these areas. For mathematics, the only difference was noted at the end of the second year, when more girls were rated at the later stages of development in work involving operations with whole numbers. This is in line with our finding of better progress by girls in mathematics.

Differences, once again in favour of girls, were also found in the stage of reading development reached, particularly at the end of the second year. By this year, significantly more girls could, in the opinion of their class teachers, follow a narrative, appraise material critically, and skim and scan material.

They also showed more proficiency in the use of dictionaries, indices, and other reference sources.

A similar difference was noted in favour of girls in records of pupils' creative abilities, particularly in dance, drama, and music. For art and craft work, there was a slight variation. More boys at the end of infant schooling had difficulties, but there were also more boys showing a particular flair in two- and three-dimensional work. In the junior years, differences in teachers' records of boys' and girls' art work were not significant.

Analyses show that teachers communicated more at an individual level with boys than with girls. This was found to be true for both female and male teachers. Differences were greatest in the third year when it was found that female teachers gave boys relatively even more attention.

The major difference concerned a greater use of criticism and neutral remarks to individual boys about their behaviour. This difference was not related to the sex of the teacher. Teachers also communicated more with boys on a non-verbal level, using both facial gestures and physical contact, and teased them more frequently. The extra behaviour control comments to boys are not surprising, given the teachers' lower assessments of boys' behaviour and the boys' tendency to be distracted more often from their work, as seen in the classroom observations. Another possibility is that the boys' poorer behaviour and attitudes to school may be related to, and exacerbated by, their treatment by teachers in the classroom. Thus, perhaps, pupils are reacting to the way they are treated by their teachers, as well as teachers responding to pupils' behaviour.

There were also differences between the sexes in their contact with teachers on work-related issues. Boys were given more work supervision, particularly in the form of extra feedback. Girls, however, received significantly more praise from teachers. Although there was no consistent pattern, there was some suggestion that teachers discussed the factual content of the work more frequently with the boys. There was no difference, however, in the frequency with which teachers heard girls and boys read throughout the day, although in sessions specifically designated for quiet reading, teachers heard more boys than girls read.

Overall, it appears that the main difference in teachers' classroom contact with girls and boys was in the greater number of negative comments, referring to their behaviour, made to boys. Boys also received more communication in general, and work feedback in particular, from their teachers. Given their poorer performance in cognitive areas this is perhaps not surprising. As far as positive work feedback was concerned, however, girls received more. It is interesting that teachers tended to rate the boys slightly more favourably than the girls in terms of ability, when account was taken of individual pupils' performance. Perhaps teachers were being influenced by the generally livelier behaviour of boys.

ETHNIC DIFFERENCES

It has also been suggested that teachers' expectations for pupils may be influenced by pupils' ethnic background. Thus, the Rampton Report (1981) proposed that the performance of ethnic minority children might be affected by low teacher expectations due to negative stereotypes about the abilities of such groups. The Swann Report (1985), while not rejecting the conclusions of the interim Rampton Report, suggested that the issues involved are complex and merit considerably more research. Eggleston *et al.* (1985) reached similar conclusions to those of Rampton about the educational and vocational experiences of young people of different ethnic groups in the secondary school context. However, an alternative interpretation was offered by Short (1985), who suggested that teachers' expectations might have been influenced by their experience of ethnic minority groups in the classroom.

The junior school project found no relationship between teachers' ratings of pupils' ability and the children's ethnic background, once account had been taken of other background factors and attainment. Ability ratings, however, were strongly related to pupil attainments. These attainments were lower in reading, writing, and mathematics for Caribbean and some Asian pupils than for other pupils. This suggests, as indicated at the beginning of this section, that for pupils from all ethnic backgrounds, teacher expectations appear to be tied to specific knowledge of previous attainment and performance in the classroom.

The data supply no evidence to support the view that teachers were withholding attention from any ethnic group. In fact they appeared to go out of their way to attend to black and ethnic minority pupils. This evidence is positive, though, quite clearly, it is not definitive. Expectations can be transmitted in subtle ways and it is possible that it was precisely through such differences in teacher attention that teachers were signalling differential expectations.

ABILITY DIFFERENCES

Most studies of teacher expectations, and the ways in which these may be mediated within the classroom, have concerned the effects of such expectations upon pupils of different abilities (see, for example, Rosenthal and Jacobson 1968; Barker Lunn 1971). Burstall (1968) found that pupils taught by teachers who believed that low ability children were able to learn French achieved better results than those whose teachers thought that such children would not be able to do so.

More recently, attention has focused on teacher behaviour in the classroom. Studies have varied in the extent to which differences in the behaviour of teachers towards high and low ability pupils have been observed. Some researchers have noted higher rates of contact with children of above average ability, more praise for correct responses, less criticism for incorrect responses, and greater opportunities to contribute in class (see the reviews by Brophy 1983; Galton and Delafield 1981). Others, however, reported no differences. Alpert (1974), for example, found as much 'good' teaching with the least able reading group as with the most able. Previous research, therefore, has produced no firm conclusions on the extent to which teacher behaviour varies towards different groups of pupils.

We found that pupils of below average ability had a higher number of individual contacts with their class teachers. This contrasts with the findings of other research quoted above. Teachers were also found to talk with the low ability pupils significantly more often about their work and to listen to them read more frequently. The less able pupils were also given more feedback on their work than more able children.

When eight teachers' contacts with a sub-sample of eighty pupils were examined in some detail, it was discovered that they criticised the higher ability pupils' work significantly more often than they criticised that of the lower ability children. Conversely, they praised the less able pupils' work more frequently than they praised that of more able children. These results are contrary to the findings of most other studies (see the review by Brophy 1983). It is possible that teachers are less prepared to accept poor work from pupils they believe are capable of producing a high standard.

It may be, however, that this seemingly positive approach to pupils considered less able demonstrates the limited expectations that teachers hold for them. Dweck and Repucci (1973) have argued along such lines in their study of girls being taught woodwork. Boys – seen as more suited to the subject – were criticised more often than girls who, in turn, were praised. The real meaning of such praise, however, may be that the performance is poor, or that expectations are lower.

On average, teachers made significantly more non-work comments to low ability pupils. These included both extra routine instructions and more neutral and negative remarks related to their behaviour. This is likely to reflect the significant relationship between teachers' ratings of pupils' behaviour and their ability, even after pupils' attainment had been taken into account. Furthermore, as a group, lower ability pupils spent less time involved in work activities. The relationship between ability and behaviour will be explored in more detail later in this section.

Differences were also identified in the ways teachers organised work and seating. Most teachers prepared different levels of work in mathematics and language according to pupils' abilities. Children were also seated according to their ability for at least some of the time in a quarter of classes.

It is possible that teachers' expectations may be influenced, at least in part, by the judgements of previous teachers. An examination of teachers' records of the progress of individual pupils showed that pupils rated as above average ability, at the beginning of the second year, were significantly more likely to have reached a further stage of development in their reading work. For example, by the end of the first year 59 per cent of the high ability pupils knew how to use a dictionary whereas the same was true for only 18 per cent of low ability pupils.

Within the classroom it appeared that, in the main, teachers responded to the needs of lower ability pupils by giving them extra support with their work and hearing them read more often. Teachers also talked to these children more frequently about their behaviour, in line with their lower assessments of these pupils' behaviour and the poorer concentration of low ability pupils observed by field officers. There was no evidence, therefore, that teachers skimped in the giving of attention. However, as was noted earlier, low expectations may be transmitted in very subtle ways.

BEHAVIOUR DIFFERENCES

Teachers make judgements not only about the ability and work habits of pupils, but also about their behaviour. In teachers' statements of aims, intellectual objectives are seen as no more important than those concerning pupils' personal and social development. Behaviour control is also seen to be an important aspect of classroom management. Much previous research has, generally, neglected the importance of behaviour when studying differences in teacher action towards various groups of children. It was decided, therefore, to examine whether teachers' behaviour varied towards pupils perceived by them as well or poorly behaved.

Teachers devoted significantly more individual attention to pupils they had rated as poorly behaved. In contrast, well-behaved pupils received more teacher contact in groups than predicted. The teachers also initiated fewer of their discussions with poorly-behaved children and more with well-behaved pupils. Calling across the room occurred more frequently with children perceived as naughtier. Either the teachers called across to pupils who were not getting on with their work, or these pupils called out to get teacher attention, rather than going up to their teachers or putting their hands up.

Teachers spent significantly more time on management and other non-work matters with poorly-behaved pupils. This included criticising their behaviour more frequently. Observations of the poorly-behaved pupils showed them to be more frequently distracted from their work than were their better-behaved peers. The extra non-work feedback given by the teachers, therefore, is likely to relate directly to pupils' behaviour in class. However, it was also found that teachers tended to praise the good behaviour of those pupils who were generally poorly behaved significantly more often than that of their well-behaved peers.

Well-behaved pupils were much less likely to receive negative comments on their work than poorly-behaved pupils, although the amount of praise for good work did not differ between the two groups. In work discussions, teachers also tended to joke with and tease naughtier pupils more than other children. There was no difference between these groups of pupils in the frequency with which teachers heard them read or in the amount of communication connected with the more detailed content of their work.

Overall, therefore, teachers' interactions with pupils they perceived to be different in terms of behaviour, tended to relate most closely to keeping the pupils 'on task'. It appears that teachers tried to achieve this end by using both positive and negative control comments.

THE LINK BETWEEN ABILITY AND BEHAVIOUR

A link between teachers' assessments of pupil ability and pupil behaviour has already been noted. The findings also indicate that teachers differentiate children in respect of their behaviour as well as their ability. Galton and Delafield (1981) suggest that, if teachers are forced to make judgements about the ability of pupils who have similar attainment levels, they do so largely on the basis of pupils' classroom behaviour. Thus, it has been argued that those nominated as of the highest ability are the quietest, most obedient pupils and those of the lowest ability are the noisiest, most disruptive children. We were able to compare teachers' ability and behaviour ratings for individual pupils. It became apparent that teachers could separate out their judgements of pupils' ability from those of behaviour.

For pupils of lower ability who also have behaviour difficulties, a greater emphasis on work rather than routine discussions may improve their performance and also the way that they feel they are perceived by teachers. It was encouraging to see that teachers were supportive of pupils with learning and behaviour difficulties when they had made a particular effort. None the less, praise was not commonly observed in classrooms for any group of children.

Two final points need to be made in relation to teachers' expectations of, and behaviour towards, different groups of pupils. First, a particular pupil may appear in a number of different groups. This has been illustrated in the analysis of pupils categorised according to behaviour and ability. It is also true for social class, sex, race, and, as pointed out earlier, for age. Any pupil appearing in the less positive category of all or most of these dimensions may be more likely to be treated differentially. Even though the teacher may go out of her or his way to give individual attention to such a pupil, the effect of such interactions may be negative. If this is the case, the message transmitted by the interactions is likely to reinforce still further the lower expectations.

The second point is that much of this process may be subconscious. Teachers may feel they are doing all they can to divide their time between all their pupils in as fair a way as possible. They may be quite unaware of the different meanings that their behaviour could convey to pupils. Some may try to give particular attention to, or be especially nice to, specific groups (girls or black pupils) without realising that, by this very action, they may be indicating lower academic expectations. The work of Dweck and Repucci (1973) provides some illustrations of the paradoxical nature of teachers' praise for the inadequate work of some groups of pupils. In considering the effects of differential expectations transmitted in the classroom it must be remembered that, for children interacting daily over a period of a year with a teacher who has a low perception of their abilities, the inhibiting effect may be stultifying. In the same way, for one of the pupils about whom the teacher holds positive views, the effect will be stimulating.

REFERENCES

Alpert, J. (1974) Teacher Behaviour Across Ability Groups: A Consideration of the Mediation of Pygmalion Effects. *Journal of Educational Psychology*. Vol. 66, No. 3, pp. 348–53.

Barker Lunn, J. (1970) *Streaming in the Primary School*, Slough, NFER.

Barker Lunn, J. (1971) *Social Class, Attitudes and Achievement*. Slough, NFER.

Barker Lunn, J. (1982) Junior Schools and their Organizational Policies. *Educational Research*. Vol. 24, No. 4, pp. 259–60.

Brophy, J. (1983) Research on the Self Fulfilling Prophecy and Teacher Expectations. *Journal of Educational Psychology*. Vol. 75, No. 5, pp. 631–61.

Brophy, J. and Good, T. (1974) *Teacher Student Relationships: Causes and Consequences*. New York, Holt, Rinehart & Winston.

Burstall, C. (1968) *French from Eight: A National Experiment*. Occasional Publication Series, No. 18, Slough, NFER.

Croll, P. (1981) Social Class, Pupil Achievement and Classroom Interaction. In B. Simon and J. Willcocks (Eds) *Research and Practice in the Primary Classroom*. London, Routledge & Kegan Paul.

Dusek, J. and Joseph, G. (1983) The Bases of Teacher Expectancies: A Meta-Analysis. *Journal of Educational Psychology*. Vol. 75, No. 3, pp. 327–46.

Dweck, C. W. and Repucci, N. D. (1973) Learned Helplessness and Reinforcement Responsibility in Children. *Journal of Personality and Social Psychology*. Vol. 25, pp. 109–16.

Eggleston S. J., Dunn, D. K. and Ajjali, M. (1985) *The Educational and Vocational Experiences of 15–18 Year Old Young People of Ethnic Minority Groups*. Department of Education, University of Keele.

Galton, M. and Delafield, A (1981) Expectancy Effects in Primary Classrooms. In B. Simon and J. Willcocks (Eds) *Research and Practice in the Primary Classroom*. London, Routledge & Kegan Paul.

Good, T. and Brophy, J. (1971) Questioned Equality for Grade One Boys and Girls. *Reading Teacher* Vol. 25, No. 3, pp. 247–52.

Goodacre, E. (1968) *Teachers and Their Pupils' Home Background*. Slough, NFER.

Meyer, W. U. (1982) Indirect Communications about Perceived Ability Estimates. *Journal of Educational Psychology*. Vol. 74, No. 6, pp. 888–97.

Murphy, J. (1974) Teacher Expectations and Working-Class Underachievement. *British Journal of Sociology*. Vol. 25, No. 3, pp. 326–44.

Nash, R. (1973) *Classrooms Observed: The Teacher's Perception and Pupil's Performance*. London, Routledge & Kegan Paul.

Palardy, J. (1969) What Teachers Believe – What Children Achieve. *Elementary*

School Journal. Vol. 69, pp. 370–4.

Pidgeon, D. (1970) *Expectations and Pupil Performance*. Slough, NFER.

Pilling, D. and Kellmer Pringle, M. (1978) *Controversial Issues in Child Development*. National Children's Bureau. London, Paul Elek.

Rampton Report (1981) *West Indian Children in Our Schools: Interim Report of the Committee from Ethnic Minority Groups*. London, HMSO.

Rosenthal, R. and Jacobson, L. (1968) *Pygmalion in the Classroom: Teacher Expectation and Pupils' Intellectual Development*. New York, Holt, Rinehart & Winston.

Serbin, L. A. (1983) The Hidden Curriculum: Academic Consequences of Teacher Expectations. In M. Marland (Ed.) *Sex Differentiation and Schooling*. London, Heinemann.

Sharp, R. and Green, A. (1975) *Education and Social Control – A Study in Progressive Primary Education*. London, Routledge & Kegan Paul.

Short, G. (1985) Teacher Expectation and West Indian Underachievement. *Educational Research*. Vol. 27, No. 2, pp. 95–101.

Swann Report (1985) *Education for All: The Report of the Committee of Inquiry into the Education of Children from Ethnic Minority Groups*. London, HMSO.

Whyte, J. (1983) *Beyond the Wendy House: Sex Role Stereotyping in Primary Schools*. York, Longman Schools Council Resources Unit.

Part III

Classrooms

Chapter 14

Life in classrooms

Philip Jackson

In this part we have brought together a collection of extracts which focus on the classroom context. To begin with, we have included an extract from Philip Jackson's classic book Life in Classrooms, *in which the sights and smells of the classroom are made both familiar and, through being brought to our attention, also strange. Why are classrooms as they are? Do they need to be that way? In whose interests do they seem to have evolved as they have? Should they be changed, and if so how? What constraints might there be on change? These are some of the issues which this part will begin to explore.*

School is a place where tests are failed and passed, where amusing things happen, where new insights are stumbled upon, and skills acquired. But it is also a place in which people sit, and listen, and wait, and raise their hands, and pass out paper, and stand in line, and sharpen pencils. School is where we encounter both friends and foes, where imagination is unleashed and misunderstanding brought to ground. But it is also a place in which yawns are stifled and initials scratched on desktops, where milk money is collected and recess lines are formed. Both aspects of school life, the celebrated and the unnoticed, are familiar to all of us, but the latter, if only because of its characteristic neglect, seems to deserve more attention than it has received to date from those who are interested in education.

In order to appreciate the significance of trivial classroom events it is necessary to consider the frequency of their occurrence, the standardisation of the school environment, and the compulsory quality of daily attendance. We must recognise, in other words, that children are in school for a long time, that the settings in which they perform are highly uniform, and that they are there whether they want to be or not. Each of these three facts, although seemingly obvious, deserves some elaboration, for each contributes to our understanding of how students feel about and cope with their school experience.

The amount of time children spend in school can be described with a fair amount of quantitative precision, although the psychological significance of the numbers involved is another matter entirely. In most US states the school year legally comprises 180 days. A full session on each of those days usually lasts about six hours (with a break for lunch), beginning somewhere around nine o'clock in the morning and ending about three o'clock in the afternoon. Thus, if a student never misses a day during the year, he spends a little more than 1,000 hours under the care and tutelage of teachers. If he has attended kindergarten and was reasonably regular in his attendance during the grades, he will have logged a little more than 7,000 classroom hours by the time he is ready for junior high school.

The magnitude of 7,000 hours spread over six or seven years of a child's life is difficult to comprehend. On the one hand, when placed beside the total number of hours the child has lived during those years it is not very great – slightly more than one-tenth of his life during the time in question, about one-third of his hours of sleep during that period. On the other hand, aside from sleeping, and perhaps playing, there is no other activity that occupies as much of the child's time as that involved in attending school. Apart from the bedroom (where he has his eyes closed most of the time) there is no single enclosure in which he spends a longer time than he does in the classroom. From the age of 6 onwards he is a more familiar sight to his teacher than to his father, and possibly even to his mother.

A classroom, like a church auditorium, is rarely seen as being anything other than that which it is. No one entering either place is likely to think that he is in a living room, or a grocery store, or a train station. Even if he entered at midnight or at some other time when the activities of the people would not give the function away, he would have no difficulty understanding what was *supposed* to go on there. Even devoid of people, a church is a church and a classroom, a classroom.

This is not to say, of course, that all classrooms are identical, any more than all churches are. Clearly there are differences, and sometimes very extreme ones, between any two settings. One has only to think of the wooden benches and planked floor of the early American classroom as compared with the plastic chairs and tile flooring in today's suburban schools. But the resemblance is still there despite the differences, and, more important, during any particular historical period the differences are not that great. Also, whether the student moves from first to sixth grade on floors of vinyl tile or oiled wood, whether he spends his days in front of a black blackboard or a green one, is not as important as the fact that the environment in which he spends these six or seven years is highly stable.

In their efforts to make their classrooms more homelike, elementary schoolteachers often spend considerable time fussing with the room's decorations. Bulletin boards are changed, new pictures are hung, and the seating arrangement is altered from circles to rows and back again. But these are surface adjustments at best, resembling the work of the inspired housewife who rearranges the living room furniture and changes the colour of the curtains in order to make the room more 'interesting'. School bulletin boards may be changed but they are never discarded, the seats may be rearranged but thirty of them are there to stay, the teacher's desk may have a new plant on it but there it sits, as ubiquitous as the roll-down maps, the olive drab wastebasket, and the pencil sharpener on the window ledge.

Even the odours of the classroom are fairly standardised. Schools may use different brands of wax and cleaning fluid, but they all seem to contain similar ingredients, a sort of universal smell which creates an aromatic background that permeates the entire building. Added to this, in each classroom, is the slightly acrid scent of chalk dust and the faint hint of fresh wood from the pencil shavings. In some rooms, especially at lunch time, there is the familiar odour of orange peels and peanut butter sandwiches, a blend that mingles in the late afternoon (following recess) with the delicate pungency of children's perspiration. If a person stumbled into a classroom blindfolded, his nose alone, if he used it carefully, would tell him where he was.

All of these sights and smells become so familiar to students and teachers alike that they exist dimly, on the periphery of awareness. Only when the classroom is encountered under somewhat unusual circumstances, does it appear, for a moment, a strange place filled with objects that command our attention. On these rare occasions when, for example, students return to school in the evening, or in the summer when the halls ring with the hammers of workmen, many features of the school environment that have merged into an undifferentiated background for its daily inhabitants suddenly stand out in sharp relief. This experience, which obviously occurs in contexts other than the classroom, can only happen in settings to which the viewer has become uncommonly habituated.

Not only is the classroom a relatively stable physical environment, it also provides a fairly constant social context. Behind the same old desks sit the same old students, in front of the familiar blackboard stands the familiar teacher. There are changes, to be sure – some students come and go during the year and on a few mornings the children are greeted at the door by a strange adult. But in most cases these events are sufficiently uncommon to create a flurry of excitement in the room. Moreover, in most elementary classrooms the social composition is not only stable, it is also physically arranged with considerable regularity. Each student has an assigned seat and, under normal circumstances, that is where he is to be found. The practice of assigning seats makes it possible for the teacher or a student to take attendance at a glance. A quick visual sweep is usually sufficient to determine who is there and who is not. The ease with which this procedure is accomplished reveals more eloquently than do words how accustomed each member of the class is to the presence of every other member.

An additional feature of the social atmosphere of elementary classrooms deserves at least passing comment. There is a social intimacy in schools that is unmatched elsewhere in our society. Buses and movie theatres may be more crowded than classrooms, but people rarely stay in such densely populated settings for extended periods of time and while there, they usually are not expected to concentrate on work or to interact with each other. Even factory workers are not clustered as close together as students in a standard classroom. Indeed, imagine what would happen if a factory the size of a typical elementary school contained three or four hundred adult workers. In all likelihood the unions would not allow it. Only in schools do thirty or more people spend several hours each day literally side by side. Once we leave the classroom we seldom again are required to have contact with so many people for so long a time.

A final aspect of the constancy experienced by young students involves the ritualistic and cyclic quality of the activities carried on in the class-room. The daily schedule, as an instance, is commonly divided into definite periods during which specific subjects are to be studied or specific activities engaged in. The content of the work surely changes from day to day and from week to week, and in this sense there is considerable variety amid the constancy. But spelling still comes after arithmetic on Tuesday morn-ing, and when the teacher says, 'All right class, now take out your spellers', his announcement comes as no surprise to the students. Further, as they search in their desks for their spelling textbooks, the children may not know what new words will be included in the day's assignment, but they have a fairly clear idea of what the next twenty minutes of class time will entail.

Despite the diversity of subject matter content, the identifiable forms of classroom activity are not great in number. The labels: 'seatwork', 'group discussion', 'teacher demonstration', and 'question-and-answer period' (which would include work 'at the board'), are sufficient to categorise most of the things that happen when class is in session. 'Audio-visual display', 'testing session', and 'games' might be added to the list, but in most elementary classrooms they occur rarely.

Each of these major activities is performed according to rather well-defined rules which the students are expected to understand and obey – for example, no loud talking during seatwork, do not interrupt someone else during discussion, keep your eyes on your own paper during tests, raise your hand if you have a question. Even in the early grades these rules are so well understood by the students (if not completely internalised) that the teacher has only to give very abbreviated signals ('Voices, class', 'Hands, please') when violations are perceived. In many classrooms a weekly time schedule is permanently posted so that everyone can tell at a glance what will happen next.

Thus, when our student enters school in the morning he is entering an environment with which he has become exceptionally familiar through prolonged exposure. Moreover, it is a fairly stable environment – one in which the physical objects, social relations, and major activities remain much the same from day to day, week to week, and even, in certain respects, from year to year. Life there resembles life in other contexts in some ways, but not all. There is, in other words, a uniqueness to the student's world. School, like church and home, is someplace special. Look where you may, you will not find another place quite like it.

There is an important fact about a student's life that teachers and parents often prefer not to talk about, at least not in front of students. This is the fact that young people have to be in school, whether they want to be or not. In this regard students have something in common with the members of two other of our social institutions that have involuntary attendance: prisons and mental hospitals. The analogy, though dramatic, is not intended to be shocking, and certainly there is no comparison between the unpleasantness of life for inmates of our prisons and mental institutions, on the one hand, and the daily travails of a first or second grader, on the other. Yet the school child, like the incarcerated adult, is, in a sense, a prisoner. He too must come to grips with the inevitability of his experience. He too must develop strategies for dealing with the conflict that frequently arises between his natural desires and interests on the one hand and institutional expectations on the other. Several of these strategies will be discussed in the chapters that follow. Here it is sufficient to note that the thousands of hours spent in the highly stylised environment of the elementary classroom are not, in an ultimate sense, a matter of choice, even though some children might prefer school to play. Many 7-year-olds skip happily to school, and as parents and teachers we are glad they do, but we stand ready to enforce the attendance of those who are more reluctant. And our vigilance does not go unnoticed by children.

In sum, classrooms are special places. The things that happen there and the ways in which they happen combine to make these settings different from all others. This is not to say, of course, that there is no similarity between what goes on in school and the students' experiences elsewhere. Classrooms are indeed like homes and churches and hospital wards in many important respects. But not in all.

The things that make schools different from other places are not only the paraphernalia of learning and teaching and the educational content of the dialogues that take place there, although these are the features that are usually singled out when we try to portray what life in school is really like. It is true that nowhere else do we find blackboards and teachers and textbooks in such abundance and nowhere else is so much time spent on reading, writing, and arithmetic. But these obvious characteristics do not constitute all that is unique about this environment. There are other features, much less obvious though equally omnipresent, that help to make up 'the facts of life', as it were, to which students must adapt. From the standpoint of understanding the impact of school life on the student some features of the classroom that are not immediately visible are fully as important as those that are.

The characteristics of school life to which we now turn our attention are not commonly mentioned by students, at least not directly, nor are they apparent to the casual observer. Yet they are as real, in a sense, as the unfinished portrait of Washington that hangs above the cloakroom door. They comprise three facts of life with which even the youngest student must learn to deal and may be introduced by the key words: *crowds, praise*, and *power*.

Learning to live in a classroom involves, among other things, learning to live in a crowd. This simple truth has already been mentioned, but it requires greater elaboration. Most of the things that are done in school are done with others, or at least in the presence of others, and this fact has profound implications for determining the quality of a student's life.

Of equal importance is the fact that schools are basically evaluative settings. The very young student may be temporarily fooled by tests that are presented as games, but it doesn't take long before he begins to see through the subterfuge and comes to realise that school, after all, is a serious business. It is not only what you do there but what others think of what you do that is important. Adaptation to school life requires the student to become used to living under the constant condition of having his words and deeds evaluated by others.

School is also a place in which the division between the weak and the powerful is clearly drawn. This may sound like a harsh way to describe the separation between teachers and students, but it serves to emphasise a fact that is often overlooked, or touched upon gingerly at best. Teachers are indeed more powerful than students, in the sense of having greater responsibility for giving shape to classroom events, and this sharp difference in authority is another feature of school life with which students must learn how to deal.

In three major ways then – as members of crowds, as potential recipients of praise or reproof, and as pawns of institutional authorities – students are confronted with aspects of reality that, at least during their childhood years, are relatively confined to the hours spent in classrooms. Admittedly, similar conditions are encountered in other environments. Students, when they are not performing as such, must often find themselves lodged within larger groups, serving as targets of praise or reproof, and being bossed around or guided by persons in positions of higher authority. But these kinds of experience are particularly frequent while school is in session and it is likely during this time that adaptive strategies having relevance for other contexts and other life periods are developed.

Chapter 15

Characteristics of good practice

Her Majesty's Inspectors of Schools

This is a short extract from a booklet produced by Her Majesty's Inspectors of Schools the year before the Education Reform Act was passed. In it, they attempted to set out common characteristics of 'good practice' in primary schools and classrooms. It thus provides a clear account of the kind of goals and provision which skilled and aware professionals were trying to achieve in the 1980s.

The examples of good practice which have been described were observed in classes which differed greatly in terms of the accommodation and facilities, the number of children in the group, the ethnic mix of the pupils, and the curricular strengths of the individual teachers. Although there were these differences some common features were apparent. It is not the intention, in what follows, to reflect a particular theory of learning but simply to point out some of the common characteristics associated with good practice in the schools. These features are discussed as two groups; the first, setting out those things which were predominantly characteristic of the whole school; the second, focusing more closely on the classroom, on what the children were doing and how the teachers were achieving a high quality of response.

CHARACTERISTICS OF THE SCHOOLS

In each school the head and staff had agreed aims relating to the academic work and the children's personal and social development. A shared sense of purpose was most evident in the way the teachers talked to their pupils. The high standard of the children's work and their sensible behaviour in the classroom and as they moved about the school were direct consequences of the teachers' expectations.

Most of the schools had curricular guidelines which had been carefully thought out. In almost all cases these guidelines had been written after staff discussions at meetings led by one teacher or a small group of teachers able to offer informed advice on the particular aspect of the curriculum. Some schools had taken the guidelines prepared by local education authority advisory groups and developed them to meet the needs of the school; some of these modifications were intended to ensure that, as the children moved through the primary age range, their teachers would make effective use of the educational opportunities offered by the environment of the school. A certain proportion of the schemes of work were being reviewed at the time of the inspections.

The work in these schools was supported by an adequate level and a suitable variety of resources. This situation reflected good management over a number of years of all the funds available to the school and a careful selection of resources on the part of the teachers. Classrooms and work areas had orderly storage arrangements and the children were taught to handle equipment safely. Books were usually available in reasonable quality and range, and stocks were supplemented by local authority library services. Where appropriate these books were carefully chosen to reflect in their texts and illustrations the variety of cultures and ethnic groups in the school and society. The schools also made good use of outside sources of materials, such as museum loan services, teachers' centres, and contributions from parents and friends and, in some instances, local shops and factories.

A number of the schools were exploring ways of deploying the staff so that more effective use was made of their abilities and curricular strengths. Their aim was to ensure in all classes that the responsibility for co-ordinating the work of the class would remain with the class teacher and that, for the most part, the class teacher would teach much of the curriculum to that group of children, while at the same time, and where there was advantage to the children, teachers with particular expertise in certain subjects might interchange classes or groups with teachers with strengths in other subjects. In this way the schools were making positive efforts to strike the delicate balance which is involved in making the best use of the curricular expertise of a primary school staff as a combined teaching unit. Staffing ratios may constrain the aspect of consulting which becomes effective only when the teacher with overall responsibility for developing an aspect of the curriculum can regularly be present in the classroom while another member of staff is teaching. Nevertheless, some teachers in these schools were acting effectively as consultants by helping to plan the work and prepare the teaching materials. Some of these teachers were responsible for the development of a single subject, others had responsibilities which related to broader aspects such as the project work described in the history and geography section of this document and others had consultancy roles which related to the teaching of literacy and mathematics.

CHARACTERISTICS OF THE WORK IN THE CLASSROOM

The examples of good practice differ in their curricular content but there are some features common to the way the children were working.

- In almost all cases first impressions were of an informality which typifies many primary classrooms. Closer investigation showed that the freedoms were not there merely by chance. They had been adopted for a variety of interrelated reasons; for example, on those occasions when children were permitted to move about the classroom so that they had access to the materials they needed and in order that they could use reference books, they were being taught, at the same time, to select from a range of materials, to behave responsibly, and to persevere with the task in hand while showing a proper consideration for others working in the same room. By these and other means a sense of self discipline was being nurtured.

- The children were keenly interested in the work. Their commitment to what they were doing extended beyond the more obviously enjoyable aspects of the practical activities. It was sustained in their efforts to achieve a high standard of 'end product', whether that was to be in the form of written recording, one or other of the modes of pictorial representation, a dramatic presentation, or a combination of these things.

- According to their age and ability and in various aspects of good practice the children were being taught to listen carefully and to speak clearly and articulately. In many cases the discussions arising from the work centred on the similarities and differences of things they had observed, the patterns they had noticed and, again according to the children's ability, the validity of the generalisations which could be drawn from their experiences. They were encouraged to read for pleasure and for information. Their written work caused them to use a variety of styles to meet a range of purposes and, in this matter, fluency and legibility were given fitting attention.

The high quality of teaching was the strongest feature common to all the examples in this publication. As might be expected there were variations in the teaching styles reflecting the needs of the situation and the personality of individual teachers. Nevertheless there were common characteristics in the intentions and the methods used.

It was evident that the teachers had a sound knowledge of their pupils' social and cultural backgrounds and this enabled them to draw upon each child's experience in order to lead them on to further learning and, in some cases, to choose starting points for studies likely to interest the majority of children.

A dominant factor in the achievement of high standards was the strength of commitment on the part of the teachers to ensure that pupils were making progress. It was characteristic that the teachers consistently faced the question, 'Is that a sufficiently high standard for that particular child?' Their answers – and perhaps even their readiness to ask the question – revealed a firm grasp of the long-term aims and the more immediate objectives of the curriculum. The various teaching methods used were all geared to making the work suitably challenging so that individually the children consolidated what they were learning and reached forward to tackle the next stage. Whether teaching the class as one unit, organising groups, or channelling special work to individuals, the matter of progression was kept in mind. Methods of evaluation and records of attainment were used as an aid to planning future activities. Challenges were set so that the work was neither too easy nor too difficult for the children. In itself, this well-matched work was a notable achievement but it was heightened by the fact that a sense of self-assessment had spread to the children. The 'climate of assessment' was accepted and many of the pupils were able to speak lucidly about what they had learned, give reasons why they were engaged in certain activities, explain what they planned to do next and, in many cases, express a reasoned view of how well they were doing. Furthermore, the teachers weighed the children's responses carefully according to individual differences in ability so that praise was not given lightly or attributed to slipshod or mediocre work. Children were nevertheless commended when their work and efforts deserved it.

In all the examples of good practice the educational objectives were firmly established. Some had been made explicit in the school's guidelines or the teacher's schemes of work; some, such as those relating to orderliness and effort, were implicit in the ethos of the school and were given expression in the teaching styles. This clear view of objectives had not in any way reduced the flexibility of the teaching arrangements. On the contrary it had provided a sure base from which the educational opportunities arising as the work progressed were taken up and used to advantage while the pace and thrust of the work were maintained.

In these examples of good practice in primary schools the overriding characteristic is that of agreed, clear aims and purposeful teaching.

Chapter 16

The rise and fall of primary education

Ellen Yeo

This chapter is an edited version of a pamphlet published by the Campaign for Real Education – an organisation which, though claiming to be politically independent, is regarded by policy analysts such as Moon (see his chapter in this reader) as a 'New Right' Conservative pressure group. It provides an excellent contrast with the views of HMI in the previous chapter and with the professional educationalist views of Hutchinson in the chapter that follows. Note the use of anecdote, assertion, and evaluation, and the attribution of all sorts of social and economic problems to educational practices in primary schools. Such writing and arguments are often picked up by the media and some politicians. They form part of what has been called a 'discourse of derision' through which teachers' professional standing has been undermined. Contrast this, too, with the principled commitments of a classroom teacher, Jane Needham, in Chapter 19. However, having done this, how justified are the criticisms which Ellen Yeo makes?

My mother went to school in London in the first years of this century. Although she must have left school at about 13 or 14 after only an elementary education, she became a clerical officer in the Civil Service. She was a beautiful writer, an avid reader, could spell as well as anyone I know and keep simple accounts. She was a cultured and eloquent person to talk to. We certainly can't say the same things about the children who have eleven years' education nowadays.

I started school in a small northern industrial town just before the Second World War. Our school life was ordered and disciplined. Every morning began with an act of worship, with a hymn, bible reading, a short talk perhaps, and the prayers and assembly notices.

Schoolwork was, of course, based on the 3Rs. Our arithmetic – mental, mechanical, and problems – was of a high standard. We chanted our tables each day so that I have never forgotten them, and by the time we reached the age of 11 we were competent at decimals and fractions and even long multiplication of money.

Reading was taught by phonetics and then continued with group reading. This has now gone out of fashion – the small group with a leader all reading in turn from the same book. It did ensure that every child read aloud each day.

The cane and the ruler were used but nobody felt aggrieved about it. I can remember having to scrub the floor all one afternoon after knocking over a jar of paint.

After passing the 11-plus, I spent the next eight years travelling a few miles by bus to the grammar school. I had an excellent education there, went on to do a degree, and then trained as a junior school teacher.

I taught for nearly twelve years in four different junior schools in my native town area until I stopped teaching when I married. I enjoyed my job and I regard that period between 1956 and 1968 as probably the golden era of primary education – the good things remained from the old schools, but better buildings and facilities and some of the new ideas had enhanced education. Even then, however, the standard of achievement was no higher than it had been ten years earlier.

The first school I taught in was an eighty-year-old school in the poorest and most deprived area of the town. Some of the children were rough and naughty – I had one child threaten me that his 'teddy boy' brother would 'get' me after school. Some gypsy children attended the school – they found it difficult to learn to read but their trading activities made them wizard mathematicians!

In spite of the difficulties it was a well-disciplined and happy school. A marvellous musical headmaster presided there. He could get a beautiful sound from a class of growlers. It is sad that nowadays so few schools sing – they spend all their time banging and blowing inexpertly at instruments instead of using the voices God gave them.

We still had group reading and history, geography, nature, art, and PE.

The great event of the year was the school trip. A large fleet of buses took everybody off to the seaside for the day – the only holiday some of them ever got.

That school was a great power for good in the area and the teachers were all held in great respect by the parents.

I am one of the people who favoured the 11-plus. I felt it was fair. I never found that the wrong children passed. There was a good mixture of rich and poor in the grammar school. Today's comprehensive system means that many parents who can afford it will opt out and choose private education. This deprives the state sector of many of the brightest children.

With the bright 11-year-olds, I did a lesson each week on current events – the elections, the EEC, the Olympic Games, the war in Laos. We had a weekly newspaper on the wall and produced a printed one for the school each term.

The school dinners were marvellous in those days – plentiful, hot, and tasty.

I taught at three other schools for long or short periods before I stopped when I married.

I think without doubt that this was the zenith of primary school or at any rate junior school education. The improvements had been achieved without the loss of standards. Teaching was still largely formal; progress was regularly tested and results were good.

And yet, even then, one could see the beginnings of the revolution that was to come. Teaching advisers and teachers fresh from college were introducing new jargon like 'the integrated day', more stress should be put on self-expression they said, there was to be less of a competitive spirit, you shouldn't expect so much of the younger children, you should not test so much.

Symptomatic of the change was the idea that children must no longer sit in rows but in cosy little groups.

This idea has prevailed ever since. This is a most invidious scheme which typifies modern educational theory. You don't look at the board, you don't listen to the teacher, you sit in little huddles with your friends, chattering, looking at other people's work or working together. It is impossible to assess what the children know or achieve – half the work is a combined effort and some children will manage to fool the teacher about what they know and will end up knowing little. The group encourages the lack of discipline. But once the group idea had come in, there was no going against it. Headteachers insisted on it to please the advisers.

After 1968, I did no more teaching for the next fourteen years. I knew very little of the changes which were coming until we moved to the Midlands. Soon after we arrived there, I was asked to go on the supply list for the local school. I was about to see what had happened to the primary education of this country. One might well say 'The glory has departed.'

Over the past six years I have taught odd days in seven local primary schools in the neighbourhood. The criticisms that I make of primary education do not apply to all of them equally. One of the Church of England-aided schools has retained some of the characteristics I hold most important – a religious ethos with a good assembly and RE lessons, good formal written work, and good discipline. The children emerge literate, numerate, and easy to talk to. Even there, however, the ideas of some of the teachers show that things may change.

Looking at the picture overall I would admit that the facilities are better, the children are happy, and the teachers are devoted to the children, even if somewhat misguided.

The criticisms are, however, far more numerous. The first is that there is no tranquillity and little obvious discipline in the schools. Instead of a quiet, ordered atmosphere conducive to work, there is perpetual noise and movement. In the classroom, children constantly move about and chatter. In many classes, groups spill out of the room with odd people making models and experimenting all over the place. Classes rush from cooking to model making to TV programmes. They charge up and down corridors; some work at their desks, while odd children may be knitting with a mother in the corridor, ostensibly looking up things in the library or counting the birds in the schoolyard. Indeed, the child who dislikes book work and is fairly astute can spend the whole day on more practical activities, and never learn the basic three Rs. Constantly there are visits to swimming baths, museums, field trips, holidays, and outings. All these may teach the children useful facts but often there is little basic teaching connected to them and they are far too frequent. Gone are the days when a trip out was a great treat.

Vast quantities of paper are used to cover display boards; the paper is then covered with beautifully mounted pictures and friezes (again on another lot of paper) – a great deal of mess, a great deal of paper used – all quite an interesting occupation for an afternoon but not to spend hours of time, day after day. There is far too little time given to formal teaching and proper formal written work in books rather than on reams of paper which either ends up on the wall or more likely in the waste-paper basket.

Formerly, as both a pupil and a teacher, I appreciated the religious side of education. Now to all intents and purposes it is non-existent in most of our schools. Obviously some of the church-aided schools are an exception although one or two of them could be better. In one large county primary school I went to, about once a month there was an excellent religious assembly taken by a gifted local clergyman in an interesting and imaginative way. Surely some of the teachers could have done something similar – but no – the rest of the time assembly was varied but all equally disappointing – some mornings the headteacher took it as though apologising for having it – two hymns, one prayer, and a moral lecture on tidiness or eating good food (with no religious connection). Some days there would be a class taking assembly as a project on electricity or French for example. This school went through the motions more than some, however.

For most schools this assembly is reckoned to be all the RE needed. There is no further religious instruction. I suspect that many parents of other faiths would prefer their children to go to Christian assembly than to have no religion in the school.

My third criticism is that the main avowed aim of one headteacher I know (and I suspect that it applies to others too) is that the children shall be happy and enjoy themselves. Nothing else matters. Consequently there is very little discipline. This belief of course means that children who cannot do work, or are bored with it, can change to something more congenial. I, like most people, am in favour of making school a happy place, but there are other things that matter. School should be a place of self-discipline and achievement. If a child always gives up on anything difficult and expects everything to be a pleasure then I am afraid he or she will find life very hard. Part of growing up is learning to cope with difficulties. The child who has all the difficulties removed will be the grown-up who will not stick at a job which involves effort and will give up on marriage as soon as the euphoria is over. He will become the person who has to have what he wants, when he wants it. Many of those who become vandals, thieves, or even rapists commit these crimes because they are doing what they want, to get what they want. The school should teach the child to discipline himself or herself.

Over the years various reading schemes came and went. Thirty years ago I used Janet and John and Wide Range Readers. Today I find very little phonetic teaching. Although the reading in some schools is quite good, this lack of phonetics means that children are unable to build up words they don't know. If you knew the phonetic alphabet, word building was possible. The most pernicious method, which I believe came from Peterborough and is sometimes called the story book method, is now sweeping through the Midlands if not through the whole country. By this method you let the child learn to love books by looking at them and by having them read to him or her. The child is then expected to learn to read the book for himself by some miraculous method. This method involves no phonetics and no word building. At one school in which I encountered the method, parents were in despair and all the children were several years behind in reading. In spite of the failure of this absolutely ridiculous method, it has become one of the sacred cows of some of the most influential educationalists. The head in the school I mentioned refused point-blank to change or modify it. This would have made him unpopular with the powers-that-be. Another school I know has recently appointed a new head, who favours this method fervently, in preference to other good candidates with more traditional methods.

If we look at writing, with a few exceptions, writing is bad. Far too little time is spent learning to write. Often children are not taught in which direction to make a letter. Nowadays very few children can copy correctly – always words are misspelt and letters or words left out. I am sure this is because very little copying from the board is done. Far too much work is photocopied on to paper for children just to fill in a word or underline something. Of course this is quicker, but copying is in itself practice which teaches writing and spelling.

Spelling is universally much worse than twenty years ago. Spelling mistakes are not usually corrected in pieces of written work.

Many schools have some sort of integrated day which means that different children will be working at different things at different times. It continually adds to the disruption of the room as children wander about to get their books from their trays. How much easier it is if a child has his or her books in a desk in front of him.

Children nowadays are given individual 'assignments' particularly at maths, so they meander on at their own speed. There is some reasonable work in some schools but it is usually, as always, from the children with better backgrounds and the whole picture is very fragmented. On the whole, if you present children of about 9 with ten mechanical sums which are fairly easy, scarcely anyone will get them right. Many will misread them, many will not connect them with similar sums they have done before.

The basic fault with most of the maths schemes seems to be that far too many methods of doing one process are taught. As in English, there is great stress on filling in answers and few children can copy down sums.

There is of course very great stress on practical work but too often the child does not see the connection with the written work. In some schools, day after day you see children trundling a wheel round the yard to measure it – but will the child ever learn to work out the perimeter without the wheel, and will he see the connection between the two methods?

Geography, history and nature are not widely taught as such but are dealt with as topics or environmental studies, often as projects. Projects are a snare and a delusion. There is much stress on making primitive cardboard models. As Dr Dennis O'Keefe, a senior lecturer in education, was reported as saying in the *Daily Telegraph*, 'A trivial "Blue Peter curriculum" of painted toilet roll tubes, montages of coloured paper and childish displays of art has come to dominate the training of Primary School teachers.'

The project method assumes that children are far more capable of abstracting material from a book than most of them are. I have seen project instructions up on the wall of a class of 10-year-olds that I would have enjoyed doing, but which are so far beyond the pupils that little of value either for teacher or child will be produced. Children are encouraged to go to the library shelves to find out things for themselves. Unfortunately this usually means that they copy an odd section out and often omit the most relevant part. Dr O'Keefe says only very intelligent children from good backgrounds benefit from finding things out by this discovery method. Most children of 7, 8, 9, or even 10 cannot do it at all adequately.

Art and craft are mostly integrated into other subjects and seem to go on all day and every day all over the school without achieving very much.

Most teachers are today very much against competition in school life. They do not favour tests or examinations of any type. Sadly, there are some children who don't do an examination at all in the whole of their school life until they come to the GCSE. Some educationalists would say 'Get rid of even these examinations', but better by far would be to get children used to tests gradually, so that by the time external examinations are encountered they hold no terrors.

There is no doubt that nowadays all teachers seem to have been brainwashed into the same views, and people just dare not oppose these views. My postgraduate course was run by quite radical professors, tutors, and lecturers but the teachers of today seem to have been completely won over by the most extreme and what one might call 'with it' views.

At one time the schoolmaster or mistress was held in great respect, on a par with the doctor and the vicar. Teachers would say that this respect was of no use to them if the scale of their salaries was not a professional one. They have therefore deliberately altered their image. They see no harm in going on demonstrations and marches and brandishing placards.

The general lack of professionalism is reflected in their appearance. Discipline is much slacker in all aspects of life but it is bound to increase the indiscipline if the teacher does not set a good example. The casual dress, the informality, even in some cases the use of Christian names when addressing teachers, will rub off on the pupil. The teacher's job is made harder without discipline and respect. How can children respect the head if he doesn't bother to keep them quiet in assembly, and if on Comic Relief Day he is got up like something out of pantomime?

The point on which I would not fault today's teachers is on their devotion to the children. They really care for them and will spend a great deal of their own time and much effort on providing for their every need. They are willing to stay at school after hours for out of school activities, and spend much time preparing work both at home and at school. Also they have untold patience in dealing with the appearance of the classroom, providing an intricate and colourful display. There is no doubt too, that the new methods put much greater strain on the teacher. It is far harder to have children working individually or in small groups rather than as a class, and project work demands far more organisation and patience than teaching the class and then setting them a piece of work. Hours of preparation are needed and there is much greater likelihood of indiscipline and naughtiness if pupils are working on their own, making things, wandering about looking things up or going to other classrooms or the library.

The modern methods certainly take their toll of teachers. More and more are taking early retirement and in some staffrooms teachers are plagued by constant colds and bad throats, and one finds many of them resorting to pills of various kinds. Teachers think they are overworked and they are right, but they do not seem to realise that the main cause is the modern methods they use. It seems a shame that so much effort should be put in for such poor results.

There is a great similarity of opinion in all staffrooms and one has the feeling that all state sector teachers have been brainwashed into the same and sometimes obviously false views.

Practically all teachers are violently against the present Conservative government, and particularly against the ideas of the education ministers. The critical remarks and scorn are constant, while the walls are festooned in every staffroom with anti-government NUT posters and slogans. Without being political, I feel they should be a little more open-minded and be prepared to give the politicians the credit for some good ideas. But any educational idea or view coming from the government is immediately regarded as misguided, impracticable, and completely unacceptable. Moreover, they are quite likely to talk in this vein to parents, probably in order that the government's ideas and lack of finance and not their teaching shall be blamed for the poor attainment of the children.

The second universal belief of the teaching profession is that the education system needs lots more money – money will solve everything. I can assure them that far more is spent on equipment of all types than twenty years ago. When I first taught, we had to send in a stock book every week listing our requirements and our demands were very closely scrutinised. In fact, things like pencils and good drawing paper were almost rationed. Today I am appalled by the wastage of paper. There are the reams of paper used for drawing and then there's the photocopier – I wonder how many sheets are duplicated each term per child – sheets which the child just uses to fill in words or underline or colour a picture.

Teachers seem to think their lot is much worse than it used to be. It is worse in some ways but the deterioration is mainly self-inflicted. Normally there are between twenty-five and thirty children in a class. When I was teaching full-time I normally had forty-five. Another improvement is the use of supply teachers. If someone was absent twenty years ago, the class was split up – we quite frequently could go up to as many as fifty-four in the class – whereas nowadays a supply teacher comes in. I feel it is a great pity that teachers will not admit these improvements in their conditions.

If teachers' lots have worsened, it is not because of the conditions but because of modern methods.

One might be able to feel that the teachers' work and suffering were worthwhile if something good was achieved, but it isn't. They wear themselves out with aims and methods that do not produce children of high educational achievement and they never will. Results of every sort have declined from the 1960s and probably from earlier. I do not encounter a single child who can match the best of the 1960s pupils at maths or English at the age of 11.

The primary school of today is not achieving its potential. It is not educating our children to a high enough standard.

School is no longer a place to learn but a place to play, to enjoy oneself and perhaps, by the way, to pick up a smattering of what is, in many cases, useless knowledge.

Even as I write, another report about the reading ability of 7-year-olds has come out, showing standards are too low in many schools.

1 Why are so many children unable to read today?
2 Why is handwriting so bad?
3 Why are so few people able to check prices or to fill in forms?
4 Why is there so much vandalism and petty crime among our young people?

5 Why are young people so easily bored by their jobs and unwilling to stick at them?

When will this country have the sense to realise what has happened and do something about it?

Chapter 17

The 'three wise men' and after

David Hutchinson

This chapter provides a considerable contrast to the previous paper by Yeo. David Hutchinson, through his review in early 1993 of the ways in which government policy continued to impact on primary education through the early 1990s, conveys much of the commonly felt frustration of professional educators at the time. His analysis articulates with Moon's chapter on the policy context of curriculum reform. However, we have placed it in this 'classroom' section because of the contrast which it provides with Yeo's work and because of Hutchinson's focus on the impact of the, so-called, 'three wise men' report (Alexander et al. 1992). This was the first attempt by government to influence actual teaching methods in classrooms. The article vividly conveys the succession of moral panics, government interventions, and expressions of professional concern which characterised the period. Hutchinson concludes, optimistically, by noting the strength of professional expertise and co-operation – but the story is far from over. . . .

Radical changes are on the way in primary teaching and teacher education. John Patten is writing to all primary schools in February 1993 asking them to consider grouping children by ability, and making more use of whole-class teaching and subject specialists. Proposals to overhaul primary teacher education in line with these aims will be produced this spring.

These changes were signalled in February 1992, when Kenneth Clarke published the 'three wise men' report, *Curriculum Organisation and Classroom Practice in Primary Schools* (Alexander *et al.* 1992). In February 1993, the National Curriculum Council and the Office for Standards in Education issued reports which Patten is using as ammunition for his policy changes. These reports, the review of the English curriculum (announced in September 1992 two years ahead of schedule) and the proposed changes in primary practice have provoked intense discussion.

A remarkable characteristic of this discussion is that everyone on all sides recognises that the educational changes are being propelled by Conservative political ideology. Since the 1944 Education Act there has been a cross-party consensus that teaching methods should not be subject to political direction. The Conservatives have broken this consensus, and are increasingly using the unprecedentedly sweeping powers given to the Secretary of State for Education in the 1988 Education Reform Act. In the *New Testament* the massacre of the innocents preceded the appearance of the three wise men, but now it could be the other way round.

I shall discuss the implications of the 'three wise men report', how these relate to the NCC and OFSTED reports, and to John Patten's proposals. But all this needs to be set in the context of the Conservatives' increasingly ideological approach to education.

The Thatcher governments set their sights on 'standards' in education. We know that the national curriculum, and the progressive diminution of local education authorities' powers through LMS and opting out, were their main policies for raising standards. Whatever their views of these policies, many schools and teachers have worked amazingly hard throughout this period to preserve and develop that old stalwart, 'good primary practice'. Despite the way the changes were imposed and rushed through, despite increasing financial constraints, schools and teachers have continued to work positively. For many years we have been used to ideological attacks on so-called 'progressive' teaching, with reading as one of the classic battlegrounds. But in schools and in teacher education we could still maintain a reasoned opposition to such attacks and develop positive alternatives.

But in Kenneth Clarke's last months as secretary of state, the ideological temperature of educational debate and policy making was significantly raised. DES press releases and circulars rounded on primary teaching methods in *Sun*-style language. Perhaps the clearest example was under-secretary of state Michael Fallon's broadside before Christmas 1991 to the effect that there was too much play, paint, and happiness in primary classrooms. It was in this atmosphere that on 3 December 1991 Clarke commissioned what became known as the 'three wise men' report. The authors were asked 'to review available evidence about the delivery of education in primary schools' and 'to make recommendations about curriculum organisation, teaching methods and classroom practice appropriate for the successful implementation of the National Curriculum, particularly at Key Stage 2'.

The authors had to compile the report in three weeks, which indicated that it was an urgent political priority, but resulted in the fact that the scope of their enquiry was limited to already published material, with no time for visits or consultations. There was then what Professor Neville Bennett called 'a cynical delay' (*TES* 24 February 1992) between a DES press conference and publication of the report. This encouraged selective and misleading media coverage before the full text was available to the public in general or to teachers in particular. Headlines in the quality media as well as the gutter press focused on 'back to the basics', blamed Plowden for teaching methods (particularly in 'topic' work) that were both dogmatic and slack, and called for a reintroduction of subject teaching in primary schools. So right from the start, debate over the report's recommendations has tended to be polarised and to obscure the issues that they raise. In various articles in the *Guardian* and the *TES*, Robin Alexander has protested against the misuse of the report and attempted to refocus the debate. Jim Rose, as a government employee, has not written publicly along these lines, but when he has spoken (e.g. at a Camden headteachers' conference in July 1992) he too has tried to steer debate away from its media polarisation, suggesting that the issues are not all cut and dried. This propaganda misuse of the report can be seen as part of a significant strategy.

In August and September 1992, three people who were centrally involved in devising the national curriculum attacked ministers and their advisers for political interference. Professor Paul Black chaired the Task Group on Assessment and Testing (TGAT) in 1987 which established the basic structure for national curriculum assessment. Later he chaired the science working group which devised the original national curriculum for science. At a conference of the British Association for the Advancement of Science, Black attacked ministers for changing the national curriculum for reasons of 'prejudice rather than evidence' (*Guardian* 26 August 1992). He also attacked the appointment and approach of Lord Griffiths, the right-wing former Downing Street adviser who now heads the rejigged School Examination and Assessment Council, saying that:

> Those who gave dire warnings that the Education Reform Act would be an instrument for direct government control in which the opinions of ministers would be insulated from professional opinion and expertise have been proved correct. . . .
>
> If the teaching profession's practices and judgements are no longer to be trusted then the fault cannot be corrected simply by giving them new orders. All those who care for education should not want them to be robots. To treat them as robots is to run the risk that they will start to behave as robots should.

These statements were echoed soon after by Eric Bolton, the former Chief HMI, and Duncan Graham, the first chief executive of the National Curriculum Council (*Guardian* 7 September 1992). Bolton told the Council of Local Education Authorities conference that:

> It is not auspicious that the formal channels of advice about education to the government appear either to be muzzled (e.g. HMI), or packed with people likely to say whatever the government wants to hear (the NCC and SEAC).

Duncan Graham later published a book on his work with the NCC which explicitly condemned government interference in the curriculum, and the way that secretaries of state could control advice-giving bodies like the NCC and SEAC by nominating and changing their constitution.

Three earlier 'wise men' – formerly key members of the educational establishment, who held almost exactly similar positions to the present incumbents – are now convinced of political interference in policy making and the curriculum. If this can now be accepted as a political fact and not just a conspiracy theory held by paranoiacs, much of the cut and thrust of recent educational events can be put into a clearer perspective.

A crucial element in this policy direction is the increasing influence of what Brian Cox calls a 'small and self-selecting group of right-wing educationalists' (Cox et al. 1992), exemplified particularly by the Centre for Policy Studies, a radical right-wing think tank. In 1991, soon after he took over as Secretary of State for Education, Clarke appointed David Pascall and Lord Griffiths to head the National Curriculum Council and the Schools Examination and Assessment Council, the two key advisory and administrative bodies in educational policy making. Both are closely associated with the Centre for Policy Studies. There will soon be a further concentration of power at the direction of John Patten, with the NCC and SEAC soon to be combined in a single body – the School Curriculum and Assessment Authority – which will offer an even more centralised means of directing education policy.

One week after praising the 'best ever' GCSE results, John Patten announced an inquiry into 'a gradual erosion of standards' (*Guardian* 2 September 1992). He wants to reduce the proportion of course work and increase the pencil and paper exam element, and he clearly distrusts teacher assessment. Two weeks later, Patten announced a review of the national curriculum in English. The consensus on English teaching which was embodied in the national curriculum (and based on the Kingman and the Cox reports published by the DES) is under attack. Kenneth Clarke's refusal in 1991 to publish LINC (Language in the National Curriculum) materials was an earlier sign that the linguistic and educational consensus approach to dialect, reading material and methods, spelling, and so on is unacceptable to many of the Tory right who are now influential in and around the DFE. Professor Cox sees this failure to publish as censorship (Cox et al. 1992).

Against this background I shall now discuss the main recommendations of the 'three wise men report'. It is important that teachers should read and discuss the report – if they find time – as it is difficult to summarise it succinctly without glossing over what the debate should be about.

Despite the media coverage, the authors say that they want to move beyond 'a simplistic dichotomy between "traditional" and "progressive" . . . to a more mature and balanced discussion of the issues' (para. 3). They point out that the fashion for knocking the Plowden Report does not contribute to such a discussion.

Their review of reports on educational standards finds 'some evidence of downward trends in important aspects of literacy and numeracy', leading them to suggest that 'whatever else they do primary schools must get their policies and practices right for teaching the basic skills of literacy and numeracy' (para. 50). This then sets the scene for a detailed discussion of the quality of teaching in primary classrooms.

There is a recognition in the report that the quality of curriculum planning, which was 'traditionally problematic, is now improving significantly' (para. 58). They see whole-school planning making it possible to combine comprehensive curriculum coverage with flexibility. These positive points were not reflected in the media, nor was there recognition that most teachers and schools are working along these lines.

They then debate the organisation of the curriculum in terms of subjects or topics. Poor topic work, such as 'aimless copying from books', is rightly criticised. They recognise that skilfully taught topic work does produce high quality results, but have reservations about it. The subject basis of the national curriculum means that 'a substantial amount of separate subject teaching will be necessary' (para. 71), particularly in key stage 2 but also in key stage 1. The crunch conclusion is that 'the class teacher system makes impossible demands on the subject knowledge of the generalist primary teacher' (para. 77), particularly with over 400 statements of attainment to be assessed at KS2. They therefore recommend 'a tendency towards specialisation in the upper years of KS2, but with specialist expertise available to provide the necessary support to teachers of younger children as well' (para. 147).

So with a subject-led curriculum the authors see no alternative to a move towards more subject specialisation. One positive corollary of this is that they can also see 'no justification for the fact that Year 6 pupils in primary schools are funded less generously than year 7 pupils in secondary schools' (para. 4). What's the betting that we get the first without the second?

These moves aim to reverse the consensus in primary schools which emphasises the integration of different subjects through well-planned cross-curricular work, taking account of process as well as content. Many investigative processes are common to maths, science, English, technology, and other subjects. For example, children who use their own developmental spelling strategies are more likely to understand algorithms in maths, to use hypotheses in science, and so on. These common learning processes are highlighted in CLPE's *Patterns of Learning* and built into *Primary Learning Record* assessment procedures. This approach aims to encourage children to develop powerful cognitive frameworks, and to promote learning through both cross-curricular and subject work. In this model, the quality of the all-round education provided by a good generalist class teacher can be more important than the problems caused by the need for them to know all there is to know about nine subjects, and more.

In a move to subject teaching, the possibilities of implementing whole-school policies on language across every curriculum area are likely to be severely diminished. A science specialist teaching in years 5 and 6 may be less able than a generalist class teacher to deal with the vast ability range in English found in most classes. Secondary colleagues have shown over the years that it is possible to work positively on 'English across the curriculum' even within a subject structure, but this would still be a real setback.

This sort of cross-curricular work is not strongly represented in the evidence the authors review, and does not figure in their discussion. Whether it can be preserved and further developed is open to question. The whole apparatus of key stage 2 assessment (being piloted this year and starting in 1994) will exert very powerful pressures towards subject teaching. Pencil and paper subject-based SATs at KS2 are likely to affect the curriculum even more than the KS1 SATs have done.

The apparatus of auditor-moderators which SEAC is developing looks as if it will be particularly powerful. Teacher assessments at KS2 will have to be moderated on the basis of the SATs, and there will be pressure to cover the curriculum through optional SATs, thus increasing the pencil and paper element in the assessments. The auditor-moderators themselves are quite likely to be secondary subject specialists with no necessary knowledge of primary teaching. In these ways, the war of attrition on GCSE course work and teacher assessment at secondary level could be continued into the primary school.

The report has interesting and provocative discussions of teaching methods, which also caught the headlines in distorted ways. The authors do not recommend a return to streaming because the evidence on under-expectation of low stream children, and its effects on achievement, is so strong. They recommend a combination of whole-class and group work (which probably reflects the pattern existing in most classrooms already). They emphasise the need for clear instruction and explanation as well as questioning, and denounce 'the belief that teachers must never point out when a pupil is wrong' (para. 104). Perhaps that is a 1960s dogma that a few teachers cherish, but it seems to me that the theory and practice embodied in CLPE's *The Reading Book* makes a nonsense of such crude stereotypes. They also lambast the 'persistent and damaging belief that pupils should never be told things, only asked questions'. It would be a very rare, and very unhappy, primary classroom where no one was ever told anything. Personally, I would be more concerned about those classrooms where no real questions are ever asked or allowed. But the balance between telling and questioning is a genuinely important and controversial area. The authors talk of 'fitness for purpose' as a useful concept by which teachers can evaluate which techniques to use.

The publication of the NCC and OFSTED reports in February 1993 moves us on significantly from the 'three wise men'. The NCC report says that the national curriculum in primary schools is 'overloaded', that key stages 1 and

2 are 'unmanageable', and 'too complex and over-prescriptive'. All primary teachers would agree with that diagnosis, while pausing to ask why the NCC was not conscious of this at an earlier stage. Like the 'three wise men', the NCC envisages more subject teaching in KS2, and more focused approaches to topic work. But it also recommends a greater use of setting than the 'three wise men', who show themselves to be much more aware of the possible crudities of setting and streaming in the primary school (para. 85).

The NCC tackles the problem of curriculum overload in two ways. It wants all the national curriculum subjects reduced to 'a core of essential knowledge, understanding and skills'. It also says that this would mean stressing 'the basics' at KS1, while at KS2 in-depth subject study would raise standards. Suddenly a prescription has emerged from the possibilities discussed by the 'three wise men'. The ideological holy grail – 'the basics' – are now to be taught in the infant school through a slimmed down national curriculum. After this they will be built on in the junior school through subject teaching, with differentiation achieved by setting, or what David Pascall (in a radio interview) called 'flexible streaming'. This would be a radical redefinition of what goes on in most primary schools.

In this context the OFSTED report makes interesting reading. HMI inspected 400 lessons in seventy-four primary schools. (Two-thirds of these were 'satisfactory' to 'good'). They recognise the problem of curriculum overload, but they do not recommend immediate changes to the national curriculum as the NCC does. They would like a reappraisal which takes particular account of good current primary practice, echoing the 'three wise men' but not the NCC, which does not appear to have any faith in gradual improvements led by teachers.

Considering that the 'three wise men' had no time to gather empirical evidence of what was going on in schools, the HMI findings on topic work are particularly interesting. Two-thirds of schools were judged to have a satisfactory balance between topic and subject teaching. (I wonder if these were the same two-thirds whose lessons were satisfactory?) The push towards subject teaching (which HMI also subscribe to) therefore seems to come from the demands of curriculum coverage rather than any intrinsic problems with integrated or thematic work. Surely there are real alternatives that need to be explored here – good thematic work and good subject-based work being further developed and shared, rather than a wholesale stampede towards 'basics' in the infants and 'subjects' with streaming in the juniors?

John Patten's letter, released at the same time as these reports, takes up some of their themes and firms up their recommendations. Schools are asked to consider more grouping by ability, more whole-class teaching, and a greater use of subject specialist teachers. He accepts the NCC's idea that the national curriculum should be reviewed and cut back, with an emphasis on 'the basics'.

What is likely to happen next and what can we do about it? Here the politics re-emerges, and the power bases of educational change become clearer.

Key stage 2 and 3 SATs are pencil and paper tests, and if they are implemented in the form of the present proposals they are likely to have as much of a knock-on effect on the primary curriculum as the old 11-plus did. The continual DFE attacks on teacher assessment, and the growing apparatus of subject-based SAT moderation, would see to that. Secondary school teachers are much more united and effective in their opposition to KS3 SATs than primary teachers have so far been, and if the proposed SATs are implemented they are likely to make primary classrooms very different places.

Privatised OFSTED inspections every four years are clearly intended by the DFE as a law enforcement device to ensure that their 'recommendations' on curriculum organisation and teaching approaches are implemented. Inspection is becoming a crucial battleground in the fight to implement right-wing policies or leave some space for alternatives. HMI have complained to the head of OFSTED that the new privatised service is 'in danger of becoming a third-rate and ill-conceived system which will be regarded as a joke in schools', according to a leaked letter (*Guardian* 11 January 1993). The place of lay inspectors on the OFSTED teams is one of the government's key measures. These lay members are there to personify a 'common sense' approach to education which their five-day training period would not do much to alter.

Yet Dr Sheila Lawlor (the deputy director of the Centre for Policy Studies) has attacked Ofsted for 'perpetuating the discredited educational orthodoxies of the recent past' (*Guardian* 18 January 1993) – in other words she doesn't trust them to do the hatchet job that the right wing wants. Her language is outspoken and immoderate. For instance, she rails against their 'anti-traditional bias . . . (such as) the recent fashions for a cross-curricular and child-centred approach, as well as theories about race and gender'.

The language of these ideological attacks resonates with New Right policies that are increasingly being highlighted in the post-Thatcher period. A party political broadcast on 20 January 1993 started with pictures of Tornadoes in action against Iraq and then moved on to show school classrooms. John Major was talking to the camera throughout and he very slowly pronounced the words 'reading, writing, and . . . adding up'. His next sentence imbued the words 'common sense' with great emphasis. This continues the ideology of Thatcherism (with its appeals to 'housewife' economics as justifications for public expenditure cuts). It must be significant that the script writers chose to reduce 'arithmetic' (already a crude reduction of 'mathematics') even further to 'adding up'. This is right-wing populism invoking traditionalist common sense.

Professor Brian Cox (chair of the original English national curriculum working group) picks up this theme in his critique of the review of the statutory orders for English (Cox *et al.* 1992). He argues that 'back to basics' in teaching reading, the insistence on speaking standard English in received pronunciation, and the construction of a 'canon' of 'great literature' are all part of a traditionalist, right-wing populism, paralleled by the pressures for Christian instead of multi-ethnic religious education. He sees this populism as the ideological heart of the Tory right. Persistent press rumours that John Major did a deal over Maastricht with his right wingers – buying their votes by giving them their head on education – may not be far off the mark.

The next stage in implementing these policies will be the review of primary teacher education, which is promised for spring 1993. The right wingers want to give teacher education to the schools, to put an end to the influence of 'trendy and progressive' college lecturers. They also want to enshrine subject teaching in the primary school by making the B.Ed. the route for infant teachers (teaching the basics), and the PGCE the route for junior teachers. On that model, PGCE students would be recruited only from strictly 'relevant' subjects, and would become specialist rather than generalist teachers.

This all seems depressing. But perhaps it helps that the political manipulations are becoming clearer, and that a non-right-wing consensus about what should be happening could also clarify as a consequence of this hardening of approaches. Presumably one way that we could stop the juggernaut rolling over primary education is to emphasise what the government at all times tries to diminish – the professional expertise of teachers. Local management – or even mass opting out, with some buying back into common support services – potentially offers schools and teachers some real autonomy. The moves towards whole-school policies, and the way in which primary teachers now work more collaboratively within these, are real and positive achievements of the last decade, and have moved teachers towards much clearer consensus approaches, which they will be reluctant to abandon.

In moving into the field of curriculum organisation and classroom practice the government is risking direct intervention in the one area that was always supposed to come outside the scope of the Secretary of State – teaching method. It is also an area that is notoriously hard to monitor. Could any OFSTED team – even one with Sheila Lawlor in it – force a primary teacher to teach in a particular way from Monday to Friday?

REFERENCES

Alexander, R., Rose, J., and Woodhead, C. (1992) *Curriculum Organisation and Classroom Practice in Primary Schools*, DES.

Cox, C. B., Dickinson, T., and Barrett, P. (1992) *Made Tongue-tied by Authority – New Orders for English?*, NATE.

National Curriculum Council (1993) *The National Curriculum at Key Stages 1 and 2*, York, NCC.

OFSTED (1993) *Curriculum Organisation and Classroom Practice in Primary Schools: A Follow-up Report*, OFSTED.

Chapter 18

Teaching strategies

Robin Alexander

*This chapter is an illustrative extract from a highly influential study con-
ducted by Robin Alexander in Leeds. The research sought to evaluate a local
education authority initiative, the 'Primary Needs Programme', which was
particularly intended to develop 'good primary practice'. The findings
reported here relate to the patterns of classroom practices which were observed and were part of the evidence which caused Alexander to review the
concept of 'good practice' itself and to argue that it is 'ideological'.*

The Primary Needs Programme was based on a list of aims rather than a
comprehensive statement of policy. The list referred only briefly and somewhat obliquely to classroom practice, recommending (but not defining): a
stimulating and challenging learning environment; flexible teaching strategies to meet the identified needs of individual pupils; and specific practical
help for individuals and small groups.

The package of suggestions, recommendations, and prescriptions was
justified in terms of a notion of 'good primary practice' which was frequently provided as a validating label but never openly defined or explored.
Consensus was assumed; the possibility that 'good practice' might be problematic was not.

THE CLASSROOM CONTEXT: DISPLAY AND LAYOUT

Leaving aside for the moment the matter of the educational validity of the
principles under discussion, their most immediately apparent influence – as
might be expected – was on the physical appearance of PNP classrooms. The
extent and quality of classroom display improved dramatically during the
period of the evaluation, though we became increasingly aware of a tendency
towards a certain repetitiveness in colour schemes and styles of mounting,
conveying a sense of conformity rather than creativity. That teachers felt
constrained in matters of display and lay-out by authority guidelines (Leeds
City Council 1989b) was confirmed in many interviews and questionnaire
responses.

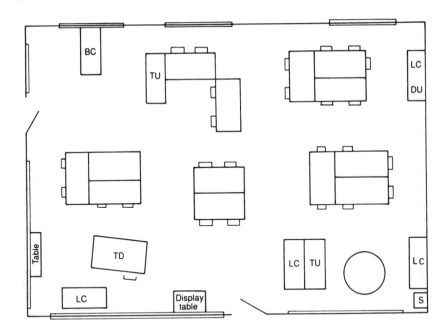

Figure 18.1 Type One classroom layout

Of the teachers we spoke to, two-fifths reported that they had rearranged their furniture, and well over nine-tenths of them had made some kind of change to their classrooms as a direct consequence of suggestions or recommendations made to them as part of the Primary Needs Programme. We were able to corroborate such claims observationally. A few of the suggestions about the deployment of furniture were fairly generally rejected. For example, only a minority of respondents were willing to abolish the teacher's desk, and very few felt able to dispense with the convention that each pupil should have his or her own place, or to accept the idea of a classroom in which there were, as a matter of policy, fewer chairs than children.

A common response to the PNP messages was to convert at least a part of the room into workbays which were generally, though not invariably, dedicated to specific areas of the curriculum. Most classrooms had at least one such area, usually a reading or library corner, and a few teachers had organised their rooms entirely in this way, forming as many as six or seven work areas. A popular arrangement involved four areas, devoted to reading, art, maths, and language. The area of the curriculum most commonly given a corner of its own was reading. Art came second, with more space devoted to it than either maths or language; it accounted for just over a quarter of all

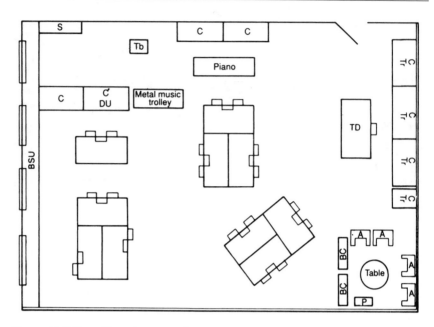

Figure 18.2 Type Two classroom layout

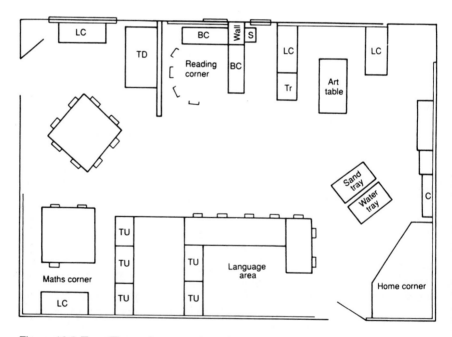

Figure 18.3 Type Three classroom layout

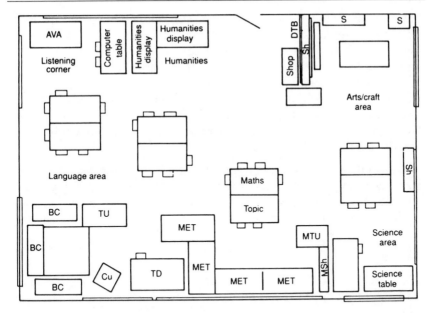

Figure 18.4 Type Four classroom layout

curriculum-specific work areas for younger pupils, and a fifth of those for older pupils. In contrast, only 4 per cent of curriculum-specific work areas were devoted to science.

In seeking to understand the extent of the LEA's influence on primary classrooms it is instructive, as we have already noted, to compare our own findings with those of Mortimore *et al.* (1988) from ILEA junior schools. In the London sample, one-tenth of classrooms had tables or desks arranged in rows: in Leeds we observed none (though that is not to say that none existed). In London, curriculum-specific lay-outs were rare: in Leeds they were the norm.

Our analysis produced four main classroom lay-out types (compared with Mortimore's three), and these are shown in Figures 18.1 to 18.4. The proportions in our sample were as follows: Type 1, 8 per cent; Type 2, 50 per cent; Type 3, 39 per cent; Type 4, 3 per cent. A more detailed analysis appears in Alexander *et al.* (1989: 247–54).

The strong emphasis on visual appeal and curriculum-specific classroom lay-out has a distinct local genealogy in the approaches inherited from the West Riding. However, not all teachers found curriculum-specific organisation easy to implement or operate, and it provides a good example of a practice commended in the name of 'flexibility' which makes the work of some teachers less, rather than more, flexible (a tension which emerges in research elsewhere – Alexander 1988). Moreover, the practice has been shown by other studies, notably those of Mortimore *et al.* (1988) and HMI (DES 1990), to reduce rather than enhance children's learning, in some situations and in the hands of some teachers, at least. If the practice is introduced from a sense of obligation rather than conviction, the adverse effects on children are likely to be even greater.

In view of the high incidence of these arrangements in Leeds, and their adoption and dissemination during a period when the massive resourcing of PNP appeared to have little impact on reading test scores, it might be worth carefully pondering HMI's finding that:

> some of the poorest work in reading occurred where the organization and management of the class were weak. Examples included too many groups of activities running at the same time and an emphasis on individual work which could not be sustained in sufficient depth for all the children in the class.
>
> (DES 1990: 15)

THE CLASSROOM CONTEXT: GROUPING

The most obvious influence of PNP on teachers' approach to the management of learning was the encouragement of group work. This was consistently commended by advisory staff throughout the period under review and still remains a central component of expected practice (for example, Leeds City Council 1989a, 1989b, 1990a, 1990b). The norm, as we have noted, was for different groups to be working in different curriculum areas simultaneously.

The most common way of grouping was to sort the children by ability (as informally rated by the teacher) and to make the groups as homogeneous as possible. Groups formed in this way tended to remain relatively stable, moving as a whole from one activity to another, although in a few classes they were formed only for specific activities (generally mathematics) and disbanded for the rest of the day. An alternative form of ability grouping was to aim for as wide a range of ability as possible in each group. A minority of teachers used other grouping criteria. An eighth of them opted for friendship groups for at least part of the time, and a few grouped their pupils by age.

We found that the larger the group, the less time its members tended to spend on task. However, against the obvious conclusion that small groups are more effective one must set the increased managerial challenges of having a larger number of groups.

It was by no means uncommon for teachers to switch from one type of grouping to another as the activities of individuals and groups of children changed. This fluidity of grouping practice, in classrooms dominated by curriculum-specific work areas in which a wide range of totally dissimilar tasks were simultaneously undertaken, occasionally led to extremely complex organisational problems and a good deal of confusion.

Though grouping of some kind was the norm in the classrooms we visited, our interview and observation data revealed it to be a somewhat problematic strategy for many teachers. Grouping children was an organisational device as much as a teaching approach, a way of maximising the opportunities for productive teacher–child interaction as well as a means of encouraging co-operation among the children and flexibility in curriculum.

However, as we show below, there could sometimes be a significant gap between intention and outcome. One-to-one teacher–child interactions were brief and (for most children) infrequent; and collaborative group work was rare (cf. Galton *et al.* 1980; Galton and Simon 1980).

As for the goal of flexibility, grouping can be distinctly double-edged, permitting teachers to concentrate as much *or as little* of their time on particular children or particular curriculum areas as they wish. The danger, witnessed sometimes in practice, is that certain children (notably the most able, the oldest, the best-behaved, and girls) are tacitly deemed 'undemanding' and may be left to their own devices for long periods, denied the kinds of challenging interaction which they, like all children, need. In turn these children may give no signals to a busy teacher 'scanning' the class while working with another group that they are other than fully and productively engaged in their learning tasks. Indeed, some will actively adopt strategies to convey this impression and secure a quiet life (Galton 1989; Bennett *et al.* 1984).

By the same token, certain curriculum areas (notably topic work and art) might be seen as of low priority and requiring little more than occasional and cursory monitoring by the teacher, with the result that unless the tasks set have an exceptionally high combination of challenge, motivating power and self-monitoring potential, children may spend excessive amounts of time either off-task or only partially engaged, or undertaking low-level learning.

In combination, this double neglect must mean that certain children, when working in certain areas of the curriculum, are getting a distinctly raw deal. Yet many of the teachers we interviewed, far from being unaware of this risk, perceived only too clearly that it was inherent to the LEA's preferred combination of group work and multiple curriculum focus teaching.

The dilemma can be expressed as follows; the more accessible teachers seek to make themselves to all their pupils as individuals, the less time they have for direct, extended, and challenging interaction with any of them; but the more time they devote to such extended interaction with some children, the less demanding on them as teachers must be the activities they give to the rest; and the less demanding an activity is of their time and attention as teachers, the more the likelihood that the activity in question will demand little of the child.

The strategy of 'unequal investment' – deliberately concentrating attention on specific groups – was a conscious response to the dilemmas of grouping. In some cases a carefully monitored rolling programme ensured that over a given period of time, say a week or a fortnight, the teacher engaged directly with every child in every area of the curriculum; but in other cases the inequality of investment was not adjusted in this way, and the result was the persistent neglect of certain children and certain areas of the curriculum.

One way through, explored by researchers like Galton (1989) and Bennett (1987), is to exploit much more fully the potential of collaborative tasks within groups. In our own studies, the ostensibly collaborative setting of the group tended to be one in which children spent most of their time on essentially individual reading and writing tasks. Much of this time could be wasted while children awaited the teacher's attention or were simply distracted. The early findings from the Leverhulme Project (Wragg and Bennett 1990) show that where learning tasks are genuinely collaborative, children will use the group rather than the teacher as their main reference point, and the ratio of work to routine interactions will improve.

Collaborative group work is not a panacea, but it is certainly a strategy worth exploring. Equally important, as we urge later on, the kinds of dilemmas and compromises associated with all teaching strategies, and perhaps especially with group work, need to be admitted and addressed. Unfortunately, the climate of PNP did not encourage this.

A final point to note on grouping is the mismatch we frequently witnessed between the ostensibly *collective* strategy of grouping and the predominance of *individualised* work tasks. Common sense dictates that task and setting should as far as possible be consistent. Just as collaborative activity is difficult in a traditionally arranged classroom, so the concentration needed for individualised tasks may be difficult within a group. We gained the impression that – like several other practices in primary education – the strategy of grouping has become an end in itself rather than a device adopted for particular educational purposes; moreover, as a strategy grouping may have become so deeply ingrained in primary consciousness and practice that to ask questions about its educational purposes may seem, to some, almost impertinent.

Our data were gathered, as we have emphasised elsewhere, during the period immediately before the introduction of the national curriculum. Since it was frequently predicted that the pressures of the latter would lead to an increase in whole-class teaching, it is useful to supplement our comments by reference to more recent data, gathered as part of another project based at Leeds University, the SEAC-funded evaluation of the 1991 key stage one national curriculum assessment directed by Diane Shorrocks and Robin Alexander. In a national sample of primary classrooms, four-fifths were divided into groups and the number of groups per class averaged four to five, with a mean group size of 6.1.

Although those who predicted that the national curriculum would cause a wholesale shift away from group work are apparently proved wrong by these figures, the matter is not that simple. The national sample of teachers spent only a third of their time interacting with groups: the bulk was divided between whole-class and individual interactions. Thus what the emerging national data seem to confirm is the Leeds data's sense of a pervasive incongruence in classroom strategies between pedagogic style and mode of organisation. The Leeds local data pointed up a mismatch between predominantly individualised learning tasks and the collaborative setting in which children were expected to undertake them. The national data suggest a further mismatch – between this same collaborative setting and the teacher's predominantly individual or whole-class mode of interaction.

Two interpretations are suggested. The first is that grouping is the ideal organisational arrangement in that it gives the teacher the flexibility to move freely between individual, group, and whole-class activities in a way which the traditional arrangement of desks in rows does not. The second, however, is that the physical arrangement of grouping in primary classrooms has acquired such a powerful doctrinal status that no other arrangement is even entertained. Whatever the interpretation, the cumulative research and survey data since 1978 suggest an urgent need to look at the justifications, dynamics, and effectiveness of grouping.

THE CLASSROOM CONTEXT: PLANNING

Teachers' planning varied greatly in its time-scale and degree of formality. The time-scale ranged from the very short-term to the comparatively long-term: from daily to yearly, with many intermediate steps. The degree of formality ranged from elaborate and schematic written documents to a simple mental rehearsal of what would happen next.

There was also considerable variation in the structure of teachers' planning. Some teachers showed a *comprehensive* awareness of the balance of different lessons and their place in the curriculum as a whole, as well as a very clear concern with progression, continuity, the acquisition of underlying skills, and the achievement of goals. Others adopted a more *incremental* approach, planning as they went along (Clark and Yinger 1987). They were much less concerned with the details or wider context of future activities, and much more interested in trying out ideas in practice before moving on to further planning. There were also teachers in the sample who were grappling with several complex long-term and short-term schedules and forecasts at a time, and others whose only apparent work plan was to set up a succession of *ad hoc* activities with little long-term coherence or progression.

Methods of curriculum planning are inseparable from teachers' thinking about what has to be planned, and the arrival of the national curriculum is dictating a much more considered and long-term approach than was adopted in at least some of the classrooms we visited (NCC 1989, 1991; Alexander *et al.* 1990).

THE CLASSROOM CONTEXT: RECORD KEEPING

We found very few teachers who kept no records of any kind. The records which were kept varied from the elaborately formal and comprehensive, involving a good deal of detailed and meticulous clerical work, to the admittedly casual and labour-saving. Some teachers were chiefly concerned to chart the acquisition of underlying skills, but many were satisfied with checklists of tasks completed.

Only about one teacher in three had any kind of supervision in the matters of planning or record keeping.

Again, the requirements of the national curriculum will make minimalist approaches to record keeping difficult to sustain, let alone justify to parents. The agenda of educational objectives to be charted – and perhaps the record-keeping format too – are now very clear.

THE WORKING DAY

On average, children in the classrooms where observation took place spent

- 59 per cent of their time working;
- 11 per cent on associated routine activities (getting out and putting away books and apparatus, sharpening pencils and so on);
- 8 per cent waiting for attention from a teacher or other adult;
- 21 per cent distracted from the task which had been set;
- 1 per cent other (unclassified).

These figures are averages which cover a very wide variation between individual classes. They are broadly consistent with those from earlier studies carried out in other parts of the country except that children in the present study spent more time waiting for attention, in spite of the presence of an unprecedented number of support teachers and other ancillary staff and helpers.

Figures like these usually occasion adverse lay comment, and these particular figures featured prominently in the press coverage of the Leeds report. The journalistic and political inference was that children in primary classrooms are not working nearly hard enough; generally this was based on an aggregation of the percentages for 'routine', 'awaiting attention' and 'distracted' to produce the claim that 40 per cent of time was 'wasted'.

We wish to distance ourselves from such inferences, even though naturally we would expect our findings to generate constructive discussion about the effective use of pupils' and teachers' time in primary schools. Quite apart from questions of sample size and representativeness, this particular aggregation is wholly inappropriate. The more legitimate aggregation is of the 'working' and 'routine' categories, since both are necessary aspects of the learning task. Moreover, it is impossible to define what constitutes the 'appropriate' proportion of time which a 5-year-old, or a 7- or 11-year-old, should spend on task in a school day of some five and a half hours.

To set the issue in its proper perspective, we might care to consider the way time is used in *adult* work settings. Adults, too, spend much time distracted and on routine activities – indeed, such time may even be dignified as 'incubation' or 'thinking time' – and few work for anything remotely approaching 100 per cent of the time they are employed. We suspect that in many work settings 70 per cent of time spent on task or on associated activities would be a remarkable achievement. Yet we are talking here not of adults but of children.

Nevertheless, the figures give pause for thought. Clearly it is important to find strategies to reduce the proportion of time children spend awaiting attention and distracted. Whole-class teaching, usually seen as the device most likely to keep children on task, may well reduce distraction (or at least distraction of an undisguised kind) but it may also increase the time children spend awaiting attention, and indeed our own figures on group sizes tend to confirm this.

In any event, the global figures above are less significant than variations which can be shown to relate to specific categories of children, kinds of learning and classroom contexts.

Thus, girls generally spent more of their time than boys on work and associated routine activities. Boys were more often distracted, and also spent more time waiting for attention from their teachers.

Older children were less inclined to wait for attention than younger children. In maths and language they were less distracted and spent more time on work and routine activities, although in art the pattern was reversed: older children were more often distracted and did less work.

Children whose teachers rated their ability as average tended to spend less time on work and routine activities and more time distracted or awaiting attention than either those who were thought to be above average in ability or those who were rated as below average. In the absence of any objective index of the children's true ability we cannot know the extent to which the teachers' ratings were themselves unduly influenced by the observed behaviour.

In classrooms where there were two adults, children were generally less distracted and spent more time working than in classrooms where there was only one. Beyond that point, however, there was no tendency for the presence of additional adults to bring about more work and less distraction, partly because extra adults tended to introduce extra challenges and more complex organisational structures. Moreover, as we shall see when we discuss collaborative teaching later in this chapter, it is much easier for two teachers than three or more to undertake the shared planning on which the success of classroom collaboration depends.

Children generally spent less time working and more time distracted as the size of their work groups increased from one to twenty. In even larger groups, however, this pattern was reversed, partly because of the nature of the tasks that were undertaken in large groups, but mainly because of the whole-class style of supervision to which they were subjected.

The large amounts of time allocated to language and mathematics were sometimes the least efficiently used. The overall percentages are shown in Table 18.1.

Table 18.1 Percentage of time spent by pupils on task-related behaviour in different areas of the curriculum

	Working	Routine	Awaiting attention	Distracted	Not observed
Language	55	11	7	26	<1
Maths	59	10	9	23	<1
Science	64	8	5	20	2
Admin.	64	5	11	18	1
Art	65	16	3	16	0
PE	51	21	18	10	0
Topic	55	21	6	16	3
Play	70	10	2	18	0
CDT	69	5	4	22	0
Choosing	63	16	7	14	0
Music	67	8	9	13	2
Environmental studies	63	6	6	26	0
Sewing	57	20	14	8	0
Table games	69	13	6	13	0
Computer	51	19	26	5	0
Cooking	55	15	0	30	0
Television	58	0	32	11	0
All curriculum areas	59	11	8	21	1

Such figures appear to challenge the conventional assumption that the way to improve standards is to give the subjects deemed most important more and more time. Perhaps familiarity breeds contempt – among teachers as well as children. Perhaps, too, there is a Parkinsonian effect at work here: the standard allocation for mathematics in primary schools, often regardless of the ground to be covered, has for decades been the equivalent of an hour a day.

A clearer understanding of such anomalies, however, comes from probing beneath the curriculum labels. We identified ten 'generic activities' which we found to underpin primary classroom practice regardless of the subject labels used by the teacher, and argued that these activities therefore constitute at least as important a curriculum reality – certainly for children – as terms like 'topic' or even 'language'. Table 18.2 shows how each of these generic activities generates different patterns of task-related behaviour.

Table 18.2 Task-related behaviour in different generic activities (percentage of pupil time)

	Working	Routine	Awaiting attention	Distracted	Not observed
Writing	52	13	8	28	<1
Apparatus	65	12	6	17	<1
Reading	57	12	6	24	<1
Listening/looking	68	6	10	15	1
Drawing/painting	55	14	5	25	1
Collaboration	67	11	6	15	<1
Movement	54	15	14	17	<1
Talking to teacher	71	11	6	10	2
Construction	70	7	3	20	0
Talking to class	100	0	0	0	0
All activities	59	11	8	21	1

Thus, children in our classroom practice sample spent a high proportion of their time working when they were engaged in tasks which involved talking to the class, talking to the teacher, construction, listening, or collaboration. Their work levels were lowest in writing, drawing/painting, or tasks which involved movement from one part of the room to another, and all three of these activities generated very high levels of routine behaviour. For the most part, high levels of distraction were found where work levels were low, and the highest distraction levels of all were in tasks involving writing, drawing/painting, and reading.

In general, the most work and the least distraction occurred in the rarest activities. The striking feature of the activities at which children worked for a high proportion of the time was involvement with other people; conversely, most of the activities at which children worked for the lowest proportion of time – writing, reading, drawing/painting – involved no other people and could have been carried out most effectively in isolation. Thus, there could be a significant mismatch between the tasks which children were given, and the setting in which they were required to undertake them.

The importance of these variations in children's use of classroom time lies less in the precise quantifications than the questions they provoke. Why do such variations occur? To what extent are they inevitable? Does the situation warrant improvement? If so, what?

There was a common sequence to nearly every teaching session observed: the teacher settled the children down; explained the tasks; allocated children to groups; interacted with one or more groups while they worked; initiated finishing off or tidying up. Whole-class sessions were very rare, though many sessions had a whole-class element, usually at the beginning and/or end. Within this basic framework the amount of time allocated to each stage varied considerably. Thus the time spent on the settling-down and clearing-up stages varied from 7 to 45 per cent of the total session, and the introductory stage varied similarly, largely because some teachers treated it as a purely administrative matter to be dealt with as succinctly as possible, while others incorporated it into the session as the whole-class teaching in an arrangement otherwise dominated by group work. Three examples, taken from our eleventh report, show something of the variation.

A class of thirty-eight 5- and 6-year-olds:

2 minutes	teacher settles class down after playtime;
2 minutes	allocates tasks;
2 minutes	works with language group;
1 minute	gives a task to an unsupervised number group and asks the nursery nurse who should be with them how long she will be;
16 minutes	returns to work with language group;
2 minutes	monitors jigsaw group;
1 minute	gives new task to computer group whose supervising nursery nurse has given them a task which is too difficult;
5 minutes	works with writing group whose teacher has been called away;
5 minutes	supervises change-over of free-choice activities and then monitors maths group and two language groups;
3 minutes	supervises tidying up;
3 minutes	children sit and sing in the book corner;
9 minutes	teacher tells a story;
5 minutes	informal activities (e.g. clapping a rhythm).

A class of twenty-nine 8- and 9-year-olds:

3 minutes	teacher talks with class about a Victorian penny brought in by a child, and about penny-farthing bicycles;
7 minutes	sorts out group choices for the afternoon session;
11 minutes	allocates tasks for current session;
11 minutes	works with maths group;
16 minutes	monitors the work of all groups and responds to individuals seeking help;
7 minutes	supervises tidying up.

A class of thirty-six 7- to 8-year-olds

8 minutes   teacher takes register and then describes and allocates tasks;
14 minutes   monitors the work of all groups and deals with individuals who seek help;
7 minutes   works with language group;
8 minutes   works with science group;
2 minutes   monitors work of language and maths groups;
7 minutes   gives new task to maths group;
11 minutes   works with science group and deals with individuals seeking help.

As Bennett (1978, 1987) points out, one of the most important determinants of pupils' learning is simply the amount of time they spend on it. In a class where almost half the time is spent on administrative matters, the time left over for active engagement in learning tasks is severely curtailed.

Though some of the foregoing indicate diversity, the questions they raise are common to all teachers:

- How can the time children spend in classrooms most effectively be used?
- How far is the fairly low proportion of time spent on task in some classrooms attributable to factors unique to those classrooms – the teacher's mode of organisation, the quality and appropriateness of the learning tasks he/she devises, the personalities of the children and adults present, and so on? How far is it attributable to more generally prevailing patterns of teaching and classroom organisation in primary schools, including those commended by Leeds LEA? We believe that our evidence suggests that the latter is indeed a critical factor.
- What can be learned from the differential figures for particular groups of children – boys and girls; older and younger children; those rated by their teachers as of average, above average and below average ability or attainment? How far such differences inevitable? How far are they a consequence of the teacher's assumptions about the expectations of the children in question?
- Do the figures on the impact of increasing the number of adults in classrooms challenge the conventional assumption that the more adults there are, the better?
- Do the figures suggest that there is an optimum size for groups?

More generally we might ask the following:

- What is the best way to introduce and allocate learning tasks?
- How can the time and opportunities for children to engage in these tasks be maximised?

- What kinds of classroom environment will most support children's learning?
- What kinds of task is it most appropriate for groups to undertake?
- How can we achieve the best possible match not only between learner and task but also between task and classroom setting?

REFERENCES

Alexander, R. J. (1988) 'Garden or jungle? Teacher development and informal primary education', in Blyth, W.A.L. (ed.) *Informal Primary Education Today: Essays and Studies*, London, Falmer Press.

Alexander, R. J., Broadhead, P., Driver, R. H., Hannaford, P., Hodgson, J., and Squires, A. (1990) 'Understanding our world: towards a framework for curriculum planning in the primary school', Leeds, University of Leeds.

Alexander, R. J., Willcocks, J., and Kinder, R. M. (1989) *Changing Primary Practice*, London, Falmer Press.

Bennett, S. N. (1978) 'Recent research on teaching: a dream, a belief and a model', *British Journal of Educational Psychology*, 48.

Bennett, S. N. (1987) 'The search for the effective primary teacher', in Delamont, S. (ed.) *The Primary School Teacher*, London, Falmer Press.

Bennett, S. N., Desforges, C., Cockburn, A., and Wilkinson, B. (1984) *The Quality of Pupil Learning Experiences*, Hove, Lawrence Erlbaum.

Clark, C. M. and Yinger, P. J. (1987) 'Teacher planning', in Calderhead, J. (ed.) *Exploring Teachers' Thinking*, London, Cassell.

Department of Education and Science (1990) *The Leaching and Learning of Reading in Primary Schools: A Report by HMI*, London, DES.

Galton, M. (1989) *Teaching in the Primary School*, London, David Fulton.

Galton, M. and Simon, B. (eds) (1980) *Progress and Performance in the Primary Classroom*, London, Routledge.

Galton, M., Simon, B., and Croll, P. (1980) *Inside the Primary Classroom*, London, Routledge.

Leeds City Council (1989a) *PNP Conference Report*, Leeds, Leeds City Council.

Leeds City Council (1989b) *A Quality Learning Environment: Display*, Leeds, Leeds City Council.

Leeds City Council (1989c) *The Primary School: A Guide for Parents*, Leeds, Leeds City Council.

Leeds City Council (1990a) *The Curriculum 5–16: A Statement of Policy*, Leeds, Leeds City Council.

Leeds City Council (1990b) *A Survey of Year 1 Pupils in Leeds Primary Schools*, Leeds, Leeds City Council.

Mortimore, P., Sammons, P., Stoll, L., Lewis, D., and Ecob, R. (1988) *School Matters: The Junior Years*, London, Open Books.

National Curriculum Council (1989) *Curriculum Guidance 1: a Framework for the Primary Curriculum*, York, NCC.

National Curriculum Council (1991) *Report on Monitoring the Implementation of the National Curriculum Core Subjects 1989–90*, York, NCC.

Wragg, E. C. and Bennett, S. N. (1990) *Leverhulme Primary Project Occasional Paper, Spring 1990*, Exeter, University of Exeter School of Education.

Chapter 19

An approach to personal and social education in the primary school

Or how one city schoolteacher tried to make sense of her job

Jane Needham

Though her article predates the Education Reform Act, Jane Needham contributes the voice of a practising classroom teacher to discussion of the issues already raised in the 'Classroom' part of this book. Her provision is thoughtful, thorough, and has been carefully matched to the needs of the children in her class. How do you feel it articulates with HMI's view of 'good practice' in Chapter 15? Do Ellen Yeo's arguments, from Chapter 16, strike home here? What do you think actual evidence of Jane Needham's classroom, such as that reviewed by Alexander in Chapter 18, would reveal?

Consideration of such questions is unlikely to produce simple answers. That is an accurate reflection of the complexities of teaching and of the need for informed professional judgement.

For the past five years I have been teaching in a large and lively inner-city primary school, containing a varied mix of people. About 40 per cent of the families are Asian (mostly Moslem) and there are a few Afro-Caribbean families, as well as English working-class and middle-class professional families. Throughout this time I have worked with 6- to 8-year-old children and each year have set about trying to provide appropriate learning situations for each child. I have also tried to provide a sense of unity among the wide range of social backgrounds, personalities, intellectual abilities, and behaviour that the children present and the varying parental expectations.

In order to do this I have had to do some careful thinking about my priorities as an educator, and this has resulted in the belief that my concern to develop the skills necessary for successful oracy, reading, writing, and numeracy should not override the promotion of the children's happiness, their belief in themselves, and their ability to relate to each other. It is the development of the whole person, myself included, that is important.

I have tried to provide a classroom environment which is an 'OK' place to be and in which children have the space to be themselves. I have tried to encourage a sense of togetherness among the children in an atmosphere of co-operation, trust, and empathy. With this has come the realisation that young children can learn a great deal from each other in an atmosphere of mutual interdependence, rather than one which revolves totally around the teacher as the giver of all things. Any competition that exists should be with oneself rather than with others – 'Is this the best I can do?' rather than 'Is mine better than anyone else's?'

The emphasis has been on learning rather than teaching and my role as teacher has focused on being an organiser of learning situations. By these I mean situations which are exciting and rewarding and which provide a realistic match to the children's abilities, but also those which are carefully thought out so that they encourage the development of personal and social skills. It is the learning process that is all-important and given this emphasis my own teaching style has, I think, become increasingly varied.

The actual choice of classroom projects needs careful consideration, bearing in mind the necessity of providing an overall well-balanced curriculum together with the incorporation of those projects which naturally lend themselves to the development and understanding of the self and empathy with others. Projects I have favoured for the latter have been those based on relationships, e.g. family, friends, ourselves; those based on child-centred activities, e.g. games, mazes; those enabling a more global approach, e.g. festivals, different types of food; and literature-based projects using appropriate books.

In what follows I have tried to pick out the key points in the process I endeavour to put into action.

FLEXIBLE GROUPINGS

Groups are organised so that all the children have the opportunity of working and playing with each other rather than keeping with one particular group all the time. Sometimes the groups are chosen by me, sometimes by the children and sometimes through random sets (e.g. all the children with the same colour shoes/hair/eyes). Sometimes the choice of activity will determine the membership of the group. I try and keep one of the groupings fairly constant for a time so that the children can build up working relationships and the membership of these groups is carefully considered so that there is an even balance as regards sex, race, and existing friendships.

POSITIVE FEEDBACK

It is important to provide an audience for the children's achievements so that their work has a sense of purpose. The nature of these feedback situations varies greatly – from 20 minutes or so at the beginning or end of a session, looking at what each other has done, to actively teaching the children to value each other's work. For example, I asked the children to read someone else's work and write a positive book review about it. One little girl ended her review with 'It's an exciting story for bedtimes and it is one of those books where you want to see the end'.

On other occasions I have linked up with another class in the school to share weekly achievements and concerns, no matter how small. I have found that the value of this type of sharing lies not only in giving the children the opportunity to appraise each other, but also in providing a situation in which they need to express themselves in the clearest way, explaining what they have done and how or why they did it. I feel that the children's work is enriched through ideas being shared and also through the desire to produce something that is worthy of sharing.

During one year my class and I were involved in a link with another school. Initially this was planned by another teacher and myself as an experiment to investigate the presence of any stereotyped attitudes among our children. It began with a swapping of photographs in which the children had the chance to choose how to present themselves to each other, wearing favourite clothes/special hats, holding favourite possessions, with different facial expressions and gestures, and so on. Gradually, special things happened; the children reached out to each other in words and pictures, writing letters, cooking and sewing presents for each other, planning and preparing surprises, learning to give and to receive.

I also think it is important to give the children the opportunity to evaluate and appraise their own work. I have used several simple ideas to facilitate this. One of the most effective was to draw a simple cartoon face with an empty speech bubble, at the end of a piece of work. The child fills in the spaces with words and/or pictures to express how they feel about what they have done. I always try to think of positive comments to write on children's work, and to make them meaningful to the particular child and appropriate to the particular context. I might ask the child which bit of the story he/she thinks is the best as well as picking out which part I like. I may sometimes use this written comment to encourage the child to explore another aspect of his/her work. Sometimes the children write back asking me questions, sometimes they discuss their comments with a friend or parent, sometimes we talk them through.

I often use more specific evaluation sheets. In one, the children complete unfinished sentences, such as 'Today I feel . . .'; 'Something I'm good at is . . .'; 'Something I'd like to be good at is . . .'. The children sometimes ask me to fill in the same sheets and we share what we think and feel in this way.

I have also asked the children to draw a map or a maze showing what has happened to them in their lives so far, the ups and downs, the dead ends, the roundabouts. They chose appropriate colours for associated feelings and wrote on personal comments. In this way some of the children were able to express their feelings about what they see as the important events of their lives. They pinpointed events like starting school, the arrival of brothers and sisters, accidents and illnesses, parents splitting up, good holidays and making good friends. When the maze or map was complete the individual child explained what he/she had done to someone else.

CLASS/GROUP CO-OPERATIVE ACTIVITIES

Class and group activities have taken many forms, from full co-operative games to co-operative group projects – making books, models, pictures, or simply working on a problem or an idea together. In each of the activities, everyone involved plays a part in bringing about the end product or solution. This is followed by a discussion and sometimes we will make a zig-zag book in which everyone involved has the chance to describe and reflect on their part in the process and any difficulties encountered. Science work, too, presents opportunities for small groups of children to work together to carry out different parts of an experiment and then to pool and compare results before coming to a conclusion. In this way we carried out experiments to find out the optimum conditions for growing turf. Using our conclusions we set up the appropriate conditions and made and mowed a miniature turf maze. At the end of last term we made a class jigsaw puzzle. It started as a large outline drawing done by one of the children of the Joybaloo creature from the book *Ned and the Joybaloo* by Hiawyn Oram and Satoshi Kitamura. I cut the picture into jigsaw-shaped pieces which we shared out. Each child involved had to decorate his/her piece with the appropriate details and patterns and this necessitated finding and matching it up with other people's pieces so that the whole picture was correctly formed. It proved to be a difficult but rewarding activity.

In other group activities the end product is for the benefit of the whole class, as when making a book or a board game to be used by everyone. I also used paired activities, e.g. paired reading partners, or one child writing a story to fit the interests and reading abilities of another, or two children writing a story together, sharing out the task and working with a joint purpose.

ROLLING ACTIVITIES

With 'rolling' activities the intention is for one group's work to act as the stimulus for another. For example, one group may collect specific information from the class, like the type of pets kept at home. This information is then passed on to another group who organise it into different graph forms which are, in turn, passed on to another group to be interpreted. The children are learning to share. A project on families began with the whole class brainstorming ideas for questions that they might ask their grand-parents about their upbringing. A group of children then went to visit one child's grandmother and asked questions about her childhood in Pakistan. The information they gained was written up and was passed on to other children to read. These children then had to answer comprehension type questions on the text.

In another useful rolling activity I ask one child to write the beginning of a story. He or she passes it on to another who reads and develops it, then passes it on again and so on around several children. I also use a version of the 'consequences' game for creative writing/picture making/affirmation work. These activities help children to share, to take turns, and to value the contribution that others can make to their own ideas.

PROVIDING OPPORTUNITIES FOR CHILDREN TO MAKE THEIR OWN DECISIONS

Many opportunities for decision making arise from everyday classroom organisation – simply asking the children to make decisions and to sort out jobs rather than me, the teacher, always delegating. Planning for such opportunities can also be more complex; in one scheme, three other teachers and myself set aside a period of time each week for our children to get together and organise activities to present to the rest of the group. The session became the high spot of the week for some children as they learnt to choose and present activities that were fun to share and watch as well as fun to do. They impressed us with the variety and quality of the activities that they organised ranging from Indian dancing and the Can Can to quizzes, telling jokes and French skipping demonstrations. The children took full responsibility for everything they did, both as performers and in learning to be part of a positive audience. Even the shyest of children became involved and parents were sometimes invited to attend. One of the children once asked me what I would do if no children prepared any activities to perform. This never happened. There was always too much.

ACTIVITIES THAT ENCOURAGE SELF-EXPRESSION

I feel it is important to give the children the time and space to express their thoughts, ideas, and feelings through a variety of creative activities, especially paint, clay, fabrics, puppets, poetry, drama, etc. We have had lots of fun with these. More structured activities have included making footprint mazes; exploding class-made ginger beer and using the experience as a stimulus for writing poetry; and designing and making Santa's castle in box model form and in cake (and eating it!).

ROLE PLAY SITUATIONS

I have found role play a valuable way of encouraging the children to put themselves into other people's shoes and to explore different ways of thinking and behaving, finding alternative solutions to problems. For example, in looking at playground problems we have explored things like: how to join in a game; how to refuse entry into a game without causing upset; how to resolve playground conflicts without always asking the teacher on duty to intervene. We have also looked at the possible causes of the conflicts to try and prevent them from happening again.

USE OF PHOTOGRAPHS

I do a lot of work using photographs. I take photographs of the children performing different activities in and around school and the children involved use them to make class and individual books. Photographs of other children in the school, past and present, and magazine photographs depicting people of different ages, social/cultural backgrounds and different sexes performing similar activities can be photocopied and used for projection work using speech and thought bubbles, or to make jigsaw puzzles and games. Somehow the use of photographs makes the conversations come alive. We have real conversations about real people and events and this also leads to more vivid and expressive writing.

LISTENING TO CHILDREN AND VALUING THEIR COMMENTS

I believe that it is vital to set aside time for children to listen and to be listened to. I sometimes use structured listening activities and games, as well as a great deal of open discussion. I have found the use of the tape-recorder to be invaluable here, enabling me to provide transcripts of the conversations we have so that the children can read and talk about each other's thoughts and ideas. The following is an extract from a class book on 'Peace'.

Instead of violence

CHILD L   'We should discuss things and say what we think and say some of that's right and some of that's wrong to make it equal: so. We should both agree, so it seems like it should be and we should be able to say what we think is wrong.'

CHILD A   'We should have a bit each.'

CHILD K   'We should sort of vote and if the people don't want that to happen we should discuss it and make it all fair. Gangs in the playground are wrong. Gangs are what started wars.'

Inevitably every primary schoolteacher is a teacher of personal and social education, not just at allocated times but at all times of each day, explicitly and implicitly. Everything you do as a teacher comes under the gaze of those eyes you encourage to observe, is heard by those ears you encourage to listen, is analysed by the mind you encourage to evaluate, and can be interpreted and challenged by those voices you encourage to ask questions.

The relationships you form, not just with the children but with their friends and their parents, their brothers and sisters, all add pieces to the picture of the child's view of him/herself and the world around him/her. The most daunting fact of all is the wide gap between the co-operative environment that I, as a teacher, try to create and the unfair world outside. Maybe I should do more to promote an intolerance of unfairness!

Part IV

Curriculum

Chapter 20

The core curriculum
An international perspective

Martin Skilbeck

We have now looked at classrooms and schools and the people who work within them. In this part we turn to examine the formal curriculum: what is taught and is intended to be learnt in school. The curriculum is not to be taken for granted. It is always a selection from the culture, whether deliberately chosen or continued from custom and tradition for reasons no longer explicitly recognised. Teachers may adapt the curriculum to the interests and perceived needs of their pupils, but it must always involve a selection, it can never be just 'natural'. In this extract, Martin Skilbeck argues that there has been a strong move in recent years for the selection of curriculum content to be taken away from individual teachers and to be centralised under State control. Simultaneously, he also notes a movement away from conceptions of the curriculum in terms of broad areas of experience or interdisciplinary studies, which might respond more flexibly to different local contexts, towards a narrower, subject-centred curriculum, pre-defined in terms of content, structure, and progression.

One of the most striking trends we are observing in the curriculum field is the renewal of interest in a firm and clear national or system-wide framework: of goals and objectives; required subjects or subject areas for study; guidelines or procedures for assessment and a range of monitoring and accountability measures. Core curriculum is a widespread phenomenon.

Changing assumptions about the nature and content of core curriculum parallel the vast expansion in the early to mid-twentieth century and onwards of our national systems of public education. This is most noticeable at the secondary school stage where the rapidly increasing number of students of much greater diversity than hitherto was, *inter alia*, a challenge to the classical model of the curriculum and pedagogy. This model presupposed a common body of knowledge, to be studied by all students, who would be taught by whole-class methods and usually in a didactic fashion. Of course, there were exceptions, but the essential point is that the core curriculum meant the whole curriculum for all students.

Historical exegesis is not our purpose here, but mention should be made of the principles that have informed core curriculum thinking. These include the beliefs that subject matter can be integrated through grouped or interdisciplinary studies; that there is a common set of social values and democratic principles that all citizens should imbibe; and that the core curriculum can be stated as a set of learning experiences and hence made personal to each and every student.[1]

These aspirations for an integrated core of socio-cultural values and meanings and a new pedagogy were to be deflected, in the United States, by the post-Sputnik drives towards a subject-centred core curriculum.[2]

CURRENT MEANINGS AND APPROACHES

First, 'core' as widely understood across different countries signifies system-wide (whether national or state/provincial) control and direction of defined, essential curriculum elements to meet national goals and objectives. Second, it signifies emphasis on pre-defined subjects or subject matter, structure, and organisation in the curriculum. Third, it encompasses not only a defined content to meet specified goals or objectives but attainment standards and means of assessing them. Fourth, the approach being taken to core, with an insistence on compulsory subjects and standards, is a reaction to the fragmentation of the curriculum resulting from the 'cafeteria' approach whereby students assemble curricula by combining their choice of the subjects that please or suit them. Fifth, there is a belief in some countries that the core curriculum movement is a covert assault on innovations in curriculum and pedagogy such as integrated studies, controversial subject matter in the social, cultural, and environmental areas, group work, and inquiry-based learning.

There is little that is novel in the core curriculum movement. In the educational literature core curriculum has an ancestry dating back to anti-quity. In all periods of history efforts have been made to analyse for purposes of schooling the fundamental elements of knowledge and under-standing: the kinds of knowledge that seem to provide foundations for further learning; the intellectual and practical skills that serve as tools; and values and attitudes that seem to be of most worth to individuals and society. Inevitably, groups with power in society – whether church or State or professional bodies – will seek to control teaching and learning and the core curriculum is an obvious mechanism.

Since interest groups are involved, and value judgements enter into all these matters – and scientific knowledge of learning processes and of knowledge itself is limited – there always has been and there remains legitimate ground for debate about the core. Moreover, until recent times the debate did not have to take into account universal, compulsory schooling. This has added a dimension which is particularly evident in present endeavours to define required learnings for all, together with more advanced and specialised pathways for individuals and particular groups. The reform of examining, assessment practices, and indicators of learning performance are also affected by extended participation in schooling. Consequently, the core is under great pressure.

In several countries where a nationally prescribed core has been a feature, reviews have recently occurred of the overall scope, shape, content, and organisation of the core to meet national priorities and needs and to respond to the changed context. Striking examples include Italy (elementary schooling), Turkey (secondary schooling), and Japan (elementary and secondary).

On the other hand, where there has been a tradition of local decision making and where there has been variety or, until recent years, perhaps a slackening of commitment to nationally declared curriculum priorities, as in the United States, England and Wales, Australia, New Zealand, and Canada, there is now a very strong revivalist movement. The core curriculum in either a stronger or weaker form has as a consequence become a major educational priority.

What is so different about the new advocacy of core? Most obvious in the United States has been the emphasis on standards of attainment in basic subjects to be achieved through:

– greater concentration on key concepts
– orderly knowledge structures
– cognitive and practical skills
– greater effort within schools by teachers and students alike
– more structured home study
– an explicit interest in cognitive learning strategies
– evaluation and application of knowledge
– more rigorous, comprehensive, and frequent testing of learning outcomes at all levels from individual schools to the whole nation.

In applying this agenda, the American public authorities and a number of private and professional organisations have embarked upon extensive critiques, reviews, and developmental programmes in the humanities, sciences, and mathematics. There has been a substantial development programme in assessment and evaluation and this has generated fierce controversy. As many commentators have pointed out, there can be a negative impact of this kind of activity upon the broader educational goals and values that have been widely promulgated across the nation. The American authorities are not blind to the dangers:

> Many educators are mindful that a great deal of instructional time has been diverted to testing. Practitioners, policy-makers, and researchers have all begun to question the appropriateness of the instruments used to gather the desired information, and the utility of the information once it is gathered.

The debate in Great Britain over the narrowness of the definition of the core and the move towards nationwide testing in the 'basic core' of English, mathematics, and sciences continues as the government proceeds from plan to consultation to legislation to implementation.[3] This debate brings out a significant issue about curriculum and pedagogy. Priorities by their nature are translated into specific cognitive and affective changes and defined skills. These are separated out from the potentially much wider range of student learnings to which curriculum and teaching should minister.

It would be advisable for governments to examine more closely the implications of the inevitable narrowing of the curriculum that results from concentration on a handful of 'basic' subjects. Selections and choices must be made, and there are necessary economies of provision to achieve. But there is a risk of retrogressive reforms, with the solutions of the 1980s and 1990s referring to the problems of the 1960s and 1970s. It is not clear how the national drive towards compulsory subjects and testing will avoid a stultifying rigidity in teaching and learning or achieve the flexibility, independence, and adaptability sought in the modern workforce or the cultivated interests needed for a leisure society. Studies in the history of pedagogy have indicated how difficult it is to achieve the experiential, student-centred learning of the kind that is needed.[4]

ADDRESSING NEW NEEDS

So far, the discussion of core has centred on the idea that fundamental and basic learnings required of all students are most readily expressed as a set of compulsory subject learnings in the framework of the school week and year. This does no more than acknowledge the way core curricula are frequently described in policy guidelines and regulations, and presented in school timetables. It is evident that there are serious limitations to this approach. These are recognised to some extent where the specification of 'essential learnings' is not subject-bound but presented in terms of general understandings, critical thinking skills, values, intellectual flexibility, and so on.

Are subjects to be abandoned, then? Certainly not. The point is, as John Dewey long ago pointed out, to draw upon subjects as a *resource* in the design of curricula and so to utilise and combine subject matters as to match the interests and experiences of learners and the socio-cultural world of which they are a part.

What is of most interest, educationally, in current debates about core curriculum are the attempts being made to introduce new forms and organisation of knowledge into the core itself: a reconceptualisation, in some measure, of basic and fundamental learnings. Noteworthy are the conceptual strategy approach adopted in the new Italian primary curriculum and the new Japanese concept of core as providing the basic building blocks of universal, lifelong learning. In Japan, there is a strong reaction to material affluence, hence a questioning of the effects of affluence on children, and a reassertion of humanistic values. *Seikatsuka* – the merging of elementary science and social-environmental studies, in the elementary school – is a bold new move. Overall, a brave effort is being made to find a central place in the core for creativity, logical thinking, imagination, inspiration, motivation to learn, enjoyment of learning, pleasure of accomplishment in face of the 'desolation' of contemporary Japanese education, and society.

NOTES

1 See Smith, B. O. Stanley, W. O., and Shores, J. H. (1957) *Fundamentals of Curriculum Development*, New York, Harcourt, Chapters 14 and 15; Skilbeck, M. (1985) *A Core Curriculum for the Common School*, London, University of London, Institute of Education.
2 Goodlad, J. (1986) 'Core Curriculum: what and for whom', in Gorter, R. J. (ed.) *Views on Core Curriculum*, Enschede, National Institute for Curriculum Development.
3 National Union of Teachers (1987) 'National Curriculum', *N.U.T. Education Review*, Vol 1, No 2, Autumn; Lawton, D. and Chitty, C. (eds) (1988) *The National Curriculum*, Bedford Way Paper 33, London, University of London Institute of Education; Simon, B. (1988) *Bending the Rules*, London, Lawrence & Wishart.
4 Instructive on this point are two American studies: Cremin, L. A. (1961) *The Transformation of the School*, New York, Alfred A. Knopf; Cuban, L. (1986) 'How did teachers teach, 1890–1980', *Theory into Practice*, XXII, 3, pp. 159–65.
   Cuban notes that teacher-centred instruction prevailed throughout this period: 'far more teacher than student talk; the predominance of questions calling for factual recall and of whole class instruction; heavy reliance on textbooks with texts emphasizing factual recall of information: the margin of classroom change available to reformers is far narrower than expected in the elementary school and even slimmer in the high school. Historically, teaching practices have hewed to a teacher-centred pattern that persistently reasserts itself after reform impulses weaken and disappear.'

Chapter 21

The national curriculum
Origins, context, and implementation

Bob Moon

This chapter explores the emergence of a national curriculum. Unlike Northern Ireland, where the curriculum has been defined in terms of broad areas of experience, the national curriculum in England and Wales was conceived of in terms of traditional 'subject' areas. Bob Moon shows how these 'subject' areas came into being, and indicates the difficulties involved in implementing the 1988 Education Act in this context, difficulties which have led to rapid and continuing revisions. The chapter provides a case study of the move to a national 'core' curriculum as described by Martin Skilbeck in the last chapter.

The Secretary of State's policies for the range and pattern of the 5 to 16 curriculum will not lead to national syllabuses. Diversity at local education authority and school level is healthy, accords well with the English and Welsh tradition of school education, and makes for liveliness and innovation.

(*Better Schools: A Summary*, March 1985: 4)

The Government has announced its intention to legislate for a national foundation curriculum for pupils of compulsory school age in England and Wales. . . . Within the secular national curriculum, the Government intends to establish essential foundation subjects – maths, English, science, foreign language, history, geography, technology in its various aspects, music, art and physical education . . . the government wishes to establish programmes of study for the subjects, describing the essential content which needs to be covered to enable pupils to reach or surpass the attainment targets.

(*The National Curriculum 5–16, A Consultation Document*,
July 1987: 35)

The English, and the Welsh, now have a national curriculum. In July 1988, just a year after the publication of a consultation document, the Education Reform Bill received Royal Assent and passed on to the statute books. The curriculum clauses survived the Commons committee stages and vigorous, early morning attacks in the House of Lords, to pass unaltered into legislation. The measures represent a remarkable political intervention to change the post-war consensus on curriculum control.

How did a centrally prescribed national curriculum come to be established and, moreover, how can the *volte-face* in policy represented in the change from Better Schools to Baker Bill be explained? The answer lies partly in the evolution of some recurring, even predictable, curriculum policies, but arguably more significantly in the political opportunism of those who achieved positions of power and influence prior to and shortly after the 1987 Election. This chapter, therefore, will examine these events and speculate on how the system worked to produce what a few years ago would have been unthinkable policies. Curriculum management, to be fully effective, requires a broad understanding of the policy context within which national policies have evolved. This is essential if *critical engagement* with implementation is to be promoted across the school or local community. It will be equally important in communicating and debating the issues with parents and others with a legitimate interest in the working out of the new programmes. Firstly, however, what form do the measures take?

Ten subjects make up the national curriculum; English,[1] mathematics and science, defined as *core foundation* subjects, alongside seven further *foundation* subjects: art, geography, history, modern languages (11–16 only), music, physical education and technology.[2] The Secretary of State is required by the 1988 Education Reform Act to establish programmes of study and define attainment targets for each of the subjects. The attainment targets provide the basis for national and school reported assessments at the ages of 7, 11, 14, and 16.

This simply stated formulation summarises the English and Welsh national curriculum. The Act states that all schools must provide a balanced and broadly based curriculum which

> promotes the spiritual, moral, cultural, mental and physical development of pupils at school and in society
>
> prepares pupils for the opportunities, responsibilities and experiences of adult life.

A NATIONAL CURRICULUM: THE LONGER VIEW

In many ways the subject basis of national curriculum is familiar, with origins stretching back at least to the nineteenth century. The historical line is traceable and well documented in general curriculum histories. The Newcastle Report of 1861, for example, led to the 1862 Revised Code of Robert Lowe and a stress on basic subjects, age-related programmes of study, and the notorious 'payments by results' system for teachers. Three years later the Clarendon Commission investigated nine leading public schools and advocated, in addition to the central study of classics, the introduction into the curriculum of mathematics, modern languages, and natural sciences.

In 1868 the Taunton Commission, after looking at 800 endowed grammar schools, recommended three types of school, serving three classes of society, with leaving ages of 18, 16, and 14. Each school would have a distinctive curriculum. The emphasis of the first grade school would be classics and preparation for university. In grade 2 the requirements of the army, business, and the professions required a stronger emphasis on practical rather than abstract activities, while the sons of artisans in grade 3 schools had a less precisely prescribed curriculum, although the basics were essential.

The latter part of the nineteenth century, and the period of this century up to the Second World War, abounds with evidence of curriculum regulations. The Revised Code went through many versions, with Gladstone's fourth administration providing a significantly liberalising influence. The 1904 Regulations for Secondary Schools included detailed syllabuses specifying the amount of time to be allocated to each subject

1904	1935
English language	English language
English literature	England literature
One language*	One language
Geography	Geography
History	History
Mathematics	Mathematics
Science	Science
Drawing	Drawing
Due provision for manual work and physical exercises	Physical exercises and organised games
(Housewifery in girls' schools)	Singing
	[Manual instruction for boys, dramatic subjects for girls]

* When two languages other than English are taken, and Latin is not one of them, the 'Board' will be required to be satisfied that the omission of Latin is for the advantage of the school.

The 1935 regulations remained in force until the Butler 1944 Education Act. The elementary codes disappeared rather earlier, to be replaced by the Board of Education Blue Book, a *Handbook of Suggestions*, which went through a number of editions again until 1944.

The 1988 specification therefore looked remarkably similar to those of 1935, although planned to cover the whole rather than secondary years of compulsory schooling.

In primary schooling the picture was more varied. The abolition of the

11-plus examination helped generate a new approach to curriculum organisation. Strong advocates for a more child-centred approach to teaching, such
as Alec Clegg in the West Riding of Yorkshire and Edith Moorhouse in
Oxfordshire, received wide publicity for the primary school reforms in their
local authorities. The Plowden Report, published in 1967, gave warm
approval to these new directions, and for a few years English primary
schools were inundated with international visitors. More recent evidence,
however, suggests that the spread of these ideas was limited. An unpublished
survey commissioned for HMI in 1988 showed that in the average primary
classroom, over half the week was devoted to studying basic mathematics
and English.

The school system therefore resolutely reflected subject traditions across
more than a century of compulsory schooling.

The first indication of the form the national curriculum would take
was published within a few months of the 1987 Conservative election
victory. The red consultation document, *The National Curriculum 5–16*,
was greeted with forceful criticism. Although the time-scale for consultation was short, two months including the summer holiday period,
thousands of responses were received. Comment ranged from the right-
wing Institute of Economic Affairs (IEA) arguing that the market, not
government, should determine curriculum, to the National Union of
Teachers' fear of uniformity and conformity. The tone of the document was
strident, and made for more interesting reading than many government
publications. A model curriculum was proposed for the secondary school
in subject terms. There was no discussion of how the subject curriculum
would apply to primary schools. The need for a ten-subject school
curriculum was boldly asserted without qualification and without
reference to the plethora of government and inspectorial publications that
had appeared in the decade following James Callaghan's Ruskin College
Speech of 1976.

PRESSURE GROUP POLITICS 1986–7

Behind this change in curriculum policy was a radical shift in the balance
of power between government and the interest groups that had been so
influential in building educational policy in the post-war period. It is now
becoming clear that in the months immediately before and after the 1987
general election, a small group of prime ministerial advisers, including or at
least influenced by the pamphleteers and polemicists of numerous right-
wing 'think tanks', exerted increasing pressure on the Prime Minister. The
ideas formulated, first for the Conservative Party election manifesto and
then the consultation document, bypassed Her Majesty's Inspectorate, the
Association of County Councils, the Association of Metropolitan
Authorities, the teachers' unions, the Society of Education Officers, and also

the Schools Curriculum Development Committee (SCDC) and Secondary Examinations Council (SEC).

Government ministers and DES officials were well aware that none of these groups could subscribe to the form and style of the 1987 Red Book proposals. It was in line with government policy to marginalise the teachers' views and those of the local authorities, but few would have predicted the ruthless exclusion of HMI or SCDC and SEC from policy formulation. This, however, represented pressure group politics of a most active form, sustained over a significant period of time.

The way the national curriculum finally came to occupy an important niche in the Education Reform Act, and the form in which it was expressed, can be seen to date back to Sir Keith Joseph's final years in office. A more precise understanding of what happened will have to await the publication of personal diaries and testimonies of the sort that are now providing further information on the Ruskin speech. At this stage, however, it appears that there was impatience and disillusion within the Tory party about policy making in the Joseph era. Despite some radical ideas (set out, for example, in his 1982 speech to the North of England conference), he had prevaricated over many decisions, and in his clumsy handling of the teachers' industrial dispute between 1984 and 1986 he had failed to show the clear and firm resolve expected of ministers in a Thatcher government. There may also have been something of a suspicion that, despite the polemic and rhetoric of the times, he had earned a grudging respect from some parts of the educational establishment. The introduction of the common 16+ GCSE examination was one major source of concern in some quarters. Rumours of his departure circulated for a long period, and the Prime Minister herself was said to be showing an interest in education, particularly as her increasing impatience with local authority levels of expenditure, linked often to policies at variance with those of the government, was most starkly illustrated within the education service. It should also be noted that her own ministerial career, when she presided in 1970–4 over a record number of grammar school closures, was seen as hardly successful against the criteria of Thatcherism in the 1980s. This was a new opportunity to make amends.

The arguments put forward to and by her advisers were opportune and congruent with the way policy was being developed towards other parts of the Welfare State, most notably the Health Service. The polemicists of the New Right had waged a well-publicised campaign for a return to what they saw as traditional values. A number had been leading contributors to the late 1960s Black Papers, an earlier polemic against progressive and egalitarian ideas, and the prospect of a third Thatcher victory and active Prime Ministerial interest offered a unique opportunity to influence policy.

It is now widely accepted that regular informal contact was maintained between the Prime Minister's Office and leading members from pressure groups such as the Centre for Policy Studies and the Hillgate Group. In formulating the election manifesto and determining the content and style of the consultation document, this influence was highly significant. A comparison between the Hillgate Group's 1986 pamphlet 'Whose Schools' and the content of the Education Reform Act shows just how significant. In their ideas Margaret Thatcher had detected a populist appeal, in public speeches she was quick to reassert the need for traditional approaches, while ridiculing certain attempts to combat some of the enduring curriculum problems. In her address to the 1987 Conservative Party conference she talked of 'children who need to be able to count and multiply learning anti-racist mathematics – whatever that might be', and promised her audience that the national curriculum would comprise 'reading, writing, spelling, grammar, arithmetic, basic science, and technology'.

The consultation document therefore reasserts the primacy of subjects. Areas of experience smacked of the educational establishment, allowed flexibility and local interpretation, and hardly made for a rousing address to the party conference. The consensus that had been building around the framework was ignored in the aftermath of a sweeping electoral victory. The symbolic importance of subjects overrode all other considerations.

THE NEW CURRICULUM – NATIONALISM, MANAGERIALISM, OR THE MARKET PLACE?

The national curriculum in the form presented surprised and offended many in the educational world. It appeared to combine the continental traditions of subject prescription and the North American predilection for testing to create a particularly powerful, and for many threatening, proposal. The level of hostility was fuelled by the scarcity of information, fears about the way the statutory orders would be produced (would the working parties be given over to Hillgate?), and rumours about the form the testing would take. It was also apparent that the measures were to be vigorously pushed through, with compromise in the climate of the late 1980s interpreted as weakness. An ambitious Secretary of State had staked his political future on the passage of the Bill.

It is difficult, close to events, to clarify the way influence was exerted and motivation tapped in establishing such a major reform of curriculum policy. A number of themes, however, in the evolution of policy generally appear to be reflected in ERA and the national curriculum clauses. A brief review suggests that the events of 1987–8 were less surprising than reactions at the time suggested. Three processes in particular appear to have fused around the national curriculum: a long-term staking-out of bureaucratic control; the drive for efficiency and accountability that had become the characteristic of government attempts to reduce public expenditure; and finally a formulation of policy that brought together competing interests among pressure groups on the right.

John Quicke (1988) has explored this final point in an interesting analysis of the politics and ideas of the 'New Right' towards education over the last decade. He points to the differences between neo-conservatives such as Roger Scruton, a member of the Hillgate Group, and neo-liberals such as Stuart Sexton, working within the Institute of Economic Affairs. Neo-conservatives, he suggests, advocate strong government and a hierarchical and disciplined view of society in which a concept of the national is central. Neo-liberals on the other hand emphasise individual freedom of choice through the free workings of the market. In terms of curriculum therefore, the neo-conservatives appeared to have been the most influential at first. A central, authoritarian prescription seems incompatible with a principle that permits the market (parents) to determine which form of curriculum prospers. The Institute of Economic Affairs in replying to the red consultation paper was clear:

> The most effective national curriculum is that set by the market, by the consumers of the education service. This will be far more responsive to children's needs and society's demands than any centrally imposed curriculum, no matter how well meant. Attempts by Government and by Parliament to impose a curriculum, no matter how 'generally agreed' they think it to be, are a poor second best in terms of quality, flexibility and responsiveness to needs than allowing the market to decide and setting the system free to respond to the overwhelming demand for higher standards. The Government must trust market forces rather than some committee of the great and good.

And the Institute sees the debate over a government-imposed national curriculum as detracting attention from what really matters, namely the proposals to devolve management to schools. In establishing the curriculum proposals, these two groups appear to have been in tension. Margaret Thatcher is reported as wavering over the degree of prescription required for the national curriculum, reaching the view at one stage that English, mathematics, and science should comprise the limits of regulation. Kenneth Baker, Secretary of State, is rumoured to have convinced her of the need for more widespread control. If Baker[3] did seek to convince in this way he may have exploited the argument of the neo-conservatives that, uncontrolled, the curriculum serves as a vehicle for the politically motivated, illiberal, and indoctrinating tendencies of the left. This is a persistent theme running through both the pamphlets (such as the Hillgate Group's determined attacks on any curriculum activity described as studies – peace studies, multicultural studies) and speeches made by Margaret Thatcher and other ministers in the pre-election period.

For Quicke, therefore, the strategy of the neo-conservatives was to highlight those elements they had in common with all forms of liberal education, and to contrast the values they jointly espoused with those underpinning the radical left-of-centre ideologies said to be dominant in educational bureaucracies, particularly at the local level. Despite the failure to convince market purists at the IEA, the approach was influential with the Prime Minister and with a minister keen to enlarge the role and responsibilities of the DES.

Hargreaves and Reynolds (1989), from a position on the left explicitly opposed to government reforms, provide a further perspective on the apparently contradictory policies of regulation and choice operating within the Act. They see nothing accidental in this juxtaposition, with centralisation and privatisation representing the co-ordinated arms of educational policy making. Centralisation of curriculum and assessment forces competitiveness around the values chosen by government. Ideological control is exerted, because to open up the next generation to socialisation by the free run of market forces runs social and political risks that no government could contemplate, particularly at a time of economic crisis and social uncertainty. For the neo-conservatives, therefore, the form and style of the national curriculum is paramount and helps explain their interest in the membership of the new national councils and their detailed scrutiny of ministerial and DES statements. It will be interesting to see how this surveillance can be sustained in the implementation of the national curriculum procedure.

A second influence on policy is the quest for measures that create accountability and efficiency within the education service. From this perspective the national curriculum 'tidies up' the ground upon which cost and personnel decisions can be made, and testing provides a basis for valid comparative judgements about efficiency of schools and classes. It is through this perspective that the DES's preference for an objectives-led curriculum, rather than HMI's 'areas of experience', becomes clear. HMI appear to have resisted many aspects of the pressure for comprehensive testing and assessment based on objectives. They would have been aware of the unresolved technical problems and the threat posed to time-honoured styles and inspection. There would also have been concern about a change in the working relationships with teachers and schools.

The curriculum clauses of ERA show, however, the DES in the ascendancy, a quite significant fight-back after years enduring Mrs Thatcher's reported suspicions of obstructionism and inaction, and the more recent activities of Lord Young who, at the Department of Industry and Employment, had launched through the Manpower Services Commission a significant challenge to DES authority over the education service. TVEI, one of the most prestigious of MSC projects, received only the briefest of mentions in the consultative process and represents another group excluded from the process of formulating policy in this period.[4] The ambitions of bureaucrats can develop a momentum of their own. Managerialism promotes bureaucratic activity and the DES prospered, not the least in new departmental structures and an expanded staffing.

The form in which the national curriculum was laid down represented a victory therefore for those on the right who had seized the political agenda for reform. It also represented a significant increase in the power and importance of the DES and it provided a yardstick against which new and more demanding forms of accountability could be introduced.

THE EARLY EXPERIENCE OF IMPLEMENTATION

The implementation phase has been characterised by an impressive weight and variety of curriculum development. Despite strident protests about the pace and extent of change, and the form of some of the subjects, surveys show that teachers have accepted the principle of a national curriculum. Professional and academic comment, however, has been critical of much of the development process. This comment has been borne out in practice by almost immediate changes in some key aspects of the structure and subject formulations. The style of development has implications for other countries contemplating core or national frameworks for curriculum. The main implementation problems therefore merit consideration.

First, the national curriculum was set up subject by subject through a series of working parties. Cross-referencing between working parties, made up of government nominees, was discouraged and the setting up and reporting took place at different times and over varying periods of time. Mathematics and science came first with physical education and music last. Each subject, in addition to being defined through attainment targets, was set out in four key stages, two for primary, two secondary, at the end of which there would be national assessments. Inevitably problems arose. Interpretation of the attainment targets varied from one group to another. The science working party defined attainment targets in terms of knowledge, the technology group by reference to processes. The number of attainment targets also varied, initially seventeen for science, fourteen for mathematics, four for English, and five for technology. The capacity to organise the whole curriculum, particularly at the primary level became increasingly problematic. Schools were given responsibility about how the curriculum structure was organised but all the attainment targets in the statutory subjects had to be covered. Planning thematically or by topic in the early years became exceedingly complex. The science and mathematics programmes were, therefore, both rewritten almost immediately to reduce the number of attainment targets.

Second, the working parties and the subsequent consultation process became an area for political interest at the highest level. Prime Minister Thatcher intervened in the orders that were laid for both English and history – and this process has continued to the time of writing. The English curriculum was reviewed in 1993 to take account of criticism from right of centre government advisers that it gives insufficient attention to basic skills. The new Secretary of State, John Patten, has indicated that Shakespeare should be a compulsory part of the curriculum for all pupils. The music curriculum, as with most other subjects, was the subject of controversial debate carried out primarily through the media. Despite the opposition of many leading music educators and musicians, led by conductor Simon Rattle, the curriculum was weighted towards musical theory and appreciation rather than practical activities.

Third, in some areas the national curriculum developed new approaches that involved a major restructuring of the organisation of the school curriculum. The thematic, topic work developed through the integrated day in most primary schools required major revision. The introduction of technology was also a new challenge for primary practitioners. Most significantly the technology statutory orders required the fixing of craft, design, technology, information technology, business studies, and home economics at the secondary stage. The subsequent confusion has received widespread criticism. A recent report appeared with the memorable phrase, 'Technology and NC is in a mess' (Smithers and Robinson 1992), and a major rewrite of the technology curriculum is now under way.

Fourth, the original subject blueprint limited the range of subjects. Dance and drama, for example, were not mentioned and had to be accommodated through English and physical education. At secondary level, given the normal English allocation of time of one tenth of the curriculum to each examined subject, it was clear that time was not available for subjects such as Latin, a second modern language, or vocational options. Ministers have had to accept that the ten subjects of the national curriculum go through to age 14 but many become optional thereafter. Policies on this issue have changed almost annually since 1989, making plans at the school level difficult to formulate. The different subjects were also expected to be implemented over differing time scales with the main pressure falling on the infant school to implement.

Fifth, the original formulation left out many curriculum issues that everyone acknowledged should be included: careers, personal and social education, for example. The National Curriculum Council has now produced a series of booklets to illustrate how these can be incorporated through the existing statutory orders, although this inevitably has led to some complex and retrospective attempts to achieve cross-curricular coherence.

Sixth, and of major significance, has been controversy surrounding assessment. The first government working party proposed assessment across ten levels (each attainment target in each subject was subsequently divided into ten levels of attainment) involving both formative and summative assessment through teacher assessment and national tests. The concept of teacher and formative assessment was accepted reluctantly by Mrs Thatcher but has subsequently been the subject of ongoing political and educational controversy. The idea of short and sharp 'pencil and paper' tests, favoured by some government politicians and all the right of centre 'think tanks', clearly clashed with the quest for more reliable and valid instruments that developments in assessment over the last decade suggested were required. In the assessment of 7-year-olds (key stage 1) the instruments used varied markedly in each of the first three years of implementation, and always towards the sort of instrument the government favoured. The well-rehearsed difficulties (Murphy 1990) of subsuming formative and summative proposals in the same instrument is being painstakingly re-learnt through the national curriculum experience. At present, however, the form of assessment is still a matter of intense debate. The use of the assessment information remains controversial with government, committed to the publication of raw score league tables, refuting any inevitably more complex plans to develop 'value added' indices of school performance.

Finally, the separation of curriculum and assessment into two separate advisory councils led to a degree of infighting, much of which has spilled out into the public domain and finally resulted in a merged Schools Curriculum and Assessment Authority (SCAA) set up in 1993.

In the design and implementation of the national curriculum, curriculum developers can pinpoint major problems that have created enormous difficulties in schools. However, despite opposition and some derision, the national curriculum is in place and is a major determinant of curriculum policy. It is a remarkable political achievement. One salutary conclusion is just how the agendas of government and most curriculum experts come to diverge so markedly. In this the judgement of history may suggest that burdens of responsibility are more equally spread than many contemporary commentators suggest.

NOTES

1 In Wales, Welsh can be an additional core or foundation subject.
2 Religious education is also compulsory, but defined by statutory requirements unique to that subject.
3 The rather obscure terminological distinction between core foundation and foundation subjects is said to date from this debate.
4 TVEI, or education relevant to working life, was strongly criticised by some traditional neo-conservative writers.

REFERENCES

Hargreaves, A. and Reynolds, D. (1989) *Education Policy: Controversies and Critiques*, Lewes, Falmer Press.
Murphy, P. (1990) 'National Curriculum assessment: has anything been learnt from the experience of APU?', *The Curriculum Journal*, 1 (2), pp. 186–98.

Quicke, J. (1988) 'The "New Right" and education', *British Journal of Educational Studies*, February.

Smithers, A. and Robinson, P. (1992) *Teaching in the National Curriculum: Getting it Right*, London, Engineering Council.

Chapter 22

Coherence and manageability
Reflections on the national curriculum and cross-curricular provision

David Hargreaves

This chapter draws attention to a number of elements of the national curriculum that schools need to integrate into their curriculum planning: the cross-curricular themes and dimensions. David Hargreaves argues here for a reformed curriculum that would both integrate subject experiences and make room for the cross-curricular themes. An argument for restructuring the curriculum was also put forward by the NCC in advice to the Secretary of State in January 1993. However, its argument was set in terms not of developing new curriculum structures, but of the need to reduce the curriculum in each subject to 'an essential core of knowledge'. In reading this chapter, how far would you feel such proposals would help teachers in developing coherent curricular plans? How far would such changes support the moves towards simplified 'testing' outlined by Martin Skilbeck in Chapter 20?

The main purpose of curriculum reform is to improve the quality of teaching and learning and thereby the achievements of pupils. In this chapter I seek to argue that, if this valuable purpose is to be realised, a reformed curriculum should become more coherent and more manageable, and I shall then examine the extent to which the introduction of the national curriculum in England and Wales appears to meet this criterion of curriculum improvement.

Let me define these terms. *Manageability* is concerned with the amount of knowledge and skills that can be put into the curriculum: if there is too much content, in relation to the allocated time, the curriculum is unmanageable for teachers and pupils. Manageability is also concerned with the capacity of teachers to relate the parts together so that they become coherent as a whole.

Coherence is about the way the curriculum as a whole hangs together. When a curriculum is coherent, the various parts of the curriculum have a clear and explicit relationship with one another. The curriculum has a rationale and can be planned so that the many different parts fit together to make it a whole. When the curriculum lacks coherence, it becomes fragmented and confusing both to teachers and to pupils.

I shall distinguish two kinds of coherence. *Content coherence* is about the relationships between the knowledge and skills involved in the curriculum. There is coherence *within* subjects, a matter which is a central part of the national curriculum, namely the attainment targets, statements of attainment, and programmes of study. There is a second form of content coherence, that *between* subjects.

In primary schools the integrated approach to the curriculum requires teachers to achieve between-subject coherence by combining the separate national curriculum subjects and the guidance for them. If the relationships between subjects are not clear and explicit, integrated work in the form of topics or themes will be (or will remain) disconnected experiences that lack coherence. However, at the same time, primary teachers need to attend to within-subject coherence to ensure progression and continuity within each subject.

A second kind of coherence I shall call *experiential coherence*, or coherence as it is experienced in the routine world of the classroom by both teachers and pupils. Primary teachers are more alert to problems of between-subject experiential coherence because of the class teacher system. They may, however, have problems with some aspects of within-subject coherence because they lack specialist knowledge, for example in science.

Experiential coherence for pupils has as its ideal that they should grasp coherence both within and between subjects. That most pupils do not currently achieve such coherence, in either primary or secondary schools, is evident. John Holt understood this very well from his observations of pupils:

> For children, the central business of schools is not learning, whatever this vague word means; it is getting these daily tasks done, or at least out of the way, with a minimum of effort and unpleasantness. Each task is an end in itself. The children don't care how they dispose of it. If they can get it out of the way by doing it, they will do it.
>
> (Holt 1964: 37)

Teachers see the curriculum as divided up into schemes of work, syllabuses, lessons, tasks. Each element is supposedly like a brick and, through schooling, the child builds the bricks into an edifice of the learnt curriculum. In reality, implies Holt, pupils stand amid a bomb-site of disconnected bricks and fragments.

A key question is: does the introduction of the national curriculum lead to an improvement in both content and experiential coherence and thus to an improvement in the quality of teaching and learning? I shall argue that the creation of a national curriculum presents an opportunity for improving curriculum coherence, but that the national curriculum for England and

Wales is being designed and implemented in a way that renders the task of achieving coherence difficult to manage in practice.

Those who devised the basic structure of the national curriculum had little regard for either coherence or manageability. In *A View of the Curriculum* (1980) HMI introduced the linked notions of breadth, balance, and coherence. Here is a happy trinity of concepts or principles to guide curriculum planning. Sadly, it did not survive for long. Five years later, in the DES document *Better Schools* (1985), breadth and balance remain as 'fundamental principles'. Two more, relevance and differentiation, are added. Coherence mysteriously disappears. Charitably, one might assume that ministers did not understand or see the significance of the concept; and, to be fair, it was not fully explained by HMI.

It is also true that breadth was the concept of most immediate concern. In many schools the curriculum was simply too narrow. 'Topic' work in primary schools often gave inadequate coverage of subjects such as science, history, and geography; and option schemes in secondary schools led to a lack of breadth and balance for many pupils in the 14–16 age range.

Thus greater breadth was a key purpose behind the national curriculum reforms. As all teachers know, the broader the curriculum becomes, the greater the problem of manageability. The problem is easily stated: how to get the quart of a desirable curriculum into the pint pot of the school timetable. To ensure that pupils receive the broad curriculum to which they are entitled requires a solution to the problem that there seems to be insufficient room for it.

The NCC's first piece of advice (November 1989) emphasised that the national curriculum is not the whole curriculum, which consists of the core and other foundation subjects, RE, additional subjects chosen by the school and cross-curricular provision. The document rightly resurrected the concept of coherence and the need to bind the strands of the curriculum together. Between-subject coherence avoids both unnecessary duplication and neglect. A whole curriculum must be a coherent curriculum.

Cross-curricular provision is divided by the NCC into three aspects – dimensions, skills, and themes. The most substantial part consists of five themes: economic and industrial understanding; careers education and guidance; health education; education for citizenship; and environmental education.

To the tasks of achieving coherence within and between (foundation) subjects, two further tasks should now be added: coherence *within* the five cross-curricular themes and coherence *between* the five themes and the foundation subjects. Coherence within cross-curricular provision is clearly desirable. Environmental education has obvious links with health education, and citizenship with economic and industrial understanding. Then each theme and cross-curricular provision as a whole needs to be linked to the foundation subjects through which they are mainly to be taught.

Content coherence remains very difficult for teachers to achieve in practice, in spite of the NCC booklets. Even when detailed advice becomes available on all foundation subjects and the five themes, most teachers will need a sound grasp of virtually *all* the advice to attempt content coherence. The scope of this task is breathtaking, both in terms of the intellectual demands and the time needed to master the material and translate it into a school curriculum.

I fear that teachers will simply treat the advice on cross-curricular provision in a mechanical way, using checklists to demonstrate that the five themes are being dealt with in the foundation subjects. This is, in practice, the way that teachers can turn an inherently unmanageable task into a manageable one. For if schools are not provided with the advice and support necessary to create a coherent whole curriculum, and are left to manage this themselves, then many schools will have subject leaders (in primary) and heads of department (in secondary) to manage within- and between-subject coherence, and cross-curriculum co-ordinators to manage coherence within the themes and between the themes and subjects, all to be co-ordinated by a head or deputy with responsibility for the curriculum as a whole. Few teachers would have an overall grasp of cross-curricular provision and its internal structure or of its relationship to the foundation subjects. Many hard-pressed heads might in any event be tempted towards the 'checklist' approach as being simpler and more manageable. If this aspect of content coherence is no more than a paper exercise, thus denying the possibility of experiential coherence, the chances of improvement in curriculum coherence for pupils are small.

REFERENCES

Department of Education and Science (1985) *Better Schools*, London, HMSO.
Her Majesty's Inspectors (1980) *A View of the Curriculum*, London, HMSO.
Holt, J. (1964) *How Children Fail*, Harmondsworth, Penguin.
National Curriculum Council (1989) *Circular No. 6: The National Curriculum and Whole Curriculum Planning: Preliminary Guidance*, York, NCC.

Chapter 23

The evolution of the topic

Trevor Kerry and Jim Eggleston

In the 1993 OFSTED Report on 'Curriculum organisation and classroom practice in primary schools', HMI noted: 'The vast majority of primary schools remain firmly committed to grouping aspects of different subjects together to be taught as "topics" ' (para. 7). In this chapter we look at one explanation for the development of an integrated 'topic' approach to the primary curriculum. In a fairly large-scale survey of what 'topic' work meant in primary schools, Eggleston and Kerry arrived at the following working definition: 'Topic work includes all those areas of the curriculum (other than basic reading and number skills) which are explored in a thematic way. Topics may be (predominantly) scientific, mathematical, or in the field of the humanities; or they may be multi-disciplinary.' Their study showed, however, that, in the majority (over 70 per cent) of schools which they surveyed, 'topic' work took the form of one of the two 'cameos' illustrated below.

Cameo 1 This class has embarked upon an interdisciplinary study of the canal system of Kendal. The teacher takes a whole-class lead lesson which is designed to draw from the children by question and answer their knowledge of the canal itself. An hour is set aside each week for a term. During this time visits are made to the canal, and the children acquire information from local sources about the local history, industrial development, and wildlife of the canal. A display of poster materials and pupils' work is mounted on the classroom walls as the weeks progress.

Cameo 2 Mr Brown is using topic work to explore the idea of colour in nature. His science lessons are given over for six weeks to various aspects of the subject: camouflage, display, threat, etc. Each week pupils are given a class introduction to the particular theme for the lesson. They then work individually or in pairs to find examples from the animal kingdom using the class and school reference libraries. Each pupil writes a short piece about, for example, animals' use of colour to camouflage themselves, and then uses drawings or cut-out pictures to illustrate his or her notes. Towards the end of each lesson the class comes together. Some pupils show the others what they have found out; and there is a general discussion led by the teacher to highlight the main points of the lesson.

THE PHILOSOPHY BEHIND TOPIC WORK

A topic-work approach in primary schools, widespread in the 1980s, is no new phenomenon. The clues as to where to look for its roots are to be found in the child-centred nature of topic work, its interdisciplinary approach, and its implied role for the teacher. These phenomena have occurred together in two famous philosophies of education: those of Rousseau and of John Dewey.

Jean Jacques Rousseau (1712–78) established a school of philosophy known as Naturalism. He declared that 'nature wants children to be children before they are men' and he adopted a stage theory of human development of a kind with which we are comparatively familiar on account of the work of psychologists such as Jean Piaget. Rousseau thought the child should be free to learn from direct experience. This maturational view of education and resulting child-centred philosophy was highly controversial in its day. It has, however, become the cornerstone of much modern theorising about primary education.

To modern primary teachers, Rousseau's dictum of discovery learning is not specially remarkable since it is so much a part of their daily presuppositions. (Of his protégé Emile, Rousseau said that he should 'not be taught science, let him discover it'.) Nevertheless, the tradition which now manifests itself in topic work cannot abandon its roots in the education of Rousseau's Emile.

Rousseau's philosophical model of education was re-interpreted into a school situation by the American John Dewey (1859–1952). He believed that the natural and spontaneous activities of children can be directed to educational ends, and that this is best done through problems of the children's own devising. In effect, Dewey (1910) was advocating a scientific approach: he believed children pursuing their own studies would be motivated to speculate, observe, gather information, and test out guesses or hypotheses to solve their own problems. This approach developed into a 'project method': a contractual approach to education wherein the child worked at his or her own pace on an assignment. The teacher played a consultative role rather than a didactic one. Similarities between this and the kinds of topic work deduced from the cameos set out above are obvious, and the direct line of influence upon primary education from Rousseau via Dewey to today's classroom practice is often acknowledged quite openly in texts (from Kilpatrick 1918 to Dearden 1976 and Stewart 1986), even if the effect on teachers is more unconscious (Plowden 1967: para. 510). Kilpatrick developed these ideas to embrace a four-stage model of learning from real situations through topics. The stages were:

1 The children specify what they want to know, ask questions, and devise ways of finding out.
2 They consult books and develop an action plan.
3 They execute that work.
4 They present findings to others, review, and make judgements.

The ethos of this philosophy, now taken so much for granted, is, typically, summed up in a few lines from Gunning et al.:

> One of the most prolific sources of such information lies within the child's own day-to-day experience. Every day the child is involved in a vast range of experiences at first hand. . . . These contacts and experiences can be used very effectively by the teacher to provide the child with a developing insight into a great range of ideas, since they provide very 'concrete' pegs on which to hang important concepts.
>
> (Gunning et al. 1981: 83, 84)

The case is even more strongly put for middle schools by Henley (1984):

> We see the middle school as providing scope to nurture the development of a child's own personality at the critical point of onset of puberty. . . . We therefore expect to find a focus on the personal and social growth of pupils as individuals . . . 'Subjects' are subordinate considerations.

So child-centred views of education are not the only philosophical pre-conditions for espousing topic work as a suitable method of teaching and learning. Topic lessons exhibit a particular attitude towards the nature of knowledge, or epistemology. The assumption is that knowledge – at least at the primary level – cannot be compartmentalised into separate subjects. Such compartmentalisation may both fail to meet face to face the questions about their world that children perceive as important and lead to inferior teaching methods (Hirst 1974). Generally, teachers would seem to grant that some *basic* knowledge of reading, writing, and numeracy needs to be taught outside the topic lesson, but hold that the topic then provides a meaningful context within which such skills are used towards wider and more significant ends. In terms of epistemology, then, exponents of topic work would seem to espouse a particular view of knowledge. Topic work, then, has philo-sophical undertones, by no means always articulated by, or overtly espoused in the thinking of, the teacher – undertones which are apparently, though, indispensable to its effective execution.

TOPIC WORK: A WAY OF ORGANISING

We have seen that one attraction of topic work for teachers – but one not necessarily consciously espoused by them – is a philosophical one: the approach accords with an integrated view of knowledge popular in primary schools. This view has become particularly associated with the Plowden Report.

The influence of the examples on subsequent practice in schools across the nation is obvious. The theme of transport is quoted (para. 540) as a suitable topic for children. Starting lessons by using first-hand experiences of the physical environment of the school is advocated (para. 543). Visits outdoors to crops, ditches, woods, and verges are suggested (543). Building sites, museums, local shops, traffic counts, and exploring sewage works are, it is said, available as starting points for town children (544). Parks, buses, classroom pets – the list is instantly recognisable twenty years on (546–8).

The implication of all this is that the subject matter of education evolves, for primary children, from immediate starting points in first-hand experiences. Thus curriculum content is 'hung on the pegs' of these experiences. By definition, the overall content of a lesson or series of lessons becomes evolutionary: one can't determine, for example, whether it will snow tomorrow and if so whether the pupils will 'take off' from this point. The end-product, if they do 'take off', may also contain elements of mystery: the teacher cannot predict with absolute certainty whether the thinking will go in the direction of measuring volumes of melting snow or drawing snow-laden landscapes. So we move closer to a definition of what Plowden means by flexibility in this context. It is the ability of the teacher to anticipate, prepare for, encourage, and pursue as many relevant avenues of thinking as emerge spontaneously from the children's excitement with the snow. In traditional terms these avenues may, or may not, provide the children with insights that might be labelled scientific, aesthetic, linguistic, or mathematical. What is important – and it is surprising that Plowden does not give a passing mention to John Dewey at this point – is the *discovery* by the child of the experience of snow: 'The sense of personal discovery influences the intensity of a child's experience, the vividness of his memory and the probability of effective transfer of learning' (para. 549).

Topic work (Plowden calls it project work) is, on this view, a way of planning and organising teaching material. The criticism to which this approach is most vulnerable is its very strength, that is, that it relies on spontaneity. For example, it is hard for such potentially random triggers to learning to be moulded into a rounded curriculum. Plowden already had the seeds of the solution to the problem. The report advocated the compilation by schools of brief schemes and of lists of themes and experiences that had proved successful. These could be sifted and revised as required, while detailed syllabus planning was to be shunned as too prescriptive. But the goals of flexibility and openness to curriculum content idealised by Plowden were a hard pill to swallow since they gave no reassurance to heads or advisers who felt accountable for curriculum matters to the wider world; they did little to bolster the work of weak teachers; they failed to guide and induct new teachers or those with less than the required sensitivity and imagination. It was easier, if not in Plowden's terms as educationally desirable, to formalise the structures of curriculum. The successful themes or topics were repeated, and became the new wisdom, the *fait accompli* of primary curriculum. Interestingly, we can track the process by which this happened in one specific curriculum area; but first it may be as well to digress for a moment lest it be thought that a Plowden curriculum was wholly without a theoretical substructure to inform it.

We have seen that topic work in the 1980s, albeit unconsciously, could be seen to rest on a particular epistemology. In the same way, the Plowden curriculum rested heavily on a specific view of educational psychology – the Piagetian. Piaget's work demonstrated, despite doubts cast on it in some quarters, the existence of psychological stages of development. The stages are well known:

0–2 years	sensori-motor stage
c. 2–7 years	pre-operational stage
7/8–11/12 years	concrete operational stage
11/12–15 years	logical or formal reasoning stage.

Robin Alexander (1984) has expressed reservations about this approach to conceptualising the primary child and the approach to teaching at this age. Nevertheless, he acknowledges the strength of its appeal. Undoubtedly, implicit in Plowden is the use of this theory of maturation as the yardstick against which the concrete experiences of the child could be turned into appropriate learning experiences (para. 522). In this psychological theory of stages, and in the concept of flexibility of a curriculum derived from concrete experiences in the immediate present, there is a potent mix that spells topic or project; by contrast, in the inability of some teachers to cope with open-endedness is the necessity to identify and define suitable learning experiences for children of this age and how to exploit them. 'Hands', 'People who help us', 'Water', 'Sheep and shepherds', 'Spring' – these and other topics became the material for the, by now, predetermined 'spontaneous' experiences of the Plowden generation of primary pupils.

Topic work can, then, be or become a way of organising learning experiences and/or materials. Under the influence of Plowden the subject base of primary learning tended to be broadened. Primary learning was becoming more interdisciplinary, or integrated.

In curriculum terms, then, the topic has tended to subsume all but basic literacy and numeracy. The traditional disciplines do contribute both to subject matter and methodology, but the topic is what gives coherence to what is studied. Whether this trend has been adequately thought through, whether the traditional disciplines have lost out, and whether the movement is soundly based on a rational philosophy are questionable.

The failure of teachers to keep records of any kind was picked up by the questionnaire research carried out for our Schools Council project: 42 per cent of our sample admitted to not keeping any record whatsoever, and less than 10 per cent recorded *children's achievements* (as opposed to work covered, for example). In the evolutionary process, assessment in topic work has a long way to go to catch up.

REFERENCES

Alexander, R. J. (1984) *Primary teaching*, Holt, Rinehart & Winston, London.

Dearden, R. (1976) *Problems in primary education*, Routledge & Kegan Paul, London.

Dewey, J. (1910) *How we think*, Harrap, London.

Gunning, S., Gunning, D., and Wilson, J. (1981) *Topic teaching in the primary school*, Croom Helm, London.

Henley, M. (1984) 'The findings of the 9–13 middle school survey: a local authority view', *Westminster Studies in Education*, vol. 7, pp. 89–93

Hirst, P. H. (1974) *Knowledge and the curriculum*, Routledge & Kegan Paul, London.

Kilpatrick, W. H. (1918) 'The project method', *Teachers' College Record*, vol. 19, September.

Plowden Report (1967) *Children and their primary schools*, vol. 1, HMSO, London.

Stewart, J. (1986) *The making of the primary school*, Open University Press, Milton Keynes.

Chapter 24

Preserving integration within the national curriculum in primary schools
Approaching a school development plan

Anna Ryan

Following on from the last chapter, we have included here one school's attempts to retain an integrated topic approach within the national curriculum framework. The rationale for the approach is given in some detail, and we think it will be useful to evaluate the school's own plans in the light of the criteria presented here. In terms of manageability and coherence, it is difficult to see how the plans would work without knowing the context of other simultaneous curriculum plans, and it would be interesting to see how the school handled progression across the age phases. But the chapter does bring out the complexity of the curriculum planning task in schools, together with a warning on the inflexibility which might result. It also indicates clearly the need for whole-school curriculum development, within which teachers can plan for their own classes.

With the introduction of the national curriculum many primary schools fear the loss of integrated topic work which for so long purported to meet the educational needs of the 'whole' child. This paper takes seriously the notion that, although the national curriculum can be conceived in terms of subjects, it need not be delivered in subject-specific terms.

One approach to preserving integration within the national curriculum in primary schools, then, could be through the careful selection of topic work which ensures integrative potential. The topic must, without contrivance, be able to embrace a range of the curriculum, embody principles of the primary ethos and it must fall within the ambit of the national curriculum. The primary ethos, which underpins primary practice, encompasses the notion of child-centredness and a recognition that education in itself is intrinsically worthwhile (Blyth 1965). It implies a need for concrete operations – the child's active involvement in constructing his own learning (Bruner 1968; Piaget 1973). It emphasises the need to relate to the immediate, local, and everyday environment and experiences of the child (Bruner 1968; Patterson 1977; DES 1985). It involves the synthesis of content and process in building curricula, in pedagogy, and in evaluation criteria (Bernstein 1977; Brogden 1983; Morrison and Ridley 1988). It demonstrates the need for broad experiential learning (Rousseau 1762; Dewey 1910; Hughes and Grieve 1983; Blenkin and Kelly 1987). It encompasses a wide view of 'the basics' (CACE 1967; DES 1985; Tickle 1985). It indicates the need for integration in planning work, since a child's experiences are integrated rather than fragmented (CACE 1967; p. 199). It portrays the need for topic work as an epistemological basis for integrated work, which draws on Hirstian 'fields of knowledge' (Hirst 1975; Waters 1982; Schools Council 1983).

The move in assessment under TGAT requires both tests and tasks (TGAT 1988: para. 152–5). This latter means that tasks will have to be provided which are more open-ended than is, perhaps, usual, since children must have the opportunity of scoring at high levels, i.e. fewer ceilings fixed on planned work. Therefore, more problem-solving, open-ended activities should be included in the primary curriculum (TGAT 1988: para. 50).

ELEMENTS OF PLANNING

How, then, do we preserve integration within the national curriculum in primary schools? There is a variety of ways of developing integration in curricula. A fully integrated curriculum will have many defining features:

1 A topic-based approach, which draws several curriculum areas into a common focus (Pring 1976; Waters 1982; Dearden 1968).
2 An identification of common threads in the topic, defined in terms of:
   (1) Content-knowledge (Taba 1962; Entwistle 1970; Pring 1976; Barrow 1984).
   (2) Skills (Schools Council 1983; Alexander 1984; Blenkin and Kelly 1987; Morrison and Ridley 1988).
   (3) Problems (Blenkin and Kelly 1987; Morrison and Ridley 1988).
   (4) Cross-curricular themes (Pring 1976; Morrison and Ridley 1988).
   (5) Key concepts (Alexander 1984; Howard 1987).
   (6) Teaching and learning styles (Bernstein 1971; Kelly 1986; Morrison and Ridley 1988).
3 A recognition that some curriculum areas are intrinsically cross-curricular, e.g. language as a focus of learning is strongly cross-curricular (DES 1987). Science and the 'scientific method' is a way of working which lends itself to history/geography/art/craft and many of the problem-solving activities where a decided outcome or product is desired (DES 1985). An investigational approach is suitable for many areas of the curriculum, explaining issues where a fixed outcome is neither desired nor, perhaps, desirable, e.g. moral issues/ethical questions, religious issues, aesthetic judgements and appreciation, literary appreciation, inter-personal relations and social development, 'political' (small p) issues, where power and decision making are involved (Dewey 1910; Entwistle 1970).

Within these areas of integration lie several issues which integrated curricula will have to address. Planners for curriculum integration will need to address the various elements of an integrated approach, for example, integration can be achieved through key concepts, skills, problem solving and investigative approaches, cross-curricular themes, and teaching and learning styles. In considering 'key concepts' planners will have to consider:

a. what they are;
b. how they operate;
c. what are their attractions;
d. what are their weaknesses.

(Taba 1962)

Key concepts are abstractions which can be understood through a variety of curriculum areas, e.g. the concept of a settlement pattern can be approached by a study of history, or geography, or housing or topology, or employment or industrialisation, etc. The key concept of, for example, 'desertification' (ILEA 1981) can be understood through geography, political decision making (e.g. the debate about deforestation, the greenhouse effect, and the effects of capitalist economies on Third World poverty). Key concepts can operate at various levels of abstraction – e.g. 'settlement patterns' is more specific than, for example, causality, power, change, continuity. (All key concepts of history.) Key concepts operate by a process of astringency – they are organisational (as well as conceptual) devices for pulling together ideas which straddle a range of curriculum areas, e.g. the key concept of 'interdependence' or 'communication' or 'conflict' (Alexander 1984; Kelly 1986).

The attraction of key concepts is that they lend/bring coherence to the curriculum; they identify priorities; they are identifiable and communicable to children; they enable progression to be built into the curriculum through the notion of a 'spiral curriculum' (Bruner 1960). The weakness of key concepts is that they can be oversimplifications of complex issues; they can become too constraining on lines of development – forcing everything into the key concept such that the concept cannot fairly carry all of the material, or that they will limit some important lateral lines of curriculum development. The key concept might be so general as to be incomprehensible to the children, e.g. what do they understand by 'power' and 'change'? Is it so general that they fail to make the links to curriculum areas? (Schools Council 1972; Blyth *et al.* 1976). The message, then, for planners using key concepts, is to ensure that the advantages of coherence and progression are not lost to constraint and incomprehensibility.

The attraction of planning for a coherent teaching and learning style is its potential for active learning – a feature which lies at the heart of TGAT proposals on assessment – (tasks and co-operative working) and which allows continuity of learning (Blenkin and Kelly 1987). Against this feature is the concern that too great a degree of inflexibility and uniformity of teaching might result in being too prescriptive on teaching and learning styles, and that the value of novel or to-be-decided pedagogical styles might be ruled out. Teachers will wish to act on the dynamism of the situation rather than have it planned for them to the last degree.

Thus, when looking at the integrative potential of teaching and learning styles, a key set of features must surely be:

flexibility;
appropriacy to content and tasks;
potential for necessary *ad hoc* planning, to respond to the needs of individual teachers, children and curricula.

(Hamilton 1981)

IMPLEMENTING A TOPIC-BASED APPROACH TO PLANNING FOR THE NATIONAL CURRICULUM

It has been argued that the selection of the topic must have integrative potential, that it must fairly and without contrivance be able to embrace a range of the curriculum. Moreover, it must also address two other considerations outlined earlier – it must embody principles of the primary ethos and it must fall within the scope of the national curriculum.

One such topic which engages all three considerations is the study of the local community and environment. This would have several attractions:

- it would involve junior age children in work in and beyond the school;
- it would provide for concrete experiences;
- it would make for a variety of learning strategies;
- it would have the potential to develop skills in a variety of fields;
- it would have immediate relevance to the children;
- it would embrace many of the concerns of the 'programmes of study' in the national curriculum;
- it would enable process and content to merge;
- it would have potential for an integrated topic;
- it would have the potential for progression, continuity, and differentiation;
- it would be task-based so that TGAT-style assessment could be practised.

Having selected the topic, then a curriculum framework can be outlined for development, to cover:

- aims and objectives of the field of study;
- the content domains, e.g. the main areas of study embraced by the topic;
- the relationship of the topic to the national curriculum;
- the content domains worked out in terms of issues previously mentioned;
- the cross-curricular links and cross-curricular issues which permeate the topic;

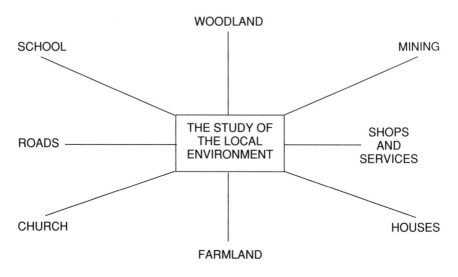

Figure 24.1 A topic web for main areas of study

- the pedagogical aspects of the content;
- the activities and tasks involved;
- the criteria for assessing and evaluating curricula and children in the topic;
- the resources (internal and external to the school) which can be used.

The task, then, of the development of a curriculum content plan will require a context of the main areas into which this project could fragment, to cover, for example, shops, houses, churches, woodland, farms, mining, and roads (see Figure 24.1). This topic web is familiar ground for primary teachers.

Within these areas, the 'thrust of the curriculum area' would have to be decided, e.g. historical/geographical/environmental/scientific. This presupposes, perhaps, an identification of key concepts in the main curriculum areas of the national curriculum. While this can be done straightforwardly for the published areas of the national curriculum to date – mathematics, English, and science – the other areas remain speculative. For example, in history, geography, and environmental studies, key concepts could be stated thus:

- communication;
- power;
- values, beliefs, and traditions;
- conflict/consensus;
- similarity/difference;
- continuity/change;
- cause and consequence;

- co-operation and interdependence;
- modification.

To give greater guidance on the initial stages of coverage, i.e. the balance of the curriculum, the notion of matrix planning can be usefully employed, where for each topic domain a set of matrices can be drawn. This is exemplified in Figure 24.2.

One can see how matrix planning will allow the content of the curriculum topic to be embraced within the national curriculum. It also enables the curriculum planner to see immediately the coverage, breadth, and balance of the topic, to highlight areas of emphasis or neglect. The next stage is to break the overall topic into specific sub-topics and set out key concepts for each specific sub-topic as in Figure 24.3.

These sub-topics can then be broken down again into smaller content areas as in Figure 24.4.

For each specific area and component element (i.e. Figures 24.3 and 24.4) the curriculum planner can then match the issue to the documentation on attainment targets given in the national curriculum, e.g. mathematics, science, and language. This has been exemplified in Figure 24.5.

Taking into account the various divisions and sub-divisions of Figures 24.3, 24.4, and 24.5, the next stage is to relate all this to the very specific attainment targets of the national curriculum.

Within this matrix of national curriculum attainment targets are specific levels for each attainment target so that, although planning starts from the very wide and general, it moves to being very specific. As part of that movement, the specificity comes through relating it to the national curriculum.

One must be aware, of course, that this approach to planning is

1 time consuming but necessary;
2 it also involves a whole-school approach to ensure continuity and progression through the various levels.

By detailing very specifically and logically the breakdown of curricula from generalities to specificities it also clarifies the criteria by which children's progress may be judged. In this respect planned teaching tasks also become planned assessment tasks (Gott 1989), perhaps one of the strengths of the national curriculum.

	Maths	Science	Lang.	Music	Geography	PE	CDT	History	Art
Houses	✓	✓	✓		✓		✓	✓	✓
Churches	✓	✓	✓	✓	✓		✓	✓	✓
Schools	✓	✓	✓	✓	✓		✓	✓	✓
Woodland	✓	✓	✓	✓	✓	✓	✓		✓
Farming	✓	✓	✓	✓	✓		✓	✓	✓
Mining	✓	✓	✓		✓		✓	✓	✓
Roads	✓	✓	✓		✓		✓		✓
Shops	✓	✓	✓		✓		✓	✓	✓

Figure 24.2 A matrix to display curriculum areas covered by the topic

	Communication	Power	Values & beliefs	Conflict/consensus	Similarity/difference	Continuity/change	Cause & consequence	Co-operation & interdependence	Modification
Houses	Telephone Postal service	Electric Gas	Council/Private housing	Location Style	House types Comparability of materials	Structure Design Sanitation Services Materials	Legislation over-crowding	Flats Maisonette Terrace	Materials Structure Design
Churches	Music liturgy	Church leaders	Religious belief	of religious beliefs	of belief and ritual	Design Function	of doctrinal issues and of design issues	The church Community	To design Belief
Schools	Written Electronic postal vocal	Authority	Ethos Aims	Values Beliefs Practices	Types of curricula	Purpose Design Curricula	of educational reform	Ethos	Design Practices Content
Woodland	Bird and animal sounds	Power saws Control of environment	Conservation and land use	Siting and land use Deforestation Conservation	Types of woodland Animal and bird life	Conservation and land use	of deforestation Acid rain	Ecology	Ecology
Farming	Vehicles cart tracks	Water power Heavy duty tractors Control of environment	Conservation and land use Conservation	Ecology Chemical agriculture methods	Types of farming and farming aids, methods	Conservation Land use Mechanical engineering	of chemical use, of genetic	Ecology	Ecology
Mining	Telephones railways road and river haulage	Coal power Oil and gas power	Land use and spoilage Opencast	Exploitation of workers Pollution	Types of mining Changes over time	Methods Conditions Output	of safety and hazards of improved technology	Working together	Technology and conditions
Roads	Major and minor motorways, location	Horse and car power Trucks	Land use Siting Location	Siting Location Leaded petrol	Types of road Location	Increase of roads, Road traffic types	of increased traffic and traffic types	Networks and services	Design Number Size
Shops	Community service	Fridges Heat Light Escalators	Competition or co-operation	Capitalism	Types Size Purpose Content	Content Wealth Selling methods	of health acts and consumer protection	Competition and service	Size Service Content

KEY CONCEPTS

Figure 24.3 A matrix to display key concepts of topic areas

Key Areas / Houses							
Structure and forces	Load bearing	Height	Materials	Lifting and covering			
Building design	changes	over	history →				↑
Amenities and services	Water	Electricity	Oil	Gas	Sanitation	Light Space Ventilation	Health
Location		House types and location	Council estates	Private/council			
Windows, doors, walls, chimneys	Windows	Doors	Walls	Chimneys	Roofs	Gates	Garden/yards
Materials	Brick, stone wood, glass, metals, tile, plastic, mud, breeze blocks	Tests for comparability strength ↑	Porosity ↑	Waterproofing Drying Insulation	Expansion Contraction	Weight and density	Flexibility/sound-proofing
Types	Terrace	Semi-detached	Detached	Maisonette	Flat	Sheltered accommodation	Castles Palaces
Size	Small →		↑	Grand			
Historical change	Mud huts and caves	Roman	Norman	Medieval	Tudor/Stuart	Georgian Regency	Victorian pre-war Modern

Figure 24.4 A matrix to display key areas within a sub-topic

Key concepts from A.T. in N.C. / Maths	Selecting, Estimating, Explaining, Testing predictions	Solving problems Knowing and recognising Choosing and interpreting Sorting, symmetry	Extracting, entering and accessing information in simple database	Using and applying maths – select, plan, understanding	Co-ordinate representation of points, angles, scale, area
	Collecting, grouping, understanding, calculating and interrogating data	Constructing and interpreting graphs, understanding and using probability	Selecting, interpreting material, using unitary ratio, calculating	Expressing simple functions symbolically	Estimating, converting scale, designing, collating, constructing
Science Compare localities		Structural features of organisms	Physical factors affecting plant growth	Environmental effects of human activity	Relationship between materials and how they are used
Materials – rocks, minerals, soils and erosion		Investigate the strength of shapes and structures	Constructing circuits and research on mains electricity	Investigating transmission and storage of information using computers, sensors and telephones	Fuels and energy sources and origin Light, sound, solar system
Language Giving and responding to increasingly precise instructions Discussion and listening		Formulating, asking and responding to questions e.g. data collecting	Group work involving predicting, speculating and hypothesising, reporting, accounting and summarising	Presenting ideas Experiences and understanding in contexts Audience awareness	Using evidence to support argument, viewpoint, developing coherent argument
Group participation Audio-visual presentation to an audience		Reading and discussion Use of reference material	Organisation of information and presentation using variety of media	understand key points in a particular passage	Reflection on reading in a thoughtful way

Figure 24.5 A matrix to link key concepts and national curriculum areas

REFERENCES

Alexander, R. J. (1984) *Primary Teaching*, Holt, Rinehart & Winston, Eastbourne.
Barrow, R. (1984) *Giving Teaching Back to Teachers*, Wheatsheaf Books, Sussex.
Bernstein, B. (1971) On the Classification and Framing of Educational Knowledge, in M. F. D. Young (ed.) *Knowledge and Control*, Collier Macmillan, London.
Bernstein, B. (1977) Class and Pedagogies: visible and invisible, in B. Bernstein (ed.) *Class, Codes and Control*, Routledge & Kegan Paul, London.
Blenkin, G. M. and Kelly, A. V. (1987) *The Primary Curriculum – a Process Approach to Curriculum Planning*, Harper & Row, London.
Blyth, W. A. L. (1965) *English Primary Education*, Vol. 1, Routledge & Kegan Paul, London.
Blyth, W. A. L. *et al.* (1976) *Place, Time and Society 8–13; Curriculum Planning in History, Geography and Social Science*, Collins and ESL Bristol, Glasgow and Bristol.
Brogden, M. (1983) Open Plan Primary Schools: rhetoric and reality. *School Organisation*, Vol. 3, No. 1, pp. 27–31.
Bruner, J. S. (1960) *The Process of Education*, Vintage Books, Random House, New York.
Bruner, J. S. (1968) *Towards a Theory of Instruction*, Norton, New York.
Central Advisory Council for Education (1967) *Children and their Primary Schools* (Plowden Report) HMSO, London.
Dearden, R. F. (1968) *The Philosophy of Primary Education*, Routledge & Kegan Paul, London.
DES (1985) *The Curriculum from 5–16*, Curriculum Matters 2, HMSO, London.
DES (1987) *The National Curriculum 5–16; A Consultation Document*, HMSO, London.
Dewey, J. (1910) *How We Think*, Boston, Heath.
Entwistle, H. (1970) *Problem-solving in the Primary School*, Blackwell, London.
Gott, R. (1989) The National Curriculum – Some Implications for Science Teachers, in *Working Within the Act*, Education Reform Act 1988–?, Educational Publishing Services, Ouston, Durham.
Hamilton, D. (1981) *In Search of Structure*, Scottish Council for Research in Education, Lindsay, Edinburgh.
Hirst, P. H. (1975) The Curriculum and Its Objectives – a defence of piecemeal rational planning. *The Doris Lee Lectures*, University of London Press.
Howard, R. W. (1987) *Concepts and Schemata – an introduction*, Cassell Education, London.
Hughes, M. and Grieve, R. (1983) On Asking Children Bizarre Questions, in Donaldson *et al.* (1983) *Early Childhood Development and Education: Readings in Psychology*, Blackwell, Oxford.
ILEA (1981) *The Study of Places in the Primary School*, ILEA Curriculum Guidelines, ILEA, London.
Kelly, A. V. (1986) *Knowledge and Curriculum Planning*, Harper & Row, London.
Morrison, K. R. B. and Ridley, K. (1988) *Curriculum Planning and the Primary School*, Paul Chapman, London.
Patterson, C. H. (1977) *Foundations for a Theory of Instruction and Educational Psychology*, Harper & Row, New York.
Piaget, J. (1973) *To Understand is to Invent*, Grossman, New York.
Pring, R. (1976) *Curriculum Organisation*, E203, Units 11–13, Open University Press, Milton Keynes.

Rousseau, J. J. (1762) *Emile* (translated by B. Foxley) London: Dent (Everyman's Library), 1911.

Schools Council (1972) *Exploration Man, An Introduction to Integrated Studies*, Oxford University Press, Oxford.

Schools Council (1983) *Primary Practice*, working paper 75, Methuen, London.

Taba, H. (1962) *Curriculum Development: Theory and Practice*, Harcourt, Brace & World, New York.

Task Group on Assessment and Testing (1988) *A Report*, London, HMSO.

Tickle, L. (1985) From Class Teachers to Specialist Teachers: curriculum continuity and school organisation, in R. Derricot (ed.) *Curriculum Continuity: Primary to Secondary*, NFER – Nelson, Windsor.

Waters, D. (1982) *Primary Schools Projects*, Heinemann Educational, London.

Chapter 25

Successful topic work

OFSTED

Following the introduction of the national curriculum, HMI identified six factors which their survey of practice in primary schools showed to be related to successful topic work. It is interesting to note that the factors relate to team work among staff, but make no reference to co-operative work among pupils or to the involvement of pupils in planning. Looking back to the earlier chapter on topic work by Kerry and Eggleston, how does the OFSTED list relate to the approach to topic work outlined there? In what ways does the structure of the national curriculum appear to have shaped and changed topic planning?

FACTORS ASSOCIATED WITH SUCCESSFUL TOPIC WORK

1 An agreed system of planning which is consistent and carefully structured, thus helping to ensure continuity and progression.
2 A degree of co-operation in planning which provides an opportunity for teachers to share the workload and their expertise.
3 Careful account taken of national curriculum requirements (the programmes of study as well as the attainment targets). Topics are usually chosen to fit national curriculum attainment targets and programmes of study, rather than the other way around. Attainment targets or aspects of attainment targets that do not fit in readily are taught separately.
4 Topics have a single subject bias or emphasise particular subjects.
5 Whole-school agreement about subject coverage and the balance between subjects and topics, the outcomes of which are monitored by members of the senior management team.
6 The planning refers to learning outcomes or objectives, activities and assessment.

Chapter 26

The classteacher and the curriculum

Robin Alexander

Here, Robin Alexander claims that there is a reason for primary teachers' commitment to topic planning other than those suggested in earlier chapters. He suggests that it is primary teachers' lack of sufficient subject knowledge which makes them enthusiastic for integrated approaches to the curriculum. Not being 'subject specialists', generalist classteachers have had to develop a role for themselves as specialists in 'child development', he argues. From our earlier chapters, it is clear that there are other advantages and rationales for an integrated approach to the curriculum (see Chapter 20 by Martin Skilbeck, for example). However, it seems true that there has been an emphasis on 'basic skills' in literacy and numeracy in most primary schools, alongside an 'integrated' approach to other subjects. In view of this, what might be the implications of a 'core' curriculum reduced to 'essentials', as proposed by the National Curriculum Council in 1993 (see introduction to Martin Skilbeck's chapter)?

The most obvious indicator of curriculum priority is the amount of time spent by the child in each area. However, while in secondary schools such calculations are straightforward, and a timetable analysis will suffice (see Wilcox and Eustace 1981), in primary schools time allocations are more difficult to ascertain. There are four reasons for this. First, the classteacher system enables teachers to be highly flexible from one day or week to the next whereas a published secondary timetable is necessarily rigid and predictable: thus the typical week, let alone the typical day, may be hard to define. Second, variation in curriculum emphasis: one child might be having extra remedial reading while others at the same time are undertaking a topic. Third, the organisational practice of having different activities going on simultaneously makes the recording of time allocations very difficult. Fourth, there is the ideological disinclination of many primary teachers to define their teaching in terms of others' curriculum labels.

These difficulties seem to be reflected most prominently in the analysis by Bassey (1978) of infant pupils' activities. Precise figures are given for the 'general activities' of 'class talk', 'play time', 'administration' and so on, but

Table 26.1

Curriculum area	Average number of hours per week for pupil	Percentage
Language	7	30.4
Mathematics	5	21.7
Thematic studies	4	17.4
Physical education	3	13.0
Art and craft	2	8.7
Music	1	4.3

Source: Bassey 1978: 28

not for the conventional curriculum areas of mathematics, language, and the rest. In contrast the figures from his junior teachers were unambiguous (see Table 26.1).

In other words, in crude numerical terms, the 'basics' of language and mathematics take up something over half the child's time, and everyday observations readily confirm in particular the practice of giving children one hour of mathematics every day of the week, usually in the morning (when the child, supposedly, is 'fresh': when he is tired he can undertake art, music, science, and the other 'non-basic' activities).

The concept of 'basics' reflects curriculum priorities, a view that certain curriculum experiences have more value than others. Educational priorities are to be expected in every society. But since our particular society is far from static or monolithic as to values, social structure, and economic circumstances, one might equally expect curriculum priorities to be neither permanent nor wholly clear-cut.

Instead we have a curriculum firmly divided, for over a century of tumultuous change, into two parts: the high priority areas of 'basic skills' which are defined as reading, writing, and mathematics, and the lower priority areas of creative and expressive arts, social and environmental studies, scientific understanding, moral and religious education, physical education, and so on. The operational divide is reinforced in primary discourse; the validity of the hierarchy, and the primacy of the activities which are defined as so much more 'basic' than others to the education of children between the ages of 5 and 11, are rarely questioned.

What the established and emerging codified, objectified quasi *a priori* primary curriculum areas have in common, therefore, is not a pre-existing 'subject' character but status as 'basics'. The pattern is clear and consistent: in acquiring 'basic' status, areas of learning divest themselves of integrationist attributes and empiricist claims and become, to all intents and purposes, separate subjects. Thus, currently, primary science is at an interim point in this process, changing from an ill-defined aspect of environmental studies into a distinctive field of activity for which the unambiguous subject label 'science' can increasingly be used in professional discourse and school timetabling without fear of that ideological backlash or professional embarrassment to which I referred earlier.

That divide between 'basics' and 'the rest', then, is accentuated structurally by a tendency for the former to have subject characteristics and for the latter to be more likely to be integrated, except in areas like music and physical education, where the necessity for a location other than the children's home base or classroom, and sometimes the use of specialist teaching, will provide at least the timetabled distinctiveness of a 'subject' if not the structural elaboration of subjects like mathematics and reading.

CURRICULUM CONCEPTIONS AND PROFESSIONAL KNOWLEDGE

The anti-subject view is strongest in relation to the 'beyond the basics' curriculum, particularly in the creative and expressive arts and social/environmental studies: in the 'basics', in contrast, we have seen that there are substantial subject divisions yet, paradoxically, the arguments about 'naturalness' 'artificiality', the 'child's view of the world', 'little boxes', and so on appear not to apply except to some extent as pedagogical rather than epistemological principles (e.g. 'concrete to abstract'). Two further points need to be noted: first, that this 'beyond the basics' area is that most heavily criticised by HMI (DES 1978, 1982) for superficiality and lack of progression in learning; and second, that this area receives the least attention in initial teacher training.

HMI's own diagnosis is that professional knowledge in arts and humanities education is insufficient for the task even of non-specialist primary teaching (DES 1978, 1982, 1983). The diagnosis is shared by Sybil Marshall:

> While 'poems' are extracted daily from anyone old enough to hold a pencil, very little poetry is pumped back into them. (The same goes, all too often, for story, drama, music and art.) Time is one enemy, but the other is quite often the paucity of the teacher's own knowledge of and liking for poetry.
>
> (Marshall 1978: 46)

Other writers and reports take a similar view. The Gulbenkian Report (1982) pursues the issue further: the teacher's curriculum knowledge and understanding influences not only the quality of children's learning but the teacher's curriculum values and priorities. Gulbenkian found art frequently perceived as a pleasurable and mildly cathartic, but, in the end, frivolous and inessential activity, given low priority in primary schools (Gulbenkian 1982: 49).

Such recent empirical study as we now have on primary practice cumulatively provokes three related hypotheses:

1 What teachers do not adequately understand they are unlikely to teach well.

2 What teachers do not value they are unlikely to teach well.

3 What teachers do not understand they are unlikely to value.

Together these hypotheses are suggestive of a downward spiral of ignorance or insecurity, low valuation and inadequate practice. On this diagnosis it will be hardly surprising if the qualitative and conceptual divide in primary education between the 'basics' and 'the rest' does not increase, for the differentiation is being reinforced at initial and in-service levels. Teachers' curriculum knowledge in mathematics, reading, written and spoken language, and latterly science, is being strengthened, but increased attention to these areas is frequently at the expense of others.

A final point on this matter: a substantial deficiency in curriculum/professional knowledge effectively negates the primary teacher's claim to be in a position to make valid judgements about priorities in the 'whole curriculum' for which, as a class teacher, he is responsible. Someone who knows little of, say, music, art, or moral education, hardly has the right, let alone the competence, to decide what proportion of the child's total curriculum shall be devoted to these areas.

'CHILD, NOT SUBJECT': A HYPOTHESIS

If at the individual classteacher level it is possible to argue a relationship between the teacher's curriculum knowledge, the quality of children's learning and the teacher's curriculum priorities, a more general hypothesis relating to 'integration' and 'subjects' becomes available.

Bernstein (1971) suggests that the breaking down of subject barriers to achieve integration is resisted because it threatens the professional identity on the basis of which the subject specialist's institutional and professional status is secured and legitimised. This hypothesis applies wherever professional expertise is defined in specialist subject terms – secondary schools and higher education, for instance. At the primary stage, one can now hypothesise, a similar process operates, but in reverse. Here, the *erection* of subject barriers poses the threat, because in this case the teacher may *lack* the requisite specialist knowledge. On the basis of such generalised curriculum knowledge as he has, the only defensible curriculum is an integrated one with low 'boundaries' or, where subject insecurity is greatest, an undifferentiated one which does not even admit the validity of subjects.

Thus 'we teach children, not subjects' becomes both defence and legitimation of the lack of curriculum knowledge, and an alternative source of professional identity and self-esteem in as far as every professional needs to rest his professional claim on 'expert' knowledge of some sort. The attraction of developmental psychology, which is widely accepted as the most essential professional knowledge for primary teaching, is that it is self-evidently 'knowledge' in the conventional academic sense, and this makes respectable what might otherwise seem mere romantic assertion. King's 'ideology' (1978) of sequential developmentalism, childhood innocence, play as learning, and individualism can thus present itself not as ideology but as a legitimate species of expert knowledge, a 'science' of teaching: 'research has proved that this is the way children are'. And, just as King postulates that the 'home/family theory' enables the blame for discrepancies between the idealised and the actual child to be shifted away from the teacher, so the anti-subject element in the ideology enables curriculum deficiencies to be explained away.

Furthermore, the alternative professional knowledge of 'children, not subjects' provides a parallel basis for boundary erection and maintenance to that of secondary subjects. For developmentalism is strongly structured, both vertically (intellectual, aesthetic, social, physical, moral, emotional, etc.) and, especially, horizontally (ages, stages, and 'levels'), so that while at secondary level it is the boundaries of subjects which are maintained, at primary level it is the boundaries of expertise relating to developmental 'levels'. On this basis, King's finding that junior teachers were regarded by infant teachers as strongly deviant is explained, as is the sometimes strong boundary maintenance of infant departments in teacher education institutions: for among staff in such departments, subject knowledge is likely to be thin.

The discrepancy I have noted between the subject characteristics of the 'basics' and the frequently integrated/undifferentiated character of much of the rest of the curriculum does not undermine the hypothesis, but supports it; for, as we have seen, professional knowledge in primary mathematics and language/literacy is relatively substantial (though not necessarily wholly adequate) and is supported by highly structured schemes and materials. Subject boundaries here pose no threat. Although primary teachers have individual curriculum strengths, reflecting interest and educational background, collectively they are best equipped in respect of the basics. Thus, they represent not so much a reversal of the Bernstein hypothesis as a more complex variant upon it: increasingly the primary teacher is both specialist (basics) and generalist (the rest), and the primary curriculum as generally enacted mirrors this exactly (basics as subjects, the rest as mostly undifferentiated or integrated). At the same time both the insecurity in respect of the generalist areas and the overall inconsistency of argument in relation to subjects/integration can be rationalised and legitimised in terms of the claim to professional expertise in children rather than subjects.

REFERENCES

Bassey, M. (1978) *Nine Hundred Primary School Teachers*. Slough: NFER.

Bernstein, B. (1971) On the classification and framing of educational knowledge. In Young. M.F.D. (ed.) *Knowledge and Control*, pp. 47–69. West Drayton: Collier Macmillan.

Department of Education and Science (1978) *Primary Education in England: a Survey by HM Inspectors of Schools*. London: HMSO.

Department of Education and Science (1982) *Education 5–9: an Illustrative Survey of 80 First Schools in England*. London: HMSO.

Department of Education and Science (1983) *Teaching in Schools: the Content of Initial Training*. London: HMSO.

Gulbenkian Foundation (1982) *The Arts in Schools: Principles, Practice and Provision*. London: Gulbenkian Foundation

King, R. (1978) *All Things Bright and Beautiful? A Sociological Study of Infants' Classrooms*. Chichester: Wiley.

Marshall, S. (1978) Language – Arts?, *Education 3–13*, 4, 1.

Wilcox, B. and Eustace, P.J. (1981) *Tooling Up for Curriculum Review*. Slough: NFER.

Chapter 27

Teachers' subject knowledge

Ted Wragg

How far is it true that primary teachers lack confidence in teaching the full primary curriculum? As part of the Leverhulme Primary Project, two national surveys were carried out immediately after the 1988 Education Act and two years later, with 901 and 433 teachers responding respectively. Perhaps unsurprisingly at a time of rapid curriculum change, the results showed most teachers uncertain about certain curriculum areas, especially those subjects with newly published programmes of study. This chapter also shows the ways in which experienced teachers went about teaching a topic for the first time, when they felt uncertain about their own subject knowledge in that area. It suggests the need for sound initial and in-service training across curriculum areas, but also the need for support easily accessible within the school, from either a subject specialist on the staff or a local authority advisory teacher. It also shows, however, the commitment of primary teachers to extend their knowledge and skills to meet the needs of their pupils. In what ways might schools respond best to this commitment while also making best use of subject specialists on the staff?

In the first stage of a two-part national survey of primary teachers in England, following the 1988 Education Act which introduced a structured national curriculum for the first time, a stratified random sample of 901 teachers in 152 schools replied to a lengthy questionnaire which sought information about how competent teachers felt to teach the ten subjects in the primary curriculum with their existing subject knowledge (Wragg et al. 1989). The response rate was 72 per cent (152 out of 212 schools approached). Teachers were asked about the nine subjects in the national curriculum – art, design and technology, English, geography, history, mathematics, music, physical education, and science, as well as religious education which had been a compulsory subject since the 1944 Education Act. Two years later, follow-up questionnaires were sent to many of the same schools, though not to all, as some had indicated that they did not wish to take part in a second survey.

Table 27.1 Percentage of teachers feeling competent with existing knowledge and skills in each of ten subjects in 1989 national survey and 1991 follow-up

Subject	1989 survey (n=901)		1991 follow-up (n=433)	
	%	Rank	%	Rank
English	81	1	77	1
Mathematics	68	2	62	2
History	54	3	38	5
Geography	48	4	36	7
Art	48	5	40	4
Physical education	47	6	37	6
Religious education	45	7	33	8
Science	34	8	41	3
Music	27	9	23	9
Technology	14	10	14	10

The results of the two surveys on the question about each of the ten subjects primary teachers are required to teach are shown in Table 27.1. Only category 1 responses are shown, that is, those believing they are competent to teach the subject with their existing knowledge.

Relatively little movement was noted in half the subjects, the rank order of English and maths (1st and 2nd), physical education (6th), and music and technology (9th and 10th) remaining the same. Science moved up from 8th position to 3rd in the two-year period, explained to some extent by the fact that many teachers had spent two years teaching the new science curriculum, but technology remained rooted firmly at the bottom of the list on 14 per cent. The percentage of teachers feeling competent dropped in all other eight subjects, and this was especially noticeable in history (54 per cent down to 38 per cent) and geography (48 per cent down to 36 per cent), where the final subject syllabuses, both of which were wide-ranging and full of subject knowledge demands, were published just before teachers filled in the follow-up questionnaire.

It was not surprising that teachers demonstrated such low confidence in their own knowledge in subjects such as science, music, and technology. Analysis of the main subject specialisms of teachers in the first sample had revealed that only 8 per cent had majored in science, only 7 per cent in music, and a tiny 0.3 per cent in technology. Over half had an arts/ humanities background. Study of responses to specific topics in science and technology showed a wide range, from about 75 per cent feeling able to teach the 'water cycle' or 'looking after living things' with their existing knowledge down to 10 or 20 per cent for topics such as 'adding to a database' or 'using graphics to develop new ideas' or 'using microelectronic kits'. Under half felt competent to teach electrical circuits or the use of power sources.

Comparisons between groups of respondents showed that male teachers expressed greater feelings of competence than female teachers in science and technology, and women felt more competent than men at art, English, music, and religious education.

In view of the special problems in science and technology, we decided to study a sample of teachers who were teaching certain topics in these fields for the very first time. This involved a study of teachers who had little or no experience of teaching a topic like electricity. Twelve schools in one region, randomly chosen from lists of schools in each of four categories, were approached. The four categories were large urban, small urban, large rural, and small rural. Ten teachers of 7- to 11-year-olds who had never, or only rarely, taught physical science topics such as magnetism and electricity agreed to be observed and interviewed about their experiences teaching the topic 'electricity'. In addition, we studied two teachers teaching technology to 6- to 8-year-olds for the first time.

TEACHING SCIENCE AND TECHNOLOGY

Most of the twelve teachers in the sample were apprehensive about teaching physical science and technology topics they had not taught before. As few primary schools had all the necessary equipment we decided to provide sets of circuit boards and components. Only two of the teachers felt they would have been able to make a start on the teaching of electricity with their school's existing equipment. Four basic kits were provided, consisting of circuit boards, batteries, bulbs, switches, and wires. Written notes for sets of activities, which covered four of the attainment statements of the national curriculum, were also offered. Teachers had a free choice about how they taught, some choosing to teach the topic as a self-contained set of activities, others incorporating it into a project on 'energy'. The two teachers who were observed teaching technology had a completely free hand in their choice of topic or activity.

Interviews were held before the teaching began and after the observation of lessons. Teachers were asked how they decided on their approach, how effectively they felt they had handled the lessons, what difficulties they had encountered, how the pupils had responded, how they handled children's questions, and what support they had found or felt they would have needed.

There was considerable apprehension before the teaching began. Comments included: 'Horror! I haven't taught it before' and 'It's a challenge. Everything in education is a challenge. Children . . . they've got to meet it, so why not the staff?' Most teachers turned to other people for help, rather than to books. Few found the children's books available in their library to be adequate for the pupils, let alone themselves, but in any case their greatest need was for a *person*, usually the school's science co-ordinator, but it could also be any fellow adult who was knowledgeable, so a spouse, a pupil's parent, a school governor who was a science graduate, and a teacher from a nearby secondary school who came in to answer questions once a month were all cited as sources of information.

Some teachers confessed their ignorance to the class immediately. One began, 'Look, I've got to be honest with you. I know nothing about electricity. I can just about change a fuse.' Classes of up to thirty-six were observed and teachers established groups of from two pupils up to six to work on the units. It soon became clear that most teachers had to spend a great deal of time on preparation, except for one who said, 'It's dreadful [laugh]. It's dreadful for two reasons. One, I haven't spent a lot of time preparing for it. It's one of the many things that are going on . . . um, what else? . . . I just feel so lacking in confidence about the whole thing . . . I don't know what I would do without David [a former school governor who had offered to help].'

The two most perplexing problems faced by these teachers were, first of all, not knowing the relevant scientific principles and, secondly, inability to cope with pupils' questions: 'Loads of questions. "Why is this happening?" "Why isn't this working?" Mostly to do with the practical and lots of questions about the actual theory of it.' One teacher simply referred children back to the written notes when any query came up and asked them to see if they could find the answer themselves. Others were perplexed and bemused by the mysteries of electricity: 'I can't understand why, when one battery (of three) is put in backwards, the lamp still lights up.'

Despite their anxieties some teachers were quite prepared to take on adventurous looking projects which took them and their class way beyond their own subject competence. The routes through the specified attainment statements were varied, but some classes went on to make a burglar alarm, dolls' house lights and one teacher even strayed, unwittingly, into topics normally covered by much older pupils, like series and parallel circuits, electricity generation and distribution to domestic and industrial premises.

The actual attainment statements which teachers had to cover included eight mentions of specific cognitive skills, such as knowing, understanding, describing, and recording. There were also the practical skills of constructing a simple electrical circuit, varying the flow of the current, and observing what was happening. Most teachers gave emphasis to the actual practical activities, but little systematic checking of understanding was observed. On the other hand, teachers' own observations influenced their judgement about how effective the lessons had been, some commenting specifically on children's enthusiasm, or the value to lower attaining pupils: 'James did *very* well the first time. He's not a high achiever usually, but I presume that was previous knowledge that he'd had. He set up a circuit very, very quickly and got the switch in, and a light-emitting diode.' Less able children performing well on a practical activity where the teacher herself was not secure was a great surprise to some teachers. One commented on the case of a boy with special educational needs who showed such manipulative skill he was appointed 'leader' by the rest of his group, an event that had not occurred previously. Another low achieving pupil asked if she could take away bulbs and batteries so she could work on them at home.

Aware of the many demands on them once the lesson started, most teachers prepared in far greater detail than for other activities in their day. One teacher described how she stayed up until past midnight practising with the electricity kits until she felt confident enough to supervise use by others. Even then she simply omitted reference to topics or concepts she did not herself understand: 'amps, volts, wattage, atomic structure. . . . Perhaps I should have. I would have gone to the *Oxford English Dictionary* if I'd had to teach it.'

Experiments in technology were similar. One teacher was observed working with children who were designing an egg holder. When one pupil decided to use the centre of a kitchen roll to hold his egg and then had to pack enormous amounts of plasticine around its base to hold it firm, eventually having to give up and even tape the egg on the top to prevent it falling off, she never discussed design principles or such notions as 'centre of gravity'. Yet in other subject areas she was competent and proficient.

Another technology lesson involved the making of kites, where children first designed and then made kites out of wood veneer and tissue paper. Seven-year-old children were not, in this school, allowed to use sharp scissors, so there was considerable frustration among them as they found the delicate paper tearing when they cut it with blunt round scissors. The teacher had little idea whether to intervene and cut out the shapes for each child or to give them extra paper so they could try again. Nor were explanations forthcoming about why some kites flew well and others did not.

Despite the difficulties most teachers claimed afterwards they had enjoyed the experience: 'We're all so excited. We've loved doing this.' 'In the main (it has gone) quite well. But, left to their own devices, we got some very complicated circuits. Everyone enjoyed it.' 'I'm quite excited about it now, because you can see their results . . . what they can discuss with you. So now I say to colleagues "Well, now look at me. I'm a prime example of someone who panicked. I'll look forward to doing it again." '

The picture in this story is a clear one. Most teachers were enthusiastic, if still apprehensive, about their experiences teaching a new topic for the first time, but their own lack of knowledge raised problems. Outside the classroom these were resolved through lengthy preparation and recourse to people such as science co-ordinator, governors, parents even, who possessed the knowledge they lacked. Inside the classroom most were perplexed by not knowing the relevant scientific principles and by pupils' questions, many of which were unanticipated or unpredictable. The most common coping strategies were evasion, that is avoiding altogether subject matter not properly known, and turning children back on their own devices, asking them to improvise a solution themselves, or offering to find out for a future lesson. Particularly bewildering, if gratifying, to some teachers was the unexpected competence of certain of their pupils, thought to be slower learners, when faced with a practical activity in which the teacher herself was not well schooled.

REFERENCE

Wragg, E. C. *et al.* (1989) 'Primary teachers and the national curriculum', *Research Papers in Education* 4(3): 17–45.

Chapter 28

Assessment and the improvement of education

Wynne Harlen, Caroline Gipps, Patricia Broadfoot, and Desmond Nuttall

This chapter starts from the assumption that assessment is essential to effective education in a number of ways. It was produced by a policy task group working for the British Educational Research Association (BERA) in 1992, in response to criticisms of the existing assessment arrangements being implemented following the 1988 Education Act. It sets out its own proposals for alternative ways of providing national assessments of learning in schools, matched to a range of different purposes. We think that this chapter offers a framework for examining national curriculum 'testing' as it evolves; allowing us to ask questions such as: For what purpose is this assessment being carried out? Is this the best form of assessment for that purpose? How much and which parts of the curriculum does it assess? How clear is this made to parents and others reading the results? What is its likely effect on the curriculum? How far is it diagnostic, thus supporting improvements in teaching? If it is to judge the effectiveness of schools, how far is it responsive to the local context in which learning is taking place?

Assessment in education is the process of gathering, interpreting, recording, and using information about pupils' responses to an educational task. At one end of a dimension of formality, the task may be normal classroom work and the process of gathering information would be the teacher reading a pupil's work or listening to what he or she has to say. At the other end of the dimension of formality, the task may be a written, timed examination which is read and marked according to certain rules and regulations. Thus assessment encompasses responses to regular work as well as to specially devised tasks.

All types of assessment, of any degree of formality, involve interpretation of a pupil's response against some standard of expectation. This standard may be set by the average performance of a particular section of the population or age group, as in norm-referenced tests. Alternatively, as in the national curriculum context, the assessment may be criterion-referenced. Here the interpretation is in terms of progression in skills, concept, or aspects of personal development which are the objectives of learning, and the assessment gives direct information which can be related to progress in learning. However, the usefulness of criterion-referenced assessment depends on the way in which the criteria are defined. Too tightly defined criteria, while facilitating easy judgement of mastery, require an extensive list which fragments the curriculum. On the other hand, more general criteria, which better reflect the overall aims of education, are much less easily and reliably used in assessing achievement.

Key principles

- Assessment must be used as a continuous part of the teaching–learning process, involving pupils, wherever possible, as well as teachers in identifying next steps.
- Assessment for any purpose should serve the purpose of improving learning by exerting a positive force on the curriculum at all levels. It must, therefore, reflect the full range of curriculum goals, including the more sophisticated skills and abilities now being taught.
- Assessment must provide an effective means of communication with parents and other partners in the learning enterprise in a way which helps them support pupils' learning.
- The choice of different assessment procedures must be decided on the basis of the purpose for which the assessment is being undertaken. This may well mean employing different techniques for different assessment purposes.
- Assessment must be used fairly as part of information for judging the effectiveness of schools. This means taking account of contextual factors which, as well as the quality of teaching, affect the achievement of pupils.
- Citizens have a right to detailed and reliable information about the standards being achieved across the nation through the educational system.

FORMATIVE ASSESSMENT

A major role identified for assessment is that of monitoring learning and informing teaching decisions on a day-to-day basis. In this role, assessment is an integral part of the interactions between teacher, pupil, and learning materials. Because of this relationship, some teachers, who practise formative assessment well, may not recognise that what they are doing includes assessing. This may partly be due to holding an image of assessment as a more formal activity, distinct from teaching (Harlen and Qualter 1991). A broader view is required, along the lines of the definition given above, which encompasses both the informal and the formal. Because of this difficulty of identifying assessment in its formative role in teaching, it seems helpful to provide a rationale and a brief illustration of its meaning in practice. These provide the basis for setting out the features of a scheme of genuinely formative assessment.

It is difficult to conceive of teaching which does not use some information about the intended learners' starting point. In some views of learning and teaching the information is likely to concern what is and is not known and to be used to fill gaps and add to what is already there. However, much more is involved when the view of learning is one which regards it as important to 'take a child's initial ideas seriously so as to ensure that any change or development of these ideas and the supporting evidence for them makes sense and, in this way, become "owned" by the child' (DES/WO 1988). For learning with understanding, according to this view, information about existing ideas and skills is essential.

In the notion of 'matching' learning experiences to pupils' abilities to benefit from them, the knowledge of pupils' present ideas and skills is a prerequisite. Here assessment is carried out to help, not to grade, pupils. Often pupils are unaware that assessment is taking place, but at other times they may take part in it explicitly through self-assessment.

Implied in these reasons for recognising assessment as essential to the educational process is that the information gathered is usable, and is indeed used, in making day-to-day classroom decisions. These decisions may be about 'the appropriate next steps' (DES/WO 1988: para. 23) or about 'appropriate remedial help and guidance' (ibid.). Success and failure are not clear-cut in the classroom, since performance is substantially influenced by context (BERA 1992), so it seems to be preferable to use the single term 'formative' to encompass and replace what the TGAT Report (DES 1988) described separately under 'formative' and 'diagnostic'.

A teacher notices that a year 7 pupil is making systematic errors in multiplying fractions. She questions him about his perception of what he understands $1/2 \times 3/8$ to mean in terms of real objects. His reply leads her to realise that he had not interpreted this as 'half of three-eighths' but was using an incorrectly remembered algorithm. The intervention informed both teacher and pupil of the problem and the remedial action to be taken was clear to both of them.

The same story could be quite different: the teacher marks the pupils' sums wrong and, as this occurs often, comes to regard him as a poor performer in mathematics. This view soon becomes communicated to the pupil, adding to his discouragement from repeated failure. Neither pupil nor teacher finds out why the pupil was having difficulty nor what action to take to help him overcome it.

This brief example illustrates some of the requirements of a system of formative assessment. The teacher who uses it successfully is looking out for progress towards intermediate goals and is aware of underlying ideas and skills which are required for success. She brings together several observations of the pupil's performance and finds patterns which help her to uncover shaky foundations by exploring understandings at earlier points. The teacher also uses techniques for uncovering these understandings which involve the pupil and avoid discouragement. She focuses on the specific aspect of response and does not label the pupil by generalising from this difficulty and making assumptions about other aspects of his mathematical ability.

Characteristics of a formative assessment scheme

Drawing together and extending points from this example leads to the suggestion that what is required from a formative assessment scheme is information that is

- gathered in a number of relevant contexts;
- criterion-referenced and related to a description of progression;
- disaggregated, which in this context means that distinct aspects of performance are reported separately and there is no attempt to combine dissimilar aspects;
- shared by both teacher and pupil;
- a basis for deciding what further learning is required;
- the basis of an on-going running record of progress.

A report of recent practice in England suggests that it falls some way short of implementing assessment of these key characteristics. HMI report that, in 1990/1:

> Many pupils were not being given a sufficiently clear idea of their progress or an indication of how they might improve the quality of their work.
>
> (DES 1992)

A scheme of formative assessment must be embedded in the structures of educational practice; it cannot be grafted on to it.

SUMMATIVE ASSESSMENT

Summative assessment is similar to formative assessment in that it concerns the performance of individual pupils, as opposed to groups. In contrast with formative assessment, however, its prime purpose is not so much to influence teaching but to summarise information about the achievements of a pupil at a particular time. The information may be for the pupils themselves, for receiving teachers, for parents, for employers, or for a combination of these.

There are two main ways of obtaining summative information about achievements: summing up and checking up (Harlen 1991). The former is some form of summary of information obtained through recording formative assessments during a particular period of time and the latter the collection of new information about what the pupil can do at the end of a period of time, usually through giving some form of test. The nature and relative advantages and disadvantages of these are now briefly reviewed.

Summing up

This provides a picture of current achievements derived from information gathered over a period of time and probably used in that time for formative purposes. It is, therefore, detailed and broadly based, encompassing all the aspects of learning which have been addressed in teaching. To retain the richness of the information it is best communicated in the form of a profile (i.e. not aggregated), to which information is added on later occasions. Records of achievement (RoA) provide a structure for recording and reporting this information, combining some of the features of formative assessment with the purposes of summative assessment in that they involve pupils in reviewing their own work and recognising where their strengths and weaknesses lie.

Their defining aims are: (a) to address the full range of desired learning outcomes; (b) to make pupils partners in assessment so that they improve their willingness and their ability to learn; and (c) to provide a basis for decisions about future courses, career options, and appropriate learning targets.

Checking up

No such additional benefits can be claimed for the 'checking up' approach to summative assessment. It is generally carried out through providing tests or tasks specially devised for the purpose of recording performance at a particular time. End of year tests or examinations are examples, as are the end of module tests for checking performance in modular programmes and external public examinations.

Checking up and summing up approaches have contrasting advantages and disadvantages. Tests used for checking up are limited in scope unless they are inordinately long and so are unlikely to cover practical skills and some of the higher level cognitive skills. On the other hand they do provide opportunities for all pupils to demonstrate what they have learned. Summative assessment which is based only on formative assessment depends on the opportunities provided in class for various skills and understandings to be displayed and, further, may be out of date in relation to parts of work covered at earlier points and perhaps not revisited.

This suggests that a combination of the two approaches may be the most appropriate solution. There are several advantages to having test materials available for teachers to use to supplement, at the end of a particular period, the information they have from on-going assessment during that time. The emphasis is on 'test materials' and not tests. These would ideally be in the form of a bank from which teachers select according to their needs. The items in the bank would cover the whole range of curriculum objectives and the whole range of procedures required for valid assessment. This provision would also serve the purposes of the non-statutory Standard Assessment Tasks (SATs).

The main advantages are that the availability of a bank of test material would provide teachers with the opportunity to check or supplement their own assessment in a particular area where they felt uncertain about what pupils can do. This would ensure that all aspects of pupils' work were adequately assessed without requiring extensive testing. Checking their own assessments against those arising from well-trialled and validated tasks would also build up teachers' expertise and lead to greater rigour in teachers' assessments.

ASSESSMENT FOR EVALUATIVE AND QUALITY ASSURANCE PURPOSES

Assessment of performance at the national level

Information about pupils' achievement is necessary in order to keep under review the performance of the system as a whole – the quality assurance role of assessment. In the absence of such information it is possible for rumour and counter-rumour to run riot. For example, the argument about the levels of performance of 7-year-olds on reading (prior to the national assessment data) would never have been possible had there been a national survey of reading performance at the age of 7.

To serve this purpose, assessment has to be carried out in a way which leads to an overall picture of achievement on a national scale. It requires measures of achievement of a large number of pupils to be obtained and summarised. For this purpose testing in controlled conditions is necessary. However, if every pupil is tested, this leads to adverse effects both on teaching practice and on the curriculum and an over-emphasis on formal testing generally. Further, surveys which test every pupil cannot provide the depth of data required to provide a wide-ranging and in-depth picture of the system. Thus testing every pupil at a particular age is not appropriate for assessing performance at the national level.

To serve the evaluative role, assessment at the national level does not need to cover all pupils nor to assess in all attainment targets those who are included. The necessary rigour and comparability in assessment for this purpose can be provided by the use of a sample of pupils undertaking different assessment tasks. Following the pioneering work of the APU, it would be possible to obviate the 'excessively complicated and time consuming' approach of the SATs and still provide the comprehensive coverage of every subject area across a satisfactorily large sample of particular age groups of pupils.

The advantages of the APU were that:

- The surveys were able to assess performance in detail and in an 'elaborate' way, covering higher order skills and including practical and oral activities. The responses were marked by trained markers and the impact on teachers was minimal. By contrast, paper-and-pencil tests for all pupils, which must be carried out under examination conditions and marked quickly by teachers (as is necessary if all pupils are included), cannot assess in such a detailed way or cover such a range of skills and activities.
- Because only light samples of pupils and schools were included, the APU surveys did not have the negative side effects of high stakes testing programmes. They did, however, produce good quality performance data which provided pointers to curriculum development and some important in-depth analysis of differences (e.g. between girls and boys) on a scale not previously possible. This underlines the point that the use of light sampling and, if necessary, the anonymity of schools, reduces the undesirable effects of the testing (e.g. teaching to the test).

The arguments in favour of using APU-type surveys for evaluative purposes extend beyond the effects on schools to the quality of the information. Unless pupils' attainments are monitored over a broad range of performance, each of which is scrutinised in depth, a thorough and useful picture of national performance cannot be obtained. A system which has to test every pupil and yet is manageable can only provide us with a superficial picture of national levels of performance.

> The APU obtained their wide-ranging picture of performance by giving each of a small sample of individuals only a small selection of the total number of questions used in a survey. Since individuals' scores were not required the overall picture of performance could be aggregated over both questions and pupils. Had an individual been given the total range of questions used in an APU survey, about 30 to 40 hours of testing would have been required in each subject area. In fact, each individual took between one and three hours of a selection of the total amount of test material used in a survey.
>
> (SEAC 1991)

In the experimental phase of SAT production, the attempt made to give every pupil a task for every aspect of performance led to the gargantuan testing of each pupil as depicted in this quotation. This was clearly not feasible, but it is equally clear that the much-reduced SATs will not give the detailed description of performance which is useful for national monitoring. The conclusion is that national curriculum assessment and testing for all pupils should be separate from and complementary to the collection of data for national monitoring.

Assessing school effectiveness

It is well established that the attainment of an individual is as much a function of his or her social circumstances and the educational experiences of his or her parents as it is of the effectiveness of the school or schools attended. To judge the effectiveness of a school by the attainment of its pupils is therefore misleading and unfair. What is wanted is a model that disentangles the effect on attainment of the school from that of the pupils' background. The value-added approach, which looks at the gain in achievement while the pupil is at a particular school (that is, the progress he or she makes there), offers a way forward and is, indeed, the basis of school effectiveness research such as that reported in *School Matters* (Mortimore *et al.* 1988; see also McPherson 1992).

The assessments of attainment used (both on entry to the school and on leaving) should be as broad as possible to ensure that school effectiveness is not reduced to efficiency in teaching test-taking skills but reflects the full range of the aims of the school. This would have been difficult to achieve even in the original plan for national curriculum assessment, which has since been abandoned as being too time-consuming, and would be far too narrow if based on the measures currently in use.

To counter the narrowness of outcomes implied by test results, even when shown in value-added form, it is suggested that schools should publish detailed reports covering such areas as:

– the aims of the schools;
– details of recent inspection reports (if any);
– particular areas of expertise offered;
– cultural and sporting achievements;
– community involvement;
– destinations of leavers.

In short, the school should show its test results as part of its record of achievement.

REFERENCES

BERA (1992) Dialogue Series: *Policy Issues in National Assessment*. Avon: Multilingual Matters Ltd.
DES (1988) *The Task Group on Assessment and Testing: A Report*. London: HMSO.
DES (1992) *Education in England 1990/1: The Annual Report of the Senior Chief Inspector of Schools*. London: DES.
DES/WO (1988) *Science for Ages 5 to 16: Proposals of the Secretary of State for Education and Science and the Secretary of State for Wales*. London: DES/WO.

Harlen, W. (1991) 'National Curriculum assessment: increasing the benefit by reducing the burden'. In *Education and Change in the 1990s*, Journal of the Educational Research Network of Northern Ireland, No. 5, February: 3–19.

Harlen, W. and Quarter, A. (1991) 'Issues in SAT development and the practice of teacher assessment'. *Cambridge Journal of Education* 21(2): 141–52.

McPherson, A. (1992) *Measuring Added Value in Schools*. National Commission on Education Briefing No. 1. London: National Commission on Education.

Mortimore, P., Sammons, P., Stoll, L., Lewis, D., and Ecob, R. (1988) *School Matters*. Wells: Open Books.

SEAC (1991) *The APU Experience 1977–1990*. Ref. D/009/B/91. London: HMSO.

Chapter 29

Target setting with young children

Yolande Muschamp

This part of the book has focused on the transmission of knowledge through the curriculum: the selection and organisation of content to be learnt by society through government, and by teachers for their pupils. The danger is that discussions of the curriculum can lose sight of the way people learn and the learners' own perceptions of the curriculum being offered to them. How far is it possible to involve learners themselves, even in the primary years, in the planning and assessment of their learning? 'Consultations' with individual pupils on their work have become an increasingly popular part of teacher assessment. (See, for example, the primary learning record produced by the Centre for Language in Primary Education.) This chapter explores one way in which learners might be supported in taking more responsibility for their own learning, while at the same time coming to understand more explicitly their teachers' plans and expectations in setting learning tasks for them.

Assessment is traditionally the teacher's prerogative but there is much to be gained by including children in this process. Assessment requires clarity of purpose, aims, and expectations and a careful analysis of performance in relation to these. These are aids to effective teaching; by involving children in their own assessment these requirements can also become aids to effective learning.

From their first day at school children are able to discover the nature of 'pupil competencies' and are influenced in their choice by background, school-generated cultures, and personal interests (Woods 1990). However, it has been suggested that the focus may not be to learn, but to cope with the complex demands of contradictory pressures of the classroom, where tasks have both an 'academic content and behavioural purpose' (Galton 1989). When 'coping strategies' such as 'testing out' are used by children as they learn the rules of the classroom, it is not without a real fear of failing (Holt 1967). As there is great potential for misinterpretation and limited communication (Bennett 1989), they have to struggle to discover the intentions and expectations of their teacher and deal with the consequences of

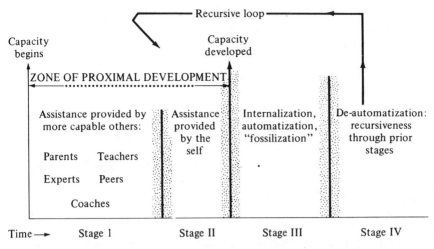

Figure 29.1 Genesis of performance capacity: progression through the ZPD and beyond

Source: Tharp and Gallimore 1988

self-image which result (Galton 1989; Pollard and Tann 1987; Lacey 1970; Burns 1979).

Tharp and Gallimore (1988) argue that the intentions and expectations of the teachers cannot be fulfilled only through instruction: 'the child is not merely a passive recipient of adult guidance and assistance.' Tharp and Gallimore provide a model of how children's performance is assisted by 'more capable others' until they can assist themselves. Eventually learning becomes internalised or automatised. Only when the learning is lost or proves inadequate does the child rely on further assistance from the more capable other – the recursive loop of the model.

Integral to this model must be the self-assessments and the awareness of competencies described above; transition from stage to stage depends on them. Tharp and Gallimore argue that this transition occurs as the children take control of their performance and they liken this to Bruner's concept of 'handover'.

The present chapter argues that by introducing pupils to self-assessment this process of taking control is hastened and enhanced. It focuses on the transition from Stage I to Stage II as seen in Figure 29.1, within the Zone of Proximal Development, and suggests that clarification and communication of purpose, aims, and expectations are central to a strategy for self-assessment. The variations in assistance to the child that Tharp and Gallimore describe permeate this account of development activities as assessment itself is treated as a performance.

My study of pupil self-assessment was a strand within a larger project on classroom-based assessment. Initially children from six classrooms were interviewed and then two classrooms become the focus for more in-depth case study investigations.

PURPOSES, AIMS, AND EXPECTATIONS

An understanding of the views that children had of their progress had already been established.

From John, aged 7, an early self-assessment revealed:

> My best subject is maths. I know all my tables. My grandad teaches me. [Is there anything that you are not good at?] Reading really. I don't know all the words. My book is a bit boring.

And from Milena, also aged 7:

> I'm not very good at maths. I find it hard. I'll make mistakes and teacher tells me to do it again. . . . My favourite is reading. I'm reading *Charlotte's Web* at the moment. Miss says I can choose what I like to read. I don't have to go to the reading shelves [reading scheme].

Even such young children, and John and Milena were typical of those interviewed, were aware of the roles that the more capable others were playing. John knew he was getting support from his grandfather; Milena perceived the control by her teacher. In performing these activities, using tables and reading *Charlotte's Web*, these children were already at Stage II of Tharp and Gallimore's model. In the other subjects, however, they did not seem in control: John found his book boring and Milena admitted she would be told to repeat her work.

The children in the six classes aged between 5 and 9, like John and Milena, could all talk to varying degrees about the progress they had made. These interviews were to provide the basis for development activities in self-assessment which began with the clarification of purposes, aims, and expectations. This was done through the use of long-term aims and short-term targets.

Long-term aims

In practical terms it was decided that a discussion with each child to review their past work would provide an opportunity to establish long-term aims for the remainder of the year. The information relating to structured schemes of work was discussed individually with the children and then noted in the portfolio in terms of learning objectives.

Although these objectives were clear and precise they were not necessarily understood or shared by the children. This conversation with Hayley illustrates some of the difficulties.

(Do you like reading?)

No not really.

(Why is that?)

It's a bit difficult, it's a bit boring.

(Do you think you'll like it more when you can read the difficult books?)

I might, no it's boring.

(How do you choose the books you read?)

I go and fetch the next one from the basket. If it's not there I can sometimes choose another from the back.

(Do you look at the more difficult books?)

I've seen them but I prefer the easy ones.

(Do you read the other books in the classroom, the ones in the book corner?)

Yes I look at the Spot books, but they're not proper reading books. They're picture books. I prefer the picture books.

This conversation was not untypical. There were many children in the class who did not enjoy some aspect of their school work. To express the long-term objectives for Hayley in terms solely of reading attainment would have been inappropriate. It was decided to include reading enjoyment and the ability to select books independently as part of the long-term aim.

An individual's needs often reflected a general need within the class. For example, the need for support in the selection and enjoyment of reading was thought to affect enough children in Hayley's class that the teacher designed activities over the term for the whole class. Over the year the traditional book reviews were revamped to include hints on choosing books by a particular author. Displays and talks about the work of a particular author were organised. The books, usually separated from the reading scheme books, were colour coded and integrated into the scheme.

These initiatives demonstrated the value of sharing long-term aims with children. The challenge of sharing the teacher's understanding and expectations with young children necessitated an examination of those aims which would not automatically have occurred. Uncovering children's confusion or lack of accord between the teachers' and children's views provided the basis for support activities while the children continued to move through Stage I of Tharp and Gallimore's model.

After the portfolio review each child had personalised long-terms aims summarised in their portfolio. This provided background information for the selection of more specific short-term targets.

Short-term targets

The setting of targets related long-terms aims to the everyday activities of the classroom and underpinned the 'hand over' from teacher to pupils.

Notes taken while sitting in on one of these portfolio reviews illustrate how short-term targets could be selected.

> Jenny was able to talk about the writing in her folder. She remembered writing all the stories and could add background information. Writing stories was one of her strengths. She was able to identify improvements which had been made over the last two years. When talking about the topic work she could recall the context but not all the detail. It was difficult for her to recall what had been the focus of the study.
>
> The plans for this term's topic, habitat, were discussed. Jenny thought that she would write a story about the animals in very bad weather. The teacher felt that she needed to move away from a continual use of a fictional form and carry out some investigation from reference texts, both books and information sheets.
>
> They were also going to create a data file on their computer. Jenny did not know very much about the habitat of the animals on the topic web (English wild animals, foxes, hedgehogs, squirrels, etc.). She agreed it would be interesting to investigate them and a list of questions was drawn up to help with this. The information would also help with her story. She would be able to put in specific detail of animal homes and habits.

The teacher was responsible for moving from a general review of progress to specific targets. Within the terms of the Tharp and Gallimore model, she is assisting Jenny's performance through the ZPD. The zone here is the setting and evaluation of targets in relation to writing. During the review she had realised the lack of detail in Jenny's writing. Jenny was unable to remember much of the content of the topic activities represented. The teacher felt that Jenny avoided the more difficult investigation of reference materials by relying on the writing of stories. The details of the investigation were decided upon together. With another child the targets chosen might be quite different within the same topic.

All of these individual targets were in addition to the targets set by the class teacher in her instructions to the class or a group. Although the review of the portfolio was a formal time when such selection of targets could be made, the reviews were not frequent enough to play a major role in the target setting week by week. Most of it had to go on in the everyday interaction between teacher and pupil. Because of the high number of pupils in the class the teacher was always anxious to deal with each child in as little a time as possible. The targets therefore had to be very clear, simple, few, and recorded so that both teacher and child could use them later to assist in assessment. The challenge to the teacher was continually to refer to and highlight the targets which had been set.

The following are the targets set and evaluated for a 7-year-old girl called

Jo. The targets were written in her exercise book. Some targets were negotiated (those starred) and others were given by the teacher when she marked the book. Jo was encouraged to add comments and increasingly assess the targets before the teacher.

Target 1:
*The garden at night. Colour in with pencil crayons. Neat labels please.

The teacher had added 'This is lovely, are you pleased?', to which Jo had given the written reply 'Yes'.

Target 2:
*Data file form. No crossings out please. Try and finish with all the facts. Use the book table.

The teacher had written 'A good try'; Jo was becoming more confident and had written 'I did not find out about the badger'.

Target 3:
Data file form. Please write smaller so the letters fit in the boxes.

Jo had written the comment 'Some letters are too big' before she presented her work to the teacher. Her teacher added 'This is much better. You have worked very hard.'

The evaluation of the folder of work on this short topic was presented as a class exercise, as each child bound their folders individually with the teacher. Jo wrote:

> I have learnt all about the garden at night. I can write and colour pictures. I used the computer. My writing is neater and smaller. We saw a stuffed owl. I liked best the hedgehogs. We read The Owl Who Was Afraid Of The Dark.

Other correction of the work had taken place which was not commented upon. Individual letters had been altered. In an attempt to fill in the data form needed for the computer data file, the words written in the boxes had been erased and rewritten in a smaller hand. Jo's attempt to meet the targets set was very serious, keeping her on task more than was usual.

The wording of the targets was important. There was clearly an overlap between the way teachers used 'instructions' and 'targets'. When planning and negotiating short-term targets, these two almost appeared synonymous. Targets could be defined and detailed with instructions. Instructions often took the form of targets. These terms were discussed with the teachers and it was decided to restrict the use of 'targets' to expressing the *purpose* of the activity in order to clarify the position. Targets such as 'finish', 'write', or 'complete' did not express the learning that was intended and therefore these terms became part of the *instructions*.

The targets above would be written in the following way to distinguish between target and instructions. The targets were always given first (underlined) and the instructions followed:

> *Learn to use a data file form*. Please write smaller so the letters fit in the boxes.

This may seem rather a pedantic alteration and yet its impact was thought to be very useful to all of us involved in trying to summarise targets. It quickly showed where there was a lack of clarity over the purpose of the activity; and it also provided a cue for helping the child to assess. The target easily became a question 'Have you learnt how to use a data file form?'

As you can see from Jo's notes above, her evaluation began with 'I have learnt all about the garden at night'. By the time this evaluation was written targets were being expressed in this way. Generally two expressions were being used, 'Learn all about . . .', 'learn how to . . .', which helped express both knowledge and skills.

The interviews of the review stage had shown how the children paid little or scant attention to instruction and clearly had developed a tacit understanding of what was required to complete a task. Writing the target and listing the instructions for the activity was an attempt to change this situation. The continual references to the summary of instructions by both teacher and pupils gradually made the tacit understanding less important and unnecessary.

ANALYSIS OF PERFORMANCE

The analysis of performance in relation to purpose, aims, and expectations became relatively straightforward once the children were practised in referring to targets they had discussed. It was useful to distinguish between two types of assessment. The first, close to the marking, which was familiar to the children, was checking the accuracy of their work and the second was deciding if it could have been made better in some way.

The first attempts at self-assessment had found predominant concern with the accuracy of the work. Targets were able to change this situation. In addition to marking the accuracy of obvious features such as spellings or the answers to calculations, there were now specific instructions to assess. The instructions relating to core subjects and study skills, if written clearly, usually entailed a yes/no answer to the question 'did I . . .?'. So, for example, in Jo's targets above designed for using a data file the instructions could be assessed by asking

> Did I do any crossing out?
> Did I finish all the boxes?
> Did I use the book table?

The target itself, 'learn how to use a data file', could be assessed by the comment 'I have learnt how to use a data file' where the task was a fairly simple one. In the case of more complex tasks these could be detailed with the aspects of the task that had been learnt. For example, 'I loaded the file myself and learnt to use the printer.'

Once each child had assessed the work in relation to the target and instructions it was decided to ask how the work might have been improved. This reflected what the teachers were doing already but in a fairly *ad hoc* manner. The purpose of this was to encourage the children to use their assessments formatively, therefore ensuring the assessment activities were not the bolt-on activity criticised in the TGAT *Report* (1987). The children were encouraged to ask themselves such questions as:

Can I think of another way I could have done this?
Could I have made this activity easier?

The question 'how could I have made this better?' was often answered by a list of the instructions if these had not been followed, but, in the situation where everything appeared correct, then the answers were often thoughtful, suggesting real improvements which provided the basis for new targets.

It was this continual use and renewal of targets that determined their success. They seemed to create a greater awareness of the processes involved in the activities set. The children became distanced from the tasks and began to develop an objective view. It clearly had an effect on their motivation, more so in the beginning when the use of targets was still novel. Over time their use became more habitual.

For the teacher they were a constant reminder of the purpose of tasks and an opportunity to increase their assessments of the children's progress. However, they were time-consuming. In classes of thirty or more children there was simply not the time to give the children the individual attention that the teachers would have liked or felt the children would have benefited from.

Tharp and Gallimore ask in this situation for the 'increased use of small groups, maintenance of a positive classroom atmosphere that will increase independent task involvement of students, new materials and technology with which students can interact independent of the teacher'.

It was possible to see some of this happening with the use of targets within a strategy for self-assessment. As children made the transition from Stage I to Stage II of Tharp and Gallimore's model they became more used to selecting targets and found that they could draw up targets from the introduction of activities given by the teacher. The teacher, using the plans for the year, was providing the content of the activities. The part of the curriculum that was to be covered was summarised as targets and evaluated first by the children. And this increasingly happened without the direct involvement of the teacher.

I know most of the time when my work is OK. But you can't be really certain until your teacher has looked at it.

Tharp and Gallimore's model provides a framework for developing the ways in which children can be encouraged to assess their own progress. The clarification and evaluation of targets become a zone in which each child's performance is assisted by their teacher. Gradually the child takes over the tasks. As they become involved in their own assessment they are provided with effective aids to learning which complement the wide range of skills and talents with which each child begins school.

REFERENCES

Bennett, N. (1989) *The Quality of Pupil Learning Experiences*, London, Lawrence Erlbaum.
Burns, J. (1979) *The Self Concept: Theory, Measurement and Behaviour*, London, Longman.
Galton, M. (1989) *Teaching in the Primary School*, London, David Fulton.
Holt, J. (1967) *How Children Fail*, New York, Pitman.
Lacey, C. (1970) *Hightown Grammar*, Manchester, Manchester University Press.
Pollard, A. and Tann, S. (1987) *Reflective Teaching in the Primary School*, London, Cassell.
Task Group on Assessment and Testing (1987) *A Report*, London, DES.
Tharp, R. and Gallimore, R. (eds) (1988) *Rousing Minds to Life: Teaching, Learning and Schooling in Social Context*, New York, Cambridge University Press.
Woods, P. (1990) *The Happiest Days?*, London, Falmer.

Part V

Schools

Chapter 30

The organisation of the primary school

Charles Handy and Robert Aitken

This chapter places the classroom within the setting of the school as a complex organisation. We chose it for the clear description it offers of the whole school at work, and for its analysis of the role of the head. In joining a new school, the beginning teacher will need to try to find out the structure of the organisation, roles and responsibilities, and systems of communication. Drawing on this chapter, it should also be possible to investigate how far a 'collective purpose' has been achieved among the staff and pupils, and how far this is shared with parents and the local community.

Schools are also organisations. Sometimes the preoccupation with so many children, with the odds and ends of schooling, with the dramas of young people's lives and all their emotions, can blind one to the fact that all the things are happening within an organisation that is itself bound by the laws of other organisations. Box 1 shows how it feels, in the words of a primary school headteacher describing a typical Monday morning in his school.

Box 1 captures the atmosphere of school, the pressure of the immediate, the intense involvement with people both inside and outside the school. The emergencies can be of intense personal concern, as with the boy whom the NSPCC inspector wanted to discuss. Always there is the human dimension that is part of the fascination of working in a school; the opportunity to be involved in the daily experiences of people – their frailties and their joys, their values and their growth.

The school in Box 1 is one of 20,384 primary schools up and down the country. It has 216 children, aged between 4 and 11. The head has a staff of nine teachers, one of whom is part-time, three nursery assistants, an education assistant to help with the reception and infant classes, a caretaker, five cleaners, a cook, and eleven kitchen staff. It is a society in miniature. It is an organisation as well as a school.

Any organisation needs systems for communicating and arranging things, as well as a structure for dividing up the work and defining the relationship of people to each other. It will require someone to set priorities and define responsibilities and duties. Someone then has to make sure that these

Box 1 Monday morning

I needn't pick up Mrs Churchill this morning. She rang at 7.30 a.m. to say her baby daughter Lisa was ill, and she would have to stay at home to look after her. Funny how calls at 7.30 a.m. at home and 8.30 a.m. at school usually mean some staff emergency!

No work on the stationery requisition today. I will take J2, and the school secretary can rough out stationery requirements after finishing the dinner money. I quite enjoy J2 – a class full of characters, and a challenge. Staff always reckon *I'm happier when I'm teaching*.

Parked at school by 8.10 a.m. As usual three staff have beaten me to it – deputy, head of infants, and nursery teacher. Talked over change of plans with Miss Butler, my deputy. Amended day's information in staff diary before she took it to send round staff prior to start of school. Checked with Mrs Griffin, head of infant department, that all was organised for the hair inspection by the district nurse at 9.30 a.m. Half-past eight has passed – no telephone call. No further staff absence today. *We'll manage.*

Children and parents already paying dinner money at secretary's window. Nursery teacher rings on internal line to say she's discovered three broken windows in her activities room. She will find caretaker. Parent arrives with son – she is taking him for a medical but would I arrange to keep a dinner for him? Secretary passes message to cook. Father arrives to ask would I act as guarantor so that he can buy clothing for children? Agree and sign. What have I let myself in for? Phone call from professional assistant in education department to ask if she could visit school later today to inspect crumbling temporary classroom and state of nursery decoration. Agreed – she knows her way around and staff and children are used to visitors.

Now to J2 . . . but no, a knock on the door, NSPCC inspector from Special Unit to discuss report from a neighbour about a possible non-accidental injury to one of our children. It is urgent I talk to him about it because *we are worried about the child too*. Quick message to Miss Butler – take assembly, please. My assembly on 'Treasures' will have to wait. She will use one of her stock for emergencies. Discussing case – panic – who is registering J2? *Panic over.* Miss North, part-time teacher, passes window with J2 on the way to assembly. I eventually get to J2 at 9.40 a.m.

Monday morning in a primary school!

responsibilities are carried out and must apportion praise or disapproval when necessary. Without these prior arrangements every problem becomes a crisis, every event something that needs the individual attention of the person at the centre.

The events in Box 1 were handled expeditiously and caringly because there was a pre-arranged organisation in the school, there were relationships that could be relied upon, and there was support for the school from parents and the wider community. Was this what the head meant when he said, 'We'll manage'? Was he referring to that pre-planned system of organisation or did he mean, 'We will cope with these problems. We'll get by'?

Is it only a British habit to use 'manage' in the second, more belittling way, to mean 'coping'? This is to relegate management to a necessary chore, something unnecessary in an ideal world. When the head said, 'I'm happier when I'm teaching', he may also have been reflecting the common feeling among heads that one is a teacher first and always, and a manager by necessity. As we shall see, it is characteristic of professionals to see management as a service function. But professionals do not like to think of themselves as members of an organisation, preferring words like 'partnership' or 'practice' or 'consortium'. The dilemma for schools is that willy-nilly they *are* organisations, not just groupings of teachers, and they have to accept that the management of these organisations is a key activity, not a mere service function.

Relegating 'managing' to 'coping' has another disadvantage. It makes it harder for the ordinary teacher to see herself or himself as a manager. Yet *every* teacher is, properly speaking, a manager of a group of children. The classroom is itself a mini-organisation in which all the laws of group behaviour, motivation, leadership, communication, and relationships apply.

In the opening example the head and his staff were able to deal with the problems that arose because they were able to rely upon:

- the organisation of the school;
- the quality of relationships within the school;
- the support of parents and the wider community.

But what, typically, would be the features of a primary school that enabled this? What choices have to be made to decide on the forms of organisation? What kind of relationships would be forged? What is the context of support from the community or world outside the organisation? How is such an organisation to be managed so that it is kept fresh, responsive, and effective?

ORGANISATION

The first and fundamental step that a head faces (and re-faces each year with changes in children and teachers) is how to *organise* the school. She or he must first decide how to divide the children into learning groups, of what

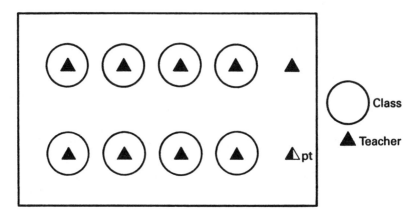

Figure 30.1 Organisation of the school

size, age, mix and for what activities, etc.; and then decide how to deploy the skills of the staff to these groups and tasks. The options are many. There is no single answer. In our example the head has chosen to organise his children into seven classes (plus a nursery) of roughly equal size (average twenty-five pupils) according to age; and to allocate each of his full-time teachers to a class, using his part-time teacher and himself to facilitate small-group work or enable teachers to take other classes for special activities. Given the current conventions of British primary education this form of organisation is typical of the majority of schools.

The basic organisational 'chart' could be depicted as in Figure 30.1. This form of organisation makes much sense and has a lot of strengths. It offers security to children and staff alike; they know their place in the order of things. Each class is like a large family with the opportunity during the course of a year to know one another and their teacher well: to know and grow together. The head knows who is responsible for what stage of development. Basic roles are clear. It is an example of what we call a 'job-shop' structure, where each unit has its own independent task to do.

Each class group could therefore be depicted as in Figure 30.2. Yet each class is but a mini-society within the larger society of the whole school, and here complications can set in. Each class is likely to develop or exhibit its own character or culture deriving from the make-up and background of the children in the group and from the person of the teacher (who herself or himself has strengths and weaknesses).

Every society has its own culture, and nothing in education is value-free. Does the class take its values from the teacher or from the group norms or from both? What if eight classes and their teachers go in differing directions? What about the inexperienced or weak teacher? There needs to be some cohesion or conformity for the whole organisation, a higher order of things

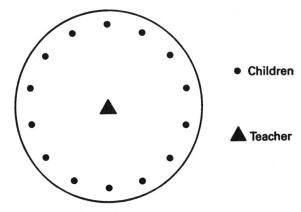

Figure 30.2 Organisation of the class

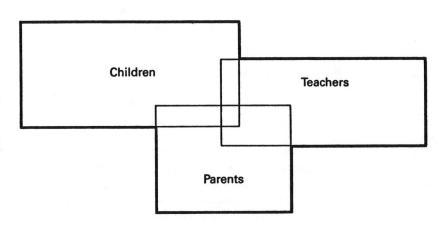

Figure 30.3 Groups within the school

than the class group, if the school is going to be more than a collection of eight different families. How is that to be achieved, and for whom?

In practice the situation is more complex than that. Within the setting of a school there are other groupings, each coming from a different position with differing experiences, expectations, and values. Children are different from adults; teachers are different (in their professional role) from parents. These form distinct 'peer groups' in the sense that one takes some of one's values and behaviour from people with a similar background. An alternative expression of such groups within a school could therefore be Figure 30.3.

There are of course other groups (including the other adults, the non-teaching staff). The caretaker who lives on site is often an influential figure with a foot in both the local community and the school. From their different vantage-points, or *roles*, these people affect and influence what happens in the classroom.

So a primary school head has a more complex task than just creating a form of organisation. She or he needs to see that the working of that organisation is informed by, and recognises, the influences of other groupings, and to guard against the inadequacies of the organisation she or he adopts. This depends a great deal upon the quality of relationships operating within the organisation.

RELATIONSHIPS

We have seen that it is one thing for a head to create an organisation; yet another to supervise its working. One of the fundamental tasks facing any head is to get the teaching staff to express a collective will. This is necessary because the teacher in her or his own classroom is *the* expression of the school. If discontinuities in the treatment, learning, or development of children are to be avoided, then a corporate purpose is needed. Yet teaching is such a personal activity; there is an interactive chemistry between learner and teacher, which depends as much on process as on content (if not more) and expresses personal values and realities as much as knowledge. There is an actor or artist in the make-up of most successful teachers, which sets great store by freedom of expression. This can be at odds with the role of teacher as the expression of the collective purpose or even as manager of the learning group.

But the head needs to ensure that there is an agreed purpose behind the structure of the organisation; a shared set of aims, a way of doing things, a means of monitoring progress. This means arriving at a shared set of values and expectations – particularly as schools are inevitably involved in the business of the development and transmission of values. How then does one combine professional autonomy and artistic freedom with a common purpose? This is the challenge that faces all schools and all professional organisations. In the setting of a primary school a head can do this by various means. She or he may choose to lay down the main content of syllabuses and schemes of work and the methods to be used, and leave the interpretation and pace to the professional competence of each teacher. This, however, is unlikely to be sufficient. Content and methods change and need updating. Even reading schemes can become quickly outdated in a multi-cultural society. The advent of computers in the classroom and the need to identify children with special learning needs are other examples of current changes that require response within the organisation.

What is important is that the organisation knows its way – where it is going – and that those working in the organisation know what it stands for and what is the shared set of values to which each is contributing. To achieve this is not easy. The head will be able to use the expertise of her or his staff by allocating leadership roles in areas of the curriculum, such as mathematics. This can be invigorating for the member of staff involved, releasing and enhancing commitment and motivation. But not all staff are equally experienced or capable of such leadership roles. Minor roles can be felt to be insignificant and demanding. The choosing of staff for responsibilities is a tightrope any head or manager has to walk, particularly if promotion remains the main reward for good teaching, for not all good teachers make good leaders of teachers. Schools, like other organisations, have to find ways to reward good performance that do not involve giving the person a different job.

The size and form of the organisation can produce imperatives, forces that can dictate unintended answers and cloud issues. The size of a primary school, with nine or so teachers and ten or twelve support staff, should mean that the head and staff are able to communicate personally and frequently, unlike in the larger organisations that many secondary schools are. But smaller organisations are not immune from contrary forces. They may become a dictatorship (owing too much for their purpose to one person) or an oligarchy. Anyone who has lived in a small-scale setting (e.g. on a ship) will know that personality conflict can be a real problem and a divisive influence. Primary schools, despite their apparent 'bonus' of relatively small scale, do not escape the need to face and work at the issue of relationships.

The definition of *roles and responsibilities* and the choosing of staff to undertake them is a crucial task for any head, and it can present difficulties. Even the basic task of allocating teachers to classes can be fraught. Heads sometimes have the difficulty of moving a teacher from, say, top juniors to second-year juniors. There are cases where a teacher has taken the same class in the same classroom for ten or more years. It has become her or his class and rightful empire – impregnable to the rest of the school and sometimes a deadweight in the evolving organisation: *Territory* is a prized possession in every organisation, with its boundaries fiercely defended.

Roles and responsibilities are important both so that tasks can be undertaken and also because they offer security and a place in the organisation for the individual. But this of itself is insufficient. *A collective purpose* is still needed. All members of the organisation need the motivation to feel they are partners in it and, particularly for teachers, that they are valued as professional people. Their views need to be heard (and if necessary challenged). This process of achieving a collective view is one of the most difficult tasks – if not *the* most difficult – of a head. It cannot be rushed or taken for granted. It is a continuous process and one that cannot be left to casual conversations or a quick discussion in the staff room at playtime – valuable as those can be. A collective purpose can be achieved only if it is truly collective, i.e. representing the considered views of all involved.

Those involved start, obviously, with the staff, but it goes further than that; parents, families, and the community have expectations of, and influence on, the organisation. Their confidence in the school is an essential ingredient in its successful functioning. They too have to share in the collective purpose if they are to be truly supportive of the organisation.

PARENTS AND THE WIDER COMMUNITY

When parents commit their children to attending primary school they do so with a sense of confidence but also with expectations and fears. Symbolically it is another expression of untying the apron-strings. Their children need to be growing in the company of other children and learning beyond the family under the guidance of specialists. But there can be a sense of loss; the influence of the family can be felt to be waning. Their children will be subjected to other values and knowledge, including those from other children from different backgrounds. This can produce tensions and dependencies of several different orders at times and an increasing need for parents to understand the 'influence' of the school system on them and their families.

So for all schools there is a bond between them and the families and communities they serve. It is a kind of bond of confidence, of trust, that exists between them. Why else does a father ask a head to act as guarantor? And why else is the head really worried about what 'I have let myself in for'?

In practice it is not as simple as that. Some parents are over-anxious and expect more from the school for their child than is realistic. But sadly too many other parents abdicate once their child is at school. Teachers know that the parents whom they really want to see, to know, and to help are often the ones who never come to school. Fortunately, the community school movement is changing this and enabling parents, especially those who are nervous of schools and teachers, to have confidence in their role. Whatever the attitudes of parents, this is a critical dimension that the school as an organisation has to *manage*, rather than accepting it as part of the scenery. Put in another way, the boundary of the system reaches out beyond the school gates. Organisations are never islands unto themselves.

If we take the class group as the basic unit of the school organisation, this 'community dimension' can be expressed as in Figure 30.4. The arrows indicate the flow of cultural forces between school and home.

It can be seen from Figure 30.4 how children are in only a relative state of relationship with the school and its ethos and its people. The children come from a variety of backgrounds: e.g. numbers in their family; their position in the family; the quality of life and material provision in the home; their religious or racial background. Such differences in cultural background produce a variety of states of learning from sources outside the school: for example, in language development, socialisation, 'street wisdom', emotional and intellectual growth. This also produces different patterns of behaviour, attitudes, needs, and dependencies.

And these are seldom consistently expressed. Children have differing

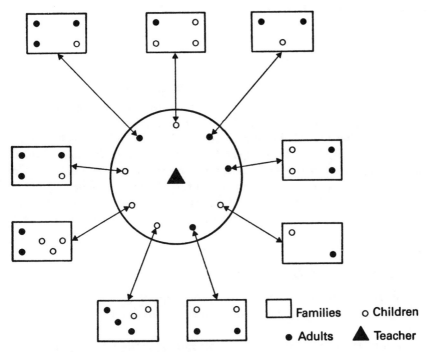

Figure 30.4 The community dimension

areas of experience and can be very adept at switching between 'cultures' and using the 'language of the situation' as it suits them. All children can be chameleons! As a result there are strong cultural influences from outside the school that are brought into the classroom daily, but the culture of the school also extends outwards and into the homes of the children. These cultural influences are expressed by the arrows in Figure 30.4.

So not only has the head of any school the problem of securing continuity in the education of pupils through differing teaching styles of her or his staff. She or he also has a need to secure as much common ground as possible between the school and home 'cultures'. She or he needs to work with the staff for a sufficient understanding between home and school so that what is done at school is not undone at home and vice versa. Thus schools and homes are increasingly readily open to parents and teachers respectively, and many schools are developing as community schools with a curriculum expressed in community/family terms.

Although a primary school may seem to be small and intimate it is in fact a complex and relatively large undertaking or *system*. The *average*-sized school will have thirty or so adults and about 200 children *within the organisation*. But, as we have seen, the school is inextricably bound up with the culture of the wider community, particularly that of the parents and families.

The primary school is a significant management task, not only for the head but also for each member of staff because each has to express the purpose of the school in managing her or his own class. Each and every primary teacher therefore has to be a manager. Every teacher has the task of setting goals and targets for a group, for organising that group and providing the sources for it, for managing the relationships within the group and the relationships between the members of the group and the other groups or families to which they belong. Every teacher has to decide how to excite and stimulate each individual, what style of behaviour to adopt, what methods of persuasion or influence to use, how to reward and punish, how to handle differences and arguments. Knowledge of one's subject counts for little if one can't do these which are *all* management functions.

THE SCHOOL AND SOCIETY

Schools are one of society's key devices for adapting to the future. As such they find themselves mirroring many of the tensions in society, for instance:

Accountability. The school is accountable to the board of governors, which must include parent, staff, and community representatives. But schools are also now required to publish annually a prospectus of their curriculum, options, activities, and examination results. This gives parents more information to choose between schools, which they are now formally encouraged to do. In effect, the gate to the secret garden of the curriculum and the internal organisation has been opened, making the leadership of the school more open to question, both within and without. This mirrors the increased pressure on all public bodies to demonstrate that they are delivering what they ought to deliver.

But the accountability remains confused. Schools are accountable to the profession, to the parents and their children, and to employers. Their interests are not always the same, nor are there easy ways of resolving any differences. Schools, like other organisations, will have to find better ways to debate and deal with these confused accountabilities.

Falling rolls. The high birth rates of the 1960s had dropped by up to 30 per cent by the end of the 1970s and have only recently begun to rise again. As a result school systems, after twenty or more years or rapid expansion, are in a period of prolonged contraction, which is likely to extend well into the 1990s.

Expansion within a system provides opportunities for creativity, experimentation, new ideas, rapid promotion. There is the stimulus of a natural yeast working within the environment. Contraction has the opposite results: closures or amalgamations of plants, redundancy or redeployment of staff, fewer opportunities for experiment or promotion. This has a dulling effect, leading to fewer risks and greater caution.

In other spheres they talk of contracting markets rather than falling rolls, but the effects are the same. Leadership has to do its best to counter the ill effects. It means working harder at the infrastructure tasks of providing opportunities for development and fulfilment, of maintaining commitment and motivation – the management tasks. It also means taking another look at the boundaries of the system in case there are opportunities in new markets. The temptation in a falling market is to retrench, but a falling market in one area often suggests that there is a rising market elsewhere. Leadership needs to look out as well as in.

Falling rolls necessarily mean falling spending on education. Money will not be available to fund the kind of slack in organisations that provides the time for development, experiment, and special projects as well as the cover for inefficiency. The necessary slack for innovation can be provided in the future only by getting rid of the inefficiencies, by the kind of inspired leadership that raises energy, reduces absenteeism, converts time into effort: by better management, in fact. Without that kind of better management as the substitute for money, the education of our young will be damaged just when it needs more than ever to be experimental and responsive to a changing society.

Chapter 31

Key factors for effective junior schooling

Peter Mortimore, Pamela Sammons, Louise Stoll, David Lewis, and Russell Ecob

This chapter identifies twelve major indicators of school effectiveness. It is derived from the largest recent research study of the issue and summarises much of the understanding about schools which developed in the 1980s. One key point from this research was that the effectiveness of different schools does vary considerably and improving organisational effectiveness must therefore be a major management goal. Of course, highlighting such factors does not show how school effectiveness is realised in practice. The other papers in this section may be helpful here, though it is probably something which has to be constantly worked towards.

By investigating the interconnections between the many factors linked with school effects on pupils' progress and development, we have been able to identify some of the mechanisms by which effective junior schooling is promoted. These factors are not purely statistical constructs. They have not been obtained solely by means of quantitative analyses. Rather, they are derived from a combination of careful examination and discussion of the statistical findings, and the use of educational and research judgement. They represent the interpretation of the research results by an inter-disciplinary team of researchers and teachers.

The twelve key factors described below are not arranged in any order of importance. However, we have grouped them into factors that concern school policy (1 to 4), those that relate to classroom policy (5 to 9), and, finally, aspects of relevance to school and class policy (10 to 12).

THE TWELVE KEY FACTORS

1 Purposeful leadership of the staff by the headteacher
2 The involvement of the deputy head
3 The involvement of teachers
4 Consistency among teachers
5 Structured sessions
6 Intellectually challenging teaching

7 The work-centred environment
8 Limited focus within sessions
9 Maximum communication between teachers and pupils
10 Record keeping
11 Parental involvement
12 Positive climate

1 Purposeful leadership of the staff by the headteacher

Purposeful leadership occurred where the headteacher understood the needs of the school and was involved actively in the school's work, without exerting total control over the rest of the staff. In effective schools, head-teachers were involved in curriculum discussions and influenced the content of guidelines drawn up within the school, without taking complete control. They also influenced the teaching strategies of teachers, but only selectively, where they judged it necessary. This leadership was demonstrated by an emphasis on the monitoring of pupils' progress, through teachers keeping individual records. Approaches varied – some schools kept written records; others passed on folders of pupils' work to their next teacher; some did both – but a systematic policy of record keeping was important. With regard to in-service training, those heads exhibiting purposeful leadership did not allow teachers total freedom to attend any course: attendance was encouraged for a good reason. None the less, most teachers in these schools had attended in-service courses.

Thus, effective headteachers were sufficiently involved in, and knowledgeable about, what went on in the classrooms and about the progress of individual pupils. They were more able to feel confident about their teaching staff and did not need to intervene constantly. At the same time, however, they were not afraid to assert their leadership where appropriate.

2 The involvement of the deputy head

Our findings indicate that the deputy head can have a major role to play in promoting the effectiveness of junior schools. Where the deputy was frequently absent, or absent for a prolonged period (due to illness, attendance on long courses, or other commitments), this was detrimental to pupils' progress and development. Moreover, a change of deputy head tended to have negative effects. The responsibilities undertaken by deputy heads also seemed to be significant. Where the head generally involved the deputy in policy decisions, it was beneficial to the pupils. This was particularly true in terms of allocating teachers to classes. Thus, it appears that a certain amount of delegation by the headteacher, and the sharing of responsibilities, promoted effectiveness.

3 The involvement of teachers

In successful schools, the teachers were involved in curriculum planning and played a major role in developing their own curriculum guidelines. As with the deputy head, teacher involvement in decisions concerning which classes they were to teach was important. Similarly, we found that consultation with teachers about decisions on spending was associated with greater effectiveness. It appears that schools in which teachers were consulted on issues affecting school policy, as well as those affecting them directly, were more likely to be successful. We found a link between schools where the deputy was involved in policy decisions and schools where teachers were involved. Thus, effective primary schools did not operate a small management team – everyone had their say.

4 Consistency among teachers

We have already shown that continuity of staffing had positive effects. Not only, however, do pupils benefit from teacher continuity, but it also appears that consistency in teacher approach is important. For example, in schools where all teachers followed guidelines in the same way (whether closely or selectively), the impact on progress was positive. Where there was variation between teachers in their usage of guidelines, this had a negative effect.

5 Structured sessions

The project findings indicate that pupils benefited when their school day was given some structure. In effective classes, pupils' work was organised in broad outline by the teacher, who ensured that there was always plenty of work to do. We also found that the progress of pupils benefited when they were not given unlimited responsibility for planning their own daily programme of work or for choosing work activities, but were guided into areas of study or exploration and taught the skills necessary for independently managing that work. In general, therefore, teachers who organised a framework within which pupils could work, and yet encouraged them to exercise a degree of independence, and allowed some freedom and choice within this structure, were more successful. Children developed and made progress particularly in classrooms where most pupils were able to work in the absence of constant support from their teachers. Clearly, when pupils can work autonomously in this way the teacher is freed to spend time in areas she or he considers a high priority.

6 Intellectually challenging teaching

Not surprisingly, the quality of teaching was very important in promoting pupil progress and development. Our findings show clearly that, in those classes where pupils were stimulated and challenged, progress was greatest. The content of teacher–pupil classroom talk was vitally important. Progress was encouraged where teachers used more higher-order questions and statements, when they encouraged pupils to use their creative imagination and powers of problem-solving. Additionally, in classrooms which were bright and interesting, where the context created by the teacher was stimulating, and where teachers communicated their own interest and enthusiasm to the children, greater pupil progress occurred. In contrast, teachers who frequently directed pupils' work without discussing it, or explaining its purpose, were less effective.

A further important feature was the expectation in the more effective classrooms that pupils could manage independently the tasks they were engaged upon. In such classes teachers only rarely intervened with instructions and directives, yet everyone in the class knew what to do and could work without close supervision.

7 Work-centred environment

In schools where teachers spent more of their time discussing the content of work with pupils, and less time on routine matters and the maintenance of work activity, the effect was positive. Time devoted to giving pupils feedback about their work also appeared to be very beneficial.

The work-centred environment was characterised by a high level of pupil industry in the classroom. Pupils appeared to enjoy their work and were eager to commence new tasks. The noise level was low, although this is not to say that there was silence in the classroom. In fact, none of the classes we visited were completely silent. Furthermore, pupil movement around the classroom was not excessive, and was generally work-related. These results receive support from the views of pupils. Even in the third year over 40 per cent of pupils reported that they had difficulty in concentrating on their work most of the time. Where levels of noise and movement were high, concentration seems to be more difficult to maintain. Work-centred classrooms, therefore, had a business-like and purposeful air, with pupils obviously enjoying the work they were doing. Furthermore, where classrooms were work-centred, lessons were found to be more challenging.

8 Limited focus within sessions

It appears that pupils made greater progress when teachers tended to organise lessons around one particular curriculum area. At times, work could be undertaken in two areas and also produce positive effects, but, where the tendency was for the teacher regularly to organise classroom work such that three or more curriculum areas were running concurrently, then pupils' progress was marred. This finding is related to a number of other factors. For example, pupil industry was lower in classrooms where mixed-activities occurred, noise and pupil movement were greater, and teachers spent less time discussing work and more time on routine issues and behaviour control. Thus, such classrooms were less likely to be work-centred. More importantly, in mixed-activity sessions the opportunities for communication between teachers and pupils were reduced (see key factor 9 below).

A focus upon one curriculum area does not imply that all the pupils should do exactly the same work. On the contrary, effects were most positive when the teacher geared the level of work to pupils' needs, but not where all pupils worked individually on exactly the same piece of work. It seems likely that, in mixed-curriculum sessions, the demands made upon the teachers' time, attention, and energy can become too great for them to ensure effective learning with all groups. Furthermore, it becomes more difficult in such sessions for the teacher to call the class together should the opportunity arise to share an interesting point that may emerge from the work of a particular group or pupil. We recognise that there are many occasions when teachers may wish to diversify the work in the classroom, and beyond, into more than one curriculum area. Sometimes such diversification is unavoidable, perhaps through the constraints of timetabling or because of the nature of the work in progress but, for the reasons cited above, we would urge the utmost caution over the adoption of a mixed-curriculum methodology as a basis for teaching and learning.

9 Maximum communication between teachers and pupils

We found evidence that pupils gained from having lots of communication with the teacher. Thus, those teachers who spent higher proportions of their time not interacting with the children were less successful in promoting progress and development. The time teachers spent on communications with the whole class was also important. Most teachers devoted most of their attention to speaking with individuals. Each child, therefore, could only expect to receive a fairly small number of individual contacts with their teacher. In fact, as we described earlier, for each pupil the average number of such contacts over a day was only eleven. Given that some children demand, and receive, more attention than the average from their teachers, this means that others have very few individual contacts per day. By speaking to the whole class, teachers increased the overall number of contacts with children, as pupils become part of the teacher's audience more often in such circumstances. Most importantly higher-order communications occurred more frequently when the teacher talked to the whole class.

We are not, however, advocating traditional class teaching. Our findings did not show any such approach to be beneficial for pupils and, in fact, we found no evidence of readily identifiable teaching styles at all. We feel that teaching is far too complex an activity for it to be categorised in this way. On the contrary, our results indicate the value of a flexible approach, that can blend individual, class, and group interaction as appropriate. Furthermore, where children worked in a single curriculum area within sessions (even if they were engaged on individual or group tasks), it was easier for teachers to raise an intellectually challenging point with all pupils. Such exchanges tended to occur when teachers were introducing a topic to the class before pupils were sent off to work individually or in groups. Class discussions were also a popular forum for gathering all pupils together, as was storytelling. These activities offered teachers a particular opportunity to challenge and stimulate their pupils.

10 Record keeping

We have already commented upon the value of record keeping in relation to the purposeful leadership of the headteacher. In addition, it was also an important aspect of teachers' planning and assessment. Where teachers reported that they kept written records of pupils' work progress, in addition to the authority's primary yearly record summary, the effect on the pupils was positive. The keeping of records concerning pupils' personal and social development was also found to be generally beneficial. Furthermore, in many effective schools, teachers kept samples of pupils' work in folders to be passed on to their next teacher.

11 Parental involvement

Our findings show parental involvement in the life of the school to be a positive influence upon pupils' progress and development. This included help in classrooms and on educational visits, and attendance at meetings to discuss children's progress. The headteacher's accessibility to parents was also important, schools operating an informal, open-door policy being more effective. Parental involvement in pupils' educational development within the home was also clearly beneficial. Parents who read to their children, heard them read, and provided them with access to books at home had a positive effect upon their children's learning. Curiously, however, formal parent–teacher associations were not found to be related to effective schooling. Although the reasons for this are not clear it could be that some parents find the formal structure of such bodies to be intimidating and are thus deterred from involvement, rather than encouraged. We also found that some parents feel that PTAs tend to be run by small cliques of parents. We would not wish to advocate, of course, that schools disband their PTAs, but if a school has an association and is not involving parents in other ways it would perhaps be worth considering how parent–school relationships could be opened up.

12 Positive climate

The Junior School Project provides confirmation that an effective school has a positive ethos. Overall, we found the atmosphere to be more pleasant in the effective schools, for a variety of reasons. Both around the school and within the classroom, less emphasis on punishment and critical control and a greater emphasis on praise and reward was beneficial. Where teachers actively encouraged self-control on the part of pupils, rather than emphasising the negative aspects of their behaviour, progress and development were enhanced. What appeared to be important was firm but fair classroom management. The class teachers' attitude to pupils was also important. Positive effects resulted where teachers obviously enjoyed teaching their classes, valued the fun factor, and communicated their enthusiasm to the children. Their interest in the children as individuals, and not just as learners, also fostered progress. Those who devoted more time to non-school chat or small talk increased pupils' progress and development. Outside the classroom, evidence of a positive climate included: the organisation of lunchtime and after-school clubs for pupils; involvement of pupils in the presentation of assemblies; teachers eating their lunch at the same tables as the children; organisation of trips and visits; and the use of the local environment as a learning resource.

It is important to note that the climate in effective schools was not only positive for the pupils. The teachers' working conditions also contributed to the creation of a positive climate. Where teachers had non-teaching periods, the impact on pupil progress and development was positive. Thus, the climate created by the teachers for the pupils, and by the head for the teachers, was an important aspect of school effectiveness. This further appeared to be reflected in effective schools by happy, well-behaved pupils who were friendly towards each other and outsiders, and by the absence of graffiti around the school.

The twelve key factors point to effective schools as being friendly, supportive environments, led by heads who are not afraid to assert their views and yet are able to share management and decision making with the staff. Class teachers within effective schools provide a structured learning situation for their pupils but give them freedom within this framework. By being flexible in their use of whole class, group, and individual contacts, they maximise communications with each pupil. Furthermore, through limiting their focus within sessions, their attention is less fragmented. Hence, the opportunities for developing a work-centred environment and for presenting challenging work to pupils are increased.

While the twelve key factors we have outlined may not constitute a recipe for effective junior schooling, they can provide a framework within which the various partners in the life of the school – headteacher and staff, parents and pupils, and governors – can operate. Each of these partners has some role to play in fostering the overall success of the school, and, when each makes a positive contribution, the result can be an increase in the school's effectiveness.

Chapter 32

The culture of collaboration

Jennifer Nias, Geoff Southworth, and Robin Yeomans

This chapter is a heavily edited extract from an influential study on staff relationships in primary schools. The work was based on case studies in five schools and a 'culture of collaboration' was identified in three of them. The key issue concerns the relationships between staff as people and the ways in which these influence their collective sense of purpose and commitment to fulfilling their roles in school. This work pre-dated the introduction of the national curriculum and research since then has identified a growth of collegiality in many schools, but with others becoming more hierarchically managed. How, for instance, would St Andrew's Primary School, in Chapter 33, compare?

All the project schools evolved their own dominant staff cultures, as over time individuals with different amounts of authority and influence chose or happened to interact with one another. But soon we also became aware that three of them – Greenfields, Lowmeadow, and Sedgemoor – were so similar in many respects that they could be described as having a particular type of culture. To be sure, this was manifested in different ways: 'the way we do it here' in relation to, say, assembly, staff meetings, or the distribution of curricular responsibilities was unique to each school. But we began to discover that, as we penetrated below these surface differences, we encountered similarities, particularly in regard to staff beliefs about the relationships which existed or should exist between individuals and groups. In consequence, the values enshrined in much of the practice of these schools were also similar.

We argue that the culture was built on four interacting beliefs. The first two specify ends: individuals should be valued but, because they are inseparable from the groups of which they are part, groups too should be fostered and valued. The second two relate to means: the most effective ways of promoting these values are through openness and a sense of mutual security.

VALUING INDIVIDUALS AS PEOPLE

In the schools where this culture existed, even the most mundane and apparently insignificant details of staff behaviour were consistent with its values. Respect for the individual cropped up in many guises. There were few signs of status consciousness within the staff groups. Headteachers freely used the staffrooms and joined in the informal conversation, joking, and teasing that were commonplace there. Probationers and newcomers to these schools were quickly made to feel valued by their colleagues (e.g., 'They [the staff] treat me as an individual here to do a job, not to be looked down upon or anything like that. I'm like anybody really' (Probationer, Sedgemoor). At Sedgemoor, Lowmeadow, Greenfields, and Hutton, the secretary and ancillary workers used the staffroom, while at Hutton the caretaker and the ancillary were members of the informal staff cricket team:

> During the evening cricket match Bill the caretaker was very prominent, not just as a player but as a member of the group. He enjoyed it hugely, saying 'I'm not competitive; but I do get involved.' He is deferred to as the expert on how to play and on the laws of this particular form of the game. Diane the ancillary is brought into the proceedings. Although she is officially reserve, she comes along and so that she can have a full part she and Maureen share the eighth place on the team, each playing for half the time.
>
> (Fieldnote, October, Hutton)

At Lavender Way, however, the caretaker was not invited to use the staffroom, and the ancillary, who had previously been a dinner supervisor, did not feel comfortable there, choosing instead to take her breaks in the kitchen because 'I was missing the company of the girls in the kitchen.'

Everyone coming to these schools was made to feel welcome:

> I don't think it matters who it is and again we say this to the children, it doesn't matter if it's the dustman, or somebody who looks terribly important, or somebody's mum, we treat them all alike and they are all made to feel welcome.
>
> (Head, Sedgemoor)

The staff were so nice, it's a very open school, you know, 'Come into the staffroom', there was no waiting around in the corridor, straight into the staffroom. Somebody was making a cup of coffee and they involved me in the conversation. They don't just do that with someone like me who came to look around the school, they do that with all the parents and with everybody. They make everybody very welcome, it's marvellous and I like the way they've got time for parents and involve the parents a lot in the school. I like the attitude towards the children. They care, and that's what came across to me.

(Recently appointed teacher, Greenfields)

The fact that staff saw one another as people rather than purely as role occupants or colleagues was also evident in the 'person-centred' nature of much of their talk:

Staffroom talk at breaks is almost always domestic and personal, e.g., broken ornaments, shopping, holidays, weddings, pets. Today, after lunch, two teachers discussed some workcards for about three minutes. It was the first curriculum conversation I've heard in the staffroom and it was rapidly overtaken by talk of a television programme shown last night.

(Fieldnote, January, Lowmeadow)

In the discussions at lunchtime there was a sense of the staff group reconvening [after a half-day strike]. It was also the first time Mary was back in school since her hospital appointment. She was warmly welcomed by both Carol and Victoria. Victoria and Mary then talked at some length with Carol about teenage children. Jim happily said hello and in a warm way noted how long it had been since they had seen each other.

(Fieldnote, November, Greenfields)

Because the lives of staff were seen to extend beyond school, allowances were made at work for domestic circumstances such as a husband's or son's redundancy, invalid relatives, children's half-terms, moving house, and for the immediate health and happiness of the individual. Staff were tolerant of each other's taciturnity, irritability, or unaccustomed inefficiency; they were quick to anticipate the help which might be needed because of, for example, a fit of depression, a painful back, a broken car, or a sleepless night. When someone was having a bad day, the appropriate response was to be sympathetic rather than offended. In the collaborative schools there was a pervasive atmosphere of consideration for others. Although it had begun to develop in the other two, it is instructive to compare:

[In the last week of term] the staff are all looking very tired and I am frankly exhausted, but everyone still deals with one another with total courtesy and painstaking consideration. I haven't heard an irritable exchange, grudging comment or expression of impatience and they continue to take a loving interest in one another's domestic doings.

(Fieldnote, December, Lowmeadow)

with the remark made by a teacher at Lavender Way as she looked back at the start of the year: 'It felt like a conscious effort to be courteous and kind to each other' (Teacher, Lavender Way).

Personal kindness sometimes also extended beyond school:

It's nice to sort of socialize really outside school . . . I've been out to people's for meals and that kind of thing. Personally I like getting to know people of all age groups – things like Josie's husband's been wonderful for mending my Hoover and putting plugs in, and I've taken Sheila's little girl swimming and that kind of thing. So we do tend to do things together.

(Probationer, Sedgemoor)

Knowledge and acceptance of people as individuals was further strengthened by getting to know and like one another's families, a reciprocal process which enabled staff members to gain insights into the broader social context in which their colleagues were set:

We all know each other's families and we've shared our problems. . . . We've all managed to share and advise each other and commiserate with each other and I think that's got a lot to do with making us into a closer community. Because of the things we know about each other . . . we've all tried to be supportive to each other and just listen. All of us feel that if we've got any problems at home we can always talk about them here and somebody will say, 'Oh that happened to me', or commiserate or help or advise or whatever.

(Teacher, Lowmeadow)

Networks of out-of-school relationships similar to the one revealed in the following extract occurred in all the schools:

INT: You have quite strong, informal social links with Jim, you're going to stay at his parents' and he's met your parents, I think, so there's a kind of outside school 'getting to know you'.

G: His daughter is my god-daughter.

INT: Right, so that's another link. I know you see Carol, because you sometimes call round of an evening to have a chat, you've said that in the past. I wonder if there are any such links with other staff?

G: The four of us, Victoria and her husband and Sally, my wife, are quite close friends and Victoria and I have been involved in activities together like school journeys which have involved chats in the evening, so there have been evening meetings with Victoria as well, probably as much as with Carol. But certainly there are times outside school when we meet – Carol, Victoria, Jim and me – not so much anybody else. We go on courses together in twos and threes and that usually means some form of socializing after the course, so there are those kinds of links.

(Head, Greenfields)

However, when a collaborative culture did not exist within a school, close or frequent out-of-school contact between individuals who were also friendly at work could be read as exclusivity rather than cohesion.

VALUING INTERDEPENDENCE

So, individual staff members at Greenfields, Lowmeadow, and Sedgemoor valued one another as people, each with his/her own identity, personality, interests, skills, experiences, and potential, but they also appreciated the diversity which this brought to the school. Similarly, the sense of collective dependence on which the 'culture of collaboration' was also built had two sides to it. Together the members of each staff made a group which they valued because it gave them a feeling of belonging. At the same time, they accepted a collective responsibility for the work of the school, so creating a strong team in which people helped, encouraged, and substituted for one another.

The staffs' awareness of belonging to a group characterised by social or emotional interdependence was expressed in two main ways. First, they saw one another as 'friends' and even, sometimes, as 'family', phrases that they repeatedly used:

> I regard them all as being friends. . . . I could go to them if anything was wrong.
>
> (Teacher, Sedgemoor)

> [The head] is like a friend, not that she's boss, she's more a friend.
>
> (Ancillary, Sedgemoor)

> I don't just look upon it so much as job as an extension of family . . . everybody is so close . . . I know I would miss it terribly if I didn't come.
>
> (Teacher, Lowmeadow)

> There's a great deal of warmth between us and it's almost like a family that closes ranks against outsiders when it's being attacked by a piece of gossip or an occasion of vandalism. We come together very closely.
>
> (Teacher, Greenfields)

> I think the friendliness more than anything else. I've worked for a long time in industry and only a short time in school, comparatively, and I don't think in industry you get the friendliness that you get in school, from the staff and pupils.
>
> (Caretaker, Lowmeadow)

Secondly, the fact that the staff saw one another as friends spilled over into the way in which they tackled their work, making it hard to maintain a distinction between personal and professional interdependence:

I went in with her and helped her put up her display that she's got to do for assembly tomorrow . . . I would have gone and helped her anyway because that's part of my job. Aside from that, I know she's not feeling very well. I know that she's got to go to the dentist at quarter to five and that she's been struggling on during the afternoon to do things, but that reinforced what I was going to do anyway. So the professional side of me going to help her is reinforced by the social side of me liking her and wanting to help her.

(Deputy, Sedgemoor)

If I just came and did the cleaning and teachers just saw you as that, just the person who comes and does the cleaning, perhaps they would treat me different, but if you give them a bit extra, then it must make your own job more enjoyable, it certainly does mine. I would hate just to be the person who comes and does the cleaning.

(Caretaker, Hutton)

Although group membership was affectively satisfying, this is not the whole story. At Greenfields, Lowmeadow, and Sedgemoor the staff also felt a sense of collective responsibility for their work and saw themselves as a team. As Isobel wrote in the Sedgemoor Curriculum Award folder: 'We feel that the consideration and closeness which characterizes relationships between adult members pervades the school as a whole. . . . Thus issues like infant–junior liaison are less important than the sense of the school as a whole team.' To be a 'team' meant to recognise and value the unique contribution of each member, teachers and non-teachers alike, to a joint enterprise. Being a team did not necessarily mean doing the same job or working in the same teaching space, but it did mean working to the same ends. At Sedgemoor:

Everyone has a function and the value of that is acknowledged – for example Josie for her language expertise, even though she is 'only' part-time, Molly the secretary for her ability to deal with administrative concerns that teachers find difficult, Polly the ancillary for her ideas and personal support.

(Yeomans 1986)

Similarly, at Lowmeadow:

Another thing I agreed with was to try and bring the caretaker and cleaning staff into the team. I firmly believe that to get the school working properly you have to have everybody working as a team and here it really works. . . . When it was Janice the cook's 21st birthday, we had a present for her and she came into the assembly. Sandra, the secretary, comes into assemblies, and when it's her birthday, she has her candle. -

(Teacher, Lowmeadow)

The sense of collective responsibility on which the teams were built showed itself in many ways. Most obviously everyone advised, supported, and helped one another so habitually and regularly that it has been difficult to select a few illustrations from among the multitude of daily examples:

> Rhoda said to me, 'I haven't done reception teaching before, could you help?' And I said, 'Absolutely, I'd love to'. So we had lots of chats at lunchtime, but it became apparent very soon that she didn't need any further help. . . . To give it and then take it away because it's not needed is much preferable to running after someone with a crutch after they've fallen over. It's too late then, it's the wrong way round.
>
> (Teacher, Lowmeadow)

> If you say 'I'm doing such and such, I haven't got any good ideas', there will be six or seven different ideas thrown at you instantly. Or if you get halfway through doing something and you happen to say 'Oh, it's not working or it's going wrong', there's always someone who is willing to help in any sort of situation. And in dealing with the children you never feel, if you have a problem, that you're cut off, there's always somebody else who is willing to help you. It's often the case [in other schools that] there is someone around who is capable of helping, but not always that they will help, but in this school that doesn't seem to be so. Everyone seems very ready to help.
>
> (Teacher, Sedgemoor)

> It is the sort of school where you can say 'I don't know what to do' in such and such a subject or how best to tackle this, or what do you suggest with this child to get him reading? And everybody will jump in with advice and help and try to be helpful, which is nice.
>
> (Teacher, Greenfields)

There was a general awareness that any member of staff might need the others at some point and that this need would be met, as a matter of course, by anyone who was available. As one teacher said:

> [You've got to be] adaptable and friendly to work here. Everyone is prepared to help everyone else out, as and when they can. If they ask you for something, you are prepared to do it, or you're prepared to volunteer something when it's required.
>
> (Teacher, Lowmeadow)

Overall, then, in Sedgemoor, Greenfields, and Lowmeadow mutuality was the norm:

> We've got to be looking for someone who will 'fit in' with the rest of the staff. They don't actually take kindly to anyone who is too shy. They don't mind somebody taking a little while to settle down,

but once they've settled down the rest of the staff here are the kind
of people who are delighted to help and give help, they like to be asked
for it.

(Head, Greenfields)

You can go round supporting everybody and expect everybody just to
listen to what you suggest and you not to take ideas, but that's unrealistic. . . . As far as supporting and influencing people [goes], it's
important that it's mutual because otherwise it doesn't work.

(Deputy, Sedgemoor)

What was less clear from our evidence was whether a sense of personal
interdependence preceded or followed the decision to work together, that is,
whether groups became teams or teams developed into groups. As someone
rhetorically reflected at Hutton:

Alison and Marion stand out, obviously, you don't really see it [team-
teaching] anywhere else. Did the friendship come first or did the partnership come first?

(Teacher, Hutton)

The answer seems to be that sometimes liking led to sharing work and
thence to a sense of belonging to a team, while at others working with
colleagues resulted in a feeling of social cohesion, and a group was formed.
Either way, '[to work closely together] you've got to respond to someone
and develop a good working relationship with them' (Teacher, Hutton).
Moreover once a 'team-group' had become established, membership of it
was so rewarding that it tended to be self-perpetuating.

VALUING SECURITY

In this section and the next we examine the two beliefs embedded in the
'culture of collaboration' which specify means rather than ends: that security
is a necessary condition for the growth of openness and that openness is the
best way of simultaneously fostering the individual and the group.

The link between beliefs relating to ends and to means lies in the notion of
interdependence which we have so far discussed as if it always and necessarily enriched those who experienced it. There is of course another side to
this: mutual dependence also means mutual constraint. To accept that one is
dependent on anyone else is to admit that there are limits to one's autonomy.
These limits might be unspoken, as they were in the team-teaching
pair at Hutton and for all the staff at Sedgemoor, they might be spelt
out by curriculum documents (such as those at Hutton and Greenfields),
or be implicit in curriculum materials (e.g., the mathematics scheme at
Lowmeadow). They might be relatively open to negotiation, as at Greenfields, or rather precise, as was the case in the Jayne–Stella partnership

at Lavender Way. Whatever their exact nature or extent, acceptance of them was mandatory:

> If you've made a conscious decision to be in the school, then you've got to make it work, you can't say 'Oh, I can't work like this and I'm not going to', because nobody has forced you to actually come to the school. You make the decision to come here, so then you've got to say 'I'm going to do my best and work with this situation as it is and not try to make it into something completely different'. . . . You can't just come storming in and do your own thing. . . . So that was it, really. I did learn a lot from Jayne and got to know her very well.
>
> (Stella, Lavender Way)

> These schemes were drawn up as a result of several staff discussions. They are not intended to be comprehensive directives, but rather to form a framework within which members of staff are free to exploit their strengths and to experiment with methods. In some cases, however, it was felt that teachers would welcome a more explicit approach as an aid to continuity. We felt that freedom of method would only be desirable within a well structured scheme, and that we should try to ensure that such freedom did not lead to omissions in the course of the school year.
>
> (Introduction to *School Schemes of Work*, Greenfields)

> To work here you'd *have* to be prepared to work as part of this team. If you persisted in not being part of a team you could exist here, but you wouldn't be happy. You could make it, but not in any satisfying sense. . . . If you're not prepared to submit, in the Biblical sense, you're not going to be an effective team member. But once you can see it's in the best interests of the children, it's easy.
>
> (Teacher, Lowmeadow)

There is no inconsistency in this position. Though to submit is to accept another's power over oneself, when all the members of a team make this submission to one another, their power over each other is evenly balanced and becomes influence instead. So within a situation of agreed interdependence, 'We're all influencing each other, I'm quite convinced of that' (Teacher, Greenfields).

But even this statement, by a member of a staff group in which dependence seemed to be evenly spread, does not reflect the whole truth. For the 'culture of collaboration' rested upon beliefs which emanated from and were exemplified in the headteacher:

> They [the staff] feel free in staff meetings or discussions with me, to make their opinions known quite clearly and they know that I'm going to accept their opinions, but that I'm not going to be swayed by them in the

'wrong way', if you like. There is no one on the staff who is going to express an opinion which will push me in a way that I don't want to go.

(Head, Greenfields)

I think you must accept that things that are done in certain classrooms . . . will be done in your classroom too. I think you have to be fairly accepting of the situation as it is. Individualistic teachers tend to leave quite quickly.

(Teacher, Lowmeadow)

The answer to this apparent contradiction between mutual constraint and deference to the head appears to lie in three interrelated facts. First, head-teachers are the main 'culture-founders' in their schools, and, provided that they exemplify in their personal and professional behaviour the beliefs that underpin this culture, they have a degree of personal authority which transcends that of other staff members, even though they can exercise effective leadership over the latter only by becoming one of them. Secondly, the mutual influence which characterises the 'culture of collaboration' is exercised within boundaries which are themselves set by and respected out of deference to the head's authority. Thirdly, primary headteachers and teachers are members not just of their schools but also of an occupation which traditionally sets much store by its members' ability to control pupils and which is, perhaps in consequence, hierarchically structured. Teachers exercise authority over others but are often themselves authority-dependent (Abercrombie 1981; Nias 1987). In other words, the 'culture of collaboration' coexisted in the project schools with a wider occupational culture that served to limit the extent to which teachers expected to be able to influence their heads. Similarly, the latter remained and expected to remain *primus inter pares*.

The fact that the heads' responsibility for the main policies in their schools was virtually unchallenged and that the staff exercised a good deal of mutual influence over one another made the collaborative schools very secure places in which to work. In addition, interpersonal familiarity helped people feel professionally at ease with one another. The personally self-confident were more disposed to speak their minds and to invite reciprocal comment than were those who felt insecure:

It's a lot to do with self-confidence, whether people can open themselves to you. If they are not very self-confident, they can't open themselves because it makes them vulnerable. But if they can, then you can have an insight into their personality and you can respond to them much better.

(Teacher, Hutton)

VALUING OPENNESS

Many of the day-to-day attitudes and actions of the staff demonstrated the value which they attached to openness. Headteachers, teachers, and ancillaries were ready to admit publicly to a sense of failure:

> This is a very unusual school because normally you don't do that. In the other schools I've taught in you *didn't* fail. If you did you kept it very quiet. It took me a good four months to realize that . . . when you had problems you didn't hide them away, you voiced them and you got them sorted out instantly instead of taking them home and worrying about them.
>
> (Teacher, Sedgemoor)

> Rosemary said, 'I don't know what all the problem is, I don't have any trouble with playground duty', but in a way that wasn't putting down and Jane felt able to respond by saying 'I feel terrible when it can take a minute or more to get the children to attend to the Stop board when I'm out there, whereas when Rosemary is on playground duty, I see her holding it up and everybody is quiet at once'. Margaret chipped in to support Jane. 'It takes me a long time too.'
>
> (Fieldnote of staff meeting, May, Lowmeadow)

> We all have to accept that mistakes are made. If that happens, we learn by our mistakes. You usually only notice that you've forgotten something if something bad happens from it. If you forget and later on it turns out that it was important, because of the atmosphere of trust in the school, you're not afraid to say, 'Well, I'm sorry', and then it becomes a point of discussion and helps everybody to see the importance of communicating carefully.
>
> (Teacher, Lowmeadow)

Staff were also ready to display other negative emotions, such as guilt, anxiety, and anger:

> We can all go in the staffroom and let off steam if we want to with each other, and really know that it's not going to go any further. You can get rid of your pent-up anxiety or whatever it happens to be, you can really let fly and they'll sympathize or agree with you. You don't have to bottle it all up and take it home with you, and take it out on somebody at home, you can talk about it here.
>
> (Teacher, Lowmeadow)

> You feel you can tell them, you're not letting yourself down. . . . You feel they will understand . . . if you didn't have the staffroom and your colleagues to go and let steam off, that's when things would get a bit much. We've got that, it's our safety valve, isn't it? Being able to sit in

there at dinner time over a cup of coffee and chat about everything and anything, whether it's related to school or not, to get things off your chest. It does help. If you've got to bottle everything up, that is when you get uptight.

(Teacher, Greenfields)

I remember once somebody saying that in one school the staff didn't think it professional to talk about the children in front of other members of staff, if they were having problems. I just said 'that's a load of nonsense', because I think that's one of the ways of getting rid of your tension, screaming about a child or joking about some child and their impossibilities.

(Teacher, Sedgemoor)

It was also regarded as normal for individual staff members to voice irritation or dissent directly to one another. Disagreements were accepted as part of human intercourse:

Differences of opinion do emerge but we're all very open, straightforward. If we don't agree with someone we do say so. You know, you just state that you didn't agree and that you thought such and such . . . it doesn't need to be argument.

(Teacher, Sedgemoor)

Some reference was made in the staffroom to politics and a teacher said, 'We have a range of opinions here. You should hear us at a general election'. [Later] I took the opportunity of asking her how 'the group of sisters' coped with differences. Her answer can be summarized as follows: 'We talk a lot, all the time, so when differences occur they can be dealt with naturally. Also, because we respect one another and respect one another's differences it's usually quite easy to talk quite openly about things. People are not afraid of speaking their mind.'

(Fieldnote, March, Lowmeadow)

By contrast, at the start of the year at Lavender Way and Hutton few people felt they could be direct with one another:

I didn't know the school he came from, but he said the staff there really did communicate with each other and you could say something to a member of staff and they didn't feel offended or you could really shout at somebody and they would bounce back the next day. It's not like that here.

(Teacher, Lavender Way)

However, would-be 'collaborators' at these schools worked during the year to establish an atmosphere in which it was seen as normal for people to disagree:

The key factor in the personal relationship side is trying to help people to understand somebody else's perception of that particular thing that has caused whatever it is. I mean, you can't possibly go through the school day term in, term out without there being problems between people. But I would hope that you could actually improve people's relationships with one another by helping that person to face it.

(New deputy, Hutton)

At Greenfields and Lowmeadow the expression of dissent was sometimes quite impassioned. From time to time pairs of teachers, or a head and a teacher, would have what they described as 'disputes', 'rows', or 'violent disagreements'. These were not, however, allowed to disrupt relationships permanently:

There was quite a severe argument between Jim and Victoria, which seemed to indicate that tempers were becoming quite frayed. We had had a very difficult couple of weeks with changing the caretaker, staff being appointed elsewhere and so on. . . . What happened was that I mentioned to Victoria that there had been an advertisement in the school list for a temporary deputy headteacher in a school at Castleton. So she was looking for the list and Jim said he had tidied it away. Victoria's rather waspish comment was 'That's the sort of thing you used to do when you were a deputy head', to which, of course, Jim took exception. . . . There was an outburst from both sides. . . . By lunchtime Jim had invited Victoria to go and have lunch with him and I went along and they both apologized and I was impressed with . . . the fact that they could be extremely angry with one another over a small thing and yet by half way through the day things had been smoothed over and they seemed to be perfectly all right.

(Head, Greenfields)

[After describing a heated difference of opinion with her head] As with all relationships, it's not having the row that counts but how you deal with it afterwards, whether you're able to build on it and go forward with the relationship.

(Deputy, Lowmeadow)

The emotions that people felt free to express were, however, positive as well as negative. Reflecting on the amount of open emotion he saw at Greenfields, Southworth (1986) wrote:

There is . . . affection. First there is affection for the children. . . . Second, there is affection amongst the adults. . . . Staff actually like each other, as professionals and as people. To talk of the school as a family is not merely to use the family as a metaphor for how the school works as an organisation, it is to imbue the school-as-an-organisation with affection. It is to recognise that working together involves an acceptance that everyone in the school has feelings, and is making an emotional as well as a professional investment. . . . On the last day of the year the emotional side of the school became particularly visible. Affection was breaking out everywhere.

The direct expression of views or feelings was not valued only for its therapeutic effect or because it eased interpersonal communication. Experienced staff members saw that it also enabled people to learn from one another in enjoyable ways. The free exchange of work-related information and ideas contributed both to the professional development of the whole staff and to its social cohesion, that is, it simultaneously built up the team and developed the group. Evidently the 'culture of collaboration' contains a potential for professional development, through the free exchange of opinions, which makes it particularly well suited to schools.

SUMMARY

Three of the project schools – Greenfields, Lowmeadow, and Sedgemoor – shared a common type of dominant culture, though it was expressed in each school in slightly different ways. The heads and deputies of Hutton and Lavender Way were trying to move their schools towards this 'culture of collaboration'. Its existence made it possible for headteachers, teachers, and ancillaries routinely and unselfconsciously to work as a team, that is, to behave, despite all their differences, as if they all shared a common goal, to feel collectively responsible for its attainment, and always to be ready to help one another towards it. It was also this culture which helped staff members, including the head, to identify as a group, that is see one another as friends and to feel a satisfying sense of social cohesion.

This culture arises from and embodies a set of social and moral beliefs about desirable relationships between individuals and the communities of which they are part, and not from beliefs about epistemology or pedagogy. It does, however, have a multiple effect, over time, on the educational practice of the schools in which it exists.

Its two main beliefs are that individuals should be accepted and valued, but that so too should interdependence, because individuals exist only in a social context. Within both beliefs one can distinguish two threads. Individuals are to be welcomed, appreciated, and fostered for their own sakes, but also for the mutual enrichment which comes from diversity. Similarly, interdependence is valued because it celebrates both the group and the team. The culture also embodies beliefs about means. Interdependence leads to mutual constraint, and it is the resulting security which encourages members of the culture to be open with one another in the expression of disagreement and of emotion.

Shared understandings and agreed behaviours enable staff in schools where this culture is dominant to trust and to learn from one another. The relationships which they create in the process are tough and flexible enough to withstand shocks and uncertainties from within and without. 'Collaborative' staffs tended to be both happy and resilient.

REFERENCES

Abercrombie, M. J. (1981) 'Changing basic assumptions about teaching and learning', in Boud, D. (ed.) *Developing Student Autonomy in Learning*, London, Kogan Page.

Nias, J. (1987) 'Learning from difference: a collegial approach to change', in Smyth, W. J. (ed.) *Changing the Nature of Pedagogical Knowledge*, Lewes, Falmer Press.

Southworth, G. W. (1986) 'A community called Greenfields: a case study of a primary school', Cambridge, Cambridge Institute of Education (mimeo).

Yeomans, R. (1986) 'The Sedgemoor way: a case study of inter-adult relationships at Sedgemoor Primary School', Cambridge, Cambridge Institute of Education (mimeo).

Chapter 33

St Andrew's Church of England Primary School

Miriam Wilcock

This is a headteacher's description of her school and her approach to management. Many of the issues raised by the other chapters in the 'schools' section of this book can be seen to be embedded in the account and the fact that it is a personal account gives it a particular interest. Note the importance of the head's values and educational philosophy, the complexity of management challenges in a period of change and the role of the head in representing the school externally as well as leading it internally.

THE SCHOOL

St Andrew's Church of England (Controlled) Primary School dates back to 1860, but a new site (single storey, flat roofed, with six classrooms) was opened in 1966. However, Chinnor was expanding close to the M40 motorway and a second building providing eight more teaching areas was completed in 1970. Both buildings have a centrally paved courtyard, one with a pond. These offer facilities for growing plants and shrubs or safe areas for keeping animals. All rooms have some carpeted areas with tiled areas for art and craft work, the remaining space being of wood-block flooring.

The grounds are spacious, offering three hard-surfaced playgrounds, with some concrete play equipment, and paved and low-walled areas with seating. Playgrounds are surrounded by open grassed areas for football and other sports. Some fifteen years ago parents raised funds and energy to build a one-metre deep, open-air swimming pool with changing rooms.

The school is situated at the foot of the Chiltern Hills and it is a ten-minute walk to the nature reserve on the hillside. Our 360 children, aged between 5 and 11 years, come from the village itself and from surrounding villages within a radius of four miles. St Andrew's is proud to have been one of the pioneering schools that have been welcoming physically handicapped children as ordinary members of the school. In addition we are the 'base' school for a unit for autistic children. These children, too, are integrated for varying periods of time into normal classes.

Chinnor is a village offering a variety of residences for those employed in

London, High Wycombe, Aylesbury, and the surrounding towns, in addition to traditional rural occupations. Families living in Chinnor tend to be in professional occupations. Parental expectations for their children are high and interest in and support of the work and activities of the school are always forthcoming.

PERSONAL PHILOSOPHY OF EDUCATION

My philosophy of education stems from the training I received at Whitelands College where the emphasis was always on meeting the needs of the individual child. Children acquire skills and knowledge when the surroundings are stimulating and purposeful. When work and effort is celebrated and valued, the child's own self-esteem is heightened and self-motivation results. I have never been happy to over-emphasize competition, preferring to encourage each individual to become independent learners, setting goals for themselves.

I have always seen my responsibility as a teacher to enable the children in my care to develop as a whole. This embraces the social, emotional, spiritual, and physical development, as well as the academic. I am concerned with children before they start school and after they leave the primary stage at 11. To this end I have sought vigorously over the last twenty-five years to create and sustain contacts across the phases of education and welcome recent initiatives that endorse this. Children have lives beyond the classroom and we cannot meet their needs if we show no interest or concerns for their activities with families and peers. The enrichment that can be brought into the classroom from the wealth of experiences children enjoy is like gold dust: it can add a dimension to learning beyond measure. It is with this firm belief that I have always encouraged the involvement of parents in schools and genuinely look towards them as co-educators, working with teachers, in the overall growth and development of their children.

Schools should be lively, busy places with the children engaged in purposeful activities. This presupposes the security of a firm underlying structure and organisation that is understood and shared by staff and children alike. Planning plays an essential part in achieving this and is, again, best brought into practice when it is shared with colleagues and the children. Evaluation should follow naturally and become the foundations of the next stage in the planning process. This is my vision and, like all visions, does not always come as fully into focus as I might wish. The pressures and calls upon personal commitments, families, outside interests, friends, which we all experience, inevitably result in periods when we as a staff know that our ideals are not being achieved. No one likes to admit that ideals are falling short and some staff find it more difficult to face shortcomings than others. These are the times when true professional support and encouragement are brought into play, and when we attempt to challenge ourselves in the light of our objectives.

ORGANISATION AND MANAGEMENT OF THE SCHOOL

I clearly recall the words of a headteacher early in my career: 'My teachers teach most effectively when encouraged to develop their own skills and personal styles.' In the schools where I have worked I have seen the truth of this. Successful schools are those that have been able to appoint staff who offer a balance of skills and styles. In any group of people there has to be a willingness to give and take, to acknowledge and respect the contributions each can make towards achieving the aims of the school.

I consider the 'staff' of the school to be all those who work alongside the children: teachers, classroom assistants, secretary, caretaker, lunchtime supervisors, voluntary helpers, and students. In the organisation and management of the school it is understandably the full-time teaching staff who carry the greater responsibilities.

In the last two years our numbers have dropped due to demographic influences, and we have twelve classes. To make the best use of the two buildings, we have reorganised into two teams, one for years 1–3 (as identified by the 1988 Act) and one for years 4–6.

Responding to reports and publications from HMI prior to the 1988 Act, we had already seen the value of identifying the strengths and skills of individual members of staff in a consultative or co-ordinating role. Given our large staff it would be surprising if we were unable to name someone to co-ordinate each of the curriculum areas. In achieving this I am confident that we are well served in mathematics, science, English, information technology, music, humanities, and religious education. But those who have undertaken to co-ordinate creative arts, physical education, and special educational needs would admit to having a committed interest rather than a high level of expertise.

In any school communication is of paramount importance, but in a large school with two separate buildings the need to implement strategies so that we all know what is happening, when, where, and why, becomes vital. We hold a weekly staff meeting, from 3.40 to 5.00 p.m. In addition, while I take an assembly with their children, each team is able to meet together for half an hour every week. Curriculum meetings have proved to be a necessity, particularly in relation to the demands of the national curriculum. At least twice a term I have a session with senior staff. Agendas are always set for these meetings at which the focus will range from planning school activities (such as sports days, concerts, and productions) to discussions on specific aspects of our teaching, the curriculum, record keeping, parental involvement, and issues raised by governors, the LEA, or government.

Almost ten years ago Oxfordshire established a scheme of whole-school self-evaluation. Every school in the county is programmed to complete this exercise within a given span of time. The first round, planned to take four years, stretched to five; we're now on the second round, which is also falling behind schedule. St Andrew's presented their first school evaluation to the County Council in 1983. When I joined the school in 1987 the document proved invaluable. I was able to discuss with the staff the changes implemented as a result of the process and consider those that still appeared to be outstanding. The greatest value of the exercise has been the long-term effect of teachers forming the habit of review and evaluation throughout the year. We have made considerable use of the devolved in-service funds (£150 for every full-time teacher), and of professional training days to release staff for additional training, to bring others with expertise to us, and to utilise our own strengths for the benefit of each other. The school development plan enables us to identify those areas that need our most urgent attention and those that may be deferred for the future. Given time, we aim to address concerns.

Time – there is always a shortage of this commodity. It seems to matter not one jot how often we reallocate time, the cry is always the same – we need more. The use of time is frequently on our agenda. With the regular use of the school by others in the evening, classrooms cannot always be left ready for the next day's activities so most staff are at school between 8.00 and 8.15. This is a time when the staff know they are able to talk to me. Several headteacher colleagues set aside one morning or afternoon when they will see visitors, in particular to show new parents round the school. This has become quite a time-consuming job, particularly as most people, quite rightly, wish to visit both schools in the village. I know this makes sense and, although at the end of a busy week I am tempted to instigate a more formalised system, I also know that it can create resentment when people ring to be told the head is not available. So I do try to deal with issues as they arise.

LOCAL MANAGEMENT OF SCHOOLS

Under the arrangements for LMS we have had control of our budget since 1 April 1990. We have received sound training from the LEA but have still become thwarted with the haste and hassle of it all. We *all* seem to be learning as we go along and this is not the best recipe for confidence building. The expectations now placed upon the secretary have grown enormously. We feel sure that we shall eventually look upon the computer as a help and a friend. However, as we struggle to familiarise ourselves with all the new jargon, software, and extended responsibilities it appears like a sword of Damocles above us. Our budget was based largely on historic figures not all of which accurately reflect actual expenditure (so the finance team tells us). We also have 60 per cent of staff at the top of their salary and only 5 per cent below point 8 on the salary scale. It is, therefore, difficult to predict how many of the things we'd like to do, such as employing more classroom assistants, redecorating, improving resources, and so on, will be achievable. What is certain is that we shall have flexibility to make decisions to meet the needs of the school as we define them (and have to bear the consequences). In itself this becomes another call upon our time in terms of planning and negotiation with staff and governors. Until we have run for at least a year and can plan on actual figures we are erring on the side of caution.

ORGANISATION AND MANAGEMENT OF LEARNING

Individual teachers have their own unique style in the classroom, and children benefit from this range of diversity in approach. All communities are made up of varied personalities and we all have to learn how to deal with each other's idiosyncrasies and foibles. Children also need to experience security so it is important that we have agreed policies on certain aspects of our activities in school. In terms of actual content of our teaching, our own curriculum guidelines and the more recent national curriculum documents set the parameters. In our attempts to implement the programmes of study in the national curriculum documents, staff are finding benefits and support from working more closely together and, in particular, with staff teaching a parallel class.

We also have agreed policies on discipline, respect and care of our environment, and health and safety. Attitudes and parity towards other adults working alongside us, or within the school as a whole, are also emphasised. We feel it is essential that children learn to respect advice, assistance, support, and discipline from all those who work with us. We are also anxious that specific threads within the curriculum, such as presentation and handwriting, are given due consideration. Finally drafted work, for display or mounting in handmade books, is double mounted and when appropriate may include some form of decorated border.

Within the classroom, organisation will vary. When it is appropriate the whole class will be taught and may work together. For a greater proportion of the day, children will be working with a partner or in small groups. There will also be times when children are engaged quite independently on their tasks. Teachers are conscious of the need to vary the groups in which children work in relation to the task. Sometimes it is beneficial for the group to consist of children with different abilities. The national curriculum places continual emphasis on the need to discuss, interpret, and relate experiences to others to demonstrate understanding. Working with others can often present meaningful circumstances in which this can occur. At other times, of course, benefits are gained from children working alongside those of similar ability.

It has been our practice to follow an integrated 'thematic approach'. In addition to recognised curriculum areas we also aim to include practical and direct experiences, which include off-site visits whenever possible. It is encouraging to see that the national curriculum documents lay stress on the need to take a cross-curricular approach. As we feel our way into these new demands, individual teachers are tending to follow the same theme as their colleagues with the same age-group. This enables them to offer support and positive, critical evaluation of each other's work.

Attainment targets, as proposed in the national curriculum, present issues that form the basis for wider discussion within team or whole-staff meetings. I ask teachers to submit forecasts to me on a regular basis, at least half termly. I am then in a position to challenge any aspects of the planned work that might appear to be unconnected and to discuss modifications with the teacher.

SPECIAL NEEDS

If we consider children as individuals then, by implication, they each have their own 'special educational needs'. This terminology has become commonplace for reference to specific groups of children, those whose needs appear to come outside the framework of education presented to the majority. It clearly includes those who have physical handicaps that inhibit their education and also those who, given the same inputs as their peers, do not make progress. I am equally concerned that we do not overlook those who fall at the other end of the continuum, who have high academic potential. As a school we need to spend time addressing our strategies and achievement in this respect.

In addition to the teacher who works with us for one-and-a-half days a week, we also benefit from a member of the special needs advisory team who comes in for one whole day a week. These two teachers work alongside the classteacher, offering specialised teaching for children, identified by the teacher, on a one-to-one or group basis. Wherever possible this will be directly related to planned work for the class and will be given in the child's teaching area.

The autistic children are integrated into classes whenever it is possible. Some are able to join in for part of the day after only a short time in the unit class; others find the company of others too disturbing and may only be able to mix at social times, such as breaks and lunchtimes.

Our two physically handicapped children (one almost blind, the other with cerebral palsy) are fully integrated in a mainstream class, with full-time welfare assistants. These women have no specialised training but are totally committed to their task. The assistant working with the blind child has taught herself Braille to enable her to meet his needs. Support and advice is given by speech, physio- and occupational therapists in addition to the special needs support team in the authority. There is very little which the children do not tackle, from participating in productions and sports, to producing work to share with others like every other child in the class.

RELATIONSHIPS WITH STAFF

I hope it will be apparent from my account that I consider all the staff in the school as a team, working together for the benefit of the children. Eight members of the teaching staff and two classroom assistants have been at St Andrew's for a considerable time and have experienced working under the direction of four headteachers – a volatile environment into which to introduce change, one might think. It did not prove to be so. When I arrived everyone was looking for some changes to be introduced. That is not to say that I didn't have to select developments with sensitivity, nor that all the new ideas I introduced were welcomed without question. But on the whole we are moving forward together with shared aspirations. I have appointed three teachers in the last three years, along with new and additional appointments of classroom and welfare assistants, lunchtime supervisors and, most recently, the caretaker. When considering applications I like to encourage people to visit prior to interview. In this way I hope to receive applications from those who feel they will be happy working alongside us. Opportunities to meet staff, formally and informally, also provide a guideline towards the possible blend of personalities. Experience has taught me that, no matter how rigorous I've tried to be, I've made a number of inappropriate appointments because none of us show our true selves until we are actually working in the school. I have been fortunate, however, to work in and to lead schools where staff have worked together conscientiously, co-operatively, and happily.

STAFF DEVELOPMENT

Having experienced the benefits of encouragement and challenge from senior personnel in education, I have always been concerned that individual members of staff have opportunities to extend and develop their personal skills and interests. The organisation of a school offers many possibilities for individuals to be given a range of responsibilities. The deputy head no longer carries the role of a team co-ordinator – that position provides another member of staff with the opportunity to augment their expertise. Incentive posts can be offered for short-term commitments, allowing me to invite staff with specific skills to share those with us and broaden their own professionalism. Teachers have always given generously of their time to fulfil roles of responsibility entrusted to them. But heads, unlike counterparts in industry, have not been able financially to reward these endeavours. Within the scope of a devolved budget it would appear that these circumstances might change, but I suspect it will be several years before we feel sufficiently competent with this unfamiliar responsibility to be able to do more than follow the established patterns of remuneration.

In-service opportunity clearly benefits both staff and children, but there are some problems too. Teachers are feeling both anxious and guilty at the amount of time they are away from their own classes. We become frustrated with the dilemma of knowing the value of in-service training and fulfilling our commitments in the classroom. Parents are confused and at times angry because they see the continuity of education for their children interrupted. In an attempt to respond to parental anxieties we invite governors, particularly parent governors, or any parent, to join us during a day's training and to judge for themselves the value of the day. Those who have taken up our offer continue to do much to 'evangelise' for us.

Despite all the perplexities I know that, if teachers are to grow and move forward in the profession, responsibility and continual training are essential for us all.

PARENTAL INVOLVEMENT

I have already indicated some ways in which we attempt to involve parents as co-educators in the education of their children. Other ways in which we encourage parents to feel valued is to welcome them into school to work alongside us. Parents are frequently found in classrooms engaged in a variety of ways. They may be working with a group of children, passing on their own skills in craft, art, music, or drama. They may be interacting with a group using the computer, following a research project in the library, engaged in some problem-solving activity set by the teacher, or they may be listening and talking to children reading. The manner in which any teacher uses parents is an individual one. Some parents will work in the classes of their own children, others will work with teachers who don't have their children at the time.

Parent–teacher interviews are held at least twice a year but parents know, and take advantage of the fact, that they can come to talk to teachers or myself at any time. We aim to have one or two open mornings when all members of the community are encouraged to come to see us in action. We have four parent governors who act rigorously on behalf of the parents and the school to become involved and informed.

The school association is well supported and actively engaged in organising fund-raising events, approximately twice termly, realising several thousands of pounds annually.

GOVERNORS

Our governing body now numbers sixteen and is playing an increasingly influential role in the life of the school. All governors attempt to participate in school activities as often as other commitments permit, which, on the whole, is not as frequently as they would like. Training sessions offered by the authority have provided valuable insight and directives towards the expected role of a governor in the 1990s. We have established sub-groups to oversee finances, curriculum, staffing, and premises. These groups are developing strategies to fulfil their terms of reference and I am confident that we shall meet the demands of ERA to the benefit of the school. I value the support and encouragement I receive from them all and look upon them as both colleagues and friends.

ADMINISTRATION AND RESOURCES

I realise I am blessed with an efficient and experienced secretary and I try hard to ensure that I spend sufficient time during the week working alongside her. There are weeks when the administration runs smoothly and I feel that I am on target but, with the plethora of paperwork that has come through the door in recent months, the box of items still requiring attention grows ever larger.

One of my most frustrating and least enjoyable tasks is having to say no to requests, from staff or children, because of lack of financial resources. We benefit enormously from the generosity of our community but classrooms and libraries still need more books, we still do not have a computer in each classroom, we would like to incorporate a wider range of media into practical skills – to name but a few of our aspirations. We have learned to prioritise and be patient until we can afford the next item on the list.

Changes which I think would help to minimise the level of stress I observe in all those who work in school are concerned with staffing. I would like to employ a full-time classroom assistant in every class and to have at least one full-time, permanent, member of staff over and above the number of class-teachers required. I see the role of this person as being able to release others in blocks of time to enable us all realistically to meet our school-based responsibilities. As a fully involved and committed member of staff, this individual would be well placed to cover more effectively for staff away on personal development courses. I look forward optimistically, with the delegation of finances, to going some way towards achieving these aims. I think there have to be realistic levels of staffing at all stages of education so that personal links can be established and maintained as children move from one educational establishment to another. Detailed records and profiles offer invaluable information but cannot replace direct contact with personnel.

At St Andrew's the one change that would make my role as head more manageable would be to link the buildings as one. Sadly, I don't think this is achievable. To be relieved of a large part of the administration by appointing a bursar would also enable me to spend more of my time with staff and children. This would help me to achieve my own goals as a head*teacher*. Perhaps this will also prove feasible under local financial management.

Chapter 34

Involving the whole staff in developing a maths curriculum

Richard McTaggart

This is a deputy headteacher's account of curriculum development work using an 'action research' project to support and monitor progress. It is worth noting the clear statement of values and aims, the use of evidence to reflect on development, and the valuing of staff colleagues as their involvement and participation was sought. This is a good example of the facilitation of whole-school development and of continuing professional reflection.

Part of my job description as a new deputy headteacher of a Group 4 Kent primary school (5–11-year-olds) is the co-ordination of a new maths policy. My initial intention, therefore, is to improve my managerial practice in relation to the formulation and implementation of the whole-school policy that must satisfy the requirements of the national curriculum.

I found no established maths scheme in operation on my arrival and a very dated policy document. There are combinations of Fletcher, Peak, Alpha/Beta, Ginn and home-made schemes mixed in all classes. Maths, in general, is formally taught, with curriculum integration occurring in possibly one or two classrooms. (My predecessor taught Alpha/Beta with all children undertaking the same page at the same time.)

The one unanimous view is the poor condition of the physical apparatus. It is extremely antiquated with no shared use and little knowledge of its extent and location.

I feel it is important to establish my beliefs and values in relation to maths teaching. I don't want this to resemble a DES curriculum document but more a set of personal values and practices that may move, or may have already moved as my work develops.

(Diary entry, September 1988)

VALUES

I believe that mathematics teaching should provide enjoyable activities that children themselves see as relevant and necessary to their place in society. These activities should provide a progressive development of the individuals' mathematical concepts. I believe the teaching should provide a solid foundation, number bonds, etc., from which problem-solving, investigational, and applied skills can be developed. Activities presented to the children should be original, child-centred, and challenging. Tasks should be both short and extended, individual and group-based, using a wide range of appropriate equipment.

I believe maths should be presented to the children with as great a variety of methods as possible. A scheme is necessary for continuity and developmental progression and a possible safety-net for teachers, but total dependency is a major worry. Mathematics should be integrated into all areas of the curriculum, but I do fear haphazard and superficial teaching. Resources should be wide and varied.

AIMS

In planning to prepare a new maths policy document, my aims are basically two-fold. Firstly, I wish to initiate a mathematics curriculum that, above all, meets the needs of children in today's society. I hope its evolution develops, enhances, and improves the practice of the teachers delivering it and that it satisfies the new requirements of the national curriculum.

My secondary aim is that, in taking an action-research approach, I hope to improve my managerial expertise and consequently address the needs of all those concerned with mathematics in Walderslade.

I believe that the issues that need to be considered if the above aims are to be achieved include the following:

- an improvement in the commitment of all staff to the consultative process;
- the production of a working mathematics document with full staff ownership;
- an improvement of resources and teachers' awareness of same;
- a development in the relationship between the staff and myself;
- an improvement in the communication within the school.

How do I see my role in the project? How will I operate?

I would like my role in the project to broaden my developing relationship with the staff. I don't yet feel I have the confidence of the staff to share and 'live' their concerns, and barriers need to be broken down. I hope the project will be seen as a sharing experience with all our fears and worries brought out into the open. My scant knowledge of infant maths is an area I feel I can utilise here to promote a whole-staff concept.

I hope to stimulate as well as co-ordinate, interpreting views, posing questions, and providing alternatives. I do, in a strange way, hope to portray my role as a learning one, working alongside the staff. I see myself as a provider of options, ideas, resources, methods, etc., and helping, advising, and reassuring staff as we progress through the project. The staff are not used to participating in policy decisions and it is necessary, therefore, to make everyone feel their contribution is valued. I do see myself as having to make critical decisions as a result of informed action, bearing in mind the end product that we, as a staff, will respect and implement.

Who is involved and what is the nature of their involvement?

The whole staff, including the head, will be involved in the project. The initial stages of the work indicate that both the desire for and the level of participation is very varied. I hope I can heighten this level by employing various strategies to increase participation.

Of the staff, I have asked the headteacher and a senior member of the staff to act as 'critical friends' to provide feedback upon the project from within the school. They were obvious choices as being both committed to the initiative and widely respected.

Forward (1989) viewed his work as 'overt' in his role as curriculum developer yet 'covert' in his role as teacher-researcher. I question his methodology, certainly in the context of 'whole-school' curriculum development. Once teachers have provided information, I feel they should be given equal access to the collective response.

INVOLVING THE STAFF

During my first term at the new school, developing the maths curriculum had to take second place to the more pressing need of establishing a working relationship with colleagues. In retrospect, I feel that not only had I to initiate new consultative processes but to involve the staff in a way that would encourage and increase their desire to take part in the decision-making process within the school. My first action was to establish regular staff meetings and develop a number of strategies to encourage colleagues to participate fully in these meetings.

STAFF MEETINGS

These were not held on a regular basis. My first action was to discuss this with the head (informal meeting 19 September 1988) and, as a result, to attempt to establish a regular pattern of meetings in consultation with staff. The first meeting of the year was on 21 September. At this meeting, at my suggestion of more regular meetings, I felt a distinct 'anti' reaction from several staff members. I can quote Mrs A – 'Some of us have family commitments'. The head described the reaction as 'latent hostility'. However, it was loosely agreed that a fortnightly meeting would be held. The fact that some members of staff saw no need for the meetings was in itself worrying and a starting point from which to work. It was evident that the consultative process, around which much of my project was to centre, was neither in operation nor deemed important. As staff meetings are surely the hub of all collaboration in schools, a clear picture of the insular and fragmented structure of the school was emerging.

After this first meeting, I spent some time reflecting over the two major issues that I felt needed to be addressed.

1 How to improve the staff's commitment to staff meetings
2 How to increase their desire to participate as one 'unit' or school

Once again, both of these targets are interrelated and achieving either would initiate a forward movement towards the other.

I felt my new role within the school prohibited any taping of meetings at this stage. It would be seen as aggressive, would inhibit the very reactions I needed to observe, and be unlikely to promote close liaison between myself and the staff.

During the next meeting, which took place on 3 October 1988, a heated discussion developed over school policy concerning parental consent for games practices/matches. Mrs S, responsible for this area of the curriculum, became upset over not knowing this issue was to be raised. My suggestion, that agendas be prepared for all staff meetings/development days and be distributed at least two/three days prior to the meeting, was unanimously agreed by the staff and has since proved very successful. 'What's this meeting about' comments have ended and, more encouragingly, some topics have been discussed in the staffroom informally beforehand. This has proved an important factor in the gradual increase in staff participation during meetings.

Another suggestion at this meeting was that points for discussion raised by staff could be submitted to head/deputy for inclusion on the next agenda. Although in the initial non-consultative climate little success was achieved here, later this 'bottom-up' policy of determining staff-meeting agendas proved far more successful.

Another development was the result of the head's perception that his 'chairing' led to a non-participatory attitude and sitting back of the staff. Outcomes could be seen to be preconceived and we wanted to share this responsibility.

The head and I discussed this and decided upon the idea of asking the staff themselves to lead all or part of future meetings. We felt that the staff would contribute more positively and freely should a meeting be led from 'within' and common ground over fears and concerns be established. Prior to a future book week, it seemed ideal for Mr A to talk to the staff about paired reading. It was interesting that Mr A, upon being asked, questioned whether his undoubted knowledge would be either interesting or relevant to the other members of staff. Was this attitude a result of the school's former autocratic decision-making process? After encouragement, particularly from the staff itself, Mr A agreed to lead the meeting on 19 October 1988.

Such was the interest and participation in this meeting that several items on the agenda had to be postponed. The recording in my learning log reads 'no time for maths input by me'. At the time, the meeting seemed a lot less significant than it does now; I regret not being able to measure the success of the participation at the time by drawing on 'hard evidence' of recorded input. What was clear, however, was that the staff reacted with enthusiasm, visibly wanting the meeting to work. Later, I was able to compare staff participation in two meetings. The findings are interesting because they show the growing confidence of staff in making contributions at staff meetings.

DEVELOPING THE MATHS INITIATIVE

My first action within the maths initiative was to ask the staff to bring all maths equipment from their huts to the hall on the morning of Development Day, 9 January 1989. We would lay this out in areas of 'time', 'money', etc., and assess needs.

First and foremost, this was to be an exercise in consultation with any other aspects (as discussed later) a welcome bonus.

What then, in detail, did I hope to achieve:

1 from the outset of the new maths policy, a consultative approach with staff. The easiest place to start, I felt, was at 'grass roots' level, i.e. teachers' classroom needs;
2 an indication to the staff of a financial commitment from the school to meeting the equipment needs that were identified;
3 a bringing together/sharing exercise to reduce the 'hut' syndrome;
4 increasing awareness of equipment around the school and therefore a route to the break-down of insular activities and interests;
5 promoting thought as to classroom method through the provision of new equipment.

The initial reaction to the intention of the morning was 'anti'. Thoughts as to the physical task of moving the equipment and 'having what I need' were muted.

However, half-an-hour saw the collection completed and, after 90 minutes of group movement around the tables, I felt much was achieved. What evidence was collected to establish whether consultation occurred?

1 I compiled a list of required equipment to which every member of staff contributed. I have analysed individual requests and a very even spread results. A number of 'all' entries represented an agreement to commit equipment to all classrooms. Eight specific requests were made by lower school staff and six by upper school. In no subsequent analysis of meetings/questionnaires, etc., has there been such a level of involvement. Albeit a simple task, this confirmed my initial thoughts as to a non-threatening first exercise in staff decision making and laid a useful foundation.
2 Useful discussion took place as to the needs and merits of certain equipment.
3 Strong consensus of opinion as to certain deficiencies brought staff together and initiated a platform for a whole-school maths policy.

QUESTIONNAIRE TO STAFF

My next action within the 'maths' sphere that directly involved the staff with a view to furthering the collaborative process was a 'maths questionnaire'.

It was the first direct *request* I made and my primary concern was an emphasis on the process, valuing everyone's involvement and opinion. How then, did I design the sheet?

In the introductory explanation, we can read 'we/our' repeated four times and 'whole-school' underlined. I worded the questions with 'you/your' to highlight their opinion and purposely chose questions that required positive replies.

I chose to introduce the questionnaire individually (to a pair in one case) and informally to each member of staff, prior to its distribution. I felt this was important as I could explain and reinforce the reasons behind the questions. I consciously emphasised the whole-school approach but also allowed the staff a 'get-out' if required. I talked of 'when you get time', 'no rush', and 'a couple of weeks', so as not to make staff wary or nervous of this new initiative.

I did consider the content of the questions important also, as I wanted to compile, unedited, the staff's broad thoughts concerning the school's maths method/organisation as a foundation document from which to move forward.

With these thoughts, I patiently waited for returns!

Of the eleven staff, three failed to return the questionnaire. Two (Mrs S and Mr B) were with me within three days but by 2 February no more had arrived. I decided to consult these two members of staff over whether to 're-ask' for the remainder. Mrs S thought they had forgotten (an indicator in itself!) and suggested I should; I did so and six others arrived by 6 February. I decided to begin my foundation document on these.

What of the three missing sheets?

> Mrs R – came to me to verbally describe her work.
>
> Miss C – 'Oh, I forgot' was her comment as the summative document was distributed.
>
> Mrs B – 0.5 teacher – little involvement in staff meetings at this stage.

I feel it is worth noting here, before comment on the content of the replies, that 6 February also saw the beginning of inter-class visits to consider maths within the school and also a smaller questionnaire relating to the usefulness of same.

I recognised the danger of 'swamping' the staff at this stage and did not want them to feel that these initiatives were enforced or, at least, pressurised in view of my position.

The replies were encouraging in many ways. An immediate thought was that establishing a consultative process may be made easier because of the degree of similarity of comment. There were many areas of agreement – i.e. continuity, lower-school strength, weakness of Peak, etc. etc.; the commitment of Mrs C, Mrs S, Mr B, and Mrs A was obvious and confidence and involvement were shown by Mrs C and Mrs A when *writing* opinion as opposed to their minimal contribution in staff meetings.

INTER-CLASS VISITS

The 6th February saw the beginning of inter-class visits, with teachers observing and participating in each other's maths teaching throughout the school. This began prior to any discussion/decisions re a new policy document. It is worth noting here:

1 After my suggestion at a staff meeting, an 'interest' survey revealed 100 per cent of staff requesting participation in the scheme, both as visitors and receivers.
2 My initial idea coincided with an A allowance award to Mrs S for staff development and also her return from a three-day course concerning same. The above idea had been strongly recommended at the course and Mrs S expressed her interest in helping its organisation.

I saw this as an ideal opportunity to involve her and extend the width of my project among the staff. We worked together on the organisation, although I very consciously took more of a 'back-seat' role.

I doubt whether evaluation of the replies concerning the visits indicates increased consultation. What it does show is a positive reaction. 'Enjoyable', 'interesting experience', 'useful', and 'particularly rewarding' are typical.

It was a positive move towards bringing the staff together around the central theme of maths.

CONCLUSION

Crucial to the action-research cycle is 'the involvement of others as collaborators in the process of managing change'. This takes on enormous significance within the context of this project when improving communication and consultation are the two claims being examined.

Obviously, I have attempted, with consultation as a focus, to involve staff in every direction the project has taken. Subsequently, the maths in the school is the only curriculum area in which staff have written any sort of curriculum document collaboratively.

However, two of the staff used as 'critical friends' have probably given extra support and guidance throughout the project and their contribution deserves a fuller acknowledgement.

The first person with whom I discussed any suggestion of action was, of course, the head. His input included:

1 regular discussion in pre-school meetings as each stage of the action-research cycle was considered;
2 willing participation in any questionnaire or staff-training exercises and freely given advice on how he felt I had conducted staff meetings;
3 knowledge of the climate of the school and the mood of staff. He acted as a 'brake' on the new deputy on several occasions when he felt I was moving too fast;
4 the initial idea of staff-led staff meetings, moving himself away from the more traditional 'chairing' role;
5 counselling – he was extremely supportive and repeatedly emphasised how severe and innovative the changes were.

My second 'critical friend' was Mrs S, an experienced teacher, respected by all the staff. My reasons for this choice were:

1 her wide experience across all age ranges of the school, something I was lacking;
2 her own commitment to change. Her ideas were compatible with mine and, working within the same hut, we began to confide, help and advise each other;
3 her knowledge of the 'hidden traps' of the school – staff quirks, parents, children, etc.

Her first reaction upon my asking her support was to suggest she was 'to be used as your spy among the staff'. The hierarchical implications are obvious.

However, her advice and help became increasingly important:

1 her reaction in one staff meeting led to the 'agenda' development;
2 we worked closely on the classroom visits development;
3 her advice on how certain staff might feel or react towards various ideas proved invaluable;
4 she met with the head and I to discuss staff comments concerning general matters and also staff development;
5 her encouragement and 'take-up' of maths ideas and suggested resources gave them an impetus and other staff followed her lead.

Lastly, my support set, the group with whom I worked at college, emerged as what I can only describe as 'my best friend'. They listened, advised, consoled, and sympathised where necessary, but proved most useful, I found, at the onset of the project when drawing the whole action-research model into perspective. Indeed, it took several meetings to establish the process and method clearly. It was the support set who, when I strayed from the 'action-research track', reinforced the need for data and thus re-channelled my thinking into the plan, act, observe, and reflect cycle.

My head, during the validation meeting which was held at college, said:

> Let me put this in context by saying that this process of staff consultation was quite novel in this academic year because it's put in a consultative framework for staff used to autocracy by another regime where comments such as 'you tell us what to do and we'll do it' were the order . . . Richard was breaking new ground for staff.

It is important to assess to what extent action-research has affected my management style.

Informed action is the most crucial change. Evaluation of data has caused me to reason more and increase my awareness of the speed with which I act. I am a naturally impatient person and the importance of evaluation has acted as a natural brake.

It has helped me in my new role of deputy head in that it has forced me to take a far wider overview of varying situations. The role of the deputy head and action-research are compatible in that they both look to take stock of the whole situation prior to further decision making.

Action-research, moreover, has given my management style a 'structure', and, rather than merely talking to others about doing 'because you feel it is right', one can, with confidence, argue the reasons why.

So what of the future? The continuing development of the policy statement and its composite parts will be the focus of future staff meetings/workshops over the next year. Certainly, teaching method is a primary concern.

REFERENCE

Forward, D. (1989) 'A guide to action research', in Lomax, P. *BERA Dialogues One: The Management of Change*, Clevedon, Multilingual Matters.

Chapter 35

Primary–secondary transfer after the national curriculum

Brian Gorwood

In part 4 we looked at different forms of curriculum organisation in the primary school and at some of the effects of the national curriculum. In this chapter, Brian Gorwood looks at continuity between the primary and secondary school, and suggests that one of the effects of more subject-focused approaches to the primary curriculum is to smooth transition across the phases. More common curriculum philosophies across the primary and secondary sectors are seen as aiding communication between schools, albeit by making primary schools more like secondaries. However, Gorwood warns that more traditional secondary teaching styles may not be able to cope with the differentiation necessary to take full account of individual pupils' achievements in the primary school.

At the time of transfer from primary to secondary schooling, many pupils experience difficulties because of extreme differences in curriculum between the two sectors. Theorists and HMI have been writing about this problem for many years, researchers have investigated it. Strategies for improving continuity have been suggested but the permissive nature of English education has resulted in piecemeal adoption. By its very nature, continuity demands that there should be general agreement to ensure that pupils move from one experience to another in a sequence of meaningful learning. General agreement about any aspect of education has always been difficult to attain, however, within a system so intent on affording freedom of choice to individual schools. With the advent of the national curriculum it was hoped that the situation would change.

When the consultation document was published in 1987, the national curriculum was presented mainly in terms of raising standards, but one of its objectives was concerned with continuity:

A national curriculum will secure that the curriculum offered in all maintained schools has sufficient in common to enable children to move from one area of the country to another with minimum disruption to their education. It will also help children's progression within and between primary and secondary education and will help to secure the continuity and coherence which is too often lacking in what they are taught.

(DES 1987)

Such a positive statement, with the affirmative 'will', gave hope of a more effective approach to achieving continuity. But there have been many similar statements in the past and yet the problem remains.

REMAINING PROBLEM OF REPETITION

It is difficult to see how the requirements of the Education Reform Act can 'secure' continuity. As in former times, central government hopes to achieve continuity by guidance rather than by legislation. The assertive tone of that guidance is deceptive. 'Continuity is no longer an optional issue in planning the curriculum' declares the National Curriculum Council (1989). Yet associated schools continue to organise their curricula without reference to each other. The national curriculum has not been in place long enough for major research to have been undertaken, but several studies by teachers in correspondence with the author suggest that it is likely to present a new variant of the 'stages' problem. In the late 1970s, I found pupils after transfer having to repeat SMP maths books they had already completed in the feeder school (1981). I now hear of secondary schools planning to start all pupils at national curriculum level three in mathematics. Their primary colleagues point out that some pupils may have reached level five, but secondary schools seem unable to adjust their teaching style to accommodate individualised approaches.

Provisions in national curriculum documents will do little to eradicate the major causes of discontinuity. There will still be unnecessary repetition and pupils will become bored; there will still be bewilderment from pupils who have missed out on previous essential learning; schools will still find it difficult to find a common starting point for pupils with different kinds of educational background. There is no legislation requiring schools to adopt particular kinds of curriculum organisation or teaching style. Yet it is these aspects of their education that cause pupils significant difficulties at the time of transition. Continuity is best achieved when receiving teachers take cognisance of what and how their pupils learned before coming to them. It is still very much an optional issue whether primary and secondary teachers communicate about the pupils in whom they have a common interest.

PLANNING BY SUBJECTS

Though the Education Reform Act may not 'secure' continuity, it will go some way to achieving it, particularly if schools move closer to each other in ethos. It is implicit in the national curriculum that subjects will form the starting point for curriculum planning (NCC 1989). That has always been the dominant approach in the secondary school but not so in the primary sector. Certainly since the time of Plowden – and probably long before that – primary schools have centred the curriculum on the child and his or her needs. Schools Council projects for primary, middle, and early secondary years rejected planning from subjects because there was too much to include if the curriculum was to be balanced. The emphasis was on skills, attitudes, and values which would eventually feed into the subject-specific curriculum. If specialist subject teachers were to be too influential in planning curriculum for younger pupils, it was thought they would lean heavily on the learning of facts and skills to the neglect of the wider range of objectives that had been revealed by the curriculum development movement (Ross *et al.* 1975). If we venture further back to the immediate post-war period, the Council for Curriculum Reform explored the relevance of subjects in the school curriculum and outlined problems of specialisation:

> Children must find the present time-table a very disjointed and piecemeal affair, mainly because of the traditional compartmentation of the subject matter. The means whereby this evil may be remedied demand careful research.
>
> (Council for Curriculum Reform 1945)

The notion of a subject, they concluded, was not a particularly helpful one. It was not until the learner moved into higher education that subjects as such started to have any real meaning. Out of such criticism there developed integrated approaches to curriculum, which seem now under threat.

There is, of course, little within the literature on the national curriculum to suggest that primary schools should modify practice. Indeed, the NCC assures, 'Planning under subject headings does not preclude flexibility of delivery across subject boundaries' (1989). It states, however, that subjects will form the starting point for curriculum *planning*. This is a significant change in method of planning for most primary schools which may, admittedly, approach mathematics and English as separate subjects, usually through the adoption of set schemes, but choose a topic method to treat other areas of the curriculum. It is difficult to see how national curriculum programmes of study in geography and history can be derived from topics such as 'toys', 'food', or 'ourselves' – themes tackled by the author's primary PGCE students during a recent teaching practice. There has been understandable criticism, particularly by HMI, of topic work which 'more often than not lacks continuity and progression, or any serious attempt to ensure that adequate time and attention are given to the elements said to comprise the topic' (1989). Even if topic methods survive, rigorous reappraisal of current forms of curriculum organisation will be needed. It is interesting to note that many of the local authority working parties set up to develop history- and geography-related in-service training are advocating either subject teaching or 'focused topic' approaches. Primary schools, therefore, are going to change and the change is likely to bring them closer to the subject-centred approach to curriculum characteristic of the secondary sector.

EFFECT ON MOTIVATION

Secondary schools are used to planning according to external criteria. The GCE and more recently GCSE have exercised a powerful influence on the curriculum not only of fifth forms but of young secondary pupils who are introduced to the techniques, if not the content, fundamental to passing external examinations. In the primary curriculum there has always been room to pick up some fortuitous happening. Children have been encouraged to talk about their interests, to bring artefacts into the classroom, and to write about matters of pertinence to them. By so doing, teachers have succeeded in spurring pupils to maintain an interest in things educational; motivation has long been accepted as a powerful determinant of what happens in primary classrooms. The demise of the 11-plus released primary schools from external influences but with the advent of the national curriculum that is changing. Primary teachers and their pupils are being made aware that time is not always available to pursue particular interests; there is the national curriculum to be discharged. It will be some time before research can suggest the likely impact of recent curricular changes on primary pupil motivation. My informal discussions in primary schools, however, suggest that pupils welcome the more structured approach which is already taking effect. 'We do the same subjects now as they do in the secondary school', replied one proud pupil in answer to my queries about national curriculum changes. 'I like learning new things rather than doing topics', was one revealing comment. Pupils are aware that primary schools are being drawn closer to styles of working customary in the secondary sector and they seem contented with this situation.

TEACHER COMMUNICATION

Although the Education Reform Act heralded significant changes in schools, potentially more extreme in the primary than in the secondary sector, it could do little to influence what has been seen in all recent research as the main cause of lack of continuity: ineffective teacher communication. Teachers in associated schools seldom come into contact with relevant colleagues and there is mutual mistrust (Stillman and Maychell 1984). There is an undoubted need for secondary teachers to have access to information concerning their pupils' achievements in the primary school but the transfer of records does not in itself ensure that such information reaches the appropriate staff or is used effectively. As Blyth points out, a teacher in a secondary school has many other things to do than to ponder over the records of new pupils (1990). Good continuity practice suggests, however, that schools which focus on transfer but fail to appreciate the need for wide discussion of curricular matters are least successful in satisfying the needs of transferred pupils. Rather than making continuity the concern of a year 7 co-ordinator, secondary schools would do better, as the ILEA secondary transfer project recommended, to organise on a departmental basis (1988). A designated key person within a secondary department would brief colleagues and keep them informed about developments and discussions between associated schools. Similarly, in the primary sector it should not always be the year 6 teacher who takes part in continuity discussions, for curriculum continuity has to be considered within a school's total policy.

Some of the early extravagant claims for the national curriculum have been moderated in more recent statements. In 1987, it was projected that the national curriculum would 'secure' continuity. More realistically, it is now said to 'provide a framework for achieving continuity'. It is doubtful that significant improvements in continuity could ever have been achieved by a British form of national curriculum *per se*; by their very training, teachers in our schools have been encouraged to maintain fundamentally different philosophies of primary and secondary schooling.

REFERENCES

Blyth, A. (1990) *Making the Grade for Primary Humanities*, p. 145 (Milton Keynes, Open University Press).

The Council for Curriculum Reform (1945) *The Content of Education*, p. 18 (London, University of London Press).

Department or Education and Science (1987) *The National Curriculum 5–16*, a consultation document, London, p. 4.

Gorwood, B. (1981) Continuity – with particular reference to the effectiveness of middle school experience upon upper school achievement in Kingston upon Hull, unpublished Ph.D. thesis, University of Hull.

Her Majesty's Inspectorate (1989) *Annual Report of HM Senior Inspector of Schools for 1987/88* (London, HMSO).

ILEA Research and Statistics Branch (1988) *Improving Secondary Transfer*, p. 26 (London, ILEA).

National Curriculum Council (1989) *A Framework for the Primary Curriculum – Curriculum Guidance One*, York, p. 9.

Ross, A., Razzell, A., and Badcock, E. (1975) *The Curriculum in the Middle Years* (Schools Council Working Paper 55) (London, Evans/Methuen).

Stillman, A.B. and Maychell, K. (1984) *School to School: LEA and teacher involvement in educational continuity* (Winsdor, NFER-Nelson).

Chapter 36

Parents' choice of school

Martin Hughes, Felicity Wikeley, and Tricia Nash

This chapter presents extracts from the interim report of a larger, long-term study, as part of which parents of 141 young children in the South West of England were interviewed on their reasons for choosing a school for their children. The data speak powerfully of the priorities for parents shown in terms of practicality and the all-round development and happiness of their children.

Recent legislation has aimed to increase the amount of choice open to parents so that they can, in theory, send their child to the school of their choice. In reality the degree of choice available to parents may vary quite widely, depending on factors such as where they live, how many schools are available within easy reach, and whether these schools have room for them or not. We therefore asked the parents how and why they had chosen the school their child attended, whether they had visited the school before making their choice, and whether they had considered or visited other schools.

Table 36.1 lists the main responses given to the question 'Why did you choose your child's school?', and shows the number of parents giving this kind of response.

As Table 36.1 shows, this question generated a wide range of responses. Most parents gave more than one kind of response, and some gave several reasons for their choice of school.

The most frequent response was that the school had been chosen on grounds of 'locality' – in other words, it was easily accessible from the child's home. Given the age of the children, this is perhaps not surprising. The school's reputation was also seen to be an important factor, mentioned by nearly half the parents: e.g. 'I asked other mothers and was told it was a good school' and 'had heard good reports'. Nine per cent of the parents mentioned that they had 'no real choice'.

As locality was the most frequently mentioned factor in parents' choice of school, we looked at how many parents sent their children to the local school and whether locality was their only reason for that choice. By 'local

Table 36.1 Why did you choose your child's school?

Locality	79
Reputation/recommendation	66
Impressed on visit	38
Size of school	25
Ethos of school	23
Did not like local school	19
Local friendships important	19
Not first choice	19
Attended playgroup/nursery connected with the school	17
No choice	13
Community-based	12
Parents went themselves	11
Village school	7
5–11 school	4
Church school	4

school' we meant the one which was geographically nearest to the child's home.

Altogether, over two-thirds (69 per cent) of the parents chose to send their child to the local school. Of these thirteen parents felt they had no real choice: other schools were either too far away, full, or refused them entry on denominational grounds or that they lived outside the school's catchment area. A further nineteen parents mentioned only the locality of the school as a reason for their choice: e.g. 'local school handy', 'nearest to home', while two parents chose the local school despite other schools having positive features: 'because closest but would rather school B because of space'. The largest group, however, were those fifty parents who mentioned positive features other than locality in choosing the local school: e.g. 'told was a very good school – in the area', 'because we live in the village – my father had said it was a good school'. A further fourteen parents gave a mixture of reasons: e.g. 'good reputation, also close – school B not much good any more', 'everyone busy, lots of unusual things, children not sitting waiting – school B nice facilities but only catered for middle ability – didn't like school C because of its ethos'.

Forty-three parents (31 per cent of the total sample) opted for a school which was not the one geographically nearest to them. In some cases it was only marginally more distant than the local school, but in others there was a significant increase in the amount of travelling involved. Four of these parents had to look elsewhere as the local school was full; while in theory they could have appealed against this, in two cases, both in different areas, they were told that such an appeal would take six weeks, which they thought was unacceptable. Another five parents felt the local school was unsatisfactory: e.g. 'just moved here, down to go to local school, lot of fuss about conditions, bad state', 'didn't like reading scheme in catchment area school'. Most of the parents, though, mentioned positive features of the chosen school, or a combination of positive features of the non-local school and negative features of the local school: e.g. 'catchment area school good but too large for timid child', 'school A caring – one in village but very church oriented, because of my background didn't want it'.

When asked why they chose their child's school, the parents produced a range of reasons. The most frequently mentioned one was the locality of the school, and over two-thirds of the parents did in fact choose the local school. Some of these parents felt they had no choice; others chose simply on the grounds of locality: but the great majority also mentioned other positive features of the local school. Just under a third of the parents did not send their child to the local school. In some cases the local school was full or considered unsatisfactory, but in other cases a positive choice was made for the non-local school. Over half the parents visited the school before making their choice, while most of the remainder obtained information about the school from other sources. Nearly half the parents did not consider any other school; those that did were more likely to visit the alternatives before making their choice, particularly if they eventually chose a non-local school.

Taken together, these findings indicate that the majority of parents are not exercising a wide range of choice. Their first preference is for the local school, and, if this seems to be a good school based on their own criteria, they will not look further afield. However, there are a minority of parents who do look elsewhere, possibly because they are looking for a particular kind of ethos in a school.

The parents were also asked whether they would consider moving their child to another school if they were not happy, and what would make them do this. Their responses are shown in Tables 36.2 and 36.3.

Table 36.2 If you were not happy would you consider moving your child to another school?

Yes	82	58%
As a last resort	43	31%
No	15	11%

Table 36.3 What would make you do that?

Child unhappy	68
Not progressing	55
Poor teaching	31
General dissatisfaction	20
Discipline/bullying	19

Table 36.4 What makes a good school?

Relationships between parents, teachers, and children	72
The staff	63
The atmosphere	53
The ethos of the school	52
Good discipline	38
Wide-ranging education offered	26
The headteacher	22
Development of the whole child	17
Academic results	16
Good resources	11
Good facilities	9
Modern methods/approach	8
Small school	8
Small classes	7

As these tables show, the majority of parents would consider moving their child if necessary. The most frequently stated reason was if their child was unhappy – e.g. 'if older would look at standard but at this age mainly happiness' or 'if he was being bullied'. However, twenty-three parents commented that they would try to sort it out first with the teacher, twelve said it would be too disruptive, six remarked that there was no guarantee it would be better elsewhere, and six pointed out that they had no real alternative.

The relative importance to parents of factors such as the child's happiness was further emphasised by their responses when asked what they thought made a good school. As can be seen in Table 36.4 a large range of features were mentioned. Over half the parents mentioned relationships between parents, teachers, and children as being an important factor in describing a good school. Other non-tangible features, such as the ethos of the school and the atmosphere, were also mentioned more frequently than physical characteristics such as facilities and resources. Nearly half the parents saw the staff as being particularly important; this was mentioned in terms of their aptitude to teach or as having a 'caring attitude'. At this stage it appears that academic results were not seen as being important, with only 11 per cent of the parents including them in their attributes of a good school.

Chapter 37

Involving parents

Alastair Macbeth

In Chapter 30 Handy and Aitken wrote of the place of parents within the organisation of the school. This chapter takes up the theme in greater detail, spelling out the legal responsibilities and rights of parents in relation to their children's education. Alastair Macbeth reviews research on the impact of the home on learning, and this raises some controversial questions; for example: Does the school exist, in part, to separate children from their families and introduce them to the wider society? Is so-called parental 'apathy' a symptom of the school system itself?

Parents are integral to schooling. Inevitably, by both example and instruction, usually for good but sometimes for ill, parents teach their children and through that teaching they influence the extent to which we, as teachers, can be effective. Further, parents, not teachers, are primarily responsible in law for the education of their individual child. They are therefore first-line clients of the school. They should not be lumped together with remoter interested parties, such as children's possible future employers or 'the community', which are largely outside the schooling process. The parental dimension of schooling is central to our professional performance as teachers. Yet it is often underrated. In my view we neglect it at our peril, for our impact as teachers and our status as professionals may substantially depend upon the extent to which we take seriously the phrase 'partnership with parents'.

The Education Reform Act of 1988 for England and Wales[1] continued a trend to give more prominence in law to the roles of parents, a trend which had started with the 1980 and 1986 Acts. Yet much of this legislative action concentrated upon parental representation on governing bodies and upon parental rights, such as to choice of school and to information. These, of course, are important but they are less concerned with partnership between teachers and parents and ways by which parents can be involved both formally and informally in the child's education.

One cannot approach the practice of home–school relations without assessing *why* there should be partnership between parents and teachers. In the past many teachers have pursued whole careers with only minimal contact with parents, and some even now continue to do so. Reasons must be compelling if practice, involving energy, time, and resources, is to be worth changing.

THE PARENTAL DIMENSION OF SCHOOLING

Parents are relevant to what happens *inside* school for five quite distinct reasons.

1 Parents are responsible in law for their child's education, and in that sense they may be regarded as the school's legal clients.
2 If most of a child's education happens outside school, especially in the home, and if parents are co-educators of the child with teachers, then it seems logical to make the two elements of school learning and home learning compatible, and for teachers to use that home learning as a resource.
3 Research indicates that family-based learning influences the effectiveness of school on a child. It may be a significant factor among the complexity of forces associated with inequality of educational opportunity.
4 Besides providing a professional service for parents, the teacher is also an agent of the education authority and the State to some degree. There are implied functions of checking upon parents' fulfilment of duties (e.g. with regard to school attendance) and, arguably, of being an educational safety-net for pupils with incompetent or uncaring parents.
5 It seems democratically reasonable, in a decentralised system in which important decisions are made at school and class levels, that those with a stake in a school should influence (though not necessarily determine) the nature of those decisions. Parents are stakeholders on behalf of their child and should be able to influence school policy through representatives.

Each of these issues warrants separate actions. For instance, to have parents on a governing body may go some way to meeting the fifth point but is largely irrelevant to the other four; or to treat parents as clients may not necessarily do anything to make home learning supportive of school objectives. Different reasons for partnership with parents require different sorts of responses at different levels of the system.

1 Parents' legal responsibility for their child's education

Freeman (1983: 4), discussing the rights of children, expresses the generally accepted principle that 'interference with a child's liberty is an inescapable consequence of the biological and physiological dependence of children'. Given that children are necessarily dependent on adults, the question becomes one of who should have responsibility for their upbringing, including education. Of course traditionally (most would say naturally) that is the family, especially parents. Yet in theory the State could take over these functions. National and international pronouncements have resisted such a radical shift. The United Nations Declaration of the Rights of the Child (1959) states:

> The best interests of the child shall be the guiding principle of those responsible for his education and guidance. That responsibility lies in the first place with his parents.

Churches tend to enunciate the same view. For instance, the Second Vatican Council in its Declaration of Christian Education asserted:

> Since it is the parents who have given life to their children, it is they who have the serious obligation of educating their offspring. Hence parents must be recognised as the first and foremost educators of their children.

Most national laws similarly place responsibility for the child's education upon his/her parents, granting rights commensurate with the duty. For example, the Basic Law of the Federal Republic of West Germany (1949, Article 6.2) states:

> The care and education of children are the natural right of parents and the duty is primarily theirs. The national community shall check upon their endeavours in this respect.

In Britain we do not have such a basic law or a bill of rights to enunciate fundamental principles. Our laws tend to be administrative rather than philosophical, but the same concept is clearly there. Section 36 of the 1944 Act answers the question: who, in law, is responsible for the education of the individual child?

> It shall be the duty of the parent of every child of compulsory school age to cause him to receive full-time education suitable to his age, ability, and aptitude, either by regular attendance at school or otherwise.[2]

It should be noted that this applies to the *individual* child, not to children in general or to the provision of facilities in general, which are central government and education authority responsibilities. It may also be noted that, although education is compulsory, schooling is not. Schooling may be (and normally is) used by parents to fulfil their legal duty minimally. That does not mean that schooling is the same thing as education, nor does it mean that schooling is obligatory.

Education authorities are required by Section 7 of the 1944 Act[3] to make educational facilities available. We may pose the question: for what purpose? If parents are responsible for their child's education, then the facilities must exist to assist parents in carrying out their legal duty. *In brief, parents may be seen as the school's prime legal clients, until the child is 16 years of age.*

That position is given emphasis by a section of the Act which is often quoted by parents, but which, in my view, is conceptually less important than the one which lays down their duty. This is Section 76[4] which requires (with qualifications about efficient instruction and the avoidance of unreasonable public expenditure) that education authorities (and therefore their school systems) are to 'have regard to the general principle that . . . pupils are to be educated in accordance with the wishes of their parents'. It is interesting that here, untypically, a general principle creeps into our law. It is not clear whether it is an inviolable and overarching principle or whether the words 'have regard to' mean, in effect, 'if it happens to be convenient', but what matters here is the relationship of parental wishes to parental duty. Educational provision according to parental wishes is a logical consequence of the fact that parents bear prime responsibility for their child's education. It reinforces parents' client status.

Laws are man-made and they can be changed. For instance, the State (through teachers as its agents) could be made responsible for the *schooling* of the individual child, leaving out-of-school education as the responsibility of the parents. Indeed many teachers behave as if that were the case now. But what would be the implications of such a change? I consider that they would be far-reaching, for they would not just set a precedent affecting parents' rights for the upbringing of their child, but would question current assumptions about the structure of our society and individual liberties within it. At present the family is regarded as the fundamental unit of our society. Parents, as the central figures in families, are given the prime right and duty to shelter, feed, clothe, educate, and secure the health of their children. The State intervenes and takes away that prime right only in cases of negligence by parents. However, it provides *services* of housing, health, education, and welfare which parents can use to carry out their duties. If those services were to be *imposed*, irrespective of whether there is negligence, that would seem to be a substantial incursion into both individual liberty and the concept of the family as the fundamental unit of society. I am not saying that such a change would necessarily be wrong. I am saying that it would be a major conceptual shift, not a minor adaptation.

Professionals, presumably, must operate within the law. If teachers are professionals, then they owe service to parents as clients (until the child is 16 years of age), and are required by law to have regard to their wishes.

2 Parents as co-educators of children in parallel with teachers

Besides being the legal clients of teachers, parents are the co-educators of children. As already mentioned, most education happens outside school. Much of it, especially in the early years, is experienced in the family, where emotional bonds make home learning especially effective. Parents also influence the sort of community learning which their child will acquire.

Since parents inescapably educate their children, surely a professional teacher cannot neglect the non-professional educators. Just as the dentist relies on parents to co-operate with regard to children's dental care, so must teachers seek to guide and to draw into partnership parents' impact on educational care. Parents are co-educators of children whether that suits our professional preferences or not.

3 The effect of home background on children's school attainment

Not only do parents largely create the nature of a child's out-of-school education, they also seem to influence (some would say determine) the extent to which their child benefits from *in*-school education. If teachers' effectiveness is linked to what families think, say, and do, then an extra professional argument for collaboration with parents emerges. Unfortunately, the evidence, substantial though it is, lacks the finality and precision which would enable us to define exactly which home-based initiatives would most heighten pupils' educational advance. It is therefore difficult to build closely specified programmes of liaison based on it. Yet lack of fine detail need not deter us from action since much is already known.

Perhaps the strongest motivation for such action comes from the evidence that aspects of home background are the causes of unfulfilled potential and unequal chances in education. Equality of educational opportunity has been at the centre of educational thinking and planning for several decades, yet it has proved an elusive goal. It is difficult to define and even more difficult to attain. Despite the abolition of 11-plus selection, the creation of comprehensive schools, the increasing deferment of separating pupils with different abilities, and other structural initiatives, certain kinds of children continue to be more successful than others. Structural steps taken within the educational system have removed some *obstacles* to attainment, but they have not sufficiently stimulated the forces which *enhance* attainment.

What are these forces? What follows is necessarily an over-simplified sketch of complex environmental processes which are still not fully understood. It should not be misinterpreted as a statement that schools make no difference. Schools *do* make a difference. Studies such as those of Rutter *et al*. (1979) and Tizard *et al*. (1988) have shown that school performance can be more or less professional and that its effects on children's attainment can vary accordingly. Although *Fifteen Thousand Hours* by Rutter *et al*. emphasised school influence, it did not deny the impact of home; indeed, having alluded to studies of home-related factors, it stated (p. 87), with tantalising brevity, 'We found the same.' It may be argued that *all* schools attain a basic level of beneficial influence and that what home learning is doing is affecting the *differences* of attainment between pupils. Yet, if equality of educational opportunity is the goal, then it is precisely those differences that matter whether they originate in homes or in schools.

The evidence of home influence on schooling began with studies which showed a general correlation between home background and in-school attainment. Home background differences often coincide with social class differences,[5] but researchers recognise that terms such as 'home background' and 'social class' are vague and difficult to measure. Further, there is some evidence that social class itself is not the causal factor (see Miller 1971) and this is the foundation for optimism for it suggests that working-class children *can* do well, given the right circumstances. Questions then emerge about which elements of home background correlate with school success, whether they are causal and whether we can influence them.

What has emerged is a complex and by no means complete picture. Part of the difficulty stems from problems of measurement. Children cannot be manipulated experimentally like rats in a laboratory. Therefore controlling variables in a physical sense has to be replaced by statistical techniques to make allowances for the multiplicity of forces which might be causing an observed outcome. Even when a correlation exists between two phenomena that does not, in itself, tell us which is causing which, and indeed it does not necessarily mean that either causes the other, since a third factor may be causing both.

Further, some of the forces which researchers would like to measure are not susceptible to direct measurement and 'proxy measures' are used instead. For instance, the attitudes of parents have been advanced as a key element in pupil attainment, and it seems likely that they are; but can attitudes be measured? Since they are invisible, the best that we can do is to measure behaviour and to make assumptions about the attitudes which may trigger that behaviour. Alternatively, we can seek expressed opinions which may or may not reflect real attitudes, and these in turn have to be assessed in regard to the circumstances in which they were expressed, their strength and their persistence, all of them elusive elements. Next, how do we assess educational attainment? Standardised test results and public examination grades are often used, but these tell us little about creativity, adaptability, determination, and other facets of achievement. To take another example, father's occupation is often used as a measure of social class, whereas clearly it is not the same thing. Further, the involvement of researchers may itself affect the outcomes, while interpretation of results always involves value judgements.

The next problem is that the socio-psychological networks involved are intricate and variable, but, as Osborne and Milbank (1987: 189) observe, enough is known to provide some guidance.

> It is important to recognise the interrelatedness of all these factors and the complex ways in which they can combine to either support or impede a child's educational progress. Each child is unique in the particular developmental path she follows yet some general principles can be dis-

cerned in the tangle of data which help to explain how some children succeed and others fail.

Thus, despite complexities, research is valuable. It provides essential indicators. Three rule-of-thumb tests may be applied which can help to decide how seriously to take a given set of findings:

1 Do several studies draw the same conclusions?
2 Is there a relative dearth of contrary evidence?
3 Do the findings accord with common sense and the experience of teachers?

The evidence that parents and family circumstances do influence children's educational attainments appears to meet these tests.

Besides broad correlations between home background and in-school attainment, research has suggested that particular features of background could be especially important. Attitudes such as parental interest in children's education[6] and aspirations[7] have attracted special attention, while a debate arose about the influence of language codes in coping with schooling.

One issue which has confused the picture has been the belief among some teachers that, because certain (often working-class) parents do not attend school functions as avidly as do others, the former are 'apathetic'. As Mays (1980) has pointed out, 'It is dangerously easy to use a phrase such as "parental apathy" and leave it at that' (p. 63). Rather, practical difficulties, deference to teachers, cynicism, and a sense of alienation from the school deter parents. Some studies (e.g. Cyster et al. 1979; Johnson and Ransom 1983) show that some parents are hesitant and unsure of themselves when confronted by the systems of schooling. But this does not necessarily mean that they lack concern for their children's welfare and there is evidence of the reverse (Lindsay 1969). As Marland (1983: 4) has written, 'not only are the huge majority of parents *not* apathetic but very concerned . . . the nature of their concerns and the modes of their support have a great deal to teach us teachers', a view more recently echoed by Tizard and Hughes (1984) and Tizard et al. (1988). Yet Wolfendale (1983: 59) is surely to some extent right when she asserts that 'between teachers' and parents' expectations and presumptions lies unexplored territory'; for there is much we still do not know about parental attitudes or actions in the home.

Several useful overviews of the evidence about the impact of homes on schooling (Marjoribanks 1979; Mortimore and Blackstone 1982; Hewison 1985) exist and it is not the purpose of the present book to summarise the large and growing body of research into the impact of home learning on school learning. However, a few generalisations do seem possible and these support (but do not determine) the practical actions discussed in later chapters.

First, Marjoribanks (1979) drew attention to the great complexity of the

INFLUENCES ON CHILD   MEDIATING ELEMENTS

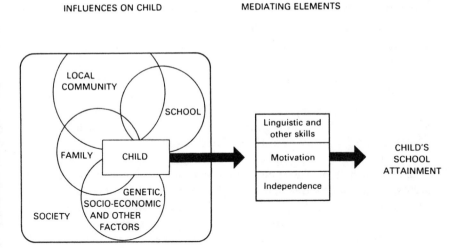

Figure 37.1

'network of interrelated family environment variables that are associated with children's cognitive and affective outcomes'. However, having assessed studies from three continents he concluded 'Environments for children's learning will become more favourable when parents and teachers act as partners in the learning process.' A model which might be sustained on the basis of existing evidence could resemble that shown in Figure 37.1.

Secondly, there are signs from several studies[8] that the early years of home learning are especially important for subsequent attainment and Tizard and Hughes concluded, 'Indeed, in our opinion, it is time to shift the emphasis away from what parents should learn from professionals, and towards what professionals can learn from studying parents and children at home' (1984: 267).

The third reasonable generalisation is that, if what happens in the home does have impact on overall educational attainment, and if average differences of attainment between children from different social class groups are linked to those home experiences, then presumably the goal of equality of educational opportunity cannot be approached merely by making changes within the system of institutional education which represents only about 15 per cent of a child's waking and therefore learning life to age 16. The debate will doubtless continue as to whether it is material circumstances or learning circumstances which have *most* effect on that inequality; but, irrespective of which is predominant, there can be no equality of educational opportunity without equality of parental input as one of the factors.

4 Teachers as agents of the education authority

I have argued that much of a child's education is provided in or influenced by the family, and I have outlined the ways by which legal systems consistently make parents responsible for their child's education. However, parents vary in the conscientiousness and the effectiveness with which they meet their obligations, and a small minority of parents might be described as incompetent or uncaring. The State, having delegated responsibility to parents, must still monitor parents' performance: in the words of the German Basic Law quoted earlier, 'The national community shall check upon their endeavours in this respect.' The most obvious way that teachers do this on behalf of the State is by reporting instances of truancy; for parents, if they opt to use schools to fulfil their legal duty of educating their child, must ensure regular attendance. Further, persistent misbehaviour of a child will be reported back to parents on the grounds that they are responsible for their child's education; again it is teachers who act as agents of the education authority in reporting it.

In two other important ways teachers may represent the education authority (or the State). One is by providing educational expertise (knowledge, skills, understanding) which most parents will not have. Usually this will be with relation to the formal curricula. But the second is a pastoral care function in providing an adult alternative to the parent to whom the child can turn in times of need. Marland (1980: 157; 1985: 82) has drawn attention to a combination of these two in what he calls the pastoral curriculum defined as 'the school curriculum looked at for the moment solely from the point of view of the personal needs of the pupil resolving his individual problems, making informed decisions, and taking his place in his personal world'. With regard to young people over the age of 16, and therefore responsible in law for their own education, there would be less or no need for teachers to involve parents in dealing with such issues. However, parents are responsible for the education (including schooling) of under-16 children and therefore whenever teachers are, as it were, filling the gaps left by parents they presumably have an obligation to contact parents on precisely those issues.

It is possible, however, to advance a quite contrary argument, namely that the school exists, in part, to *separate* the child from the family and to provide an induction to society. Taylor (1980: 12) has written:

> The primary school class emancipates the child from the basic emotional ties with his own family, encourages the internalization of social values and norms other than those current in the family home, and begins the process of selection and allocation relative to the adult role-system that will be continued and given great emphasis in the later stages of schooling.

This may be valid to some degree as a description of some current practice, but if rejection of family were to be an aim of the school, not only would it seem to be contrary to the spirit of current law, but it could well damage children's education. It is a major misconception, in my opinion, but a common one, to assume that being an agent of the education authority or State confers autonomy of action on the teacher. On the contrary, it implies an increased obligation to collaborate with parents.

5 Parents as stakeholders in their child's school

The fifth and final main reason why parents matter to schools is of an entirely different nature to the first four. It is democratic rather than educational. The principle is generally accepted in Western democracies that those with a stake in an enterprise should have the opportunity to influence (though not necessarily to determine) decisions affecting that enterprise in proportion to their stake in it. We have a highly decentralised school system, and important decisions are taken at school, department, and class levels. Politicians have a stake in the school as elected representatives of the community. Teachers have a stake in the school as employees, as co-educators, and as taxpayers, among other criteria. Parents might claim to have a stake as clients, as co-educators, and as taxpayers. The governing body is the main mechanism to enable those with a stake in a school to influence decisions about the school. However, it is worth noting that the families which jointly have children in one class might also have a similar stake in that class (or group) and the decisions made for it.

In one sense a school system is like an airline: it likes to create an image of individual service in what is, essentially, a group process. Perhaps parents should have more right to discuss and influence internal school processes than has hitherto been accorded to them for, whereas in an airline the passengers choose where to go and when, in a school parents have little choice.

NOTES

1 Scottish and Northern Irish reforms have been developing rather differently and comparisons are made at appropriate points in the book from which this extract is taken.
2 Counterpart clauses in Scotland and Northern Ireland are Section 30 of The Education (Scotland) Act, 1980, and Section 35 of The Education and Libraries (Northern Ireland) Order, 1972. Wording is not identical but is similar.
3 And section 1 of the Education (Scotland) Act, 1980.
4 And section 28 of the Education (Scotland) Act, 1980.
5 e.g. Floud et al. 1957; Fraser 1959; Mays 1962; Douglas 1964; Douglas et al. 1968; Miller 1971; Davie et al. 1972.
6 Fraser 1959; Wiseman 1964; Douglas 1964; Miller 1971; Osborne and Milbank 1987.

7 Rosen 1961; McClelland 1961; Miller 1971.
8 Wiseman 1964; Davie *et al.* 1972; Schweinhart and Weikart 1980; Tizard and Hughes 1984; Osborne and Milbank 1987.

REFERENCES

Cyster, R., Clift, P. S., and Battle, S. (1979) *Parental Involvement in Primary Schools*. NFER.

Davie, R., Butler, N., and Goldstein, H. (1972) *From Birth to Seven*. National Children's Bureau/Longman.

Douglas, J. W. B. (1964) *The Home and the School*. MacGibbon & Kee.

Douglas, J. W. B., Ross, J. M., and Simpson, H. R. (1968) *All Our Future: A Longitudinal Study of Secondary Education*. Peter Davies.

Floud, J., Halsey, A. H., and Martin, F. M. (1957) *Social Class and Educational Opportunity*. Heinemann.

Fraser, E. (1959) *Home Environment and the School*. University of London Press.

Freeman, M. D. A. (1983) *The Rights and Wrongs of Children*. Pinter.

Gould, R. (1973) 'The Teaching Profession', in Lomax, D. E. (Ed.) *The Education of Teachers in Britain*. Wiley.

Hewison, J. (1985) 'The evidence of case studies of parents' involvement in schools', Ch. 3 in Cullingford, C. G. (Ed.) *Parents, Teachers and Schools*, Royce.

Johnson, D. and Ransom, E. (1983) *Family and School*. Croom Helm.

Lees, D. S. (1966) *Economic Consequences of the Professions*. Institute of Economic Affairs.

Lindsay, C. (1969) *School and Community*. Pergamon.

McClelland, D. (1961) *The Achieving Society*. Van Nostrand.

Marjoribanks, K. (1979) *Families and their Learning Environments: An Empirical Analysis*. Routledge & Kegan Paul.

Marland, M. (Ed.) (1980) *Education for the Inner City*. Heinemann.

Marland, M. (1983) *Parenting, Schooling and Mutual Learning: A Teacher's Viewpoint*, advance paper for the EEC School and Family Conference, Luxembourg, 1983. Also published in Bastiani, J. (Ed.) (1988) *Parents and Teachers 2: From Policy to Practice*, pp. 232–42. NFER-Nelson.

Marland, M. (1985) 'Our needs in schools', pp. 67–91 in Lang, P. and Marland, M. (Eds) *New Directions in Pastoral Care*. Blackwell.

Mays, J. B. (1962) *Education and the Urban Child*. University of Liverpool.

Mays, J. B. (1980) 'The Impact of Neighbourhood Values', ch. 4 in Craft, M., Raynor, J., and Cohen, L. (Eds) *Linking Home and School*. Harper & Row.

Miller, G. W. (1971) *Educational Opportunity and the Home*. Longman.

Millerson, G. (1973) 'Education in the Professions' in History of Education Society *Education and the Professions*. Methuen.

Mortimore, J. and Blackstone, T. (1982) *Disadvantage and Education*, DHSS/Heinemann.

Osborne, A. F. and Milbank, J. E. (1987) *The Effects of Early Education: A Report from the Child Health and Education Study*. Clarendon Press.

Rosen, B. C. (1961) 'Family structure and achievement motivation' in *American Sociological Review*, 26, 574–84.

Rutter, M., Maughan, B., Mortimore, P., and Ouston, J. (1979) *Fifteen Thousand Hours. Secondary Schools and their effects on Children*. Open Books.

Schweinhart, L. J. and Weikart, D. P. (1980) *Young Children Grow Up: The Effects of the Perry Preschool Program on Youths Through Age 15*. High Scope Press.

Taylor, W. (1980) Family, school and society. Ch. 1 in Craft *et al.* (Eds) *Linking Home and School*. Harper & Row.

Tizard, B. and Hughes, M. (1984) *Young Children Learning, Talking and Thinking at Home and at School*. Fontana.

Tizard, B., Mortimore, J. and Burchell, B. (1988) 'Involving parents from minority groups', pp. 72–83 in Bastiani, J. (Ed.) *Parents and Teachers 2: From Policy to Practice*. NFER-Nelson.

Wiseman, S. (1964) *Education and Environment*. Manchester University Press.

Wolfendale, S. (1983) *Parental Participation in Children's Development and Education*. Gordon & Breach.

Acknowledgements

Chapter 1 From *How Children Fail*, by John Holt (1982), pp. 263–5 and *How Children Learn*, by John Holt (1983), pp. 146–55 reproduced by permission of John Holt and Penguin.

Chapter 2 'Towards a sociology of learning in primary schools', by Andrew Pollard from *British Journal of Sociology of Education* (1982/3), reproduced by permission of Carfax Publishing Company.

Chapter 3 'Wally' pp. 5–10 by Vivian Gussin Paley, from *Wally's Stories* (1981), reproduced by permission of Harvard University Press.

Chapter 4 'Bilingual by rights', by Helen Savva, from *Language and Learning Magazine*, vol. 5, pp. 17–21, reproduced by permission of The Questions Publishing Company Ltd., 6–7 Hockley Hill, Hockley, Birmingham B18 5AA.

Chapter 5 'Sex roles in the formative years', from *Sex Roles and the School*, by Sara Delamont (1990), reproduced by permission of Routledge and by the author.

Chapter 6 'Learner needs or learner rights?', by Caroline Roaf and Hazel Bines, from *Needs, Rights, and Opportunities in Special Education* (1989), reproduced by permission of Falmer Press.

Chapter 7 'Total teachers', from *What's Worth Fighting for in Your School?*, by Michael Fullan and Andy Hargreaves (1991), reproduced by permission of Open University Press.

Chapter 8 Adaptation of 'Implications of studies of expertise in pedagogy for teacher education and evaluation', by David Berliner, © 1993 by Educational Testing Service. All rights reserved. Adapted and reproduced under licence.

Chapter 9 'Teaching as a professional activity', by James Calderhead, from *Exploring Teachers' Thinking* (1987), pp. 1–3, reproduced by permission of Cassell.

Chapter 10 'Those who understand: knowledge growth in teaching', from *Educational Researcher*, by Lee Shulman (1986), reproduced by permission of American Educational Research Association.

Chapter 11 'A first try: starting the day', from *Doing Teaching: The Practical Management of Classrooms*, by Carol Cummings (1982), reproduced by permission of Batsford.

Chapter 12 'Akemi', pp. 121–6, by Vivian Gussin Paley, from *Wally's Stories* (1981), reproduced by permission of Harvard University Press.

Chapter 13 'Teacher expectations', from *School Matters: The Junior Years*, by Peter Mortimore, Pamela Simmons, Louise Stoll, David Lewis and Russell Ecob (1988), reproduced by permission of Open Books.

Chapter 14 'Life in the classrooms', by Philip Jackson from *Focus on Teaching*, by N. Bennett and D. McNamara (1979), reproduced by permission of Longman

Group UK.

Chapter 15 'Characteristics of good practice', from *Primary Schools: Some Aspects of Good Practice*, by Her Majesty's Inspectors of Schools (1987), reproduced by permission of HMSO.

Chapter 16 'The rise and fall of primary education', from *Value for Money in Education*, by Ellen Yeo (1991), reproduced by permission of Campaign for Real Education.

Chapter 17 'The "three wise men" and after', from *Language Matters 2*, by David Hutchinson (1988), pp. 11–18, reproduced by permission of the author.

Chapter 18 'Teaching strategies' from *Policy and Practice in Primary Education*, by Robin Alexander (1992), reproduced by permission of Routledge and by the author.

Chapter 19 'An approach to personal and social education in the primary school: or how one city school teacher tried to make sense of her job', from *Thinking about Personal and Social Education in the Primary School*, by Jane Needham (1988), reproduced by permission of Simon & Schuster Education, Hemel Hempstead, UK.

Chapter 20 'The core curriculum: an international perspective', from *Curriculum Reform: An Overview of Trends*, by Martin Skilbeck (1990), reproduced by permission of OECD, Paris.

Chapter 21 'The national curriculum: origins, context and implementation', by Bob Moon from *Managing the National Curriculum: Some Critical Perspectives*, T. Brighouse and R. Moon (1990), reproduced by permission of Longman Group UK.

Chapter 22 'Coherence and manageability: reflections on the national curriculum and cross-curricular provision', from *The Curriculum Journal* 2 (1), by David Hargreaves, reproduced by permission of Routledge.

Chapter 23 'The evolution of the topic', from *Topic Work in the Primary School*, by Trevor Kerry and Jim Eggleston (1988), reproduced by permission of Routledge.

Chapter 24 'Preserving integration with the national curriculum in primary schools: approaching a school development plan', from *The Curriculum Journal* 1 (3), by Anna Ryan, reproduced by permission of Routledge.

Chapter 25 'Successful topic work', from *Curriculum Organisation and Classroom Practice in Primary Schools* (1993), reproduced by permission of OFSTED.

Chapter 26 'The class teacher and the curriculum', reproduced by Robin Alexander, from *Primary Teaching* (1984), reproduced by permission of Cassell.

Chapter 27 'Teachers' subject knowledge', from *Primary Teaching Skills*, by Ted Wragg (1993), reproduced by permission of Routledge.

Chapter 28 'Assessment and the improvement of education', from *The Curriculum Journal*, by Wynne Harlen, Caroline Gipps, Patricia Broadfoot, and Desmond Nuttall, reproduced by permission of Routledge.

Chapter 30 'The organisation of the primary school', from *Understanding Schools as Organisations*, by Charles Handy and Robert Aitken (1986), reproduced by permission of Penguin Books Ltd.

Chapter 31 'Key factors for effective junior schooling', by Peter Mortimore, Pamela Sammons, Louise Stoll, David Lewis and Russell Ecob, from *School Matters: The Junior Years* (1988), reproduced by permission of Open Books.

Chapter 32 'The culture of collaboration', by Jennifer Nias, Geoff Southworth and Robin Yeomans, from *Staff Relationships in the Primary School: A Study of Organisational Culture* (1989), reproduced by permission of Cassell.

Chapter 33 'St Andrews Church of England Primary School', by Miriam Wilcock from *The Primary Head: roles, responsibilities and reflections*, by P. Mortimore and J. Mortimore (1991), reproduced by permission of Paul Chapman Publishing Ltd.

Chapter 34 'Involving the whole staff in developing a maths curriculum', by Richard McTaggart, from *Managing Staff Development in Schools*, by P. Lomax (1990), reproduced by permission of Multilingual Matters Ltd.

Chapter 35 'Primary–secondary transfer after the national curriculum', by Brian Gorwood, from *School Organisation* 11 (3), pp. 283–90 (1990), reproduced by permission of Carfax Publishing Company.

Chapter 36 Edited version of *Parents and the National Curriculum: An Interim Report* (1990), by M. Hughes, F. Wikley and T. Nash, reproduced by permission of the authors.

Chapter 37 'Involving parents', from *Involving Parents* by Alastair Macbeth (1989), reproduced by permission of Heinemann Publishers (Oxford) Ltd.

Notes on sources

Chapter 1   J. Holt, *How Children Fail*, Penguin, 1982, pp. 263–5; *How Children Learn*, Penguin, 1983, pp. 146–55.

Chapter 2   *British Journal of Sociology of Education* 11 (3): 241–56.

Chapter 3   V. G. Paley, *Wally's Stories*, London: Harvard University Press, 1981, pp. 5–10.

Chapter 4   *Language and Learning* 5: 17–21.

Chapter 5   Sara Delamont, *Sex Roles and the School*, London: Routledge, 2nd edn 1990, pp. 25–40.

Chapter 6   C. Roaf and H. Bines (eds), *Needs, Rights and Opportunities in Special Education*, Falmer, 1989, pp. 5–19.

Chapter 7   *What's Worth Fighting for in Your School?*, Open University Press, 1991, pp. 25–44.

Chapter 8   *New Directions for Teacher Assessment*, Educational Testing Service, 1988, pp. 39–65.

Chapter 9   *Exploring Teachers' Thinking*, Cassell, pp. 1–3.

Chapter 10   *Educational Researcher*, February 1986, 4–14.

Chapter 11   G. C. F. Payne and E. C. Cuff (eds), *Doing Teaching: The Practical Management of Classrooms*, Batsford, 1982, pp. 148–56.

Chapter 12   V. G. Paley, *Wally's Stories*, London: Harvard University Press, 1981, pp. 121–6.

Chapter 13   *School Matters: The Junior Years*, Open Books, 1988, pp. 163–75.

Chapter 14   N. Bennett and D. MacNamara (eds), *Focus on Teaching*, Longman, 1979, pp. 21–5.

Chapter 15   *Primary Schools: Some Aspects of Good Practice*, HMSO, 1987, pp. 31–4.

Chapter 16   Campaign for Real Education, 1991.

Chapter 17   *Language Matters* 2 (1988): 11–18.

Chapter 18   *Policy and Practice in Primary Education*, London: Routledge, 1992, pp. 59–83.

Chapter 19   P. Lang (ed.), *Thinking about Personal and Social Education in the Primary School*, Blackwell, 1988, pp. 144–51.

Chapter 20   *Curriculum Reform: An Overview of Trends*, OECD/CERI, 1990, pp. 45–8.

Chapter 21   T. Brighouse and R. Moon (eds), *Managing the National Curriculum: Some Critical Perspectives*, Longman, 1990, pp. 11–24.

Chapter 22   *The Curriculum Journal* 2 (1): 33–40.

Chapter 23   *Topic Work in the Primary School*, London: Routledge, 1988, pp. 16–41.

Chapter 24   *The Curriculum Journal* 1 (3): 127–36.

Chapter 25   *Curriculum Organisation and Classroom Practice in Primary Schools,* 1993.

Chapter 26   *Primary Teaching,* Holt, Rinehart & Winston, 1984, pp. 54–75.

Chapter 27   E. C. Wragg, *Primary Teaching Skills,* London: Routledge, 1993, pp. 153–63

Chapter 28   *The Curriculum Journal* 3 (3): 214–30.

Chapter 29   Commissioned for this volume.

Chapter 30   C. Handy and R. Aitken, *Understanding Schools as Organisations,* Penguin, 1986, pp. 11–21.

Chapter 31   *School Matters: The Junior Years,* Open Books, 1988, pp. 248–62.

Chapter 32   *Staff Relationships in the Primary School: A Study of Organisational Culture,* Cassell, 1989, pp. 46–74.

Chapter 33   P. and J. Mortimore (eds), *The Primary Head: Roles, Responsibilities and Reflections,* Paul Chapman, 1991, pp. 52–70.

Chapter 34   P. Lomax (ed.), *Managing Staff Development in Schools: An Action Research Approach,* Multilingual Matters, 1990, pp. 70–81.

Chapter 35   *School Organisation* 11 (3): 283–90.

Chapter 36   M. Hughes, F. Wikeley and T. Nash, *Parents and the National Curriculum: An Interim Report,* University of Exeter, 1990.

Chapter 37   *Involving Parents,* Heinemann, 1989, pp. 1–13.

Index

ability: grouping by 132, 138, 146; link to behaviour in teacher expectations 105, 107; teacher expectations 104–6, 151; and teachers in 'insecure' subjects 216–17
access, equality of opportunity and 59–60
accountability 179, 248
action research 283–91
administration, school 281–2
'advanced beginners' 74, 75
age: differences and teacher expectations 100; and waiting for attention 151
ageing, teachers and 69
aims: long-term and target-setting 230–1; shared 119, 122, 244, 245
apathy, parental 308
APU surveys 224–5
art 128, 173, 209, 214, 215
assembly 126
assessment 219–26; bilingual children 37–8; 'climate of' 122; criterion-referenced 219–20; formative 220–2; key principles 220; national curriculum and 181–2, 199, 219, 225–6; at national level 224–6; norm-referenced 219; school effectiveness 226; summative 222–4; target-setting and self- 228–36; topic work 192–3, 199
attainment: home background and 306–9; standards of 169
attainment targets 173, 180, 206
attendance, involuntary 117
auditor-moderators 137

Baker, Kenneth 178–9

balance 186
'basic' core subjects 138, 170, 208–9
B.Ed. 140
behaviour: link to ability in teacher expectations 105, 107; sex roles reinforced by teaching 45; teacher expectations 106–7
bilingual children 32–41; assessment 37–8; multilingual classroom 38–41; multilingual diversity 34–6; national curriculum and 32, 36–7, 37–8, 41; positive practice and negative attitudes 32–4
boredom 10–11
breadth 186

careers education 181
case knowledge 87
Centre for Policy Studies 135, 176
checking up 222–3, 223–4
child-centred teaching 175, 189–90
child-initiated talk 90–4
child psychology 12–13, 192, 210–11
children's rights 303–4
choice, parents' and school 298–301
Clarendon Commission 174
class, social: and attainment 307; sex roles 42–3; teacher expectations 42–3, 100–2
class co-operative activities 160
classroom environment 113–18; complexity of 81–2; display 142; layout 142–6; work-centred 253
classroom management: good practice 120–2; group work see group work; sex roles 43–4; St Andrew's C of E Primary School 277–8; working day 150–6; see also teaching strategies

classroom phenomena, interpreting 77
classroom tasks: 'quality' 16;
  routinisation 17–18
classteachers, generalist 207–11
co-educators 305–6
coherence 184–7
collaboration, culture of see culture of
  collaboration
collaborative group work 148
collaborative teaching 151–2
collective purpose 119, 122, 244, 245
collective responsibility 263–5
commitment: pupils' 121; teachers' 70,
  71, 121–2
common learning processes 136
communication 275; between primary
  and secondary teachers 296–7;
  between teachers 245, 268–71;
  between teachers and pupils 254–5
community: school and 246–8; topic
  work based on local 197–9
community schools 36, 246, 247
'competent performers' 74, 75–6
competition 128, 158; sex roles and 43,
  49
concepts, key 196, 199, 201
Conservative Government: educational
  reforms 1–2, 16; intervention in
  delivery of education 132–5, 139–40,
  180–1; 'New Right' 178–9; pressure
  group influences 175–7; teachers'
  antipathy to 129–30
content coherence 185, 187
content knowledge 84–6
context, learning and 16–19, 26
continuity, curriculum 293–7
contraction of education system 248–9
control: class 43–4, 92–3 (see also
  discipline); of learning 19, 22, 24, 25
cookery 44
co-operative activities: gender and 50,
  51; personal and social education 160
coping strategies 24–5
core curriculum 167–71
core foundation subjects 173
criterion-referenced assessment 219–20
'critical friends' 285, 290–1
cross-curricular provision 136–7, 186–7,
  195
crowds 118
cultural diversity 34–6, 40–1
cultural influences 246–7

culture of collaboration 258–72;
  individuals as people 259–62;
  interdependence 262–5; openness
  268–71; security 265–7
curricular knowledge 85–6
curriculum 16; continuity 293–7; core
  167–71; national see national
  curriculum; pastoral 310; special
  education 54–5
curriculum areas, classroom layout and
  143–6
curriculum co-ordinators 275
curriculum development, whole-school
  283–91
curriculum planning: 'good practice'
  119–20; by subjects 294–6; teaching
  strategies 149–50; 'three wise men'
  report 136; topic work 195–7, 206;
  topic work and national curriculum
  197–9, 200–3

dance 181
decision-making: opportunities for
  children's own 161; teachers and
  personal 75–6
Department of Education and Science
  (DES) 179–80
deputy heads 251
developmental psychology 12–13, 192,
  210–11
Dewey, John 189
diagnostic assessment 220–2
differentiation: national curriculum 186;
  social 12
disagreements 269–70
disappointment, teachers and 69
discipline: lack of in present-day
  schools 125–6, 129; self- 126–7; sex
  roles and 43–4
discovery learning 189
discussion 90–4
disillusioned teachers 69
display, classroom 142
drama 181

education, legal responsibility for 303–5
Education Act (1944) 304–5
Education Act (1981) 54, 57, 61
education expenditure 130, 249
Education Reform Act (1988): and
  government interference in teaching
  133, 134; national curriculum 172–3,

173, 176, 177; and parents 302
effective schools see school effectiveness
'effective' teachers 16
electricity 215–17
eleven-plus 124, 174–5, 296
emotionality: culture of collaboration
    270–1; expert teachers 78–9
English: assessment of bilingual
    children 38; language across the
    curriculum 136–7; national
    curriculum 135, 173, 180–1; teachers'
    feelings of competence in 214, 215
environment: classroom see classroom
    environment; work-centred 253
equal opportunities: equality of
    parental input 309; special education
    53, 56, 59–60
equality 55–6, 59–60
ethnic minority children: special needs
    61–2; teacher expectations 42, 104;
    see also bilingual children
evaluative assessment 224–6
examinations 128, 223, 296
experience: sociology of learning 23,
    23–4; topic work and 190, 191
experiential coherence 185
expert teachers 74, 76–7, 78–9
expertise, teacher 73–9; classroom
    routines 77–8; development stages
    74–7; emotionality 78–9; interpreting
    classroom phenomena 77

failing, learning and 7–11
falling rolls 248–9
feedback, positive 158–60
'feigning ignorance' 93
flexible groupings 158
flexibility 191
fluid performance 76–7
'focused topic' approach 296
formative assessment 220–2
foundation subjects 173

GCE 296
GCSE 135, 176, 296
gender 42–51, 61–2; classroom
    management 43–4; pupils' views
    48–51; staff development and 70;
    subject competence 215; teacher
    expectations 42–3, 102–3; teaching
    45–8; time spent in waiting 151
generalist classteachers 207–11

generic activities 153
geography 173, 214
goal-orientation 81
good practice 119–22; classroom work
    characteristics 120–2; school
    characteristics 119–20
'good schools', parents' views on 301
governing body 281, 311
government policy see Conservative
    Government
group size, use of time and 152
group work 137; co-operative activities
    148, 160; modern educational theory
    124; national curriculum and 148–9;
    rolling activities 160–1; teaching
    strategies 146–9
grouping: by ability 132, 138, 146;
    flexible 158
groups within a school 242–3

headteacher: culture of collaboration
    259, 266–7; organisation of school
    239–49; purposeful leadership 251; St
    Andrew's C of E Primary School
    274–5
Her Majesty's Inspectorate (HMI)
    175–6, 179
Hillgate Group 176–7
history 173, 214
home background, effect of 306–9; see
    also parents

identity 20–2, 24, 25
'ignorance, feigning' 93
imagination 28–31
incompetent teachers 68
individualised tasks 148
individuals, valuing 259–62, 271
informality 121
inspections 139
instructions, targets and 233–4
integrated day 127; see also topic work
integration, special needs provision and
    54, 55–6
inter-class links 159
inter-class visits 289–90
interdependence 262–5, 265–6, 267, 271
interest groups 168, 175–7
interpersonal domain 14–15
interpreting classroom phenomena 77
inter-school links 159
intimacy 115–16

intra-individual domain 13–15
intuition 76
investigation 195
involuntary attendance 117

Japan 170–1
Joseph, Sir Keith 176
judgement: needs and 58; professional
87; teachers' of colleagues 68

key concepts 196, 199, 201
knowledge 84–8; content 84–6; forms
needed by teachers 86–7; pedagogical
of teaching 88; subject 213–18;
teachers' professional 80–1, 82–3;
teachers' and topic work 190–1,
209–11
knowledge in action 83

language problems 95–8; see also
bilingual children, English
languages, modern 173
layout, classroom 142–6
leadership 244–5; purposeful 251
learning: common learning processes
136; and failing 7–11; model for topic
work 189–90;
organisation/management in St
Andrew's C of E Primary School
277–8; pre-school 309; in primary
schools 12–16; sociology of see
sociology of learning
learning difficulty 57; see also special
education
legal responsibility for education 303–5
limited focus 253–4
LINC (Language in the National
Curriculum) materials 135
linguistic diversity 34–6, 40–1
listening to children 162
literacy 136
local community topic work 197–9
local education authorities (LEAs) 304;
diminution of powers 133; influence
on classroom layout 145; teachers as
agents of 310–11
local management of schools (LMS)
133, 140, 276–7
locality of school 298–300

manageability 184–7
management: classroom see classroom

management; St Andrew's C of E
Primary School 275–6; teachers and
241, 248; see also organisation
managerialism 177–80
Manpower Services Commission 179
market place 177–80
mathematics 123; falling standards
127–8; national curriculum 173, 180;
primary-secondary transition 294;
teachers' feelings of competence to
teach 214; time allocation 152;
whole-school curriculum
development 283–91
matrix planning 199, 200–3
mistakes, making 7–8
modern languages 173
modern methods 125–31
motivation: gender and 43–4;
primary–secondary transfer 296
multilingual classroom 38–41
music 173, 181, 214, 215
mutual constraint 265–6, 267, 271
mutual dependence 262–5, 271

national curriculum 133, 172–82, 278;
assessment 181–2, 199, 219, 225–6;
and bilingual children 32, 36–7,
37–8, 41; coherence and
manageability 185–7; continuity
293–7; and group work 148–9;
implementation 180–2; nationalism,
managerialism and the market place
177–80; origins 173–5; overload
137–8; and planning 149–50;
political interference 134, 135;
pressure group politics 175–7; and
record keeping 150; topic-based
approach to planning 197–9, 200–3;
and topic work 206
National Curriculum Council (NCC)
134–5; report 132, 137–8
national level, assessment at 224–6
nationalism 177–80
Naturalism 189
needs 53–5, 56, 57–9, 60–1, 62
networks 260–2
'New Right' 178–9
new teachers 69–70
Newcastle Report 173
norm-referenced assessment 219
novices 74
numeracy 136

Office for Standards in Education (OFSTED): inspections 139; report 132, 138
openness 268–71, 271
'opportunities to learn' model 16
opportunity 59–60, 60–1, 62; see also equal opportunities
opting out 133, 140
organisation, school 239–49, 275–6
out-of-school relationships 260–2

paper, wastage of 126, 130
parent-teacher associations (PTAs) 255–6
parents: apathy 308; attitudes of 307; choice of school 298–300; as co-educators 305–6; equality of input 309; features of good schools 301; involvement and school effectiveness 255–6; involving 280, 302–11; legal responsibility for education 303–5; reasons for moving child's school 300–1; school's relationship with 246–8; as stakeholders 311; St Andrew's C of E Primary School and 280
pastoral curriculum 310
Patten, John 132, 135, 138, 181
pedagogical content knowledge 85
pedagogical knowledge of teaching 88
performance: genesis of capacity 229; targetsetting and analysis of 234–6; see also assessment
personal and social education 157–63, 181; co-operative activities 160; decision-making by children 161; flexible groupings 158; listening to children 162; photographs 162; positive feedback 158–60; role play 161–2; rolling activities 160–1; self-expression 161
PGCE 140
photographs 162
physical education 173, 214
Piaget, Jean 13, 192
planning, curriculum see curriculum planning
play 45–6
Plowden Report 175, 191–2
poetry 209
polarisation by sex 49–51
political intervention in education

132–5, 139–40, 180–1
populism, right-wing 139–40
positive climate 256
positive feedback 158–60
power 118
practical work 128
praise 118
pre-school learning 309
primary education, rise and fall of 123–31
primary-secondary transfer 293–7; motivation 296; planning by subjects 294–6; repetition problem 294; teacher communication 296–7
problem-solving 195
profession, teaching as 80–3
professional judgement 87
proficient teachers 74, 76
progression 121–2, 219–20
'project method' 128, 189; see also topic work
propositional knowledge 86–7
psychology, developmental 12–13, 192, 210–11
'pupil career' 24
pupils: commitment 121; communication with teachers 254–5; opportunities for decisionmaking 161; self-evaluation 159; targetsetting 228–36; views on sex roles 48–51; see also teacher–pupil interaction
purposeful leadership 251

quality assurance 224
'quality' of classroom tasks 16
questioning, telling and 137
questionnaire 288–9
questions, answering 7–9

racism 33–4
reading 124, 127
record keeping 150; school effectiveness 251, 255; topic work and 192–3
Records of Achievement (RoA) 223
'reflective agent' 22–3
relationships 244–6, 279; see also culture of collaboration
relevance 186
religious education 126, 182, 214, 215
repetition 294
resources 120, 281–2
Revised Code 173, 174

right-wing populism 139–40
rights: children's 303–4; special
    education 53, 55–6, 60–1, 62
risk-taking, learning and 18–19
role play 161–2
rolling activities 160–1
Rousseau, Jean Jacques 189
routines, classroom 77–8
routinisation of tasks 17–18
rules, classroom 116

school effectiveness: assessing 226; key
    factors 250–7
'school stupidity' 8–11
schools: characteristics and good
    practice 119–20; organisation of
    239–49, 275–6; parental reasons for
    moving children 300–1; parents'
    choice of 298–300; parents'
    perception of good 301; self-
    evaluation by 275–6; stakeholders in
    311
Schools Curriculum and Assessment
    Authority (SCAA) 135, 182
Schools Curriculum Development
    Committee (SCDC) 176
Schools Examination and Assessment
    Council (SEAC) 134–5
science 160, 208–9; national curriculum
    173, 180; teachers' feelings of
    competence to teach 214, 215;
    teaching for first time 215–17; topic
    work and 195
secondary education: national
    curriculum 181; transfer to 293–7
Secondary Examinations Council (SEC)
    176
security 265–7, 271
segregation, by pupils 49–51
self-assessment see target-setting
self-evaluation: by pupils 159; by
    schools 275–6; by teachers from tape-
    recorded data 89–94
self-expression 161
setting 138
sex roles see gender
shared aims 119, 122, 244, 245
shared values 244
skills see expertise, knowledge
smells, classroom 115
social class see class
social constructivism 13, 15, 16, 19–26

social differentiation 12
society, school and 248–9
socio-historical domain 14–15
sociology of learning 12–26; analytical
    framework 22–6; developing an
    identity 20–2; learning in primary
    schools 12–16; longitudinal
    ethnography 19–20; policy and
    substantive contexts 16–19
special education 53–62; equality and
    rights 55–6; integrated approach
    60–1; needs 53–5, 57–9; opportunity
    and equality 59–60; rights 60; St
    Andrew's C of E Primary School
    278–9; trends in 53–6
spelling 127
spontaneity 191
St Andrew's C of E Primary School
    273–82; administration and resources
    281–2; governors 281; head's
    philosophy of education 274–5; LMS
    276–7; organisation and management
    of learning 277–8; organisation and
    management of school 275–6;
    parental involvement 280;
    relationships 279; the school 273–4;
    special needs 278–9; staff
    development 279–80
staff development 279–80; teacher as a
    person 67–71
staff meetings 285–7
staffroom talk 260
stakeholders in schools 311
Standard Assessment Tasks (SATs) 139,
    224, 225
standards 133, 135–6, 219
standards of attainment 169
start of the day 89–94
State: legal responsibility for education
    304–5; teachers as agents of 310–11
stereotyping, sex 46–9, 102; see also
    gender
stories 95–8
strategic knowledge 87, 88
streaming 137, 138
structured sessions 252
'stupidity, school' 8–11
subject matter content knowledge 84–5
subject specialists 132, 138
subject teaching 136, 138
subjects: curriculum planning by 294–6;
    generalist classteacher and curriculum

208–10; teachers' feelings of competence with existing knowledge 213–15; teaching for the first time 215–18

summative assessment 222–4

summing up 222–3

supply teachers 130

symbolic interactionism 15, 16, 19–26

tape-recorded classroom data 162; self-evaluation from 89–94

target-setting 228–36; analysis of performance 234–6; long-term aims 230–1; short-term 231–4

Taunton Commission 174

teacher-centred instruction 171

teacher expectations 99–108; ability 104–6, 151; age 100; behaviour 106–7; effect on pupils of transmitting 107–8; ethnic differences 42, 104; gender differences 42–3, 102–3; link between ability and behaviour 107; social class 42–3, 100–2

teacher expertise see expertise

teacher intentions 17

teacher–pupil interaction: gender differences 45; unequal investment 147–8

teacher ratings 42–3

teachers: agents of education authority 310–11; antipathy to government 129–30; co-educators 305–6; commitment 70, 71, 121–2; communication between primary and secondary 296–7; communication with pupils 254–5; consistency 252; culture of collaboration see culture of collaboration; deployment in good primary practice 120; deterioration of lot owing to modern methods 130; devotion to children 129; 'effective' 16; generalist and curriculum 207–11; involvement 252; lack of professionalism 129; and management 241, 248; as people 67–71; positive climate 256; reinforcing sex roles 45–8; relationships in school 244–5; and school effectiveness 252, 254–5, 256; subject knowledge 213–18

teachers' roles: consultancy 120; curriculum co-ordinators 275; special education 54–5

teaching: intellectually challenging 253; as a professional activity 80–3

teaching strategies 142–56; display and layout 142–6; grouping 146–9; planning 149–50; record keeping 150; working day 150–6

technology: national curriculum 173, 181; teachers' feelings of competence to teach 214, 215; teaching for first time 217

telling, questioning and 137

test materials 223–4

testing 169–70, 223; national curriculum 177, 179; see also assessment, Standard Assessment Tasks

Thatcher, Margaret 176, 177, 178–9, 180

themes 186–7

'three wise men' report 132; propaganda misuse 133–4; recommendations 135–7

time 276; children's use of 150–3, 155; curriculum area allocations 207–8; spent in school by children 113–14

topic work 138, 181, 188–99, 278, 295; 'basics' and other curriculum 208–9; developmental psychology as justification for 210–11; factors associated with successful 206; lack of subject knowledge and 209–10; personal and social education 158; philosophy behind 189–90; planning 195–7, 206; planning for national curriculum 197–9, 200–3; way of organising 190–3

trips/visits 124, 126

TVEI 179, 182

'unequal investment' strategy 147–8

United States (US) 114, 169

value-added approach 226

values, shared 244

valuing teachers 71

visits/trips 124, 126

Wales 37, 182

Warnock Report 54, 57, 61

whole-class teaching 132, 137, 138, 151

'whole school approach' 54

whole-school curriculum development 283–91; consultation 287–8; inter-

class visits 289–90; questionnaire 288–9; staff meetings 285–7
work areas, curriculum-specific 143–5
work-centred environment 253
working day: structured 252; teaching strategies 150–6

world view 39–40
writing 127
written work 9

Zone of Proximal Development 229